Foundations of Education

A companion website to accompany this book is available online at:
http://education.craverphilipsen.continuumbooks.com

Please visit the link and register with us to receive your password and access these downloadable resources.

If you experience any problems accessing the resources, please contact Continuum at:
info@continuumbooks.com

Foundations of Education

Problems and Possibilities in American Education

Samuel M. Craver and Maike Ingrid Philipsen

continuum

2011

Continuum International Publishing Group
80 Maiden Lane, New York, NY 10038
The Tower Building, 11 York Road, London SE1 7NX

www.continuumbooks.com

Library of Congress Cataloging-in-Publication Data
Craver, Samuel M.
Foundations of education : problems and possibilities in American education / by Samuel M. Craver and Maike Ingrid Philipsen.
    p. cm.
Includes bibliographical references and index.
ISBN-13: 978-1-4411-9748-1 (hardcover : alk. paper)
ISBN-10: 1-4411-9748-6 (hardcover : alk. paper)
ISBN-13: 978-1-4411-4095-1 (pbk. : alk. paper)
ISBN-10: 1-4411-4095-6 (pbk. : alk. paper) 1. Education – United States – Textbooks. I. Philipsen, Maike. II. Title.

LA212.C725 2011
370.973—dc22

ISBN: 978-1-4411-9748-1 (hardcover)
       978-1-4411-4095-1 (paperback)

Typeset by Newgen Imaging Systems Pvt Ltd, Chennai, India
Printed and bound in the United States of America

We dedicate this book to our spouses: Sam's wife, Jeanie, and Maike's husband, Jon.

Contents

Acknowledgments

We gratefully acknowledge the scholarly advice and feedback we received from unknown reviewers and the following colleagues: Thomas Gumpel of the Hebrew University of Jerusalem and Kurt Stemhagen and Kevin Sutherland of Virginia Commonwealth University. Their insights were invaluable. Many thanks also to the countless students with whom much of this material was field tested over the years. They informed our understanding of the type of learning material students need. In addition, we recognize the professional consideration and courtesy of Director David Barker at Continuum Publishing. We want to thank Stan Wakefield for his services, assistants Leigh Pottle and Kevin Reeves for their aid, and the Department of Foundations at Virginia Commonwealth University for its support.

List of Figure and Tables

Figure

Tables

Preface

In writing this book, we had our own students in mind. They are typically at the beginning of their journey into educational careers. Some of them are uncertain about what or whom to teach or whether to teach at all, while others can hardly wait to enter the classroom. Still others may decide at some later point to become school counselors, administrators, or librarians or to serve students in other ways. This book was written as a foundation for understanding important issues that transcend grade levels, disciplines, and specific job descriptions, for these issues are central to all educators' professional preparation. They are enduring rather than faddish, big rather than small, and they affect each and every one of us insofar as they shape the context in which we practice our professions as educators.

Our intention is to provide thoughtful analysis that will allow both critical reflection and the construction of an interpretive framework giving structure to professional practice. The book is an outgrowth of our deep conviction that, no matter what specific challenge educators face during these times of political contentiousness and economic upheaval, they must still understand that professional work is more than a job with a prescribed set of activities. Teachers are and always have been professionals, and in order to act as such they must understand relationships between school and society. This includes not only relationships in classrooms, playgrounds, or school hallways but those in the larger political, economic, and social framework that impact the places where education occurs. Good professional teaching necessitates reflective decision-making that depends on a thorough understanding of the historical and contemporary nature of the issues that influence professional practice. Prospective educators need familiarity with existing scholarship that sheds light on what shapes education. They need to see beyond their own immediate experience and situate their practice within the wealth of knowledge accumulated over time by scholars and fellow practitioners.

The book is organized by chapters focusing on issues that continue to play significant roles in schooling. These issues include teaching as a profession and school governance and control. They involve race, ethnicity, social class, gender, and special needs, all connected with the quest for equal educational opportunities. They also touch on ideas of freedom of thought and belief, which roils contemporary education no less than the contemporary world of politics and diplomacy. The analytic approach is a multidisciplinary one in which, rather than devoting one chapter to "the history of education," another to "the philosophy of education," and still another to "the sociology of education" and so on, these disciplinary lenses are used where appropriate for a richer treatment. Each chapter draws on relevant historical, philosophical, and sociological research of sufficient breadth and depth to ground prospective educators for subsequent professional studies, and each chapter provides an international comparison to show how a given issue plays out in selected countries. In a rapidly globalizing world, it is necessary for educators to step out of comfortable cultural and national confines to understand how other countries struggle with the same problems and how they may approach them. Such international glimpses might confirm traditions as well as provide insights on how to do things differently or at least appreciate the variety of approaches people use to educate. Countries were selected in an effort to represent a variety of geographic, political, and economic systems.

The book is organized into eight chapters. Chapter 1 (Teaching as a Profession) introduces readers to the profession they are about to enter. It provides historical and philosophical background on how the role of teachers evolved over time, and it explores the struggle to be recognized as a profession and the efforts to find a more unified voice at the present time. Readers are presented with a demographic profile of the profession, daily realities teachers face, selected ethical aspects of teaching, and analysis of how the teaching profession serves the common good. Chapter 2 (School Governance and Control) includes the evolution of school governance and how schools are currently controlled, encompassing the role of school funding and the interplay of different stakeholders, reform efforts, and legislation.

Chapters 3 through 7 focus on specific aspects of equal educational opportunity: social class, race, ethnicity, gender, and disabilities. Each chapter examines how its particular topic is engaged in the struggle for equal educational opportunity, and how that engagement has shaped educational theory and practice. The chapters also address ideas and conditions that illuminate both the successes and the continuing impediments to equal educational opportunity, with description and analysis of various policy initiatives and reform proposals aimed at change. Chapter 3 (Social Class) concerns how social class connects, historically and currently, with school funding, tracking, ability grouping, and school choice. Chapter 4 (Race and the Education of African Americans) examines the impact of race on American education in terms of racial socialization, social stratification, segregation/desegregation, and multicultural and Afrocentric education. Chapter 5 (Ethnicity and Education) addresses the history of the unity- diversity tension in American society and education, including the education of Native Americans and selected immigrant groups (Polish, Italian, Chinese, and Mexicans) as well as the controversial reform policies of bilingual and multicultural education. Next, Chapter 6 (Gender and Education) delves into gendered approaches to schooling, thinking and knowing, and learning and achievement, as well as how both females and males fare in today's schools. Chapter 7 (Education of People with Disabilities) examines the development of leading theories and practices on the education of special needs learners, including mainstreaming and inclusion.

Chapter 8 looks at a fundamental aspect of freedom, the freedom of conscience, belief, or thought. If class, race, and gender are thought to be essential aspects of personal and group identity, so is freedom of thought. The chapter examines the historical and contemporary place of religion in education, including conflicting intellectual views, important legal and ethical aspects, leading policy initiatives and proposals, and analysis of why the issue has proved to be so sensitive in the educational arena.

The style of the book is meant to be clear and informative, with a concerted effort to avoid jargon but without an overly simplistic prose or pages overloaded with graphics. The text is designed to provide foundational preparation for readers about to embark on what the authors hope will be fulfilling professional lives as teachers and other education professionals. Such students need material that avoids sugarcoating contentious issues, but they also need analysis that offers a sense of possibility for those who want to journey into the nation's classrooms and schools.

To aid reading and study, each chapter begins with objectives and a list of questions to prepare readers for what is to come. Brief tables and text boxes are used throughout to provide details to textual content. In addition, strategically placed marginal notes are provided with questions for class discussion, suggestions for relating text material to personal experiences, and activities for further investigation and reflection. Key terms are bolded throughout the text, with an appropriate and alphabetized vocabulary list provided at the end of each chapter. There are also indications in the text where additional information and further readings can be found on the publisher's website.

All in all, the book is an invitation to think, discuss, and engage in friendly debates with classmates and professors, not only for the stimulation and fun of it, but also for increased awareness of the complex nature of contemporary education. Indeed, as in so many other spheres of life, absolute certainty is scarce in education, while differences of opinion are plentiful. The conditions in which contemporary education exists seem to breed contention, but they also appear to generate suggested solutions. The authors hope the text will encourage readers to become intellectually involved, and those who truly want to be educators are invited to join the efforts to better understand the world of education and to add their own voices to those trying to make sense of it all.

Teaching as a Profession

Chapter contents

Chapter objectives

- To sketch the history of the teaching profession.
- To develop appreciation of teachers' struggles for professional status and control over time.
- To increase understanding of what it means to be a "professional."
- To present a profile of "who teaches" with demographic data such as teachers' race, gender, age, and income distribution.
- To analyze daily realities faced by many teachers in their workplaces.
- To increase understanding of teachers' professional societies and unions.
- To provide an international perspective on teaching in China.

Opening questions

1. What were the historical challenges teachers faced in becoming established and recognized as professionals?
2. What is the meaning of "profession" and does the term best capture the status of teachers?
3. What is the makeup of the teaching profession and what are the implications of its demographic characteristics?
4. How do teachers experience the world of work?
5. How are teachers organized, and what are the debates surrounding these organizations?
6. How does teaching in the United States compare to teaching in China?

The issue

Is teaching truly a **profession**, is it a mere vocation, or is it a "calling"?[1] While teachers are perceived as crucial to societal well-being, they lack the extrinsic rewards enjoyed by professions such as engineering or medicine. Teachers often face contradictory public perceptions: They are praised for their efforts to educate the young but also pitied for their lack of recognition or reward. Curiously, while teaching is seen as demanding, the old saying persists that "anyone can teach." Proponents insist that the teaching profession can transform society, while critics deplore teaching as a job for drudges unqualified for the lucrative professions. In other words, the teaching profession faces a significant **status discrepancy**. Teaching has high status if measured by public admiration, low status if measured by professional autonomy and salary.

What is effective teaching, and who defines "effective"? Much current debate focuses on high-stakes testing and teacher accountability, but there is a human component to good teaching. Those hoping to become effective teachers need subject-matter preparation, foundation understandings, teaching methods, and classroom management skills, but they also need charisma, compassion, egalitarianism, a sense of humor, and the ability to work with diverse people, to name a few.[2]

In short, debate surrounds what characterizes the teaching profession. Some critics declare that teaching should not be considered a true profession at all but a "quasi-" or "managed" profession. Others call the entire debate superfluous and argue that teachers should focus on the valuable things they do rather than argumentative definitions. The point of departure taken here is that teaching is, indeed, a genuine profession, but some unique characteristics as well as contentious points of view swirl around its status.

Background

Teaching has traditions going back across the centuries. Of course, gifted teachers develop their own effective approaches, but much of what we do in education comes not from creativity so much as from social and cultural traditions. In fact, many of our ideas about education are like mother tongues not consciously chosen but handed down.

Suggested Activity: Compose an "educational biography." How were you taught throughout your educational journey? What teacher(s) left the deepest impressions, both positively and negatively? What have you learned from these role models, and how might your experience shape the way you will treat your own students?

European heritage

Key elements of the European educational tradition come from ancient Greece and Rome. For the Greeks, language and literature as well as philosophical and mathematical studies were central to their concept of a proper education. Roman educators used this tradition to develop an education based on what came to be called the **liberal arts**. The concept of **liberal education** is derived from the Greco-Roman **classical tradition**, that is, an education that "liberates" the mind through the study of important branches of knowledge. By the Middle Ages, the curriculum was formalized into the "seven liberal arts" (arithmetic, geometry, music, astronomy, grammar, rhetoric, and logic or dialectic), but it also became heavily supplemented by Christian doctrines that emphasized education for the salvation of the soul. The study of classical languages, particularly Latin, retained supremacy in formal education, even as the **vernacular** (or native) languages of Europe expanded, primarily because Latin was the official language of the Roman Catholic Church, the chief provider of formal education in medieval Europe, but also because Latin continued to be used in such pursuits as scholarly writing and international diplomacy.[3]

As the era of exploration dawned, Europe underwent social and intellectual changes that stimulated colonization in the Americas and elsewhere. The Renaissance and the Reformation were two such changes, each in its own way adding to the educational assumptions and expectations of teachers in colonial America.

Cross Reference: For a more extended discussion of European influences on American education, see Chapter 8, Religion and Education, pp. 355–410.

Originating in Italy probably in the late fourteenth century, the Renaissance eventually swept across Europe and invigorated intellectual curiosity. "*Renaissance*" means "rebirth," but for education it was not solely a rebirth of classical studies. It helped to revive the liberal arts, with its emphasis on the humanities, and spurred new interest in astronomy, mathematics, and knowledge of the natural world. Liberal education became imbued with the goal of producing well-rounded individuals pursuing excellence in a wide range of artistic, intellectual, and cultural endeavors. The present-day view of liberal education encompasses the liberal arts, human cultures, and scientific and mathematical studies, sometimes collectively referred to as the **arts** (or **humanities**) **and sciences**.[4]

For Further Reflection: Consider your own college experience with course requirements that were supposed to broaden your horizons. Does liberal education truly "liberate" the person, or does it put a greater premium on loyalty to the past and to cultural traditions and old ways of thinking? Should higher education seek to broaden prospective teachers, or should it train them for the job market for teachers?

As the Renaissance gained headway, Europe also experienced the Protestant Reformation and the Catholic Counter Reformation. Among other things each movement emphasized, the Protestants advocated widespread literacy to enable as many as possible to read the Bible, while the Catholics renewed secondary and higher education to strengthen their institutions and adherents. Such emphases, along with the invention of the printing press and other developments, stimulated the growth of elementary education in the vernacular languages, with classical and vernacular studies boosted in secondary and higher education. Although Protestantism was dominant in the English colonies of North America, Catholic educational ideals would exert a degree of influence on later American education.[5]

> **For Further Reflection:** Did literacy for common people become important only after religious leaders connected reading with salvation, or did it have other sources as well? Is there any difference between literacy for religious salvation and literacy for individual and social well-being? Why or why not?

> WEB: Additional Information 1.1.: JOHN AMOS COMENIUS

Thus, many educational ideas were brought from Europe that shaped American education. Teaching in the United States did not start with a blank slate but with traditions from across the centuries. Americans built on these traditions and made their own educational contributions in the process.

American education

As the English colonies in North America became established, at least three levels of schooling developed, each with its own kind of teachers: elementary "petty" schools, secondary "grammar" schools, and colleges. Various schemes were tried, but perhaps the most notable departure came in Massachusetts with a 1647 law that helped foster petty schools in its requirement that every township of at least 50 households should appoint someone "to teach all such children as shall resort to him to write and read." Once a town increased to 100 households, it should "set up a grammar school" to educate youth to be "fitted for the university." The law was followed in some jurisdictions and virtually ignored in others, but it set a pattern used throughout New England by the end of the colonial period.[6] Indeed, most colonies had at least a few petty and grammar schools, although not on the scale of New England.

Colonial teachers

Background preparation of petty school teachers was varied; some had suitable background while others were barely adequate. One form of petty school was the "dame school," usually conducted in a household by a literate woman, sometimes a mother who took in a few children along with her own to provide rudimentary instruction (and perhaps a small income). Other petty schools were more formal. The manner in which petty schools were financed differed: Some were given public support by towns, some charged tuition fees, and some were "charity" schools, free of charge to poor children and financed by endowments from benefactors. Some petty schools might only teach reading, others might offer both reading and writing, and still others might have a more complex curriculum. Despite variability, petty school teachers taught a relatively common curriculum in the sense that students were started on simple hornbooks of the ABCs, then moved to spelling, psalters and catechisms, and then possibly to more advanced reading, writing, arithmetic, and religion.

Suggested Activity: Use the internet to locate definitions, descriptions, and illustrations of historic educational terms. See, for example, "The Hornbook," at http://www. iupui.edu/~engwft/hornbook.html (accessed on September 23, 2010); and "Introduction to Psalters," at http://www.leavesofgold.org/gallery/psalters/index.html (accessed on September 23, 2010). For facsimile reprints of pages from the *New England Primer*, see Paul Leicester Ford, ed., *The New England Primer: A History of Its Origin and Development* (New York: Dodd, Mead and Co., 1897) at http://www.archive.org/stream/newenglandprimer00ford (accessed on September 23, 2010).

A famous colonial textbook was the ***New England Primer***, used for reading, vocabulary development, and moral and religious instruction. For example, the 1737 edition of the *Primer* began with letters of the alphabet, each followed by a verse or moral dictum and an illustration to drive home the meaning: On the left of the page was the letter "*A*," with a small drawing of a man and woman contemplating an apple, accompanied on the right with the verse, "In Adam's Fall, We Sinned all." Next came the letter "*B*," with a small image of an open book fortified by "Thy Life to mend, This Book attend." For the letter "*C*", with an illustration of a cat playing with a mouse, the admonition read, "The Cat doth play, And after slay." The *Primer* proceeded all the way through the alphabet, then to syllabic pronunciation tables, stories, and other material.[7]

For Further Reflection: Early in American educational history teachers relied on textbooks such as the *New England Primer*. Schools continue to rely on textbooks. Is this a good thing? Should a variety of reading materials be used in classrooms, and if so, what kinds should they be? Should textbooks still have an essential place?

Grammar (or secondary) school teachers were expected to have more advanced academic preparation than petty school teachers. Preparation for secondary teachers grew out of the European university tradition. It was comprised of undergraduate study in the liberal arts (leading to the bachelor of arts degree) and graduate study in liberal arts (leading to the master of arts degree) as well as professional studies in law, medicine, or theology. Although there were no specific courses on how to teach, universities contributed to secondary teacher preparation by providing the liberal arts background that was expected and the bachelor of arts degree that was highly desired.

This tradition was reflected in what secondary teachers were expected to know: They should be able to speak and write Latin, understand some Greek and perhaps some Hebrew, and have capacity in English usage as well. They also needed general knowledge of history, mathematics, and perhaps a bit of science.[8] There were expectations concerning teachers' religious qualifications, too, as reflected by Massachusetts in a 1654 law that required the overseers of Harvard College and the selectmen of the towns to prohibit anyone from teaching school children or college youth if the applicant demonstrated unsound belief, scandalous behavior, or "'not giving due satisfaction according to the rules of Christ,'"[9] presumably meaning untrustworthy performance. Both the depth of preparation and the performance of teachers were uneven; consequently, colonial schools experienced frequent **teacher turnover**, not only because well-qualified grammar school teachers were difficult to find and retain but also because of a persistent labor shortage during the time, with many teachers moving on as more promising job prospects became available.

> **For Further Reflection:** Topics of great relevance today, such as teacher turnover and variation in teacher preparedness, obviously have a long history. How should we attract and retain qualified teachers today?

In the eighteenth century, petty schools continued as before, but grammar schools actually declined. One reason was a decrease in value placed on classical learning. Another was the growth of town-supported "writing schools" that emphasized more advanced instruction in English, arithmetic (or "ciphering"), and accounting, all subjects that had greater practical application. As the colonial economy expanded, private "vocational" schools arose that taught such subjects as geometry, trigonometry, navigation, surveying, double-entry bookkeeping, foreign languages, and foreign currency exchange, all of which found practical application in the growth of American business, industry, and shipping and trade.[10]

WEB: Additional Information 1.2.:
SOME COLONIAL AMERICAN TEACHERS

Teachers for the new nation

In hindsight it may appear that after the American Revolution the success of the United States was a foregone conclusion, but its existence was actually precarious. Numerous efforts were made to remedy this, not only with the adoption of the Constitution in 1789 but also with pleas for greater educational opportunity as one of the surest ways to strengthen the new republic. For example, Noah Webster called on education to develop a national unity around "the American tongue," while Benjamin Rush advocated an education to "convert men into republican machines" to bind the country together.[11] However, questions about the preparation of teachers did not receive similar examination.

Suggested Activity: Apply the ideas of Webster and Rush to contemporary contexts and discuss to what extent modern schools perceive their mission as being to prepare students to develop national unity around "the American tongue," and to "convert men to republican machines" to bind the country together? Are these ideas quaint and dated, or do they still hold relevance today? Why or why not?

As the nineteenth century dawned, the belief was that a good grounding in reading, writing, arithmetic, some religion, and a smattering of history and geography were sufficient preparation for most elementary teachers. For secondary teachers, a liberal arts education seemed sufficient to provide all the moral, social, psychological, and academic knowledge needed. Educational theory and teaching methodology, if studied at all, were to be gained from personal study and on-the-job experience.[12]

For Further Reflection: What do teachers need to know and experience in order to be competent professionals?

With the passage of time, teaching came under increased scrutiny. One reason was the growing awareness that for the new republic to succeed, as many citizens as possible should be educated as far as practicable. This led to the establishment of statewide systems of public schools, a significant phase of which was the **common school movement**, a widespread development of public elementary schools from the 1830s up to about 1860. A second phase was the spread of public high schools after the Civil War, a movement that lasted well into the twentieth century. An essential need was a sufficient supply of properly educated teachers to make the public schools successful, which also spurred the growth of teacher education institutions.

Why did the United States move from a mixed bag of sectarian schools, private schools, charity schools, and municipal public schools inherited from the colonial period toward the eventual founding of statewide systems of locally controlled public schools? A simple answer is that by the 1830s there was public demand for more widely available educational opportunities, with emphasis not so much on producing refined scholars as on forming virtuous and morally upstanding citizens. A more complex answer is that more people came to believe that a truly educated person must not only be literate but possess culture and character as well. The goal was as much social and cultural as it was literary and intellectual, views that also spilled over into the preparation of teachers. Thus, the push became to prepare teachers not only to develop the mental capacities of their students, but also to serve as proper role models for them and to maintain discipline while implanting desired character traits in them.[13]

> **For Further Reflection:** To what extent do we still expect teachers to be ethical role models who adhere to higher moral standards than citizens working in other professions? Should this be the case? Why or why not?

Women enter teaching

In earlier times, teaching was mainly a male occupation. It was believed that men were more suitable because they were better educated, more intellectually capable, and made of the stern temperament and physical strength needed to quell unruly pupils and demand achievement. Such beliefs would undergo change as growing numbers of women became teachers in the nineteenth century.[14]

Educational opportunity remained limited for females when the United States was young. Of course, wealthier parents had long secured private tutors for their daughters, and there were a limited number of "finishing schools" that polished the social graces of young ladies and provided a veneer of intellectual training. But a more rigorous academic preparation became the rallying point for reformers who believed that females were as intellectually capable as males.[15] Indeed, women increasingly entered the teaching profession as the public school movement gained momentum. Although denied access to most professions at the time, it is arguable that their entry into teaching helped women also enter other professions later on.

There were strong economic reasons for women becoming teachers: When the public common schools appeared in the nineteenth century, the Industrial Revolution was a growing force. Developments such as the electric telegraph, the steam engine, and the mass production of goods rapidly changed social and economic life. Consider textile production as an example: Old-fashioned spinning wheels and hand-operated looms disappeared from the home as mechanized factories mass-produced high-quality cloth that consumers could buy more cheaply than make at home. Where teaching once attracted the likes of a John Adams, young men were now attracted to more lucrative jobs in an expanding industrial economy. With industries producing affordable household goods, more women became available for jobs outside the home and family. Connect these factors with the growth of the common schools and the need for more teachers, and connect public opposition to higher taxes with the fact that women were paid less than men, and it is a small step to see one reason women teachers gained acceptance—they were cheaper. As reformer Alonzo Potter dryly noted at the time, local school districts wanted the best teachers possible—as long as they were the cheapest.[16]

Even more important was the growing belief that, contrary to tradition, women were actually suited by temperament to teach. Just as men were better for action in the outside world by virtue of their traditional roles as warriors and hunters (the thinking went), women were more understanding and sympathetic to children because of their softer temperaments and natural capacities as mothers. At a time when people were questioning the extensive use of corporal punishment in schools, there was increasing acceptance that most women preferred moral suasion over physical force; therefore, they were desirable additions to the teaching profession. In many respects this change was due to the Enlightenment, an intellectual movement that swept Europe and America from the late seventeenth through the early nineteenth centuries and produced philosophers such as John Locke (seventeenth century), social critics such as Jean-Jacques Rousseau (eighteenth century), and educators such as Johann Pestalozzi (early nineteenth century). These thinkers promoted such ideas as children being educated according to the natural developmental processes of childhood, with their natural traits recognized, their manners and morals sympathetically nurtured, and their characters shaped through rational, humane instruction rather than physical force.[17]

For Further Reflection: Do men and women truly differ in their natural, inborn capacities to teach? If so, in what ways? Have you personally encountered beliefs and attitudes that portray women as nurturers and men as disciplinarians? What is your reaction to such views?

WEB: Suggested Reading 1.1.

Teacher preparation

As the school age population grew, there were never enough qualified teachers to fill the demand in the schools. It had long been the expectation that secondary school teachers should have, if not a full academic degree, at least some higher education preparation. As many educational reformers saw it, elementary teachers needed more extensive preparation too. It was not until the appearance of the **normal school** that an institution dedicated to elementary teacher preparation appeared in the United States.

Normal schools

Why the term "*normal*" for a teacher-training institution? The idea for such a school probably originated with the Prussian "teacher seminaries" of the mid-eighteenth century, but the specific term *normal school* apparently was derived from the French, the first being the *École Normale Supérieure*, founded in 1794 during the French Revolution to serve as the model for other such schools across France. In the United States, the Model School of Philadelphia opened in 1818 to train teachers in that city; in 1823, a private teacher-training institution was opened in Concord, Vermont; and in 1826, two others were opened, one in New Harmony, Indiana, and the other in Lancaster, Massachusetts. But the term "*normal school*" did not gain common American usage until the founding of the state-supported Lexington Normal School in Lexington, Massachusetts in 1839.[18] The growth of the public common schools and their demand for greater numbers of teachers subsequently spurred the opening of many normal schools throughout the remainder of the nineteenth century.

Most normal schools followed a four-point plan of study: a review of the branches of knowledge, the study of pedagogy (the art or science of teaching), some training in classroom/school management, and practice teaching. At first, normal schools used the secondary school curriculum, along with some pedagogical applications, to train teachers for the elementary common schools, but as public high schools increased, many normal schools added the training of high school teachers and school administrators as well. Over time, some normal schools took on collegiate functions, particularly where there was little or no postsecondary education available within reasonable geographic proximity.[19] In some cases, this expansion of mission served to weaken normal schools because it detracted from their original objectives.

> **For Further Reflection:** Educational hierarchies have a long history, and the status of elementary school teachers has suffered in comparison to secondary teachers. Turn this type of thinking upside down and construct a rationale for why young children might need teachers whose preparation is even more sophisticated than that of teachers of older students.

By the beginning of the twentieth century, normal schools were fairly common. In 1860, there were only 11 nationwide, but by 1898 there were 166 public and 165 private normal schools, with a combined graduation total of 11,255 students in that year. Between 1870 and 1900, normal school enrollments grew from 10,000 to 70,000 students, but normal schools never provided more than about half the teachers actually needed in most states. Consequently, many poorer school districts, particularly rural ones, had to employ teachers with no more preparation than an elementary school background. Even in Massachusetts, with its reputation for educational innovation, more than 60 percent of teachers had no pedagogical training at all. By 1900, the normal schools faced stiff competition from the growing number of state colleges and universities, many of which claimed teacher preparation as one of their missions. As colleges and universities increasingly took over the preparation of teachers, normal schools closed, merged with existing higher-education institutions, or became four-year **state teachers colleges** themselves.[20]

State colleges and universities

Traditionally, colleges and universities prepared secondary school teachers as a by- product of their regular liberal education programs, but not with any special emphasis on pedagogy per se. By the twentieth century, most state colleges and universities assumed the primary responsibility of preparing both elementary and secondary teachers. This involved establishing departments and schools of education to deliver courses in the foundations of education, curriculum, teaching methods, student teaching, school administration, school counseling, and other specialized studies.

At those state teachers colleges that had developed out of normal schools, there was usually a strong carryover of commitment to teacher education. Commitment was also present in some new, general-purpose state colleges and universities, but not in all. It was probably strongest in those institutions where the presidents had backgrounds as schoolteachers and administrators or were graduates of departments or schools of education. Such presidents often stayed in their posts for years, and where there were good relationships between top administrators and schools or departments of education, the latter enjoyed greater support and stability.[21]

However, teacher education did not fare so well in those institutions accepting it reluctantly. As public school enrollments grew, state governments often assigned teacher preparation to their public colleges and universities as a duty to taxpayers, whether or not those institutions were willing. Thus, the marriage of teacher education to a reluctant institution was not always a happy one. For one thing, some liberal arts professors saw teacher education as tainted by its inferior normal school origins, and they scorned it as a result. For another, teaching did not wield the economic clout of other professions such as law or medicine, and it suffered in comparison. Also, some aspects of teacher education lacked the scholarly research base of the traditional professions, and this reinforced biases that teacher education lacked intellectual substance. Indeed, there were teacher education faculty more interested in how-to techniques than intellectual substance and, in turn, some of them dismissed their academic critics as impractical bookworms and out-of-touch intellectuals. Where there were failures on the part of both academic and teacher education faculties to cultivate common interests, teacher preparation and the public interest were probably not well served.

Suggested Activity: On your own campus, examine the relationship between the teacher preparation program and other degree programs and disciplines. Does your institution have its roots in a normal school or teachers college, and what difference does this make for the current status of teacher education? How do your observations compare with the accounts given in this book?

Professionalism and professionalization

There was an additional factor at work, too, and this was the drive to "professionalize" public education. According to Jurgen Herbst, there are two essential distinctions to be made—**professionalism** and **professionalization**. Teacher *professionalism* is something to be valued: Among other things, it involves the teacher's fundamental duty to be well-prepared in both subject matter and teaching skills in order to provide competent educational service to students, and to exercise responsible professional judgment in regard to teaching, curriculum, and evaluation of student progress. This view borrows heavily from traditions in the historic **learned professions** trained in the universities (ministers, lawyers, physicians, and college and university professors), whose professional status grew from their extended preparation that allowed them to exercise judgment and a high degree of autonomy in professional practice. In this view, true professionals collectively determine admission criteria and the ethical standards of good practice. Properly trained members of the profession should be allowed to carry out their duties, as guided by expertise and professional ethical standards, taking responsibility for results without intrusive external supervision. Such a strong tradition was not established when pedagogical training was transferred from the normal schools to the colleges and universities. For a long time, teacher preparation remained at the undergraduate rather than the graduate level where other learned professions were taught. Efforts to achieve greater depth in professional preparation, which might have boosted teacher claims to professional autonomy and judgment, were restricted rather than enlarged.

> **Suggested Activity:** Use your imagination and rewrite history. What path would the teaching profession have had to take in order to achieve similar status as other professions?

At that time, what enjoyed far greater success was the *professionalization* of school administrators and specialists. Such factors as graduate training, workplace autonomy, peer evaluation, and accountability to society—all recognized traits of the learned professions—became common features for administrators and educational specialists but not classroom teachers. The policy makers who controlled the schools established a hierarchical, bureaucratic form of corporate organization in which teachers were defined as employees who carried out directives, not professionals who exercised judgment or autonomy in their work.

Incentives for teachers to pursue greater professionalism were curtailed if not eliminated outright. As the twentieth century advanced, teacher education did move toward the graduate level, but by then a pervasive pattern of administrative control was firmly entrenched. For teachers to get "promoted" to "full" professional status, they had to leave the classroom and enter the ranks of administrators and specialists.[22]

Teachers organize

Soon after the advent of public school systems in the nineteenth century, teachers, administrators, reformers, and education-minded citizens began forming educational associations, which arose from the need to seek workable solutions to problems, share successful ideas, and influence public policy on education. Some of the participants, including many teachers, also believed there was a need to promote the interests of the teaching profession itself, including better pay, improved working conditions, and the protection of professional autonomy.

National Education Association

Today's largest teacher organization traces its origins to 1857 and the founding of the National Teachers Association. In 1870, this group merged with the National Association of School Superintendents and the American Normal School Association to form the **National Education Association (NEA)**. The NEA supported public and private schooling at all levels, but it was mainly devoted to the goals of reformers, school superintendents, and college presidents, not classroom teachers. In 1917, the NEA reorganized itself into a trilevel organization of local, state, and national divisions. Teachers gained some influence through the "classroom teachers' associations" formed at the local and state levels, but traditional interests maintained organizational dominance at the national level.[23]

> **Suggested Activity:** Compare the NEA to other professional organizations and unions. To what extent do leaders of professional organizations perceive themselves as the avant-garde rather than the representatives of the membership? Is there often a disconnect between leaders and ordinary members?

Teachers and bureaucratic controls

One of the issues that generated teacher unrest was the controversy over "merit rating," one of the practices superintendents instituted to get more "efficiency" out of classroom teachers. As school bureaucracies grew, additional layers of administration exercised control over teachers. In some school systems, teachers might be rated by four or more layers, from the building principal to grade or subject supervisor to assistant superintendent to superintendent. In some systems the rating criteria were kept secret, with teachers not knowing what they were rated on or how results were decided. Needless to say, this created teacher distrust.[24]

The NEA made some efforts to improve relations, but tensions remained. During the Great Depression, the NEA conducted a national salary study in 1935. Findings revealed pay discrepancies between elementary and secondary teachers, male and female teachers, and black and white teachers. The NEA recommended salary equity for the elementary-secondary and male-female discrepancies, but the issue of race-based salaries was deferred to the prerogatives of local education authorities.[25]

The NEA would later change many of its positions and become a stalwart defender of teacher interests. Such changes occurred not only because of conditions but also because of agitation from dissatisfied members and from outside competition.

Suggested Activity: Research current debates about merit rating, merit pay, and career ladders. What are valid arguments for and against these practices?

Margaret Haley, a Chicago classroom teacher-advocate

Margaret Haley was an elementary school teacher from the tough "stockyards" district of Chicago and also a longtime member of the National Education Association (NEA). Goaded by underfunded schools and cynical city policies, she and other elementary teachers formed the first union for teachers, the Chicago Teachers Federation (CTF) in 1897. In 1901, Haley became the first elementary teacher (and also the first woman) to speak from the floor during a general session of the NEA. The featured speaker was William T. Harris, a former superintendent of the St. Louis schools and then U.S. commissioner of education. When Harris argued that the most important thing for schools was to strengthen their ties with the business community, Haley rose to challenge him, saying that, on the contrary, the top priority should be higher salaries for teachers. Harris retorted that delegates should not listen to the speaker, obviously a "grade teacher. . . worn out, tired and hysterical," words that probably only strengthened Haley's resolve. Under her leadership, the CTF grew rapidly and affiliated with the Chicago Federation of Labor in 1902. Haley delivered a formal speech at the NEA convention of 1904, calling on the delegates to address the poor working conditions and "wholly inadequate" salaries of teachers. She also criticized the corporate model of school organization, charging that it produced factorylike mechanical processes in schools and unthinking minds in students.[a]

[a]Sources: "Margaret Haley becomes the first woman and first teacher to speak at the NEA," http://fcis.oise.utoronto.ca/~dschugurensky/assignment1/1901haley.html (accessed on September 23, 2010); and Margaret Haley, "Why Teachers Should Organize [1904]," *Woman's True Profession: Voices from the History of Teaching*, Nancy Hoffman, ed. (Old Westbury, NY: The Feminist Press, 1981), 289–95.

Suggested Activity: Extreme discrepancies in pay existed between white and black teachers in the past, particularly during the times prior to the Supreme Court decision of *Brown v. Board of Education of Topeka* (1954). Civil rights lawyer Charles Hamilton Houston documented race-based pay scales and other such discrepancies in building his legal argument that "separate is not equal." What was his role in ending legally sanctioned school segregation? For help, view the video recording "The Road to *Brown*," San Francisco: California Newsreel, distributor, 1990. Compare also with Chapter 5: Race and the Education of African Americans, pp. 208–256.

American Federation of Teachers

From its beginnings the **American Federation of Teachers (AFT)** identified with the labor movement, and it took strong positions on better pay and working conditions for teachers. The first successful effort at forming a union for classroom teachers started in Chicago where poorly supplied classrooms, inadequate facilities, meager salaries, ineffective administration, and politically motivated board policies led to the founding of the Chicago Teachers Federation (CTF) in 1897. When the CTF sued the Chicago Board of Education for reneging on a promised pay raise for teachers, the board claimed lack of funds. After it was discovered that the board allowed some Chicago corporations to escape paying their lawful city taxes, the court ordered the corporations to pay up and the board to deliver its promised pay raise. CTF membership grew rapidly and, on April 15, 1916, the organization joined with the Chicago Federation of Men Teachers, the Chicago Federation of Women High School Teachers, and the Teachers Federation of Gary, Indiana, to form the American Federation of Teachers (AFT). Joined by other locals in New York City, Oklahoma, Pennsylvania, and Washington, D.C., the AFT was admitted into the American Federation of Labor on May 19, 1916.[26]

Some boards of education fired teachers who joined the AFT, but it still projected an image of teachers as upstanding citizens rather than mere servants. It also advocated popular election of school boards, free textbooks for school pupils, job tenure for teachers with meritorious service, and adequate pensions for teachers.[27]

The salary issue and union status

Despite their differences, at first both the NEA and the AFT rejected the use of "withdrawal of professional service" (or **strikes**) to get improvements in salaries, working conditions, or resources for schoolchildren. Indeed, the AFT had a no-strike policy for many years. However, due to Depression-era cutbacks in the 1930s and war-related cutbacks from 1941 to 1945, American schools were in poor straits. During the 1950s, school enrollments climbed dramatically from the World War II "baby boom," and when state and local authorities proved reluctant to increase funding to meet conditions, the AFT decided to resort to strikes and **collective bargaining**.

> ### WEB: Additional Information 1.3.: COLLECTIVE BARGAINING

> **For Further Reflection:** Should teachers strike or are strikes anathema to professionalism? Justify your position.

The influx of "baby boomers" into the schools in the 1950s and 1960s meant overcrowding, poor working conditions, low teacher morale, and increased public criticism of schools. In 1953 there were almost 60,000 one-room schools still in existence, and in 1957 the nation had an estimated shortage of around 247,000 classrooms. By 1958, there were 47,564 schools districts with 42.4 million students and 1,644,000 teachers. Under these conditions, the idea of strikes gained popularity among members, particularly after the 1960 formation of the United Federation of Teachers (UFT), a new AFT local in New York City. Over the next several years, successful UFT strikes brought the AFT to national prominence as never before.[28]

Meanwhile, in lieu of strikes, the NEA recommended "sanctions" (issuing a warning about substandard conditions in a school system and advising teachers against accepting employment there) and "professional negotiations" (negotiating contracts with local school systems without resorting to strikes). In actual practice, both tactics made the NEA appear weak because, in the absence of strikes, there was no incentive for school boards to negotiate in good faith or make the changes necessary to lift NEA sanctions. The NEA finally decided that to negotiate successful contracts it had to change, and in 1973 it adopted a new constitution that made it a union.[29]

Several attempts were made by the AFT to merge the two organizations, but each time it fell through. Sticking points included NEA members who refused to affiliate with the AFT's parent organization, the American Federation of Labor and the Congress of Industrial Organization (AFL-CIO). In addition, the NEA favored secret ballots and term limits for union presidents, while the AFT did not. While both organizations signed a "NEAFT partnership agreement" in 2001, whether an actual merger will occur remains to be seen.[30]

Professionalization and teacher education reforms

After World War II, the United States experienced domestic and international tensions from the Cold War that fed increased criticisms of teachers and schools. The relative stability teacher education programs once received in many colleges and universities gave way to instability. At several times over the years, powerful economic and political interests launched reforms of both school curricula and teacher education that created new uncertainties.

Teacher preparation after 1950

During the 1950s, both teacher education and the teaching profession were pummeled by harsh criticisms from political ideologists, business interests, tax-cut lobbyists, national defense advocates, and academic critics. Teachers and schools were accused of weakening scholastic standards and failing to teach the "basics" in the curriculum. Accusations from the political right that American youth were being endangered by subversive left wing forces in education only increased the public's fears. This was the era of high-pressure political tactics called "McCarthyism," (named after U.S. senator Joseph McCarthy of Wisconsin, who claimed that communists had infiltrated important American institutions). Fears led to greater emphasis on patriotic symbols and increased censorship of textbooks, curriculum materials, and school library holdings. In some jurisdictions, schoolteachers were required to sign loyalty oaths in order to keep their jobs.[31]

> **Suggested Activity:** Research McCarthyism and how it affected society in general and educators in particular. What is the debate today about the relationship between citizens' rights and threats to national security from external forces?

In little more than a decade, however, teachers had to face strong political criticisms from another direction, this time from the left. During the Vietnam War era (roughly, the mid-1960s to the mid-1970s), there was a rising level of criticism directed at traditional society, including condemnations of teachers and schools as insensitive tools of the "power establishment." Teachers were admonished to become more attentive to student needs, to provide "soft" teaching styles and curricular programs that recognized different interests, and to be more critical of the status quo.[32]

By the 1980s, conservative politics returned with renewed vigor, and teachers and schools were once again castigated for pampering students, weakening academic standards, and failing to teach the basics. In 1983, during Ronald Reagan's first term, the U.S. Department of Education released a critical national report, *A Nation at Risk*, that claimed "the educational foundations of our society are presently being eroded by a rising tide of mediocrity that threatens our very future as a Nation and a people."[33] This was followed by other reports, such as those released by the Education Commission of the States, various private foundations, and other interest groups. In the calls for reform a term emerged that became a mantra for many reformers—*teacher accountability*. By the 1990s, state-mandated high-stakes testing programs were widely implemented as ways to hold teachers and schools accountable for how students were taught and what students retained. Teacher education programs were once again forced, not only by political pressure but also by state and federal laws, to revise certification and graduation standards, irrespective of whether the imposed changes had adequate research behind them. Efforts increased to move teacher preparation programs to the graduate level, although the economic remuneration and professional status of teachers in the educational hierarchy did not noticeably improve as a result.[34]

For Further Reflection: Based on the historical evidence, it seems obvious that the preparation of teachers is directly connected to political developments outside education. Discuss the implications for educators.

Among the criticisms of teaching that arose in the 1980s and 1990s was the claim that, when compared to other learned professions, teaching simply does not measure up. Another was that too many teacher education students lack the intellectual background of students in other professional programs. Still another was that education research only produces "soft" knowledge, and few if any causal claims can be drawn from it. Of course, this could be said about research in the social and behavioral sciences generally, as opposed to the more predictable, "hard" knowledge of the physical sciences. Indeed, education research mostly deals with human factors that tend to be unpredictable and difficult to control; hence, an extensive body of stable professional knowledge has been difficult to produce. But there may be issues beyond intellectual substance or stable professional knowledge that impact teaching's status more than in other professions: Most teachers come from working- or lower-middle-class backgrounds, and the majority of them are women; therefore, social class and gender biases may exert more adverse effects on the status of teaching than on other professions.[35]

In the last few decades several groups have sought to elevate teaching through professionalization reforms. Three of the more significant are the **Holmes Partnership**, the **Carnegie Corporation**, and the **National Board for Professional Teaching Standards (NBPTS)**.

Suggested Activity: Conduct an informal poll in your college/university asking faculty and students who are not involved in teacher preparation about how they view the quality of teacher education programs. Analyze and discuss the results.

Holmes partnership

Launched by a consortium of schools of education in leading research universities in 1986, the Holmes Partnership began as the Holmes Group, a major advocate of teacher professionalization that gained wide attention with its 1989 publication titled *Tomorrow's Teachers*. Attempting to reform both teacher education and the teaching profession, the Holmes Group sought to improve teacher preparation by toughening entry standards, increasing candidates' command of academic subjects and teaching practices, cultivating stronger cooperation between the public schools and the teacher preparation programs in the colleges and universities, and encouraging more research and its dissemination. It also pushed the identification of "professional development schools" in cooperating school systems where student teachers, experienced teachers, and university professors could work together to solve "real world" teaching and learning problems. In 1996, the Holmes Group changed its name to the "Holmes Partnership," but it continues to promote high-quality professional preparation, strong partnerships among public schools and teacher preparation institutions, and more research and its dissemination.[36]

Carnegie corporation

An influential 1986 publication that heightened interest in the professionalization of teaching was *A Nation Prepared: Teachers for the 21st Century*. Issued by the Carnegie Corporation's Forum on Education and the Economy, the report proposed that teacher preparation should include both a bachelor degree in the arts or sciences and a master of teaching degree based on a new graduate curriculum in both the arts and sciences and in teacher education. Although the report's focus was on the economic aspects of education, and although it proposed more centralization of teaching and more accountability for student progress, it also pushed for greater decision-making power for teachers, increased resources and technology to enhance teacher productivity, and major improvements in teachers' salaries and career opportunities on par with other professions.[37]

National Board for Professional Teaching Standards

One of the important results flowing from teacher education reform initiatives was the creation of the National Board for Professional Teaching Standards (NBPTS) in 1987. NBPTS established a program through which a number of teachers have since pursued studies leading to **National Board Certification (NBC)**. The voluntary program takes a year or more of concerted effort, during which teachers must demonstrate how their teaching activities result in improved student achievement. NBC is the only available national teacher certificate, and it is recognized by an increasing number of states as an advanced level beyond state certification. Many states use it as an additional criterion in recruitment, and some provide financial rewards for those who hold it. In 2009, almost 82,000 teachers held NBC. It has also been endorsed by such organizations as the National Council for Accreditation of Teacher Education (NCATE), the National School Boards Association (NSBA), and the AFT and the NEA, among others.[38]

For Further Reflection: Are such efforts as those by the Holmes Group to enhance the status of teaching a promising development? Is the Carnegie-backed National Board Certification idea a good thing? Justify your position. What other possibilities can you suggest to achieve the goals of improving and strengthening the teaching profession?

Impact of professionalization

The 1980s and 1990s witnessed a flurry of reports that questioned the effectiveness of schools and teachers and put forward various reform proposals. An obvious question is, how much actually changed as a result of late twentieth-century professionalization reforms?

In a 1999 study, two-thirds of the teachers interviewed indicated that some aspects of the various reforms had been incorporated into practice, a trend reflected at the national level as well. Although most resulting reforms were imposed by policy makers, the study found that reforms incorporating active teacher involvement were more successfully implemented than those pushed from the top down. However, little has been done to remove major obstacles to teacher involvement, including the rigid structure of the workday that severely restricts teacher participation in professional planning or collaboration, lack of resources committed to high-quality faculty development, reluctance to establish genuine peer evaluation (where teachers systematically evaluate one another), and unwillingness to allow teachers to exercise any significant control over their own professional practice. Most participants doubted that any substantial increase in teacher power would take place, and some felt that what actually occurred was only a slight increase in their advisory role. Many crucial decisions on budget, curriculum, and personnel continue to be made at the district and state levels rather than the individual school level.[39]

It has been observed that, in terms of the professional working life of teachers, little improvement has been made since the early 1980s, and many teachers perceive additional erosion of professionalism due to the continuing imposition of a "factory model" on teaching. Today, control is exerted over teachers by entities far removed from classrooms, often making it difficult for teachers to make professional judgments. Teachers often lack the time and space to discuss problems with colleagues or to implement innovative ideas. In addition, given the increasing complexity and intensity of teaching, teachers are often required to "multitask" in ways that interrupt instruction, create stress, and result in less effective teaching.[40]

Cross-reference: For a discussion of school governance and decision making, see Chapter 2: School Governance and Control, pp. 54–103.

Portrayal of teaching in popular culture

Popular media tend to idealize good teachers, portraying them as heroes and saviors, a limited understanding at best. The image of the heroic teacher usually projects an entrepreneurial, independent individual who works in isolation from others, which is not necessarily typical of how most teachers work, including the most capable and effective ones. Heroic teachers also are often portrayed as maverick outsiders with little or no formal professional preparation.[a]

⇨

One example is the movie *"Stand and Deliver."*[b] The main character is Jaime Escalante (played by Edward James Olmos), a computer expert seeking to become a teacher. He lands a job in a barrio in Los Angeles, teaching a group of underprivileged, underachieving students who always seem to live down to the low expectations of their teachers. His colleagues argue that high expectations only set up the students for failure. The students doubt themselves as well, and they challenge Escalante's authority as they contend with the crushing weight of family and community problems. Escalante rejects low expectations and challenges the students to take calculus and prove themselves on national exams. In the end, the students do rise to their teacher's challenge and gain a sense of accomplishment, and Escalante prevails after devoting all of his energy to the task, even suffering a stress-induced heart attack in the process. Overall, throughout the film, Escalante is portrayed as a heroic, highly successful teacher who, after defying colleagues and the entrenched educational bureaucracy, helps a group of marginalized students learn that they can succeed. And he accomplishes all this without any formal teacher preparation or attention to educational theory and methodology. Once again comes the message that formal teacher preparation is superfluous, that what teachers really need to know is the "common sense" they presumably learn on the job.

[a]Sari Knopp Biklen, *School Work: Gender and the Cultural Construction of Teaching* (New York: Teachers College Press, 1995),1–6.

[b]*"Stand and Deliver,"* American Playhouse, Warner Brothers Pictures, 1988.

Contemporary conditions

Teacher profiles: who teaches?

In the United States, the teaching profession at the elementary and secondary levels is pursued predominantly by white females, two demographic characteristics that have not shown any significant change in recent times. For that reason, each needs further explanation.

Ethnic identity

In 2001, an NEA survey showed that 90 percent of all teachers were classified as Caucasian/white, 5 percent were African American, 1 percent were Asian, 1 percent were American Indian/Alaska Native, 1 percent belonged in more than one category, and 1 percent were "other." In addition, 5 percent also identified themselves as "Hispanic," which cuts across the other categories (that is, one could be white or black but also Hispanic). It appears, furthermore, that the percentage of African American teachers has decreased since 1991, and even then it was only 9 percent. All of these percentages are important, given that the student population as well as the population at large have become more racially and ethnically diverse while the teaching profession remains predominantly white.[41]

> **Suggested Activity:** Discuss with other prospective teachers how, given their own particular backgrounds and beliefs, they are preparing to teach a racially and ethnically diverse student population. How are perceptions similar or different, and why?

Gender

According to the NEA survey, 79 percent of all American public school teachers in 2001 were female, and only 21 percent male. It should be understood, however, that these numbers varied by geographic region, age, district size, minority status, school level, and other factors. For example, there were fewer males among minority teachers than among white teachers; conversely, the older the students, male teachers were more likely to be their instructors: 43 percent of all teachers at the high school level were male, as compared to 25 percent at the middle or junior high level, and 9 percent at the elementary level. Finally, the percentage of males has generally declined since 1981. Table 1.1 illustrates these points, providing the gender of all teachers and selected subgroups of age, school type and size of system, and geographical region.[42]

> **For Further Reflection:** Does it make any difference that the majority of teachers are women? How do you explain the tendency that the older the students the more frequently they are being taught by men?

Table 1.1 Percentage of male and female teachers, 1961–2001 (at ten-year intervals)

Group and year	1961	1971	1981	1991	2001
% Males:	31	34	33	28	21
Elementary	12	10	18	12	9
Secondary	57	54	47	44	35
% Females:	69	69	67	72	79
Elementary	88	90	82	88	91
Secondary	43	45	53	56	65

Adapted from "Table 70, Males and Females, All Teachers and Selected Subgroups, 1961–2000," in *Status of the American School Teacher, 2000–2001*, NEA Research 2003 (Washington, DC: National Education Association, 2003), 91, at http://www.nea.org/home/2233.htm (accessed on February 9, 2009).

Teacher salary

Teachers' salaries vary considerably, depending on such factors as school level, geographical location, and years of experience, but in recent years teacher pay slightly improved, according to a 2007 survey conducted by the American Federation of Teachers (AFT). Elementary school teachers still made less than middle and high school teachers, beginning teachers less than veterans, and rural teachers less than urban. In terms of geographical location, for example, South Dakota paid 69.4 percent of the national average salary, while California paid 124.8 percent.[43]

Compared to other professionals employed in public school systems, teacher salaries lagged. During the 2006–2007 school year, for instance, teachers earned an average of $49,295 while principals at the high school level made $92,964 and superintendents earned $141,191 (see Table 1.2).

Of course, opportunities may exist for some teachers to earn additional income by serving as mentors or staff developers, teaching in those subject areas experiencing teacher shortages, working in schools where improved student performance is most needed, or engaging in other efforts such as acquiring additional special qualifications and/or achieving National Board Certification.[44]

For Further Reflection: Teaching has been referred to as a "labor of love." What is your response to this statement?

Table 1.2 Average professional salaries of selected positions in public school systems[a] in the 1999–2000 and 2006–2007 school years

Position	1999–2000	2006–2007
Central office		
Superintendent	$112,158	$141, 191
Assistant Supt.	88,913	111,963
Finance Administrator	73,499	91,718
Subject Area Supervisors	63,103	75,982
School principals		
Sr. High	79,839	92,965
Jr. High/Mid. Sch.	73,877	87,866
Elementary	68,407	82,414
Auxiliary school personnel		
Counselors	48,195	55,930
Librarians	46,732	54,881
Classroom Teachers	**32,213**	**49,294**

[a]Data from a stratified sample of school systems enrolling more than 300 pupils.
Source: Adapted from "Table 247: Average Salary and Wages Paid in Public School Systems: 1985 to 2007," *Statistical Abstract of the United States, 2009*, 160, at http://www.census.gov/prod/2008pubs/09statab/educ.pdf (accessed on September 23, 2010).

Choosing to become a teacher

Why do people choose to enter the teaching profession, and why do they stay or leave? The NEA found that 73 percent of all respondents reported the "desire to work with young people" as a major reason to enter the profession, followed by "the value or significance of education in society," "interest in subject matter," and "the influence of a teacher or advisor in elementary or secondary school." The first three responses were also given as reasons why teachers stayed in the profession, in addition to "having too much invested to leave now."[45]

Observers such as Lee Shulman and Gloria Ladson-Billings have expressed concern that more teachers do not emphasize intellectual goals as important reasons for entering the teaching profession. Shulman maintains that this lack of intellectual emphasis strikes at the status of teaching as a learned profession, and it also shows the need for teachers to see themselves as members of a scholarly community. In her research, Ladson-Billings asked why prospective teacher education candidates wanted to become teachers, and the typical replies included "loving kids" or wanting to "be with young people." These are desirable attributes for teachers, of course, but Ladson-Billings was troubled by the lack of intellectual goals, such as the desire to empower students with a love of knowledge.[46]

Suggested Activity: Discuss with others the meaning of being part of a learned profession and a scholarly community. Elaborate on whether you believe students preparing to be teachers think of themselves in these terms. Should they, and why or why not?

On the contrary, evidence can also be found that many teachers have strong orientations toward improving society, even as they face accountability measures, are made to follow business models, and have to prepare students for high-stakes testing. Running parallel to official pronouncements about accountability, however, is a "discourse of possibility" in which teachers continue to view public education as an avenue to greater equality and social justice.[47]

New teachers may be excited by the prospects of making differences in students' lives, but they may also become frustrated by such things as limited opportunities for advancement and fellow teachers who seem unable or unwilling to improve their practice. New teachers are usually inclined to initiate changes, but they often become discouraged by climates of conformity, some becoming disillusioned and dropping out after only a few years. It has been suggested that some teachers should leave the profession if their effectiveness has been exhausted, but others may simply need ways to reenergize and renew their efforts to become better teachers. Under these conditions, teachers are better able to carefully choose practices for best effects on students, take calculated risks, and seek support from colleagues and give it freely in turn. In addition, society itself has obligations to prevent teacher burnout by providing better working conditions and salaries commensurate with similar professions.[48]

Teaching as a profession

Today it seems easy to forget that when statewide systems of American public schools first emerged in the 1830s and 1840s, society was mostly rural, government was miniscule, and industry was composed of small independent companies. By 1900, Americans had built a network of public school systems that provided more schooling for more of its people than any other nation on earth. Decentralized and locally controlled, the typical public school for most of the nineteenth century was a small, one-room building. As late as 1890, more than 71 percent of the population still lived in sparsely populated rural areas. Most teachers were young and poorly paid, and if they had any professional preparation, it was probably a few normal school courses, some occasional lectures, or maybe a short summer training session or two. Teacher turnover was high and a lifelong teaching career was the exception rather than the rule. In the twentieth century, this American "system" of schools was transformed by urbanization and industrialization, which brought structural uniformity to American education.[49]

In the process, teacher preparation moved from normal schools to the colleges and universities, and an undergraduate degree became the minimal level of professional preparation, with movement toward the master degree as an entry-level requirement by the end of the twentieth century. Looking at this track record, it would appear that teaching was indeed moving to full professional status, but the question of whether teaching is a genuine profession continues to spark debate and proposals.

Teaching as a traditional profession

Some observers maintain that teaching must claim its place among the traditional learned professions. For example, Lee Shulman argues that teachers are professionals because their work is guided by standards rather than mere rules. Their work requires them to make informed decisions when confronted with unpredictable situations and challenging teaching-learning conditions. Rather than following static guidelines, teachers must respond frequently to unexpected circumstances by using expertise derived from professional standards, something they share in common with other learned professions.[50]

Teachers as intellectuals

Some observers would like to see the teaching profession adopt a model of teachers as **transformative intellectuals**. Henry Giroux has long argued that teachers should be involved in debates about educational policy and school reform, and he has been highly critical of the model of teachers as technicians who simply follow other people's orders. He maintains that teachers perform *intellectual* labor rather than purely *technical* (or instrumental) labor. Furthermore, teachers play a distinctive political role because they are morally obligated to raise questions about the curriculum and about what and how they teach, rather than uncritically teaching everything handed to them. They also should not accept being relegated to "mere employee" status, but should link their preparation and professional knowledge to the goals of education for a more democratic society. Schools are not isolated institutions immune to politics, because political power is so often used to control them; instead, they should be places where knowledge and values from the past and present are taught to rising generations to help them shape their own visions of the future, particularly when powerful interest groups try to dictate what is taught in schools and exert control over the minds of the young. This is apparent in curriculum controversies over such issues as school prayer, evolution, patriotism, and censorship of materials. Neutrality may be difficult, but rather than partisanship, teachers should be dedicated to preparing students for active roles as democratic citizens who try to understand issues, solve problems, and achieve a more just society. As Giroux sees it, this is the crucial transformative role of teachers.[51]

> **For Further Reflection:** Should teachers be transformative intellectuals, and if so, what does that mean in the specific context of the daily routines of schooling?

Teachers, technical expertise, and moral agency

Certainly there is ample historical and contemporary evidence to show that technical expertise has helped accomplish advances in many areas of life. As Robert Welker points out, however, sometimes these accomplishments get mythologized into a belief that technical expertise ultimately will solve our problems. Such a viewpoint fails to recognize the realities faced by teachers in actual classrooms and schools. Clearly, teachers gain from acquiring better technical expertise, but they also face problems that do not simply reduce to technical solutions. For example, teaching a child to read is helped by a teacher's technical know-how, but bridging the gap between teaching a child to read and other, sometimes conflicting societal expectations requires more than just technical skill. Society's expectation that schools should build a strong sense of identity with the greater community may actually come into conflict with society's expectation that schools also should build a strong sense of individual freedom. Community identity and individual freedom do not have to be in conflict, but they often are. It is one thing to teach a child to read (which may be difficult enough), but educating a child to accept a strong community identity while at the same time imbuing that child with an equally strong sense of individual freedom may be far more difficult and take longer to accomplish. "Community identity" and "individual freedom" are primarily moral goals, not technical ones. Their achievement depends not only on what teachers do but on society clarifying its moral and social expectations and achieving a better understanding of what schools may reasonably accomplish. Complex educational goals are likely to call for complex solutions, and while technical efficiency helps, by itself it is not sufficient. The technical expertise model for the teaching profession remains strong, however, for if teachers are seen as technical experts (the thinking goes), then they will gain a place among the more exclusive professions whose technical proficiencies have brought them high status and credibility (such as the engineering profession). A problem with such a view is that teaching is not the same as engineering, for no particular teaching technique has yet been devised that is as predictably successful as the mathematical precision of many engineering techniques. The language of technical expertise promises predictable, consistent success, but as experienced teachers well know, perseverance, patience, humor, and good will, which are moral and social qualities, play a vitally important role in good teaching. In sum, teaching is different from professions defined primarily by technical expertise; hence, we must recognize the moral basis of teaching, not in some sentimental sense, but in the larger sense of what kind of person or citizen we want to develop and what kind of individual and social life we want to cultivate, questions that are as fundamental now as when they were first raised centuries ago.[52]

WEB: Suggested Reading 1.2.

Teaching as a unique profession

There are various ways of defining the term *"profession."* It may mean doing something for pay, as in "professional athlete." It could connote objective detachment, disinterest, or technical excellence. It might indicate the results of prolonged and rigorous study of a particular field or simply a high level of competence at certain tasks. According to Roger Soder, such an array of definitions not only allows neurosurgeons to be considered professionals but also football players and car thieves. In other words, the term *"profession"* is a social construct, carrying particular meanings according to usage and context. Despite these variations, however, there are characteristics most people associate with the term *"learned" profession,* that is, a profession based on knowledge, training, ethical conduct, status, rewards, and a degree of autonomous control of the work. By and large, to be a member of a learned profession has positive connotations as something desirable in both an individual and a social sense. Various professional groups, such as physicians, have invested much time, effort, and resources in pursuing public respect and protecting their professional status with both public relations and legal safeguards. Teachers are not very different, for while they may not enjoy as much status, remuneration, or legal protection as physicians, teachers have long claimed professional status and have sought to establish themselves as a full-fledged profession.[53]

Soder argues, however, that teachers err when attempting to emulate established professions such as medicine, because teachers are simply unable to replicate the same path that medicine took. Physicians once had to contend with a historic image that included incompetent quacks who sullied the medical profession's reputation to the detriment of its competent practitioners. Medicine's image improved significantly only after two major developments: scientific and technological advances that brought more predictable results to the practice of medicine and tougher entry requirements for medical school students and their more rigorous preparation in appropriate scientific and technical knowledge. These changes noticeably improved the services provided by physicians, and they also helped give the medical profession an authoritative image.

An outpouring of new educational science and technology that yields similar results for teaching seems unlikely in the foreseeable future. Teachers should bury the dream of becoming like physicians, mainly because comparing physicians and teachers is akin to comparing apples and oranges: They are not the same kinds of things, either logically or practically. Soder recommends that teachers should drop such comparisons and focus instead on what is unique and applicable to teaching itself, such as its moral basis. Students are sent to school in compliance with compulsory attendance laws, and they are placed in the charge of teachers who may be virtual strangers to both the parents and the students. In turn, teachers are supposed to give competent, ethically committed instruction to all students equally, providing them with opportunities to grow intellectually and to develop their humanity. These particular traits are unique to the teaching profession and make teaching an inherently moral endeavor.[54]

> **Suggested Activity:** Interview three people at random about their definitions of *"professional."* Compare their responses and analyze what the differences and similarities mean.

This line of argument is bolstered by Gary D. Fenstermacher, who points to three significant factors that make the teaching profession fundamentally different from other learned professions. The first factor is the **mystification of knowledge** found in traditional learned professions such as medicine and law. For example, physicians and lawyers "mystify" knowledge when they embrace claims that only they know how to diagnose and treat illnesses or interpret and argue points of law. In education, however, teachers strive to give away their knowledge. The second factor deals with **social distance**, something other professions maintain by avoiding involvement in the lives of clients/patients beyond specific conditions (i.e., a client's property rights, a patient's liver condition). Teachers, however, cannot ignore the life experiences of learners. The third factor is **reciprocity of effort**. Those in other learned professions usually want the client or patient to defer to their professional judgments without fully understanding either the reasoning or the knowledge behind those judgments. In teaching, however, reciprocity of effort is central because success depends on the active involvement of students in learning the teacher's field of knowledge and becoming skillful in applying its concepts.[55] Paolo Freire goes even further and argues that not only must students actively participate in the learning process, but teachers also must be active learners concerning what and who they teach and how they and their students might grow from the process. In other words, both students and teachers must be involved in one another's intellectual growth.[56]

Professional ethics and the teaching profession

A long recognized feature of any learned profession is to be guided by ethical standards. The relation of ethics to education is a very old concern, for just as people today encounter controversy over what a proper education ought to be, so did people in ancient times. For example, in the fourth century B.C.E., Aristotle complained that there were "no generally accepted assumptions about what the young should learn" or whether education should be directed "at things useful in life, or at those conducive to virtue, or at exceptional accomplishments."[57] Today, debate continues to surround what should be taught, what its purpose should be, and whether the chief result should be job preparation, intellectual achievement, virtuous moral character, or a combination of such ends.

Part of the debate concerns the preparation of professional educators themselves. Some observers argue that what teachers most need is practical "hands-on" experience in the "real" world of schools, not time spent on "theoretical" studies such as professional ethics. Others argue that while teachers need practical preparation, they also need the intellectual depth that comes from reading, debating, and reflecting on the ethical issues of their profession and the larger society. The position taken here is that members of the teaching profession not only need to know what to teach and how to teach it but also the ethical standards for good professional practice and how to apply them.

WEB: Suggested Reading 1.3.

What is professional ethics?

Aristotle claimed that all human conduct aims at some notion of "the good," but the pursuit of a good (such as wealth, power, or respect) may be used for evil purposes. What we need is a better understanding of "the good" in the general sense, which for Aristotle was "the good of the human community or society." The way we define *good* in ordinary life is related to specific practical goods, such as health, success, and the enjoyment of life. For Aristotle, the pursuit of all goods should aim at one end, "happiness," by which he did not mean mere pleasure but ways of living chosen for their inherent goodness. This involves avoiding the excesses of too much (overindulgence, compulsiveness) and too little (insufficient effort, shallowness); instead it means seeking the ethical "golden mean" between extremes and pursuing moderation in life situations by using rational thought and ethical principles to guide conduct and achieve happiness.[58]

Nel Noddings has articulated a contemporary view of Aristotelian happiness, with application to certain educational issues. She argues against the current emphasis on higher test scores as the ultimate aim and proposes instead an earnest debate on the aims of education. One central aim should be to help students work toward happiness, not as frivolous pleasure but as an essential life goal. In this sense, "happiness" is the avoidance of fatalism and the development of talents (such as learning to appreciate what is morally valuable and increasing knowledge of life and the world). All of us need to understand that, while we cannot solve every problem confronting us, we are not totally helpless and can work toward at least some improvements in personal and social life. However, caught up in today's test-driven mentality (a singular focus on measurement and quantification), schools are forced to ignore such moral aims. What the curriculum should reflect is helping students better understand, appreciate, and become more skillfully engaged in life in communities, civic responsibilities, friendships, and meaningful occupations. This does not mean weakening the curriculum with simplistic "how-to" courses, but—for example—using good literature to help students explore life experiences reflecting both happiness and tragedy. Rather than test score mania, students should be taught a challenging academic curriculum that builds the kinds of understandings, appreciations, and skills needed in life.[59] When education is considered from the ethical standpoint of happiness as one of its ultimate aims, it leads to useful conceptions of value that far outweigh test scores.

According to John Dewey, the origin of the English word "*ethics*" is derived from the Greek word *ethos,* which originally meant the customs and usages of a society, including its views on character and disposition. Similarly, in Latin the word for those concepts was *mores,* from which the English word "*moral*" is derived. The meanings of both terms cover ways of behaving that are approved by a society, and to act against the ethos (ethics) or mores (morals) of a society is to violate norms of "good" and "bad," "right" and "wrong."[60] Today, ethics is still concerned with right or wrong and the good or bad of human conduct. It involves thinking critically about what we do and how we do it in order to clarify our ethical principles and moral understandings and thus make sound judgments and take good or right actions.

Ethical thought and action involve both the "inner" life of individual reflection and the "outer" life of social relationships. Ethical life involves interactions with other people, especially how we should treat others and how we expect to be treated by them in turn. Factual knowledge about individual and societal conditions (or "what is") may help us make ethical judgments, but facts alone rarely solve ethical dilemmas. A condition long recognized by ethicists is that factual claims try to describe the world as it is, and they are true if the world is as described. Ethical claims, however, are different: They do not describe the world as it is, factually speaking, but how personal and social life should or ought to be lived. In short, factual claims *describe,* ethical claims *prescribe* ways to help us reflect on how we should live; therefore, we need to be informed by ethical traditions and customs, by great moral teachers and moral teachings, and by our own critical (or reflective) thought and experience.[61]

> **For Further Reflection:** Are people born with an innate sense of right and wrong, or are these things learned from one's environment? Do teachers need specific preparation in professional ethics, or do they learn all they need to know about ethics and moral reasoning from ordinary life experiences? Consider arguments both for and against your own conclusions.

Professional ethics is the application of general ethical principles to professional conduct and to solving ethical dilemmas encountered in professional practice. Working for good and doing right may seem to be clear-cut things: We should simply choose the good and right and act accordingly. Of course, many aspects of daily personal and professional life are quickly decided and do not rise to the level of ethical dilemmas, but despite our best efforts difficult problems often arise and a clear path is not readily apparent. One good may conflict with another, or we may find ourselves facing only bad choices (being "caught between the devil and the deep blue sea") in which all the likely options we can devise seem seriously flawed. When good and right actions are difficult to discern, that is when we need a background in ethical knowledge and reflective thinking skills to help us choose wisely. Unerring moral clarity and pristine ethical purity are terribly scarce; consequently, most teachers need background preparation to help them understand ethical issues in professional practice and to develop better reasoning skills. Professional practice, as life itself, requires us to make ethical choices and decisions.

Teacher professionalism, ethics, and teaching as a moral activity

When teaching is understood as a moral activity that impacts people, it provides a more helpful view of the profession. Teaching shapes and influences students, but it ought not to be forced on students in ways over which they have no reasonable level of assent or control. As Hugh Sockett points out, it seems that we do not want to talk about teaching in moral terms or discuss the important moral and ethical responsibilities that go along with it. Examine any number of contemporary writings on teaching and the language is full of psychological, technological, and even economic terms: We seem intent on producing graduates for job markets, but we seem embarrassed to talk about straightforward moral outcomes, such as compassion, patience, honesty, courage, and kindness. This is curious, particularly if we recognize that teaching is a moral activity that helps shape the growth of persons. Of course, teachers are only one influence in the development of persons, but the moral good of every student ought to be important and ought to be recognized by every teacher.[62]

WEB: Suggested Reading 1.4.

Ethical obligations of the teaching profession

According to Michael Bayles, professional ethics is concerned with the trust-worthy performance of professional obligations to clients, patients, customers, or in our case, students or pupils. For teachers and other educators, the primary ethical obligation is the educational well-being and growth of students. A related obligation is met in serving student growth, because in doing so educators are serving society itself (including third parties such as parents, citizens, and tax-payers). Closely related are obligations to the employer and to the profession itself and how these impact students and third parties. In other words, profes-sional ethical obligations serve to prescribe (or even to proscribe) certain pro-fessional actions or character traits of professionals.[63]

Obligations to students: the bond of trust

"Trust" refers to students' (and the public's) moral right to expect (or trust) that professional educators will work to promote the educational growth of each student. The teacher's overall ethical obligation is to provide professional services worthy of student and public trust. This obligation is sometimes called "beneficence", and it is a major reason why professional standing is granted by society through certification or licensure, which is supposed to signify that the holder is competent to deliver good professional service.[64]

Ethical values and professional educators

There is a need to be wary of mere lists of values and virtues because they might lull us into assuming they contain all we need to solve any ethical dilemma. In fact, solving ethical dilemmas is hard work, and difficult ethical problems rarely have simplistic solutions. Reflecting on values never hurts, however, and the following list provides some well-known examples to consider in both professional and personal life:

- *Honesty.* Truthful, honest conduct in professional interactions with students and others, including judgments on student progress and teaching the curriculum without intentionally distorting subject matter.
- *Candor.* Being forthright when a student thinks he or she is performing satisfactorily but is not. Candor should be provided in helpful, supportive ways that foster student growth, not in punitive ways that diminish the student.
- *Competence.* Competence is not a moral virtue per se, but an incompetent professional cannot deliver trustworthy professional service. Becoming more competent should be a constant goal.

⇨

- *Diligence*. Carrying out professional duties and obligations in timely ways, such as always being prepared for class and evaluating student work in timely fashion.
- *Discretion (or Confidentiality)*. Care of personal knowledge and opinions professionals gain of students as well as official school records. It is the educator's obligation to protect confidential information about students in accordance with law and school policy.
- *Fairness*. Treatment of an individual student or group of students in comparison with other individuals and groups of students. The educator's obligation to fairness stems from the principle of democratic equality.
- *Loyalty*. Working for the good of students but not in unethical ways (such as glowing but untruthful recommendations to a student's prospective employers). Ordinarily, the educator's foremost loyalty should be to the student, but this may sometimes conflict with obligations to third parties such as parents.

Sources: Adapted from material in Michael D. Bayles, *Professional Ethics*, 2nd Edition, Belmont, Calif.: Wadsworth, Inc., 1989, 79–99; and the National Education Association, *Code of Ethics for the Education Profession*, (adopted 1975), at http://www.nea.org/home/30442.htm (accessed on September 23, 2010).

Obligations to others

Although a professional educator's primary obligations are to students, there are also obligations to third parties, such as parents, taxpayers, citizens, and prospective employers. This means that professional service ought to be delivered in ways that serve not only the good of students but also the public good (or the good of the wider society). In other words, ethical obligations to students must be reasonably balanced with obligations to others.[65]

Obligations to employers

Professional educators are expected to act in the best interest of their employers as well, and for most teachers this is usually a board of education. In public education, administrators are not, strictly speaking, the legal employers but are hired supervisory personnel who carry out the employer's policies and directives.

Obligations to fellow professionals and to the profession

Sometimes professionals provide services to other professionals, such as serving on committees that evaluate peers for awards, promotions, or other personnel-related tasks. One should protect confidential information about fellow employees, but one should be candid and truthful to the employer concerning relevant information about other employees encountered in legitimate personnel deliberations.[66]

Obligations to the profession include engaging in research and study for knowledge acquisition, skill development, and other improvements in one's competence and encouraging the same commitment among colleagues. A professional is also obligated to improve the status, working conditions, remuneration, and prestige of the profession because public respect enhances professional effectiveness; however, this should not be merely self-serving. Positive public opinion is extremely important for the teaching profession, because it cannot effectively provide professional services without ethical and competent members and without public respect and support.[67]

Daily realities of teaching

Teaching has frequently been examined concerning what teachers do, how they do it, and how it compares to other occupations. Writings by teachers about their professional experiences and insights into successful teaching have also been published. Sundry efforts have defined, labeled, and described teachers' daily activities and their world of work.[68] Generally speaking, the professional and economic status of teachers may contain some puzzling contradictions, but in most communities teachers are viewed as reliable and dedicated people of good character whose professional service is crucial to the good of society.

> **Suggested Activity:** Talk to relatives and friends about how they view teachers. To what extent do your conversations reveal the existence of "status discrepancy" and in what ways? See "The issue" at the beginning of this chapter.

Teachers themselves give divergent answers when asked how they feel about their daily work. These include how they must often work in isolation from other adults, how their workdays are fragmented, and how they are expected to play multiple roles of educator, therapist, surrogate parent, even police officer and social worker. Some teachers are dismayed by how their work has been **deskilled** by "teacher-proof" curricula and how they must follow prescribed directives in which they were not consulted and had no input.[69] Stressful working conditions force some members of the profession to leave altogether; however, some teachers provide positive accounts of their professional experience. One is the pleasure they derive from interactions with young people. Another is that teaching is filled with many intrinsic rewards, including the satisfaction of knowing that the work is meaningful for students and the larger society. However, too much reliance on intrinsic rewards for job satisfaction may make teachers too vulnerable and dependent on their students. After all, teacher success rarely depends solely on personal efforts alone but on the cooperative efforts of students as well. Student roles lead to a paradoxical situation concerning the teacher's authority and vulnerability. On the one hand, the teacher needs to control the classroom and secure sufficient compliance from students for effective teaching and learning to occur. On the other hand, teacher control is fragile because it is so dependent on student cooperation. In other words, the dependence on student cooperation and the necessary exercise of sufficient classroom control may create additional stress for teachers.[70]

There are various proposals to reform and restructure the teaching profession, but which is best to advance the profession is hotly contested. For example, is teaching a collegial effort, and should teachers engage in greater collegial collaboration than is currently practiced? Or, has the value of collaboration been overemphasized in the past, and does teacher individualism remain highly important to how teachers operate?[71]

One study of teachers' workplaces concludes that teachers are "brokers" who must deal with society's goals, student characteristics, personal professional judgments, and workplace attributes. Multiple variables come into play, including teacher conceptions of the subject matter being taught (is it fixed or malleable?) and how they view students as learners (are they motivated, academically able, proficient?). Relationships among teachers, students, and subject matter constitute the "stuff of schooling," and these things all occur within a "professional community" that plays a large role in whether teachers succeed or get burned out. Hence, **reflective professional communities** must be nurtured to encourage critical inquiry, focus on solving classroom problems, and support professional growth and change. Teachers tend to thrive in supportive environments of this kind, as opposed to those characterized by a lack of intellectual stimulation, overly individualistic norms of privacy, lack of collegial interaction and feedback, and lack of exposure to new ideas. Instead of schools as organizations where success depends on top-down tinkering with administrative structures, technological gimmicks, and teacher accountability measures, work environments in schools ought to be seen as professional communities where reflective professional practice, collegial collaboration, and mutual responsibility in educating students are the norms.[72]

Schools are usually crowded places where space is scarce, and this makes reflective teaching difficult. While teachers belong to a "school community," the typical school is often organized with classrooms and labs located along long hallways and with the central office, auditorium, cafeteria, gym, and art and band rooms at a distance. There is a scarcity of space for teachers to meet and collegially plan or evaluate their work. Teachers spend most of their time with students, sometimes even during lunch breaks, with little time for collegial interactions and no place to have them.[73]

Of course, many teachers favor a more individualistic style, and the profession itself simply may attract those who desire autonomy over their work, a factor that can complicate professional cooperation and collaboration. Despite all the calls for a stronger professional community, a more fitting image of teachers might be that of independent artisans, or those who develop teaching strategies and learning activities for their own students and classrooms. They usually prefer to work alone, but when the need arises they will collaborate, particularly with colleagues who teach the same subject matter or grade level or who share the same pedagogical style. There may be merit in operating schools as loosely coupled systems, because they allow teachers to coordinate to the degree necessary without giving up highly valued classroom autonomy. Over time many schools develop effective internal mechanisms, and they prove quite resilient to reformist efforts bent on changing them into idealistic visions of "good" schools. Effective teachers establish ways of working individually and collegially that should be respected, and instead of forcing collaboration, teachers should be respected as artisans who collaborate when needed and share collegially when asked, whether within a school or across schools and systems.[74]

> **Suggested Activity:** Speak with experienced teachers about the issues of collegial collaboration and individual preference and what they prefer concerning their own work, its challenges and rewards. What conclusions can you draw from their responses that might help you prepare for your own professional future?

Professional organizations and societies

Teachers have long come together in professional organizations or societies to learn from colleagues and researchers, and these organizations are important tools in maintaining and extending professional understandings and skills. They range in size, scope, and mission. Almost all of them are engaged in supporting and enhancing the professional work of teachers. For example, some organizations are devoted to broad teaching fields, such as the National Council for the Social Studies (history, geography, civics or government), the American Council on the Teaching of Foreign Languages (French, Spanish, German, etc.), or the National Science Teachers Association (biology, chemistry, physics, etc.). Others are dedicated to specific disciplines or subjects in the curriculum, such as the National Council for Teachers of English and the National Association of Biology Teachers. Some are national in focus while others are international, such as the Association for Childhood Education International or the International Reading Association. Some organizations focus on a specific age or school level while others concentrate on certain needs, such as the Council for Exceptional Children. All of the major professional organizations have central goals of disseminating research, information, publications (reports, white papers, newsletters, journals). Almost all major organizations also have state and local chapters, so wherever teachers are located there will likely be chapters within reasonable geographical access that hold meetings and disseminate publications and other materials. See examples on the web.

WEB: Additional Information 1.4.: SELECTED LEADING PROFESSIONAL SOCIETIES FOR TEACHERS

Suggested Activity: Visit the website of the professional organization that most closely represents your own professional interests. See what helpful information you can find.

Educators forming and joining professional societies organized around subjects, student ages or school levels, or other specific professional interests seems to generate little or no controversy. Such organizations appear to be clearly dedicated to the development of professional competencies or the extension of education to more people. Controversy tends to emerge only when educators join groups that speak out forcefully for advancing the economic interests of the profession.

For Further Reflection: Why does a teacher's right to organize in unions seem more controversial than other people's rights to do the same? What is your opinion about the issue, and why?

Should professionals belong to unions?

When the topic of teacher unions is raised, it is usually collective bargaining that comes to mind. To be fair, teacher unions do far more than advocate collective bargaining on economic issues, but the use of strikes is usually one of the features of being a union.[75]

In early 2009, the NEA claimed 3.2 million members and the AFT claimed 1.4 million. As these numbers attest, many teachers apparently value unions, not only for their focus on research, publications, and teaching-learning issues, but also the benefits that may come from collective bargaining. Salary and fringe benefits are certainly important aspects of collective bargaining but so are issues such as educators being required to teach subjects for which they are not qualified, or situations where the health and safety of students and teachers are threatened by unsafe conditions, to name but two.[76] Without collective bargaining, teachers individually would have to confront powerful forces and bear the full costs of legal fees and loss of personal time.

Teacher unions also have vociferous critics. For example, one critic calls teacher unions the "worms in the American Education Apple" and the NEA the "National Extortion Association." Another accusation is that teacher unions misuse public resources because, instead of emphasizing greater educational output to meet public needs, they seek more money for schools in order to build power bases for themselves.[77]

Teachers have long come together in professional organizations and societies, but whether they should join unions remains a contested issue both inside and outside the profession. Perhaps the central question ought to be: What is the best way to pursue professional growth and improve educational results while also attracting and retaining the best teachers possible?

International comparison: China

China is the world's most populous country, with more than 1.33 billion people. In international terms, it has the second-largest economy (after the United States) and the fourth-largest landmass (after Russia, Canada, and the United States). China is located on the coast of eastern Asia, facing the Yellow Sea, the East China Sea, and the South China Sea. Its coastline stretches from North Korea southward to Vietnam, and it shares land borders with 14 countries, the longest with Kazakhstan, Mongolia, and Russia to the north and India, Nepal, and Burma to the south. Its climate ranges from the subtropical in the south, Siberian-like winters in the north, and desert conditions in the far west.[78]

China has a long history as one of the world's great civilizations. For centuries it was ruled by imperial dynasties, the last of which (the Qing or Manchu Dynasty) ended in 1911. Efforts to establish a republican form of government were led by Sun Yat-sen, founder of the Kuomintang or Nationalist Party, but he was unable to form a stable government before his death in 1925. His successor was Chiang Kai-shek, who was thwarted by a civil war with the Chinese communists and by the Japanese invasion beginning in 1937. Chiang's Nationalist government was toppled by the communists under Mao Zedong, who established the People's Republic of China under the Communist Party in 1949. The Nationalists fled to the island of Taiwan and established the Republic of China. Although a truce holds presently, both governments continue to view each other with suspicion.[79]

Revolution of 1949 and its aftermath

Under Mao Zedong and the Communist Party, mainland China became a state-controlled, collectivized system. The popular respect given Mao enabled him to unleash several massive reforms attempting to improve agriculture, force rapid industrial development, and abolish illiteracy. Some efforts proved helpful, but the "Great Proletarian Cultural Revolution" launched in 1966 resulted in many school closings, harsh treatment of educators and intellectuals, and damage to numerous cultural treasures, all of which weakened China's educational system until the movement ended in 1976.[80]

After 1978, reforms begun under Deng Xiaoping and expanded under Jiang Zemin and then Hu Jintao relaxed economic controls and stimulated considerable growth, such that China has become a major economic power. Centralized controls, however, continued to be exercised over political activity and intellectual freedom.[81]

Education in China today

One of the major problems facing China's educational system today is the sheer size of its population. A brief glimpse helps illustrate the scale: In 2002 (the most recent statistics provided by China's Ministry of Education), there were approximately 318 million students enrolled in China's primary, secondary, and higher educational institutions. In comparison, the total 2002 population for the United States was approximately 288.6 million, with approximately 71 million students enrolled from prekindergarten through degree-granting higher education institutions.[82]

Teacher education

Following the reforms begun in 1978, the Chinese government recognized that national development depended on education, and education depended on teachers. National efforts were made to upgrade teacher education in 1980, 1985, and again in 1996. Today, teacher education in China is divided into pre-service and in-service components. The pre-service phase is initiated at "secondary normal schools," with additional preparation provided by "normal colleges," "normal universities," and "teacher training institutes." Most secondary normal schools prepare both pre-school and primary school teachers, but a limited number are devoted to preparing special education teachers for the primary schools. The normal colleges and universities offer preparatory programs for teachers of junior secondary schools (similar to American middle schools) and senior secondary schools (similar to American high schools).[83]

While significant efforts have been made to provide better teacher education, not all teachers possess the academic credentials required by law, particularly in some rural areas. In 2003, the highest percentage of credentialed teachers was in the primary schools (96 percent), with the junior secondary schools having the next highest percentage (87 percent). The lowest percentage occurred in the vocational high schools (44 percent). A recently expressed goal of the Chinese government is for all teachers to possess the required credentials.[84]

Importance of the teaching profession

China has a centuries-old tradition of respect for teachers, at least as old as the teachings of Confucius and the rise of the Chinese "civil service" examinations for public service. Nevertheless, present-day teachers face major challenges in educating China's massive population. That China recently emerged as a leading world economy might, at least in part, be testimony to the successful effort of its teachers. Despite the official recognition of their importance, Chinese teachers still face problems related to their social and economic status, such as a shortage of housing for teachers. Recently the Chinese government reiterated the need to provide greater respect, better pay, and improved housing for all its teachers.[85]

China clearly wants to close the education gap between itself and other industrialized nations of the world. Against daunting odds, it has increased educational funding, provided greater access to schools, and improved teacher preparation. However, greater academic freedom, which could improve the professional effectiveness of educators and researchers, might help China close that gap more quickly.[86]

For Cross-Reference: Compare China's contemporary educational reforms of teaching with its ancient reforms in the Confucian era discussed in Chapter 5: Ethnicity and Education, pp. 208–256.

For Further Reflection: Some observers predict that China will become the dominant nation of the world. Will China's recent reforms in education help further that development, or are additional major changes needed? React to this prediction, and explain your reasoning.

Summary and conclusions

How the teaching profession is viewed today is conditioned by centuries of traditions. The conditions encountered in establishing a new nation and subsequent efforts to build widespread public schools added some unique American innovations as well, including higher numbers of women admitted to the teaching profession. Along with the growth of schooling came an increased need for better teacher preparation and institutional frameworks to carry out the task. Normal schools played an important role, but teacher education was eventually assumed by colleges and universities.

Efforts to elevate the teaching profession by improving teacher knowledge and expertise (professionalism) helped strengthen teaching's ethical claims to professional autonomy, but this was hindered by the bureaucratization of school systems along corporate organizational lines in the late nineteenth and early twentieth centuries. The growth of bureaucratic educational hierarchies and the professionalization of administrators and educational specialists served to reduce teacher autonomy and make efforts to elevate teacher status more difficult. These developments encouraged many teachers to form organizations, but there was disagreement over whether professional societies or unions best served teacher interests. During its first century of operation, the National Education Association (NEA) rejected a union identity, but the regulation and control imposed on teachers by bureaucratic hierarchies encouraged the founding of the American Federation of Teachers (AFT), which embraced union identity, even though it had a no-strike policy until the 1960s. In 1973 the NEA transformed itself into a union as well. Efforts to merge the two into a single organization have not succeeded, but greater collaboration seemed to emerge in the early twenty-first century.

Class and gender composition of the teaching profession continues to have implications for its professional status and remuneration. The relative racial homogeneity of the profession also poses questions about how to best serve an increasingly diverse society. Efforts toward professionalism in teaching may well depend on whether teachers truly see themselves as professionals. Some participants want to achieve status parity with other learned professions through more rigorous preparation programs and competitive career ladders, while others argue that teaching should stop comparing itself to other professions; instead, teaching should build on the particular professional and ethical characteristics that make it unique among the learned professions.

The debate over the teaching profession's status apparently has made an impact. Many teacher preparation programs have moved to the graduate level, which may elevate their status. In addition, research indicates that teachers feel more empowered when they participate in educational decision making, and if such participation becomes the norm it could strengthen the profession. However, many teachers continue to see themselves left out of decisions directly affecting their professional duties and obligations.

Today there are numerous professional organizations striving to advance education and promote teachers' professional growth. Among them are those devoted to academic subject areas, pupil age levels, and other such specialized interests. Through them, opportunities to collaborate and share ideas within the profession are probably greater than ever before. Here, as with many other aspects of education, differences of opinion are encountered but also a high degree of commitment to common goals.

A better understanding of the teaching profession may be gained through international comparison. China is currently undergoing major social and economic changes it hopes will improve its standing in the world. It sees its teaching profession as having an important role in building that future, but China's teachers face continuing challenges in teacher preparation, teacher status, and providing better educational services to China's massive population.

Teaching is a multifaceted profession central to any society. That its status often suffers is only part of the story, because there are those who continue their efforts to improve it, just as they also seek to understand more fully its future possibilities.

Vocabulary

A Nation at Risk
American Federation of Teachers (AFT)
arts and sciences
Carnegie Corporation
classical tradition
collective bargaining
common school movement
deskilled

Holmes Partnership
humanities
learned professions
liberal arts
liberal education
mystification of knowledge
National Board Certification (NBC)
National Board for Professional Teaching Standards (NBPTS)
National Education Association (NEA)
New England Primer
normal school
profession
professionalism
professionalization
reciprocity of effort
reflective professional communities
social distance
state teachers colleges
status discrepancy
strikes
teacher accountability
teacher turnover
transformative intellectuals
vernacular language

Notes

1 David T. Hansen, *The Call to Teach* (New York: Teachers College Press, 1995).

2 Jeffrey A. Kottler, Stanley J. Zehm, and Ellen Kottler. *On Being a Teacher: The Human Dimension*, 3rd edn (Thousand Oaks, CA: Corwin Press, 2005).

3 Gerald L. Gutek, *Historical and Philosophical Foundations of Education; A Biographical Approach* (Upper Saddle River, NJ: Pearson/Merrill, 2005); Christopher J. Lucas, *Our Western Educational Heritage* (New York: Macmillan, 1972); and James Mulhern, *A History of Education: A Social Interpretation* (New York: Ronald Press, 1959).

4 See also W. H. Stahl, *Martianus Capella and the Seven Liberal Arts*. Records of Civilization, No. 84 (New York: Columbia University Press, 1971); and William Harrison Woodward, *Desiderius Erasmus Concerning the Aim and Method of Education*, Classics in Education, No. 19 (New York: Teachers College Press, 1964).

5 Frederick Eby, *Early Protestant Educators: The Educational Writings of Martin Luther, John Calvin, and Other Leaders of Protestant Thought* (Chicago: American Theological Library, 1962); and Neil G. McCluskey, S. J., ed., *Catholic Education in America: A Documentary History* (New York: Bureau of Publications, Teachers College, 1964).

6 Lawrence A. Cremin, *American Education: The Colonial Experience, 1607–1783* (New York: Harper Torchbooks, 1970), 176–184.

7 Ibid., 185; and Timothy J. Shannon, "Pages of the 1805 New England Primer," History 341: Colonial America Homepage, at http://www.gettysburg.edu/~tshannon/his341/nep1805contents.html (accessed on January 20, 2010).

8 Merle Borrowman, "Liberal Education and the Professional Preparation of Teachers," *Teacher Education in America: A Documentary History*, Classics in Education, No. 24 (New York: Teachers College Press, 1965), vii.

9 Cremin, 187.

10 Jon Teaford, "The Transformation of Massachusetts Education, 1670–1780," in *The Social History of American Education*, B. Edward McClellan and William J. Reese, eds (Chicago: University of Illinois Press, 1988), 31–35.

11 Thomas Jefferson, *Notes on the State of Virginia*, William Peden, ed. (1787, reprint, New York: W. W. Norton and Co., 1972), 146–149; Noah Webster, "The Call for a National Culture [1789]," in *The Educating of Americans: A Documentary History*, Daniel Calhoun, ed. (Boston: Houghton Mifflin, 1969), 89, 94; and Benjamin Rush, "Of the Mode of Education Proper in a Republic [1798]," in *The Founders' Constitution*, vol. 1, Philip B. Kurland and Ralph Lerner, eds (Chicago: University of Chicago Press, 1987), at http://press-pubs.uchicago.edu/founders/print_documents/v1ch18s30.html (accessed January 20, 2010).

12 Borrowman, 2–4.

13 Paul H. Mattingly, *The Classless Profession: American Schoolmen in the Nineteenth Century* (New York: New York University Press, 1975), 45–47.

14 Donald H. Parkerson and Jo Ann Parkerson, *Transitions in American Education: A Social History of Teaching* (New York: Routledge Falmer, 2001), 63.

15 Willystine Goodsell, ed. *Pioneers of Women's Education in the United States: Emma Willard, Catherine Beecher, Mary Lyon* (1931, reprint, New York: AMS Press, 1970).

16 Parkerson and Parkerson, 70–71.

17 Ibid., 129–131; and Robert Welker, *The Teacher as Expert: A Theoretical and Historical Examination* (Albany: State University of New York Press, 1992), 46–47.

18 Richard J. Altenbaugh and Kathleen Underwood, "The Evolution of Normal Schools," in *Places Where Teachers Are Taught*, John I. Goodlad et al., eds (San Francisco: Jossey-Bass, Inc., Publishers, 1990), 137–138; and James W. Fraser, *Preparing America's Teachers: A History* (New York: Teachers College Press, 2007), 45–55.

19 Jurgen Herbst, *And Sadly Teach: Teacher Education and Professionalization in American Culture* (Madison: University of Wisconsin Press, 1989), 4–6.

20 Herbst, 140–160; Altenbaugh and Underwood, 139–144; and William S. Learned et al., "Purpose of the Normal School," in *Teacher Education in America: A Documentary History*, 184–207.

21 John Goodlad, "Connecting the Present to the Past," *Places Where Teachers Are Taught*, 18–19.

22 Herbst, 6–8.

23 Wayne J. Urban, *Gender, Race, and the National Education Association* (New York: Routledge and Falmer, 2000), 3–9.

24 ———, *Why Teachers Organized* (Detroit: Wayne State University Press, 1982), 154–172.

25 ———, *Gender, Race, and the NEA*, 57–74.

26 William Edward Eaton, *The American Federation of Teachers, 1916–1961: A History of the Movement* (Carbondale: Southern Illinois University, 1975), 2–17; and see George Herbert Mead, "The Educational Situation in the Chicago Public Schools [1907]," at http://www.brocku.ca/MeadProject/Mead/pubs/Mead_1907f.html (accessed on January 20, 2010).

27 Eaton, 19–29, 35.

28 Ibid., 140–155, 161–166.

29 Urban, *Gender, Race, and the NEA*, 177–179.

30 Ibid., 267–274; Jeff Archer, "NEA Board Approves AFT Partnership Pact," *Newsweek*, vol. 20, no. 23: 3 (February 21, 2001); and NEAFT Merger Caucus, at http://www.neaft.org (accessed on January 20, 2010).

31 Stuart J. Foster, *Red Alert!: Educators Confront the Red Scare in American Public Schools, 1947–1954* (New York : Peter Lang, 2000); and Fraser, 207–213.

32 See Jonathan Kozol, *Death at an Early Age: the Destruction of the Hearts and Minds of Negro Children in the Boston Public Schools* (Boston: Houghton Mifflin, 1967); Nat Hentoff, *Our Children Are Dying* (New York: Viking Press, 1966); and Colin Greer, *The Solution as Part of the Problem: Urban Education Reform in the 1960s* (New York, Harper & Row, 1973).

33 National Commission on Excellence in Education, *A Nation at Risk: The Imperative of Educational Reform, An Open Letter to the American People* (Washington, DC: The Commission [distributed by the U.S. Government Printing Office], 1983), 5.

34 Arthur Bestor, *Educational Wastelands: the Retreat from Learning in our Public Schools* (Urbana: University of Illinois Press, 1953); Kozol, *Death at an Early Age*; National Commission on Excellence in Education, *A Nation at Risk: the Imperative for Educational Reform*, a report to the Nation and the Secretary of Education, United States Department of Education (Washington, DC: The Commission, 1983); Chester E. Finn, Jr., et al., eds, *Against Mediocrity: the Humanities in America's High Schools*, foreword by William Bennett (New York: Holmes and Meier, 1984).

35 David F. Labaree, "Educational Researchers: Living with a Lesser Form of Knowledge," in *The Life and Work of Teachers: International Perspectives in Changing Times*, Christopher Day et al., eds (London and New York: Falmer Press, 2000), 55–58.

36 The Holmes Group, *Tomorrow's Teachers: A Report of the Holmes Group* (East Lansing, MI: The Holmes Group, Inc., 1989), 4.

37 Carnegie Forum on Education and the Economy: Task Force on Teaching as a Profession, *A Nation Prepared: Teachers for the 21st Century: the Report of the Task Force on Teaching as a Profession* (Washington: The Forum, May 1986), 2, 3; and "The Corporation's Program: A Report to the Board by Vartan Gregorian, President, February 2, 1999," Carnegie Foundation, at http://www.carnegie.org/sub/program/ndpage2.html (accessed on January 17, 2009).

38 "National Board Certification Statistics," NBPTS, at http://www.nbpts.org/about_us/2009_national_board_cert/national_board_certifica (accessed on January 20, 2010); "History: The Beginnings of a Movement," NBPTS, at http://www.nbpts.org/about_us/mission_and_history (accessed on January 02, 2010); "National Board Certification," AFT, at http://archive.aft.org/topics/teacher-quality/nationalboard.htm (accessed on January 20, 2010); and "National Board Certification," NEA, at http://www.nea.org/home/31738.htm (accessed on January 20, 2010).

39 Gerald Grant and Christine E. Murray, *Teaching in America: The Slow Revolution* (Cambridge, MA: Harvard University Press, 1999), 182–185.

40 Michael P. Grady, Kristine C. Helbling, and Dennis R. Lubeck, "Teacher Professionalism since *A Nation at Risk*," *Phi Delta Kappan*, April 2008, 603–607; and Göran Brante, "Multitasking and Synchronous Work: Complexities in Teacher Work," *Teaching and Teacher Education*, vol. 25, no. 3: 430–436 (April 2009).

41 National Education Association, *Status of the American Public School Teacher 2000–2001*. (Washington: NEA, 2003), 89, at http://www.nea.org/assets/docs/Status_of_the_American_Public_School_Teacher_2000–2001.pdf (accessed on January 20, 2010).

42 Ibid., 90–92.

43 American Federation of Teachers, Survey and Analysis of Teacher Salary Trends 2007, at http://archive.aft.org/salary/2007/download/AFT2007SalarySurvey.pdf (accessed October 20, 2010).

44 National Education Association, 79.

45 Ibid., 67–69.

46 Lee Shulman, "Knowledge and Teaching: Foundations of the New Reform," *Harvard Educational Review*, vol. 57, no. 1 (Spring 1987), 9; and Gloria Ladson-Billings, *The Dreamkeepers: Successful Teachers of African American Children* (San Francisco: Jossey-Bass, 1994), 94–95.

47 Sonia Nieto (ed.), *Why We Teach* (New York: Teachers College Press, 2005), 4–5.

48 Dominic Belmonte, *Teaching From the Deep End* (Thousand Oaks: Corwin Press, 2003), 67–72.

49 Welker, 17–18; and David Tyack and Elizabeth Hansot, *Managers of Virtue: Public School Leadership in America, 1820–1980* (New York: Basic Books, 1982), 4.

50 Lee S. Shulman, "Foreword," *Teaching as the Learning Profession: Handbook of Policy and Practice*, Linda Darling-Hammond and Gary Sykes, eds (San Francisco: Jossey-Bass Publishers), xiii.

51 Henry A. Giroux, *Teachers as Intellectuals: Toward a Critical Pedagogy of Learning* (New York: Bergin & Garvey, 1988), 121–128.

52 Welker, 129–130, 132, 134–135.

53 Roger Soder, "The Rhetoric of Teacher Professionalization," in *The Moral Dimensions of Teaching*, edited by John I. Goodlad, Roger Soder, and Kenneth A. Sirotnik (San Francisco: Jossey-Bass Publishers, 1990), 35–86.

54 Soder, 35–86.

55 Gary D. Fenstermacher, "Some Moral Considerations on Teaching as a Profession," in *The Moral Dimensions of Teaching*, John I. Goodlad et al., eds (San Francisco: Jossey-Bass Publishers, 1991), 136–138.

56 Paolo Freire, *Pedagogy of Freedom: Ethics, Democracy, and Civic Courage* (Lanham, MD: Rowman & Littlefield, 1998).

57 Aristotle, *The Politics*, Trevor J. Saunders, trans. (London: Penguin Books, 1981), 453–454.

58 Aristotle, *Ethics*, J.A.K. Thomson, trans. (London: Penguin Books, 1976), 64, 66, 69, 73–76, and 100–110.

59 Nel Noddings, *Happiness and Education* (New York: Cambridge University Press, 2003).

60 John Dewey, *Theory of the Moral Life* (Reprint, New York: Holt, Rinehart and Winston [1932] 1960), viii.

61 Ibid., ix–xii; and Kenneth A. Strike and Jonas F. Soltis, *The Ethics of Teaching*, 3rd edn, Thinking About Education Series (New York: Teachers College Press, 1998), 6.

62 Hugh Sockett, *The Moral Base for Teacher Professionalism*, Professional Ethics in Education Series, Kenneth Strike, ed. (New York: Teachers College Press, 1993), ix–x.

63 Michael D. Bayles, *Professional Ethics*, 2nd edn (Belmont, CA: Wadsworth, Inc., 1989), 17–27ff. Indebtedness in this and the following paragraphs is acknowledged to Bayles, particularly terminology related to general ethical obligations, which here are adapted to the teaching profession.

64 This idea dates back to Hippocrates, a physician in ancient Greece. See N. S. Gill, "Is 'First Do No Harm' From the Hippocratic Oath? Myth vs. Fact," at http://ancienthistory.about.com/od/greekmedicine/f/HippocraticOath.htm (accessed on January 20, 2010).

65 Bayles, 111–127.

66 Ibid., 136–157.

67 Ibid., 166–178.

68 See Gregory Michie, *See You When you Get There: Teaching for Change in Urban Schools* (New York: Teachers College Press, 2004); Laurel Schmidt, *Classroom Confidential: The 12 Secrets of Great Teachers* (Portsmouth, NH: Heinemann, 2004); Randi Stone, *Best Teaching Practices for Reaching All Learners: What Award-Winning Classroom Teachers Do* (Thousand Oaks, CA: Corwin Press, 2004); and Kathleen Bennett deMarrais and Margaret D. LeCompte, *The Way Schools Work: A Sociological Analysis of Education* (White Plains, NY: Longman Publishers, 1995), 145.

69 DeMarris and LeCompte, 146–151.

70 Mary Haywood Metz, "Teachers' Ultimate Dependence on Their Students," in *Teachers' Work: Individuals, Colleagues, and Contexts*, Judith Warren Little and Milbrey Wallin McLaughlin, eds (New York and London: Teachers College Press, 1993), 104–136.

71 Andy Hargreaves, "Individualism and Individuality: Reinterpreting the Teacher Culture," *Teachers' Work*, 51–76.

72 Milbrey Wallin McLaughlin, "What Matters Most in Teachers' Workplace Context?" *Teachers' Work*, 79–103.

73 Milton E. Rosenthal, *Reality 101: What It's Really Like to Be a Teacher . . . and Teach, too* (Lanham, MD: The Scarecrow Press: 2003), 3–4.

74 Michael Huberman, "The Model of the Independent Artisan in Teachers' Professional Relation," *Teachers' Work*, 11–50.

75 National Education Association, "About NEA," at http://www.nea.org/home/2580.htm (accessed on January 20, 2010); and American Federation of Teachers, "About AFT," at http://www.aft.org/about/ (accessed on January 20, 2010).

76 "About NEA;" "About AFT;" and Nina Bascia, *Unions in Teachers' Professional Lives: Social, Intellectual, and Practical Concerns* (New York: Teachers College Press, 1994), 58–74.

77 Peter Brimelow, *The Worm in the Apple: How the Teachers Unions are Destroying American Education* (New York: HarperCollins, 2003); G. Gregory Moo, *Power Grab: How the National Education Association is Betraying Our Children* (Washington: Regnery Publishing, 1999), xi–xii; and Myron Lieberman, *The Teacher Unions: How the NEA and AFT Sabotage Reform and Hold Students, Parents, and Teachers, and Taxpayers Hostage to Bureaucracy* (New York: The Free Press, 1997).

78 "China," *The World Factbook*, at https://www.cia.gov/library/publications/the-world-factbook/geos/ch.html (accessed on October 19, 2010). For current population figures, see the dynamic population clock, "China Population," at http://www.cpirc.org.cn/en/eindex.htm (accessed on January 20, 2010).

79 Jonathan D. Spence, "Sun Yat-sen," at http://www.time.com/time/asia/asia/magazine/1999/990823/sun_yat_sen1.html (accessed on January 20, 2010); Lori Reese, "China's Christian Warrior [Chiang Kai-shek]," at http://www.time.com/time/asia/asia/magazine/1999/990823/cks.html (accessed on January 20, 2010); and Zhang Hanzhi, "Mao Zedong," at http://www.time.com/time/asia/asia/magazine/1999/990823/mao1.html (accessed on January 20, 2010).

80 Yinghong Cheng and Patrick Manning, "Revolution in Education: China and Cuba in Global Context, 1957–76," *Journal of World History*, vol. 14, no. 3: 367–374 (September 2003); Suzanne Pepper, *Radicalism and Education Reform in 20th-Century China: The Search for an Ideal Development Model* (New York: Cambridge University Press, 1996), 279–283, 352–364, 381–393, and 466–474; Satya J. Gabriel, "Political Economy of the Great Leap Forward: Permanent Revolution and State Feudal Communes," at http://www.mtholyoke.edu/courses/sgabriel/economics/china-essays/4.html (accessed on January 20, 2010); Youqin Wang, "Student Attacks Against Teachers: the Revolution of 1966," at http://humanities.uchicago.edu/faculty/ywang/history/1966teacher.htm, and "The Second Wave of Violent Persecution of Teachers: the Revolution of 1968," at http://humanities.uchicago.edu/faculty/ywang/history/1968teacher.htm (both accessed on January 20, 2010).

81 Jonathan D. Spence, "Deng Xiaoping: The Maoist who reinvented himself, transformed a nation, and changed the world," at http://www.time.com/time/asia/2006/heroes/nb_deng.html (accessed on January 20, 2010); "Jiang Zemin, at http://www.answers.com/topic/jiang-zemin (accessed on January 20, 2010); Kallie Szczepanski, "Biography of Hu Jintao," at http://asianhistory.about.com/od/profilesofasianleaders/p/HuJinTaoProfile.htm (accessed on January 20, 2010).

82 China Education and Research Network (CERNET), "MOE: Survey of the Educational Reform and Development in China," at http://www.edu.cn/Researchedu_1498/20060323/t20060323_113688.shtml (accessed on January 20, 2010); CERNET, "Basic Statistics on Education," at http://www.edu.cn/20050119/3127194.shtml (accessed on January 20, 2010); U.S. Census Bureau (USCB), "US and

World Population Clocks," at http://www.census.gov/main/www/popclock.html, and USCB, "Countries and Areas Ranked by Population, 2010," at http://www.census.gov/cgi-bin/broker (all three sites accessed on January 20, 2010).

83 CERNET, "Teacher Education in China (I)," at www.edu.cn/20010101/21923.shtml, and "Teacher Education in China (II)," at www.edu.cn/20010101/21924.shtml (both accessed on January 20, 2010).

84 Xuifang Wang, *Education in China since 1976* (Jefferson, NC: McFarland and Company, Inc., Publishers, 2003), 93–94, 120–123.

85 Wang, 124–125; and The Ministry of Education, People's Republic of China, "The Development of Education for All in China," UNESCO (International Conference on Education, 46th Session, Geneva, Switzerland, 2001), 12–13, at http://www.ibe.unesco.org/International/ICE/natrap/China_Scan_1.pdf, and http://www.ibe.unesco.org/International/ICE/natrap/China_Scan_2.pdf (both accessed on January 20, 2010).

86 Wang, 169–172; Teresa Wright, "The Limits of Political Loosening: CCP Restraints on Student Behaviour in the Spring of 1989," *Higher Education in Post-Mao China*, Michael Agelasto and Bob Adamson, eds (Hong Kong: Hong Kong University Press, 1998), 375–394; and Michael Agelasto and Bob Adamson, "Editors' Conclusion—the State of Chinese Higher Education Today," *Higher Education in Post-Mao China*, 410–413.

2

School Governance and Control

Chapter objectives

Readers should be able to:

- understand the concept of school governance and varying viewpoints on it.
- explore the history of school governance to uncover the roots of school governance today.
- analyze the current governance structure, its strengths and weaknesses.
- gain an understanding of how funding sources impact school governance.
- become attuned to contemporary reform issues and their impact on school governance.
- gain insight into school governance through international comparisons.

Opening questions

1. What characteristics of school governance have changed most, and what has endured? Why and how have leading economic and political theories shaped school governance?
2. What are the major factors of continuity and change in contemporary school governance?
3. How are the schools funded, and what consequences for governance flow from the existing funding system?
4. In what ways should both school governance and funding be reformed?
5. What are the pros and cons of both existing governance practices and leading reforms that impact how schools are governed?
6. What lessons about school governance can be learned from international comparisons?

The issue

Prior to the American Revolution, responsibility for education was considered an individual, family or church concern, with little government involvement. The end of the eighteenth century saw rising calls for greater educational opportunity, but how to organize and finance it remained elusive. A major nineteenth-century development was the common school movement (from the late 1830s into the 1850s), which resulted in state systems of tax-supported, public elementary schools. Although these systems were created by legislation on a state-by-state basis, they were typically financed by local taxes and overseen by local **school boards** or **school committees**. After the 1870s, public high schools were added to this configuration. In the early twentieth century, critics of the organizational frameworks of school systems carried out school governance reforms modeled after corporations, which they believed would make school operations more efficient. With persistent tinkering, public school systems continue to operate within this kind of hierarchical structure.

According to David Tyack, in the twentieth century, Americans built a network of public school systems that made education available to more people of greater diversity than in any previous period, an accomplishment in which they rightly could take pride. Yet, criticism of the schools has not diminished. For example, how funds are allocated is one issue, with some critics arguing that public school systems are **bureaucratic** and limit parental choices of the schools their children may attend. As taxpayers, parents (or guardians) should have public funds made available for the schools of their choice, including private schools. Others want publicly financed school systems to remain the option of choice, but they argue for more choice within that framework. Some see public charter schools that operate independently of local boards and central offices as a good expansion of choice. There are also concerns about whether existing forms of governance adequately address educational needs, and whether the schools use what they now receive to best effect.[1]

Criticism also emerges over what roles local, state, and federal governments should have, not only in funding but also in curriculum requirements, testing and evaluation, and other details of school operation. Critics aside, there are many who favor public, tax-supported schools, and they make strong arguments that the schools must represent all of society and expose all students to common experiences. Students need to understand local conditions and cultural communities, of course, but they also need the benefits of state and national participation and support too. Some supporters caution against too much centralized control, however. It weakens direct accountability of schools to their local communities at a time when citizens need to "own" their schools, not surrender them to distant bureaucracies. As can be seen, debate swirls around governance and control from one side of the spectrum to the other. It is a controversy prospective educators will almost certainly face as professionals.

> **For Further Reflection:** What is a healthy balance between the power of parents and citizens versus that of educational professionals concerning school governance? What factors need to be taken into account in order to achieve such balance?

Background

There is difficulty in concisely describing the American system of educational governance and control, because in actuality there are 50 state systems, with each state further subdivided into numerous local systems (except Hawaii, which has one statewide system of 285 schools on seven islands).[2] All the state systems share much in common, but each also has its unique characteristics.

Origins of American school governance and control

Although there were educational commonalities among the British colonies in what is now the United States, there were also significant differences. The New England colonies (Connecticut, Massachusetts, New Hampshire, and Rhode Island) shared important cultural and religious assumptions that helped unify attitudes about education. The middle colonies (New York, Pennsylvania, New Jersey, Delaware, and Maryland) were more diverse. New York, for example, began as a Dutch colony, then came under British control, and attracted people from various other cultural origins, in addition to being the home of a sizable portion of Native Americans. Similarly, Pennsylvania began under the Quakers but welcomed other religious persuasions and national origins as well. Likewise, the population of Maryland was comprised of a mixture of national origins composed of Protestants and a sizable number of Catholics. Such conditions meant diversity in educational provisions in the middle colonies.[3] The southern colonies also contained religious and cultural variety, but most southern colonists accepted the English tradition of schooling as a duty of home and church, not government.

Colonial Massachusetts and Virginia: a comparison

In 1647, the General Court of the Massachusetts Bay Colony passed a law fixing responsibility for education with the townships and, in turn, left each township relatively free to meet requirements as it saw fit. In Virginia, the House of Burgesses placed responsibility for education on various sources, including families, masters, local pastors, justices of the peace, and county commissioners.[4] Although there were similarities among the colonies in following the English tradition of parish (township) and shire (county) forms of organization, differences still occurred in how schools were governed.

In Massachusetts, the local governing body for schools became the "school committee" and, depending on the township, its members were either locally elected or appointed by a township's selectmen or governing council. Some townships ignored elements of the 1647 law, particularly secondary grammar schools with a Latin and classics-based curriculum, but this was partially offset by the development of township-supported English-based "writing" schools, as well as private "venture" schools that usually emphasized mathematical and technical studies (e.g., geometry, surveying, navigation, bookkeeping, foreign currency exchange rates, and languages). Despite the decline of grammar schools, Massachusetts achieved a high degree of literacy by the 1770s.[5]

In comparison, Virginia relied primarily on private initiatives, with school governance evolving along the lines of the privately endowed "free schools," the first of which was established in a 1635 bequeath of 200 acres of land and the "increase and produce" of eight cows to support the education of poor children in the Hampton area. In 1659, a heftier bequeath left 500 acres, two slaves, 20 hogs, 12 cows, and two bulls for another free school for poor children in the same county but in a different parish. Each school was governed by a board of trustees composed of the county commissioners and the ministers and churchwardens of each respective parish. Important as these schools were, however, only a small number of children benefited while most Virginia youngsters received little or no education beyond what an individual family, local church, or private tutor might provide. Private venture schools also developed, but most were short lived and never extensive.[6]

Variety in school governance and control

During colonial times, no single widespread mode of governance and financial support emerged, and this probably discouraged greater uniformity in the methods of control. Thus, school governance varied from one region, locale, and school to the next. Despite the lack of uniformity, however, some aspects of school governance at the time endured One was a growing recognition that responsibility for education rested with society as a whole, not only portions of it. A pattern was emerging of school committees and boards of trustees, which set the stage for school boards today.[7]

> **Suggested Activity:** Discuss with other students to what extent ideas about school governance still vary among localities or regions today. Compare experiences and views that may differ in your group, depending on where individual members grew up.

Emergence of public school systems

In the decades following the American Revolution, the United States adopted a new constitution, extended its territory, and fought a second war with the British, but as the nineteenth century unfolded, attention was given to education. At first, there was a mixture of sectarian schools, elite academies, private venture schools, charity schools, and municipal schools inherited from colonial times, but state systems of public schools would become dominant by midcentury.

Jeffersonian model

One of the first attempts at a statewide system of public schools was made by Thomas Jefferson in Virginia. As Jefferson envisioned it, each county would elect three aldermen who would divide their county into small geographical units (or "hundreds," Jefferson called them), each containing enough free (not slave) children to justify a school. The aldermen were also to select a site and erect a schoolhouse where the children could be taught reading, writing, and common arithmetic, with reading materials to be drawn from Greek, Roman, English, and American history. Finally, for every ten "hundreds" in a county, the aldermen were to appoint a qualified "visitor" to hire and oversee teachers and to visit each school periodically to examine students and see that the curriculum was followed.[8] Although Jefferson's plan never materialized, it provided ideas for others to consider. One can see hints of his proposal today: the aldermen are similar to local boards of education, the hundreds akin to school attendance zones, and the visitors similar to superintendents.

Public schools and local control

After experience with various private and public ventures, most Americans embraced the idea of public, tax-supported "common schools." Public common schools gained wide acceptance by the 1850s as significant instruments for producing virtuous citizens at the local level, supplementing the roles of families and churches. Perhaps these kinds of connections helped solidify public opinion that the schools should be locally controlled. As it evolved, the ideal (if not always the reality) was nonsectarian and nonpartisan local boards. Although the legal authority to establish public schools came from the state, the source of financial and moral support came from local citizens, and **local control** became the operational mode of governance.[9]

Local control was not without its problems, however. As noted by Horace Mann, as crucial as local control was, it could be deleterious if a local community was apathetic, riven by partisan divisions, or fearful of public expenditures for education. There was need for at least some state control to invigorate local support, not replace it.[10]

Suggested Activity: Discuss the following statements: While the concept of community conjures up many positive associations such as family and friends, togetherness and support, sometimes communities can be oppressive and suspicious of differences. These two sides of local community need to be considered when deciding how best to balance localized and centralized controls over schooling.

Local school boards

Four out of five citizens lived in rural areas by 1860, but the leading developments in school governance emerged from urban areas. Between 1818 and 1853, most cities established some form of citywide school board. Large cities typically divided themselves into wards (or districts) that, in turn, provided local school governance, usually by means of an elected school committee in each ward. This body was responsible for collecting school taxes, purchasing sites, constructing and maintaining school buildings, and hiring and supervising teachers. Many cities also allowed a ward to elect a representative to serve on central city school boards. In big cities with numerous wards, this meant large, unwieldy central school boards where political bickering and competition for city resources sometimes paralyzed effective action. In addition, some wards were dominated by corrupt political machines that used political patronage to control contracts for school supplies, the hiring of personnel, and other such functions. Reformers, dissatisfied with what they called the "inefficiencies" of ward control, successfully pushed for smaller, more powerful central city boards of education.[11] As it turned out, however, this proved to be double edged, for as ward control weakened, so also did local citizen feelings about ownership and control of the neighborhood schools.

Origins of the school superintendency

A second major development was to place administrative control in the hands of a single person, from which the modern school **superintendent** emerged. Before, local boards of education did the supervisory work, usually with one or more members doing the actual on-site visits and other supervisory duties. As population increased and school-age children became more numerous, supervision consumed more time than most board members (usually unpaid for their services) were willing to provide, and so the idea of a paid, full-time school supervisor or superintendent became an attractive alternative for most boards.

It was in 1837 that the first superintendents were hired, in Buffalo, New York, and Louisville, Kentucky. In the 1840s, St. Louis, Missouri, appointed a superintendent, followed in due course by Boston, Chicago, Cleveland, Detroit, New York City, and San Francisco. By the 1880s, Pittsburgh, Philadelphia, and Los Angeles also joined the trend. At first the job was ill-defined: Buffalo desired someone to gather reliable information about the schools for board deliberations, Baltimore wanted someone to provide oversight of textbook adoptions, while San Francisco sought someone to take charge of renting and provisioning adequate schoolhouses. Other places needed a full-time board secretary. By 1900, the title of superintendent (or some other approximation such as director or secretary of the board) was common. As the job evolved, it took several forms: In some locales, boards directly hired superintendents as employees; in others, superintendents were elected officials. Regardless of title or method of appointment, the idea of having a full-time person responsible for general administrative duties of public school systems gained popularity.[12]

What's in a name?

Pennsylvania enacted its Free School Law on April 1, 1834, with the Secretary of the Commonwealth also acting as the head of that state's free schools. In 1837, Pennsylvania created a Department of Schools with a superintendent of common schools as its top official. In 1873, it changed the top official's title to superintendent of public instruction and the department was renamed the Department of Public Instruction. Almost a century later, in 1969, the Department of Public Instruction was changed to Department of Education, and the superintendent's title was changed to secretary of education. Such changes seem to lend credence to the old saying that, "The more things change, the more they stay the same."

Source: Pennsylvania Department of Education, "About the Department of Education," at http://www.pdeinfo.state.pa.us/depart_edu/site/default.asp?g=0 (accessed on March 10, 2006).

Urbanization, industrialization, and school reform

The *Gilded Age* is a term coined by Mark Twain in an 1873 book about the rampant materialism and corruption in the years following the Civil War,[13] and it has since been used to designate the period from roughly 1865 to 1900, when American society experienced rapid urban and industrial development that brought far-reaching changes to institutions and social life.

Population growth and urbanization

One important change was massive population growth, which made it difficult for existing institutions to meet increased demands. Population in the United States almost doubled in the 30 years from 1870 to 1900 (see Table 2.1). Some of this increase was due to higher fertility rates, but a significant part was from immigration. Although a portion of the population growth stretched to the rural frontiers, most centered on the urban areas, which attracted both foreign and domestic newcomers. The number of foreign immigrants greatly changed

Table 2.1 United States population, 1870–1900

Year	Total population	Numerical increase	Percent increase
1870	38,558,371	N/A	N/A
1880	50,189,209	11,630,838	23%
1890	62,979,766	12,790,557	20%
1900	76,212,168	13,232,402	17%

Note: Adapted from U.S. Census Bureau, "Table 2: Population, Housing, Unit Area Measurements, and Density," Selected Historical Decennial Census Population and Housing Counts (1990), at http://www.census.gov/population/censusdata/table-2.pdf (accessed on March 20, 2009).

the United States, and its ethnic variety has become an oft-told part of the American story. Less well known was the migration of native-born farm workers and marginal farmers from the rural areas into the cities, particularly during periods of agricultural recession or depression. Both foreign-born immigrants and native-born migrants were lured to the cities by the promise of better jobs and greater economic opportunity. As the cities experienced this growth, however, there were shortages as existing institutions struggled to meet the new demands. In addition, the newcomers—many of whom came from rural backgrounds—often faced difficulties adjusting to city life as they confronted unfamiliar customs and lifestyles. As they poured into the cities, they also faced insufficient numbers of schools to meet their needs because educational institutions and their governance structures were unable to respond effectively.

> **Suggested Activity for Further Reflection:** Consider the economic impact of different immigrant groups on the United States, both historically and currently. One hears these observations made about immigrants: They provide cheap labor that native-born Americans refuse to perform; they use much-needed resources and take away jobs from American workers; they add to the economic productivity of the United States; and they help rejuvenate society by bringing new ideas and perspectives. Do such generalizations have validity, or are they flawed? Why or why not? What is prejudiced, what is fact, and how do such views affect education?

Compulsory attendance

In a time of subsistence wages for the working class and extreme wealth for a small group of industrialists and investors, many working-class families needed income from all family members, including their children. Some reformers saw this as child exploitation, and they pushed compulsory attendance laws as a way to get children in schools and out of factories and sweatshops. However, due to a combination of factors, including rapid changes and ineffective political leadership, many hard-pressed city school systems were unable to accommodate all eligible children. Though well-intentioned, compulsory attendance laws sometimes exacerbated the hardships of working-class families. Not only did poor families need the extra income children earned, but poor children themselves often resisted attending because they found schools unpleasant places biased against poor and immigrant children.[14]

Compulsory attendance was also complicated by legal variations from state to state. Some states required as much as full nine-month terms, some required no more than 16 weeks, while others had no attendance laws at all. Legal age of compulsory attendance also varied, from 7 to 16 in Wyoming but only 10 to 14 in Utah. Few states provided any serious enforcement, and many laws included exemptions ranging from travel distance, poverty, and lack of clothing (commonly recognized exemptions), to such vague ones as "inability to send" and "urgent reasons."[15]

In addition, many cities proved so unable (or unwilling) to provide adequate financial support that schools were forced to operate on double sessions each day and on shortened annual terms just to keep expenditures in line with funding. While the boom-and-bust economic fluctuations of that era made financial planning difficult for schools, many Gilded Age school "reforms" were little more than cutbacks driven by political resistance to school taxes. Simply put, inadequate financial resources meant the lack of facilities, materials, and professional personnel sufficient to accommodate all eligible children.[16]

> **For Further Reflection:** Look at compulsory school attendance from an ethical perspective; human beings are forced to do something (go to school) regardless of their wishes. How can such laws be ethically justified given the infringement on the liberties of individuals? Does society have an obligation to educate children whether they want it or not? Does the social group have ethical responsibilities for its individual members?

> **For Further Reflection:** Although the phenomena described here date back more than a century, some of the problems sound quite familiar today. Is history repeating itself? Do certain things never change, or do we simply fail to solve problems? How else can apparent similarities between the early twentieth century and the early twenty-first century in regard to the problems of education be explained?

Progressive education reform

At the close of the nineteenth century, progressivism became the name for a series of reforms that affected many areas of American life. The progressive movement was not anchored in a single philosophy, and progressive education was only one part of the larger movement.[17] For purposes of illustration, two broad philosophical views on school governance are examined: the pedagogical progressives and the administrative progressives.[18]

Pedagogical progressives

One of the hallmarks of pedagogical progressivism was "child-centered" education, and it helped make progressive education a household term at the time. Child-centered education had its roots in European educational thought, particularly that of Jean-Jacques Rousseau and his followers Johann Pestalozzi and Friedrich Froebel.

Rousseau rejected the old theological doctrine of original sin, that the child was corrupted by Adam and Eve's behavior in the Garden of Eden. On the contrary, Rousseau maintained that the child was innately good in its original natural state and was only corrupted by the artifices of society, such as an overly bookish, abstract, and unnatural education; therefore, the child's education should occur in natural settings away from society. Of course, Rousseau did not reject all civilization, but he insisted on education where the child is free to explore and learn from its experiences, with adult intervention limited to such things as safety, well-being, and educational guidance as needed. Implements of civilization, such as books, should be introduced only when the child is able developmentally to benefit.[19] This may seem highly impractical, but what attracted educational thinkers to Rousseau was his insight into the need to fit education to the child's natural growth stages, learning from experiences, and higher levels of intellectual education as development allows.

Pestalozzi put Rousseau's ideas into practice with child activities, observations, and manipulations of instructional objects at the schools he ran. He encouraged child-initiated activities but also teacher-designed activities that respected the child's natural development. A properly educated child's potential would develop naturally, as a sprouting seed unfolds its full potential as a mature plant. To aid the child's development, its natural senses should be stimulated through observations and hands-on activities that gradually move from concrete experience to abstract, reflective thought. Pestalozzi emphasized that kindness rather than harshness must be the rule. From such ideas, Friedrich Froebel developed the idea of the kindergarten, a "garden" for children replete with carefully structured activities and instructional objects in a nurturing environment. Froebel believed that a child is in harmony with God's natural order, and he stressed the need for play and learning activities to stimulate the physical and intellectual growth of the child.[20]

Suggested Activity: Investigate some schools in your local areas, particularly Waldorf or Montessori schools, to find out to what extent the philosophies discussed above can be found in their curricula.

These theories were among the educational outlooks of American pedagogical progressives, or what some proponents called the "new education." Among the contributors were educator Francis W. Parker and psychologist G. Stanley Hall. As superintendent of schools in Quincy, Massachusetts, Parker stressed that, rather than primary reliance on textbooks, students should also use supplementary materials such as newspapers, magazines, and teacher-devised materials; rather than memorizing scientific laws and principles, they should be taken on field trips for direct observations and specimen collection; and rather than rote learning of such things as multiplication tables, they should learn inductive problem solving with objects and examples. The Quincy System, as it was called, emphasized learning through observation, description, and understanding before moving students into more abstract approaches. G. Stanley Hall did pioneering work in child development that had a major impact on progressive education. Although influenced by predecessors, Hall's psychological research convinced him that the content of the curriculum should be determined by the developmental needs of the child. As Hall viewed it, education was too school centered, with the child forced to adapt to school demands; instead, school should be adapted to the child's-needs. Hall's use of empirical research gave him an aura of scientific legitimacy, and his child-centered views appealed to the pedagogical progressives.[21]

Perhaps the person most often identified with pedagogical progressivism, however, is John Dewey, who believed that philosophers should help people break from outmoded ways of thinking in order to solve major problems they actually faced. While Dewey valued child-centeredness, he took a broadened approach that included the social as well as the individual needs of the children, who become educated through their experiences of both the natural and the social world. The urban, corporate, industrial society of Dewey's day contained the elements for increased communication and interaction, but it was also too ruthless, competitive, and inhumane. Changes were needed so that schools could operate as protective environments where the capacities of children could be developed. To accomplish this, schools must be environments where, instead of imposing traditional rote instruction and harsh discipline, pupils can learn, shape, and test ideas in humane environments that foster the development of reflective personal and social judgment.[22]

For Further Reflection: Discuss the notion of children being "natural" and "social" creatures. What is the relationship between the two?

Dewey's philosophy was complex and his writings not always easily understood, but he also had followers who sometimes took his ideas in directions he never intended. For example, some disciples understood Dewey's criticism of traditional education to mean that knowledge acquisition was unimportant. Some took his stress on the social to mean children should mainly be taught social roles and relationships. A closer reading, however, shows Dewey's firm insistence that education should help the young understand the world and the changes it undergoes by such things as scientific and technological development, industrialization, and urbanization. He placed particular focus on the social nature of education because he saw it as an important pathway to build a more democratic society with humane social conditions. New approaches to organizing and teaching the curriculum were needed, and they should begin with children's ordinary shared experiences. As their intellectual skills and social understandings grew, they should increasingly become immersed in the cumulative knowledge of the human race and in using it to better understand the larger society and its problems. Dewey thought that the true value of administration, curriculum, and instruction resided in operating schools as learning communities animated by a democratic social spirit and shared learning experiences.[23]

In many respects, World War I was a watershed for progressivism. After several decades of reform, topped off by a war that was supposed to "make the world safe for democracy," many Americans were weary of reformist slogans, and a new generation was ascending that was attuned to jazz music, get-rich-quick schemes, Prohibition and bootleggers, and other excitements of the Roaring Twenties, all of which took people's attention away from educational reform.

Pedagogical progressivism did not disappear, but in the struggle to control the governance and direction of American schools, pedagogical progressivism lost out to administrative progressivism.[24] In other words, pedagogical progressivism helped shape how we continue to think and talk about curriculum and instruction, but administrative progressivism shaped how we actually govern and control the schools.

Of course, obituaries of pedagogical progressivism may be, as Mark Twain once said about news reports of his death, "greatly exaggerated." There have been revivals, such as the open education movement of the late 1960s and early 1970s, which focused on the active engagement of children in the learning process. The movement faltered in the mid-1970s, however, as economic stagnation and the war in Vietnam drew public attention away from children's education. By the 1980s, the country was in a conservative, "back to basics" swing, with high-stakes testing and accountability becoming reform bywords.

Still, pedagogical progressivism's legacy continues in such emphases as active student learning, small group projects, and cross-disciplinary studies.[25]

Administrative progressives

Many administrative progressives found child-centered education lacking when it came to learning the prescribed curriculum. They also found the views on democracy—such as Dewey's—too impractical for what they believed the "real" world required. They saw themselves as men of action akin to the corporate captains of industry who supposedly saw the world as it truly was. They formed what Raymond Callahan termed the "cult of efficiency."[26]

The administrative progressives were concerned about the problems facing large urban school systems, but where pedagogical progressives looked to democratic expansion for remedies, administrative progressives sought answers in what they believed were the most successful institutions of their time, the industrial corporations. Like Dewey, they worried that the country's rapidly growing urban population was swamping existing institutions, but they thought local neighborhood control was both corrupt and inefficient, and it should be replaced by centralized expert management. They believed their approach was progressive because, guided by their scientific and technological expertise, it would lead to efficiently managed schools systems.

The administrative progressives were attracted to philosophical realism, a view that ultimate reality is external to human consciousness and independent of internal human needs and desires. A branch of philosophical realism is scientific realism (sometimes called positivism), which holds that the material world is the only objective reality, it can be measured and quantified, and rigorous scientific investigation uncovers the operating principles of that reality. Moreover, human well-being depends on understanding those operating principles and bringing human behavior into conformity with them.[27]

Although most administrative progressives were not philosophers, they reflected some of the main currents of philosophical realism during their time. In addition, the administrative and management theories from which they borrowed or which they created also reflected important elements of realist thinking.

Scientific, technological, and industrial developments

Most administrative progressives believed that the truly successful changes in modern society appeared to be based on scientific "laws." The thinking went something like this: Since the corporation was the most successful institution of the day, and since it used scientific management and technology to operate in predictable and efficient ways, then the corporate form of organization must reflect the correct way to operate all kinds of institutions, even schools.

Likewise, since "survival of the fittest" seemed to be a "law of nature" (as backed by some scientific claims of the times), then it must also be a law of human nature as well. These kinds of assumptions led some to conclude that, if science measured natural conditions and reduced them to their true descriptions and classifications, then properly trained educational experts should be able to measure (test) and classify (group) pupils from their "lower" to their "higher" forms, and schools would then operate predictably and educate efficiently at the lowest possible cost.[28]

Efficiency movement

One development in American business that gained the attention of many administrative progressives, and one with mixed blessings, was "scientific management," or simply "Taylorism" after its prime spokesman, industrial engineer Frederick W. Taylor. Scientific management involved time-motion studies of how workers performed their jobs, along with detailed recommendations on how they might become more productive in less time and with less wasted motion. Indeed, scientific management helped make American industries among the most productive in the world, and its success attracted followers, including many administrative progressives who hoped it might bring similar gains to school systems.

> **For Further Reflection:** To what extent can today's testing and accountability movement be traced back to the social efficiency movement just described? To put it differently, what are the parallels between the two movements and eras?

Corporate model of school governance and control

Armed with a strong belief in the power of their ideas and assuming that scientific management and the corporate model would help them better organize schools and instruct pupils, administrative progressives set out to discover the "one best system" for urban schools and to implement it everywhere.[29]

However, the mixed-blessing by-products were centralized authority, hierarchical divisions, organizational stratification, and increased specialization among administrators and support staff. In 1920, for example, there was one supervisor for every 35 teachers; by 1930, it had increased to one for every 22 teachers; by 1974, it was one for every 16 teachers; and by 1985, it was one for every 11 teachers.[30]

The drive toward the "one best system" of schools was characterized by an **ideological orientation**—a set of beliefs about social institutions, human behavior, and knowledge. "One best" advocates believed that, with the right kinds of knowledge about organizational structures and human psychological and social conditioning, they could solve troubling educational problems by making schools more efficient.

School systems came to look like corporations: a small board of directors at the top (the school board), a chief executive officer (the superintendent), professional managers (various levels of administrators), experts (specialists and supervisors), and assembly line workers (classroom teachers). The new structures brought changes many teachers welcomed, including specialized courses, subject-area departments, and classes organized by age and grade levels, but gradually new stresses emerged as bureaucratic controls eroded teacher autonomy and professional judgment in classrooms. Teacher objections to the contrary, by the 1950s the organizational revolution was fairly complete: Centralized, bureaucratic, and corporation-mimicking organizational patterns became deeply rooted in every major school system in the United States.[31]

For Further Reflection: Does the corporate model actually work efficiently and effectively for schools, or are there distinct differences between schools, on the one hand, and businesses and industries, on the other hand, that make such comparisons between the two problematic? In other words, is educating children and youth the same as making automobiles, or are the two operations distinctly different?

School board change

As originally intended, school committees or boards of education were to provide representative public control over schools at the local level. Despite the dedicated public service demonstrated by most boards, some systems experienced corruption and political favoritism, which helped fuel reformist fires. Consider, for example, the situations in San Francisco and Philadelphia. At one point, the San Francisco school board hired and fired teachers as much for political connections as professional competence. Also, teachers were hired on annual contracts only, and every year the board divided the hiring task equally among its 12 members. Those wishing to be re-employed had to take an annual examination with questions so arbitrary that the board could pass or fail applicants at will. Arbitrary control was also present in Philadelphia, divided into 42 wards, each with its own school committee. Ward bosses often intervened in such matters as hiring or firing and who got lucrative school contracts (for school repairs, heating, and supplies, for example). Such conditions hastened calls for civil service reform, merit-based hiring, elimination of graft and corruption, and rational management by qualified professionals. The goal was laudable: incorruptible, orderly, and efficient school systems.[32]

One outcome was the reduction of ward control in favor of centralized city school boards. The idea caught on that central school boards, composed of only 7 to 15 leading citizens chosen at large rather than by ward, would be as efficient as reformers believed corporate boards to be. As early as 1872, San Francisco and Chicago abolished ward representation and reduced the size of their central school boards. Boston reduced its level of ward representation in 1875, and Detroit followed in 1881 (only to restore it in 1889). By the early twentieth century, most major cities had either modified or abolished ward representation, and small central school boards with elite memberships, whether elected or appointed, became the chief educational policy-making bodies in most American cities.[33]

This was a pattern that would, with periodic tinkering, remain intact into the twenty-first century. A major problem, however, was that elite centralized school boards meant elite viewpoints (and biases) in the making of educational policies and directions.

The changing superintendency

The superintendent's job became more complex, involving not only the business end of school operations but also oversight of instruction, curriculum development, and personnel. Reformers successfully argued that superintendents should be in charge of all school operations, and in large school systems, assistant superintendents and other assorted administrative support staff were added. With the growth of large administrative bureaucracies, school superintendents truly became chief executive officers (CEOs), as bureaucratic in some respects as corporations.

Trained in the universities and armed with "scientific" psychology and testing technology, the new breed of school superintendents organized urban school systems into corporate-style bureaucracies with educational production separated into three lines: elementary schools, junior high schools, and high schools. Curriculum and instruction at the secondary levels were organized like assembly lines, with curriculum divided into discrete subjects taught by teachers specialized in those areas, with bells ringing to signal class changes and students marching from one specialized teacher and classroom to another. Quality control was managed by grouping students according to age and tested abilities, and with curriculum specifically designed (or "differentiated") so that each ability level received the kind of academic or vocational preparation deemed appropriate. Such developments, with structural tinkering and terminological changes over succeeding decades, set the standards by which most school systems continue to operate today. Improvements were made, but reformers failed to recognize that centralized school boards and powerful superintendents meant neighborhood control and citizen identity with the schools would wither.[34]

Suggested Activity: Discuss with others: Well-intended structural changes often produce results neither planned nor desired. Brainstorm examples related to education, historical and contemporary, that illustrate this phenomenon, and discuss whether or not things could have been done differently.

WEB: Additional Information 2.1.:
SHOULD SCHOOLS BE MORE LIKE BUSINESSES?

Teachers and school reform

There is a need to recognize that teachers—not administrators, supervisors, specialists, boards, scholars, reformers, or critics—are the ones who actually deliver instruction. This is not meant to imply that the other components fail in providing important services, but since instruction is the central function of schools, then teachers ought to be recognized as the significant professionals in the schooling process. Powerful representatives of the elite and centralized bureaucracies continue to control American public schools in ways that leave teachers out of the loop. Until better engagement of teachers occurs, instructional reforms orchestrated by elites in government, corporations, academia, and superintendents' offices will probably continue top-down. If the historical record is any indication, it promises little more than "tinkering toward Utopia," an approach that "has rarely worked well."[35]

Financial control of education

In many ways, the most powerful aspect of control is school finance. As can be seen in Table 2.2, the bulk of school finance continues to come from the state and local levels, with the federal government being the third. It is said that "he who pays the piper calls the tune," so it would appear that the state and local levels exert the most control over schools. The way federal control is exercised

Table 2.2 Percentage of revenues provided to elementary and secondary schools by government level in selected academic years in the United States

School year	Federal %	State %	Local %
1919–20	0.3	16.5	83
1929–30	0.4	16.9	82.7
1939–40	1.8	30.3	68
1949–50	2.9	39.8	57.3
1959–60	4.4	39.1	56.5
1969–70	8.0	39.9	52.1
1979–80	9.8	46.8	42.4
1989–90	6.1	47.1	46.6
1990–2000	7.3	49.5	43.2
2000–2001	7.3	49.7	43.0
2001–2002	7.9	49.2	42.9
2002–2003	8.5	48.7	42.8
2003–2004	9.1	47.1	43.9
2004–2005	9.2	46.9	44.0
2005–2006	9.1	46.5	44.4
2006–2007	8.5	47.6	43.9

Source: Adapted from National Center for Educational Statistics, "Table 172: Revenues for Public Elementary and Secondary Schools, by Source of Funds: Selected Years, 1919–20 to 2006–2007," *Digest of Educational Statistics, 2009,* at http://nces.ed.gov/programs/digest/d09/tables/dt09_172.asp (accessed on January 1, 2010).

over education, however, cannot be so neatly drawn, because its influence over policy is far heftier than its percentage of financial contribution would suggest.

In early twentieth-century reforms, educational governance was devised for boards and superintendents that served to shield them from interference by mayors and city councils. Similar shields existed for state superintendents and state boards as well. Most local boards were elected rather than appointed, and so also were some superintendents. Election by voters entailed loyalty to constituents, and it provided a degree of independence from higher authorities. Prior to the 1950s, most state and federal authorities were content to allow localities to exert the lion's share of control over curriculum, personnel, and finances. In the second half of the twentieth century, however, governors found good schools to be a major lure to bring businesses and jobs to their states, and achieving a competitive edge helped push states toward more control of schools. During the Cold War, federal leaders faced increased international scrutiny when, for example, the United States was compared unfavorably to the Soviet Union over racially segregated schools. Later, as global economic competition threatened American power, unfavorable international comparisons of American educational achievement with those of competitor nations stimulated even greater federal control of education. Thus, state and national controls over the schools increased in the latter half of the twentieth century.[36]

There was an important shift in financial control from localities to state and federal levels, with a growing gap occurring between those who made school policy and those held accountable for results. Since the early 1980s, governors and state legislators have imposed statewide reforms to raise student achievement and require high stakes testing. In addition, U.S presidents since the 1980s—Ronald Reagan, George H. W. Bush, William J. Clinton, George W. Bush, and Barack H. Obama—all pushed national education reforms and policies. When such state and federal demands lack adequate funding, however, critics hurl the charge of "unfunded mandates." Schools, teachers, and even students get blamed if they do not meet the demands, but the evidence is thin that governors, state legislatures, presidents or congresses ever accept blame when school performance does not improve under policies they imposed.[37]

Local control

Although local control has popular appeal, from a legal standpoint the constitutional power to establish public schools is a state responsibility. Historically, most governance and control were delegated to localities, and so it was well into the twentieth century.

The growth of state control over education was never a straight line of progression, but more of a perpetual balancing act between state and local authority.[38] From colonial times through the first decades of the twentieth century, localities maintained dominant control but with a slow drain of power toward the state level by the middle decades of the twentieth century. During the 1930s, local control was particularly eroded when Depression-wracked localities had to appeal to state governments for financial aid. Financial outlays are highly significant ways and means of governance. As seen in Table 2, during the 1929–1930 school year (the beginning of the Great Depression), local financial outlays were a whopping 82.7 percent, with state outlays only 16.9 percent, but by the 1939–1940 school year (as the Great Depression was coming to an end), local outlays had shrunk to 68 percent, while state outlays almost doubled to 30.3 percent. By 1949–1950, state outlays increased to 39.8%, where they more or less hovered until the 1979–1980 school year, when for the first time state financial outlays (46.8 percent) actually exceeded those of the localities (42.4 percent). In the 1980s, the local share increased slightly as federal contributions decreased, but by the 2000–2001 school year, the state clearly had the lion's share at 49.7 percent. At present it remains to be seen what impact the recession beginning in 2007 will have on local, state, and federal funding, but it appears to be significant.

State control

The idea of ultimate state responsibility for public education has long been recognized by the courts. In the landmark decision of *Brown v. Board of Education, Topeka* (1954), for example, the U.S. Supreme Court held that a state may delegate responsibility for public schools to its local governments, but it cannot abrogate its ultimate responsibility for those schools and, therefore, a state must ensure that its laws and policies are consistent with the requirements of the Constitution.[39] The force of court decisions along such lines has contributed to an increase of state control of public education.

However, this is not as clear-cut as it seems. Two notable decisions on financial resources for schools, one by a state supreme court (*Serrano v. Priest* [1971]) and the other by the U.S. Supreme Court (*San Antonio Independent School District v. Rodriguez* [1973]) help illustrate the point. The Serrano case, brought before the California State Supreme Court in 1971, concerned that state's heavy reliance on local property taxes to finance education and how this method of financing created educational inequalities between wealthy and poor school districts. Although the case would reassert itself in the California courts several times over the years, *Serrano v. Priest* helped focus nationwide attention on state responsibility for equitable public education provisions at the local level.[40]

The issues were similar in *Rodriguez,* a case originating in Texas, particularly the inequities from relying on local property taxes, except *Rodriguez* was appealed to the U.S. Supreme Court, which held that, while education is one of the most important services provided by a state, it is not a federal right guaranteed by the Constitution. The court concluded that issues of taxation for public education are reserved to state legislatures, in effect upholding state responsibility for public education.[41]

Both of these cases reinforce the view that public education is squarely the responsibility of states; however, criticisms continue. For example, there is the argument that state responsibility under the Tenth Amendment is no match for the spending power of the U.S. Congress. Over time, the federal government has slowly increased expenditures for schools, and Congress has come to exert growing influence over education through the **power of the purse**, even moving toward a national curriculum and a national testing program. Viewed in this light, the tradition of strong local and state control is facing increasing pressure.[42]

Perhaps there has been a loss of confidence in local control by both the state and federal levels of policy making. Near the end of the twentieth century, driven by fears of global competition and domestic economic decline, many states instituted massive statewide testing programs to make local educational authorities and teachers accountable for the educational achievement of their students. At its onset, this movement was spurred by critics charging that the schools were failing to meet the challenges of global market competition. There was also an intense economic rivalry among the states for businesses and jobs, and strong accountability and testing programs were seen as indicators of good schools. Pressures to lower local property taxes and the clamor over standards and accountability only encouraged more centralization, an enhancement of state and federal control and a diminution of local control.[43]

For those who fear federal control, however, it should be kept in mind that as late as the academic year 2006–2007, the federal government contributed only 8.5 percent of the nation's public school funding, while state governments contributed, on average, 47.6 percent, and local governments put up 43.9 percent (see Table 2.2). The lion's share (91.5 percent) was still provided by localities and states.

Federal control

Although the federal government has no specific constitutional authority for schools, it has long been involved. Although never as substantial as local or state involvement (see Table 2), federal involvement came about primarily in initiating or providing crucial support for educational activities that state and local governments could not or would not undertake.

In its earliest educational forays following the American Revolution, the federal government was debt ridden and short of cash, but it had one asset in abundance—federal land. While still operating under the Articles of Confederation, Congress passed the Ordinance of 1785, concerning the Northwest Territory between the Ohio River and the Great Lakes, to wit: "There shall be reserved the lot No. 16, of every township, for the maintenance of public schools, within the said township. . ."[44] In 1862, Congress passed the Morrill Act to dispense unsettled land in the Louisiana Purchase by apportioning large swaths to each individual state to sell, using the proceeds for "the endowment, support, and maintenance of at least one college" to provide instruction in "agriculture and the mechanic arts" (not excluding other "scientific or classical subjects"), to promote "the liberal and practical education of the industrial classes."[45] Through the late eighteenth and into the nineteenth centuries, most federal support for education came through federal lands. While these actions also intended to encourage territorial settlement, bring unsettled lands into economic production, and relieve population pressures east of the Mississippi River, educational objectives were clearly important.

Federal funds for education were extended by the Smith-Hughes Act of 1917, which helped (and pushed) states to provide high school vocational and technical education "in agriculture and the trades and industries" and which also included funds for "the preparation of teachers of vocational subjects" at the higher education level.[46] Most federal education legislation coming after 1917 continued to provide financial aid, one of the more significant being the G.I. Bill (officially the Serviceman's Readjustment Act of 1944), which provided financial support for World War II veterans to attend postsecondary educational institutions.[47]

More federal financial aid came after World War II in legislation such as the National Defense Education Act of 1958 (NDEA), which supported math, science, and foreign language instruction, to some extent an outgrowth of the Cold War "space race" with the Soviet Union. Another major expansion occurred with the Elementary and Secondary Education Act of 1965 (ESEA), which was a significant part of President Lyndon Johnson's Great Society program and what he called the War on Poverty. A decade later came the Education for All Handicapped Children Act of 1975 (later revised and renamed the Individuals with Disabilities Act [IDEA] in 1990), which expanded federal aid to include equal educational opportunities for persons with disabilities. All these acts expanded federal involvement, and they also increased federal controls as well.

Since there is no explicit education power laid out in the Constitution, federal aid must be channeled through other powers, such as national defense (the National Defense Education Act of 1958), general welfare (the Elementary and Secondary Education Act of 1965), and equal protection of the laws (the Individuals with Disabilities Education Act of 1990).[48] Federal funds must be allocated according to the Constitution and as specified by congressional legislation; consequently, most federal funding for education is through **categorical grants**, or federal funding of education for narrowly defined purposes and programs, rather than **general grants** (as provided by state and local governments), although there has been some loosening of that restriction in recent years.

In sum, general financial support for education continues to rest with local and state governments, but pressures for greater federal aid have grown. In the 1980s, there was an effort to relax restrictions on federal funding with block grants, or grants that allow more state and local discretion to spend federal funds. Although **block grants** did not loosen restrictions as much as supporters hoped, they were extended by the **No Child Left Behind (NCLB)** act of 2002 under President George W. Bush.[49] In 2009, President Barack Obama made it clear that strong federal involvement in education would continue during his administration.

Contemporary conditions

Schools are institutions controlled at several levels in both direct and indirect ways, but the most direct form of control comes at the local level. The primary policy-making local body is the school board, which provides general oversight of policies, operations, and professional personnel (superintendents, other administrators and support personnel, and classroom teachers) to deliver day-to-day operations and instruction; however, local school systems must not only carry out local board policies and directives but also state and federal laws and regulations as well. State governance is more indirect than local, but local schools are dependent on the state, because it is the significant source of policy, legislation, and funding. In comparison, the federal government has been a secondary player, but its influence over educational policies and practices often exceeds the financial support it actually provides.

Local school systems

While schools differ by state and locality, they share much in common in regard to organizational and physical structures as well as curriculum and instruction. For example, local school systems are organized hierarchically, with the school board setting policy at the top and the superintendent serving as the chief administrative (or executive) officer. Authority and power flow downward to central office staff and outward to building principals and then to teachers. In physical structure, schools are typically constructed with individual classrooms along hallways in a configuration that has been likened to an "egg crate" or "motel-like" design, a feature that has utility but may hamper communication among teachers and serve as a physical barrier to innovative instructional practices. In addition to classrooms, there is usually a central office and an auditorium, cafeteria, and gymnasium and perhaps spaces designed specifically for music, theatre, art, shop, and other activities. In other words, the typical school is arranged by the functions and activities that take place.[50]

Suggested Activity: Consider the high school you attended and describe the physical layout. Compare notes with other students and discuss your findings.

The "motel-like" structure of many school buildings facilitates what has been described as the "autonomy of the closed door."[51] In other words, teachers may have limited control over the curriculum and other factors impacting their

professional lives, but when classroom doors are closed, they are able to determine much of what goes on within.

School districts

While states set the general parameters for school operations, significant
control is still exercised at the local level. **Local school districts** (sometimes
school divisions or similar terms) vary by size, number of schools served, and
function. In addition, there is variation in terminology: As used here, a school
district is a local school system with a board, superintendent, administrative
support staff, and classroom teachers in a network of elementary, middle, and
high schools (see Figure 2.1).

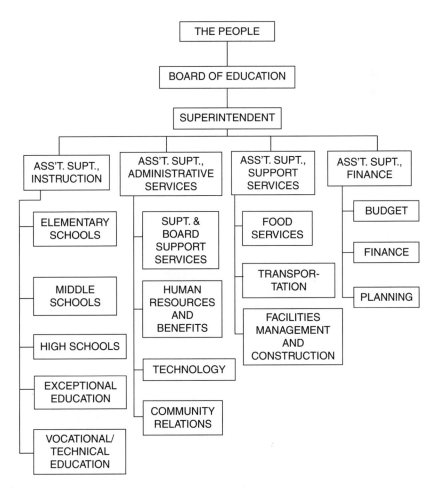

Figure 2.1 Organizational chart for a typical school district

Of course, large school systems are more complex and subdivided than smaller ones. The Denver Public Schools, for example, is a single system divided into five director districts. An immense and subdivided school system like Los Angeles might also be called a unified school district. New York City, the country's largest school system, is subdivided into ten regions that are further subdivided into school districts.[52]

Among the variety of school districts, student enrollments range from a few hundred students in the smaller districts that may serve only a handful of schools to thousands of students in the larger ones serving hundreds of schools. For example, New York City has more than 1,600 schools currently serving approximately 1.1 million students in grades kindergarten through 12; on the other hand, Winooski, Vermont, encompasses approximately 1 square mile of territory served by a single school complex housing all grade levels.[53]

The organizational structure of local school districts varies according to such things as state requirements and local needs and conditions. Generally, local school districts mirror state law requirements; states usually define in general terms how their local school systems must be structured, how school board members must be selected, and what their general roles and responsibilities must be.

School boards

The majority of **local school boards** are elected by local citizens, although in some instances boards may be appointed by local judges, mayors, city councils, or county commissioners or supervisors. Elected or appointed, however, school board members are supposed to be public servants representing the people, rather than a narrowly defined constituency (see Figure 2.1 for a flow chart illustration). Sometimes professional educators may serve on boards but may not serve on boards that employ them because of conflict of interest laws. The idea is that education should serve the public interest and public school systems should be governed by citizens, not professional employees. Professionals certainly exercise influence through their services and advice, but according to democratic theory, citizens are the ultimate source of legal authority, not professionals.[54]

The roles and responsibilities of local school boards may vary by state, but usually boards operate at the level of policy and not of hands-on daily operations. Although local board controls diminished as state and federal control grew over the years, boards still exercise significant influence. In many respects, democratically elected school boards provide a "nursery" for self-government, allowing citizens an opportunity for direct involvement in public policy making that impacts their lives in the close personal terms of children, families, and homes. School board meetings are always open to the public, except when addressing such legally protected areas as confidential personnel matters. Local school boards must be conducted in accordance with applicable local, state, and federal statutes. Typically, school boards make budgetary decisions, purchase property, authorize school construction and repair, deal with policy issues concerning curriculum and instruction, and personnel matters (such as contracts, pay scales, fringe benefits), to name a few. According to the **National School Boards Association (NSBA)**, a school board should:

- Establish a vision for the district through thoughtful, innovative planning and broad community involvement.
- Focus on improving student learning and pushing achievement to higher levels.
- Provide a management system using thoughtful decision-making processes.
- Advocate for education by securing local community support.
- Involve the community in providing strong financial support of local schools.
- Account for educational results by establishing clear objectives and reporting procedures.
- Encourage greater power and accountability at the building and classroom levels.
- Give guidance and direction for the superintendent and central office staff.
- Collaborate with other child development, health, and welfare agencies providing professional services to children and their families.[55]

Suggested Activity: Attend a school board meeting, take notes of any discussions related to governance, and discuss your observations and reflections in class.

Superintendents

Traditionally, some of the earliest **local superintendents** were elected by voters, but in most states today they are directly hired by school boards; consequently, superintendents and local school boards typically share similar educational philosophies, and superintendents tend to be concerned with maintaining the support of their board. Superintendents serve as chief executive officers of local school districts, their primary responsibility to keep the schools working smoothly and lawfully. They also provide professional advice and data to their boards to help them shape policies, plan budgets, and articulate educational goals. Superintendents serve at the pleasure of the board, and they should be cognizant of community constituencies and interest groups, understanding that they will often face forceful special interests that try to influence curriculum, policies, personnel, and operations. Not surprisingly, the turnover rate for local superintendents tends to be high, particularly in large school districts.[56]

Local school systems are hierarchical in nature and typically employ both **line officers** and **administrative staff**. Line officers hold positions in the chain of command below the superintendent, from assistant superintendents down to school principals and teachers (see Figure 2.1). A line officer (for example, a school principal) reports to a superior (for example, the assistant superintendent for curriculum and instruction) who, in turn, reports to the school superintendent who reports to the board. Although librarians, counselors, and specialists provide vital services, they are usually neither administrators nor teachers, but a third category called professional support staff.[57]

Principals

At the school level, the principal must see that the policies of the board and the administrative directives of the superintendent are carried out and then report the effects and needs back. In another sense, however, the term *principal* means "first" teacher (or sometimes "head" teacher), that is, one who serves as the **instructional leader** who also has duties as the **school administrator**. Principals are instructional leaders who must encourage professional growth, commitment to goals, and innovative teaching and curriculum practices, and they are school administrators who must manage professional staff, students, programs, community relationships, and the general operation of the school. Principals report directly to the local superintendent or a designated assistant superintendent. Depending on the number of faculty, students, and the needs of a school, principals may be supported by assistant principals and other support staff.[58]

Teachers

Schools are often organized by departments, particularly at the high school level, although they may be present in middle and elementary schools as well. However, middle and elementary schools are more typically organized by subject or grade level teams, with team leaders who are full-time teachers that facilitate team efforts and communications to and from the principal's office. High school departments are typically organized around subjects or disciplines.

Teachers comprise the largest group of professionals in any school, yet they may work independently of one another in their individual classrooms. Individualization of work affords teachers a certain degree of autonomy, but this can foster professional isolation if it restricts cooperative interaction with professional colleagues.[59] Interactive collaboration and professional autonomy are matters of debate, but the two need not be mutually exclusive. Professional autonomy does not mean all-powerful teachers in isolated classrooms; instead, it means competent teachers using their best professional judgment in conducting professional duties and activities in line with the lawful directives of employers and administrative supervisors.

Cross-Reference: see Chapter 1: The Teaching Profession for a discussion of professional organizations and unions. pp. 1–53.

For Further Discussion: Think about the potential ethical dilemmas resulting from the tension between professional autonomy and democratic control over education. How much input should laypersons have when it comes to educational decision making? How would you, as a teacher, feel if your opinion ran counter to the opinion of the local school board, which does not consist of educational professionals but of local citizens? How would you feel as a parent?

Special interest groups

Every community has **special interests**, and they emerge from parents, local communities, and/or the larger society. Special interest individuals and groups exert pressures on schools by pleading various causes and ideologies. They lobby legislatures, school boards, councils, and individuals; and they speak out at public meetings, circulate petitions, organize media campaigns, and work behind the scenes to further their agendas.

Cross-Reference: For a discussion of the relationship between religion and schools, see Chapter 8: Religion and Education. pp. 355–410.

The existence of special interest groups can be a sign of a healthy democracy in action where various elements of the community play vital roles in educational decision making, but some special interests can become obstructive or even destructive of the public interest, particularly when they dominate public dialogue to the detriment of vital but less vociferous views. When this occurs, there is a need for both patience and a concerted effort to ensure public participation under rules of fair play.

Parents

Parents might be involved in schools in many ways, but it is particularly important for them to see that their children have a caring and supportive home environment that encourages learning and that fulfills such specific practical needs as getting the children ready and prepared for school each day. It is also crucial for parents to attend parent-teacher conferences and to work supportively with teachers to ensure their children's success. Other forms of parental participation include occasional community service activities, such as chaperoning fieldtrips, helping with special classroom or school events, or providing volunteer work in the classroom, library, or computer lab. Parents often organize fundraisers, support teams and the band, work in parent-teacher organizations, and even beautify school grounds. These types of parental participation are important and are generally seen by educators as extremely valuable; however, parental participation in sensitive policy and personnel issues is sometimes resisted, as is an excessive advocacy on behalf of one's own children, both of which may become parental interference rather than support.

Nevertheless, it must also be recognized that parents have rights and duties as well as professionals. After all, the schools actually belong to citizens and taxpayers, including parents, and they, too, have ethical obligations and feelings of responsibility for their children that must not be undervalued by professionals. Despite the drawbacks that sometimes occur, parental involvement in schools is almost always a good thing, including significant correlations of parental participation with the academic success of their children.[60]

For Further Reflection: How would you define the most productive form of parental involvement in schools that is not only in the best interest of children but also respects teacher professionalism as well as parental rights?

For Further Reflection: To what extent should parents be advocates for their children? Should they influence school governance and shape educational policy?

Accreditation agencies

In addition to the quality controls over schools exercised by local and state authorities, there are also independent, peer-review **accreditation agencies** that monitor such things as academic standards and quality of instruction. Similar to practices in higher education, these agencies conduct school visits to assess course offerings and instruction, evaluate curriculum requirements, and ensure a certain degree of standardization, especially among secondary schools and college-preparatory programs.

State governance of schools

As noted, states have the implied power to establish public schools under the Tenth Amendment of the U.S. Constitution. "Implied" means the power is not explicitly stated; in fact, the Constitution does not contain the word *education*. The Tenth Amendment simply states that "the powers not delegated to the United States by the Constitution, nor prohibited by it to the States, are reserved to the States respectively, or to the People."

At the present time, the most significant source of governance and control over education remains at the state level. State legislatures are by far the most influential because they control the most important purse strings. Governors also play significant roles through executive powers and personal powers of persuasion that can stir public opinion to action. State governance is also exercised through a **state board of education**, a **state superintendent**, and a **state department of education**, which provide central state-level oversight and regulatory roles concerning state laws, policies, regulations, and general operations. State government decides crucial aspects of funding, curriculum requirements, student promotion and graduation requirements, and teacher licensing. Over the past few decades, state power has expanded not only in funding but also in curriculum requirements, promotion and graduation standards, and high-stakes testing results that have state funds and sanctions tied to them.

Suggested Activity: Review the literature on testing and begin to form your own viewpoint on the pros and cons of a pronounced testing system.

Federal control of schools

Although federal government participation is limited, it does have power and influence through Congressional funding. Four important ways are:

- Categorical aid—funding that supports specific programs, such as compensatory education, bilingual education, special needs education, and vocational-technical education.
- Power of the purse—technically, all federal funds to education are "purse" related, but here the expression reflects funding to uphold constitutional powers and the laws of Congress, such as the Fourteenth Amendment's "equal protection of the laws" and congressional statutes supporting equal educational opportunity.
- Education research—funding of research on federally endorsed educational projects, the collection and dispersal of national education statistics and other general information useful to citizens, educators, and all levels of government.
- Moral suasion—developing a national vision for education by example through leadership, programs and policies, national discussion and debate, law making, and the collection and dispersal of information.[61]

No Child Left Behind

Until after World War II, education was rarely if ever a national political issue, but beginning in the 1950s education gained increasing national importance, even becoming the source of major initiatives in presidential administrations. One of the most ambitious presidential initiatives was President Lyndon Johnson's Great Society, of which the 1965 Elementary and Secondary Education Act (ESEA) was a part. There have been a number of other federal education reform efforts, an example being President George W. Bush's No Child Left Behind (NCLB), a revision of ESEA. NCLB was to be a cornerstone of the Bush administration, but the violent attacks of September 11, 2001, forced a change in priorities. Nevertheless, Bush was able to steer NCLB through Congress (with bipartisan support) and sign it into law on January 2, 2002. It contained four key elements:

- Stronger accountability—schools are accountable for closing the achievement gap and ensuring that all students become academically proficient. States and school districts must release public information annually about school progress, and underperforming schools must take corrective actions (such as tutoring and after-school and summer programs).
- Increased flexibility for school districts—in exchange for stronger accountability, states and school districts must have more freedom to shift and combine funds to serve different purposes (such as hiring, salaries, and professional development).
- Scientifically supported educational methods—rigorous research should determine the effectiveness of programs and practices (such as teaching skills in preschool and elementary reading instruction), and federal funds will be targeted at successful ones.

- School choice—families should be able to choose a different school or free tutoring if their child attends a school deemed unsafe or in need of improvement. The law encourages charter schools and supports selected services in private schools as well as home schooling.[62]

At the presidential signing, Senator Edward Kennedy (a liberal Democrat who provided key support) stood side by side with President George W. Bush (a conservative Republican), each smiling broadly. Bipartisanship soon slackened as provisions took effect, however.

Federal financing

Legal challenges have been launched against the way American schools are financed, although their full impact remains to be seen. Since the late 1980s, following a pattern set by the Serrano case in 1971, but also reflecting the more recent accountability movement, state supreme courts in Kentucky, New Hampshire, Tennessee, Arkansas, Ohio, and New Jersey have ruled that their respective state constitutions require each state to provide resources necessary to meet state-mandated standards. In other words, if a state is going to require higher standards, and if it expects schools actually to achieve them, then it must provide the requisite financial resources. However, if it is difficult for a state to determine what it will cost to meet its own standards, it is even more difficult for the federal government, because it must adapt its requirements to each state's unique educational system and each state's unique accountability standards, and this makes it challenging to determine a fair mode of dispensing federal funds.[63]

For example, a study on state accountability funding illustrates some of the states' difficulties to meet NCLB requirements, and what follows includes findings on three states as examples:

- Indiana: For the year 2001–2002, Indiana estimated that it would have to increase funding from $5,468 to $7,142 per pupil per year (an increase of 34 percent), with an additional $7,500 to $8,300 per special education pupil, and $4,200 to 5,300 for "'hard-to-serve'" students.
- Maryland: For the fiscal year 2000, the state estimated the cost at $12,060 per elementary student, $9,000 per middle school pupil, and $9,599 per high school student. No estimate was included for special education, but for low-income students an additional $7,748 per pupil was projected. Altogether, Maryland would have to increase its expenditures between 34 percent and 49 percent.
- Montana: In 2002, with a then-current base of $4,471 per pupil, Montana estimated it would take between $6,004 to $8,041 per pupil, with special needs pupils requiring an additional $8,000 each and with remedial needs an additional $2,000 per pupil. Montana would need to boost its education expenditures between 34 percent and 80 percent.

The study concluded that for states to meet their own accountability standards there would have to be massive new education investments.[64]

This points to a major school governance dilemma: How do localities, states, and the federal government sort through all the pressures from politically hot education issues and the economic realities faced in funding/governing education? This was further complicated by the economic recession beginning in 2007, because by the 2009–2010 school year, all governance levels—local, state, and federal—were financially strapped. Perhaps some school governance changes will emerge from this, but perhaps American education will return to its well-worn path.

NCLB and federal accountability measures

The emphasis by the federal government on standards, accountability, and testing has certainly affected public education. Some observers see federal accountability measures as welcome reform, but others are skeptical or even opposed, and some have changed their minds over time. Diane Ravitch, for instance, who was initially instrumental in paving the way for NCLB, now views the legislation's narrow focus on testing as undermining what public education really needs: a focus on the aims of education and a strong curriculum. Other critics argue that NCLB fails to address social and emotional risk factors that prevent student success in school. Some maintain that the statistical procedures used to measure student proficiency are flawed. Still others complain that the system of local-state-federal control is too complex for top-down management, and high-stakes testing is problematic because there is little agreement on the best way to measure school performance. A great deal of criticism is directed at high-stakes testing itself: It does not effectively measure what students actually learn; it skews instruction toward teaching to the test, which distracts teachers from helping students pursue knowledge of interest; and there is a "saw-tooth-effect" of testing in which performance improves over time because both teachers and students become "test smart," rather than students actually learning and retaining knowledge. Finally, critics point out that the punitive provisions in NCLB encourage states to lower standards so enough students pass to keep federal funds flowing.[65]

Of course, such problems do not mean accountability should be discarded; rather, it should be studied carefully for its effects on teaching and learning and on local-state-federal governance. Local and state school systems are **loosely coupled systems**, that is, they are such diverse systems that stringent federal control becomes difficult if not counterproductive. Instead of rigid control, perhaps the federal government should partner with the states to develop new knowledge through federally funded **education research** and develop from it some helpful accountability measures designed for each of the 50 state systems and their even more diverse local systems.[66]

> WEB: Suggested Reading 2.1.

One troublesome problem is that accountability measured by test scores may be particularly detrimental to low-income, culturally and linguistically diverse (LI/CLD) children, because LI/CLD students are not underprivileged by their own doings but by life circumstances. Instead of diminishing inequities, accountability exacerbates them with its sorting and ranking, which determine how federal funding rewards and penalties are doled out to the schools. In its accountability measures, NCLB seems to assume that low academic achievement results from personal irresponsibility and that poverty results from the poor choices of individual children rather than pre-existing economic inequities. In other words, while LI/CLD children might eventually shape their own destinies, as children they have no choice about their socioeconomic conditions, which impact their test performance differently than those students whose luck of birth environment makes school achievement more likely. In sum, NCLB accountability encourages moral and academic judgments about LI/LCD students and their teachers and schools but not about children's socioeconomic conditions and the adult world of power that created them.[67]

According to some observers, President Obama's educational plan will address some of NCLB's weaknesses. In particular, the plan promises to give greater attention to data (including test scores and other measures) affected by such things as race, ethnicity, English learner status, and family income. In general, it calls for rigorous accountability to continue but with greater attention to fairness.[68]

> WEB: Suggested Reading 2.2.

Debate over school governance reform

Public school governance has been criticized for years from a variety of vantage points, and numerous reforms have been suggested. Some proposals advocate a simplified reform that leaves some traditional structure while increasing local community and even individual school control over curriculum and teaching. Others call for a more radical restructuring that seems to leave few vestiges of traditional modes of governance.

For example, there are critics who argue that public schools are top-down, hierarchical systems that overload teachers with supervisors and negate teacher professionalism, but the primary reason this approach continues is the "the trap of favored ways of thinking." The greatest concentration of bureaucratic decision-making power has occurred at the state level, when what is needed is more control over curriculum and instruction at the local level. The role of school principals must be redefined as facilitators of teaching, and teachers must be more fully engaged in decisions not only on curriculum and instruction but also on administrative acts impacting their professional duties. If teachers had more control they could break out of their current isolation and work in teams to meet unique needs at each individual school. Old ways of scheduling class periods and organizing by age-grade levels should be scrapped in favor of organizing around student needs and progress. Parents should be more involved in governance, with individual schools deciding how to define this involvement.[69]

Other critics, however, propose not simply restructuring but complete reshaping. For example, it has been observed that existing school systems are not, and never were intended to be, very efficacious. In the early 1900s, they were designed as an assembly line approach to socialize large numbers of immigrant children to the urban industrial environment, without much regard for productive learning. What is needed now is a new school governance system designed for productive learning, with teachers and parents exercising far more authority over local schools than currently. More research and evaluation should be conducted to better understand how teachers and students interact and how productive learning occurs. Schools should be open to public scrutiny and be accountable to the communities they serve. School principals might become superfluous, because faculty would be directly involved in running schools and could assume administrative responsibilities.[70]

For Further Reflection: Consider how "the trap of favored ways of thinking" might get in the way of innovation and reform in many spheres of life, not only education. How does one get out of such traps and develop visions of what might be more effective or humane?

For Further Reflection: Making school principals largely superfluous seems like a radical idea. Consider whether it would lead to better schools or to chaos. Would schools be more effective if teachers themselves assumed school management responsibilities?

Other critics idealize the past, seeking to recover lost traditions and better times. Advocates of school vouchers and stringent accountability standards, for example, appear to believe that education was once wide open to private choice, and academic standards were once very high. As the historical record shows, however, before there were any public school systems, school choice was mostly dependent on the ability to pay at a time when few could afford it. No serious effort was made to educate everyone, and there never were enough private schools to accommodate the demand if all parents had tried to enroll their children. Criticism of schools for lack of academic achievement has a long history, and would-be reformers who seek to return to a golden age of academic achievement actually look for a past that never existed.[71]

Although criticism has a valuable role to play, it sometimes seems the critics know everything about public school improvement but very little about financing it. For example, in the 1980s critics proclaimed that global economic competitors were surpassing the United States and pointed their fingers at the schools. About a decade later, however, the National Assessment of Educational Progress (NAEP) reported that reading and math scores were at a 30-year high, and by 2000 the dropout rate neared an all-time low. Critics then complained about the "merely average" performance of American students on international tests of reading, math, and science achievement. These same critics seemed strangely silent when an international comparison showed the United States rated only average in the percentage of gross domestic product invested in elementary education, and well into the bottom half in secondary education.[72]

Some assumptions of reformers

Sometimes it helps to examine reform vocabulary and rhetoric. It has been observed that the current school accountability movement is based less on accountability to the public (which ordinary citizens might expect the term to mean), and more on technical-managerial accountability in which auditable accounts are reviewed by state or federal authorities instead of parents or community. It is a market-style view of accountability that defines schools as producers of commodities and students and parents as consumers; hence, educational quality is associated with accounting processes and procedures rather than academic substance. Parents are made to feel that they should be preoccupied with whether their children are prepared for the needs of competitive economic interests rather than their children's own educational growth and development or the larger common good.[73]

Defining school accountability in terms of market theory reflects what has been called the consumerization of citizenship. It is based on promotional, top-down communication, with service delivery geared at maximizing customer preferences based on market competition. A singular emphasis on consumer preference, however, undermines democracy because it makes it difficult to counter bad consumer choices or to create desirable stability in educational institutions.[74]

New Public Management

Just as "scientific management" and the corporate business model of organization had a great impact on public school governance in the twentieth century, there is a new wave of management theories seeking to influence educational debates, policies, and programs in the twenty-first century. A leading theory indicative of that trend is called New Public Management (NPM), and it is concerned with the management of public-sector institutions rather than private ones. NPM is based on public service management ideas developed mostly since the early 1980s. It first took root in the United Kingdom and rapidly spread to Australia and New Zealand, then to the United States, Scandinavia, and elsewhere. Its central doctrine reflects a business-corporate orientation that public service sectors (including public education) should be seen as "quasi-markets," but it extends its reach into government-wide management systems such as finance, procurement, and audits. Advocates claim that, if properly conceived and executed, NPM would reduce government costs and contain growth in the public sector.[75]

NPM harkens back to the scientific management theory (or Taylorism) of the early twentieth century, particularly its measurement and efficiency emphases. The influence of market theory on school governance has been tighter state and federal controls over public schools, while the impact of market ideology on the public possibly helps explain such developments as school choice, voucher plans, and charter schools, which are all consumer-driven views of education. Many NPM advocates champion corporate deregulation and privatization of public services, a view echoed by taxpayer-funded school vouchers for use in private schools. As a result, NPM has been variously described as a popularized mixture of management, psychological, and market theories that blur public and private distinctions.[76]

This ideological orientation lies behind claims that public schools exist fundamentally to serve economic ends, but what gets lost in this drumbeat of economic determinism is public education's vital importance in preparing future citizens of a democratic society. Schools never had and do not now have the singular, eternal purpose of serving economic interests, despite what is loudly proclaimed. The historical record shows no such singular purpose. What it actually reveals is multiple purposes in which economic benefit was only one (and very often *not* the most important one). In the end, the fact remains that values are not biologically transmitted; they must be passed from one generation to the next through some means of education. Education to develop competent and knowledgeable citizens may be the *most* important goal of education in any society that aspires to be democratic.[77]

Rather than mere submission to the drumbeat of market ideologues, greater emphasis is needed on education for a deliberative democracy. Perhaps the greatest need is the education of future citizens who take citizenship responsibilities as seriously as private rights and privileges.[78]

Value of criticism

While school critics might need criticism themselves, and while they might seem to ignore too easily the accomplishments of schools and their governing agencies, it still remains that the schools face daunting problems that need serious attention. In the final analysis, American education is neither as hopeless as detractors proclaim nor as flawless as admirers soothingly pronounce. Both the public and professional educators alike need to understand that valuable service is provided by critics when their efforts become stimuli for creative thought and action about the aims of education and better ways to accomplish them.

International perspective: Argentine Republic

The Argentine Republic is the second-largest country in South America (after Brazil). On its western side it borders Chile and on the eastern side the South Atlantic Ocean. It is also bordered by Bolivia in the north and Paraguay, Brazil, and Uruguay in the northeast. Argentina has a population of approximately 40.9 million (a July 2009 estimate); the majority (97 percent) is mostly of Spanish and Italian ancestry, with the remaining 3 percent composed of mestizo (mixed white and Amerindian ancestry), Amerindians, and other non-European groups. Argentina gained independence from Spain in 1816, and today it has a republican form of government, with 24 provinces and with Buenos Aires as its capital city. It is one of the wealthier countries in Latin America, possessing rich natural resources along with diversified industries and a strong agricultural base. It claims a high literacy rate of 97.2 percent, among both males and females, age 15 and older.[79]

Governance and the Argentine education system

Argentina has a history of political instability but also of strong public interest in national education. A major political problem has been frequent military interference in government, probably the worst instance occurring when a military junta seized power in 1976 and subjected the country to brutal repression. Citizens were imprisoned, and many were killed, with thousands unaccounted for to this day. In education, junta control was so complete that virtually no initiative was given to national, provincial, or local education officials. A rigid curriculum was enforced, teachers were reduced to inculcating officially approved knowledge, students were stifled by extensive rules (even how to carry books to and from school), and school officials were forbidden to discuss educational issues with citizens. Independent-minded educators were treated as national security risks; thousands were fired, and many fled the country in fear of their lives. Public outrage over the brutality, widespread social and economic deterioration, and warfare finally brought the junta down in 1983.[80]

In the aftermath, reforms were undertaken to decentralize the education system, strengthen greater regional and local control, and bring school governance closer to the people. Indeed, primary school financing was transferred to the provinces by the junta in 1978, and in 1991 a new law transferred secondary and some postsecondary education (such as teacher-training institutes) to the provinces. Without adequate national funding to cover the expenses, however, this move only put additional burdens on provincial and local sources of revenue. More extensive changes came with the National Law of Education in 1993, which gave central curriculum planning and goal-setting responsibilities to the Ministry of Education and additional management and funding responsibilities to the provinces and localities. The ministry planned a broad general education curriculum called the Common Basic Contents (CBC), and each province had to develop its own detailed curriculum plan within CBC guidelines, while each district was to refine its province's plan to meet local needs. The 1993 law also changed the structure of primary and secondary education from the traditional seven years primary and five years secondary to nine years primary (divided into 3 three-year "cycles") and three years secondary (with options of a humanities and sciences mode or one of several vocational and/or technical modes). Finally, the law extended compulsory education from ages 6 to 12 to ages 5 to 14.[81]

A 1995 law brought related changes to tertiary (postsecondary and higher) education, with additional provincial funding responsibilities and new institutional performance expectations. These efforts had adherents but also generated opposition fearful that the changes would negatively impact institutions and diminish the favorable international reputation of Argentina's national universities. Despite crippling economic recessions (1999–2002, and another beginning in 2007), by 2009 Argentina had 40 national, tuition-free public universities and 46 tuition-charging private universities. There was also an international university (the Latin American Faculty of the Social Sciences), a branch of a foreign university (the University of Bologna), and a number of public and private institutes that provided advanced professional preparation.[82]

Changes in national political leadership and rising resistance to decentralization led to the repeal of the 1993 law when the National Education Law of 2006 was passed. Among other things, it changed the structure of elementary and secondary schooling back to the traditional seven- and five-year structure. It also extended compulsory attendance to age 17, in effect pushing it to the end of secondary education.[83]

> **For Further Reflection:** In Argentina, military and democratic governments alike have used their educational systems to instill specific values. Do school systems in the United States do the same? Is this desirable or undesirable, and does it depend on what values are taught and how they are taught? What values should be fostered in schools, and what should not?

School governance issues

A leading justification for decentralization was that greater control would flow to the local level where schooling most affected people's lives, but control seemed to recentralize at the provincial level instead. Part of this was due to traditional reliance on central authorities for policy directives, while provinces and localities simply carried them out. Reform was hindered by a lack of provincial and local experience with major policy making and funding responsibilities, and by reduced national financing and increased demands for provincial and local financing. A few provinces and localities could handle this, but others simply lacked the necessary resources of taxable wealth.[84]

Some of the motivation behind decentralization was driven by so-called neo-liberal market ideology. One aspect was a belief that the transfer of financing from national to provincial and local levels was right and that development of greater public reliance on private education instead of public education was desirable. Put into practice, these ideologies led to a reduction of national funding for public schools and an increase for private schools. At the same time, public schools were given higher performance expectations and increased workloads for educators, all of which meant fewer educational services and less effective delivery. Such conditions helped secure the passage of the National Education Law of 2006, which promised such things as an increase of national support for education and a return to the old structure of seven years of primary and five years of secondary education. Unfortunately, the worldwide recession that began in 2007 slammed the Argentine economy, shriveled economic resources for education, and hamstrung the government's ability to implement the law.[85]

As it neared the second decade of the twenty-first century, Argentina faced mixed messages about its educational system. A 2006 study by the United Nations Educational, Scientific, and Cultural Organization (UNESCO) ranked Argentina's educational system to be twenty-seventh out of 129 countries, especially for its favorable school enrollments and tuition-free public universities; however, that same year the Organization for Economic and Cultural Development (OECD) compared 57 countries on student performance in math, science and reading, and it found Argentina's schools placing near the bottom in those particular areas.[86]

It seems clear that Argentina's current economic woes help explain some of its educational difficulties. When economic prosperity returns, a 2009 UNESCO study could potentially point to where the country might want to focus. This concerns the problems of low teacher morale due to insufficient pay, lack of resources to help low-income students, poor school facilities, and inadequate instructional materials. According to the report, evidence indicates that teachers with high morale make a difference in student achievement and program success, while low teacher morale is indicative of the school governance problems facing many countries, including Argentina.[87]

Summary and conclusions

Understanding school governance and control is central to comprehending the ways schools work today. Prior to the emergence of public school systems, there was considerable variety in how American schools were governed. For the most part, education was seen as the responsibility of individuals, families, or religions, not governments. The nineteenth-century idea of universal, tax-supported public schools, available to virtually all children, became accepted and widely implemented. Among the driving forces were industrialization, urbanization, and the immigration of diverse peoples. As the population became more heterogeneous, it soon became obvious that some common experiences were needed to reduce social divisions and provide a stronger sense of the common good. Public common schools were considered a central part of such reform efforts, with most of the financial support and governance provided by localities and with oversight by local boards of education or school committees. The idea of public, tax-supported education eventually spread to secondary and higher education as well.

High fertility rates and increasing immigration caused rapid population growth in the late nineteenth and early twentieth centuries, and public schools had to expand accordingly. Seeking to manage this population impact on schools, progressive reformers opted for the corporate model of governance, which resulted in bureaucratized school systems governed by small elite boards and operated by trained professionals, a development that shaped the kinds of school governance existing today.

An important aspect of school control is finance, and while the proportions provided by the local, state, and federal levels have changed over time, the lion's share of funding continues to come from the local and state levels. Traditionally, the power to establish public schools was a state responsibility, with actual control delegated to the local levels. At one time, localities were the major source of funding, but by the late twentieth century, state funding exceeded those of local funding. Federal funding has always been less than that contributed on the local and state levels, and it usually provides only categorical rather than general funding. In earlier times, the federal government gave public lands to encourage educational development, but in the twentieth century it started contributing funds for certain specific programs. Today the federal government is involved in significant ways, with such programs as the Individuals with Disabilities Act (IDEA) and No Child Left Behind (NCLB).

Individual schools are administered by principals and assistant principals who function as instructional leaders, supervise teachers, deal with student discipline, manage school budgets, maintain good community relations, and more. Department chairs and team leaders facilitate coordination and communication among teachers and administrators, while support staff help ensure smooth operation. At the local level, school boards make budgets, purchase school sites, decide curriculum questions, among many other duties. The boards hire local superintendents who serve as chief administrators of the schools. Interest groups also shape school governance through such activities as lobbying and raising public attention. Accreditation agencies exert control through monitoring activities at the local, state, regional and national levels.

At the state level, governance is performed through legislatures, governors, courts, state superintendents, state boards of education, and state departments of education. Crucial decisions are made involving such issues as state financial support for schools, content of the curriculum, teacher licensure, and student promotion and graduation criteria. Finally, the federal level shapes education through promoting a national perspective for schools across the country, gathering educational data, providing categorical aid, and funding education research, among other things.

Throughout history, school governance has been modified, overhauled, and reformed. Reform proposals during recent years encompass ideas ranging from centralization to decentralization, from increasing the scope of public options to privatization and school choice, and from strengthening the status quo to completely rebuilding it. Despite all the criticism, debate, and reforms over the years, schools and school governance seem to be fairly resistant to radical change. Perhaps some fundamental change will come, but time will tell what changes take root and what conditions remain the same.

In comparison, Argentina's school system has undergone greater political turmoil and more dramatic change than the American system. During the twentieth century, Argentina was alternately governed by civilian and military governments, and its education system suffered from that instability. The nation has made great efforts to rebuild its educational system and was making good headway until the world economy went into recession beginning in 2007. Despite the difficulties, the Argentine people highly value education and seem determined to bring about their planned educational reforms.

Vocabulary

accreditation agencies
administrative staff
bureaucratic
categorical aid
centralized control
education research
ideological orientation
instructional leader
line officers
local control
loosely coupled systems
National School Boards Association (NSBA)
No Child Left Behind (NCLB)
power of the purse
school administrator
school board
school committee
school district
special interests
state board of education
state department of education
state superintendent
superintendent

Notes

1 David Tyack, *Seeking Common Ground: Public Schools in a Diverse Society* (Cambridge: Harvard University Press, 2003).

2 U.S. Department of Education (USDOE), "About Us," at http://doe.k12.hi.us/about/index.htm (accessed on February 1, 2010).

3 Glenn Weaver, "Benjamin Franklin and the Pennsylvania Germans," *The William and Mary Quarterly*, 3rd ser., vol. 14, no. 4: 536–559 (October, 1957); and Patricia U. Bonomi, "The Middle Colonies as the Birthplace of American Religious Pluralism," at http://nationalhumanitiescenter.org/tserve/eighteen/ekeyinfo/midcol.htm (accessed on February 2, 2010).

4 "The Massachusetts School Law of 1647," in *Educational Ideas in America: A Documentary History*, S. Alexander Rippa, ed. (New York: David McKay Co., Inc., 1969), 162; "Enforcement of Pious Teaching [*Laws of Virginia*, March 1645–6]," in *The Educating of Americans: A Documentary History*, Daniel Calhoun, ed. (Boston: Houghton Mifflin, 1969), 18; and "Labor for Poor Children [*Laws of Virginia*, October 1646]," in Calhoun, 18.

5 Jon Teaford, "The Transformation of Massachusetts Education, 1670–1780," in *The Social History of American Education*, B. Edward McClellan and William J. Reese, eds (Chicago: University of Illinois Press, 1988), 31–35; and William J. Gilmore, "Elementary Literacy on the Eve of the Industrial Revolution: Trends in Rural New England" (Worchester, MA: American Antiquarian Society, 1982), 87–178.

6 Lawrence Cremin, *American Education: The Colonial Experience, 1607–1783* (New York: Harper Torchbooks, Harper and Row, 1970), 177–178, 530–531; and J. L. Blair Buck, *The Development of Public Schools in Virginia, 1607–1952* (Richmond: Commonwealth of Virginia State Board of Education, 1952), 14–18. In 1805, the Syms and Eaton schools combined to form Hampton Academy, which in 1852 became a part of the public school system of the city of Hampton, Virginia.

7 Cremin, 517–543, and 544–563; R. Freeman Butts and Lawrence A. Cremin, *A History of Education in American Culture* (New York: Holt, Rinehart and Winston, 1953), 97–115.

8 Thomas Jefferson, *Crusade Against Ignorance: Thomas Jefferson on Education*, Gordon C. Lee, ed., Classics in Education, No. 6 (New York: Teachers College Press, 1961), 84–86.

9 Thomas Timar and David Tyack, *The Invisible Hand of Ideology: Perspectives from the History of School Governance* (Denver: Education Commission of the States, 1999), 11.

10 Lawrence Cremin, "Horace Mann's Legacy," in Horace Mann, *The Republic and the School Horace Mann on the Education of Free Men*, Lawrence Cremin, ed., Classics in Education, No. 1 (New York: Teachers College Press, 1957), 20; Horace Mann, "First Annual Report (1837)," in ibid., 29–30.

11 Joseph M. Cronin, *The Control of Urban Schools: Perspectives on the Power of Educational Reformers* (New York: The Free Press, 1973), 39–52.

12 Ibid., 52–57; and Joseph M. Cronin and Michael D. Usdan, "Rethinking the Urban School Superintendency: Non-Traditional Leaders and New Models of Leadership," in *American Educational Governance on Trial: Change and Challenges*, William Lowe Boyd and Debra Miretsky, eds (Chicago: National Society for the Study of Education, 2003), 177–178.

13 Mark Twain (Samuel Clemens) and Charles Dudley White, *The Gilded Age: A Tale of To-Day* (Hartford: American Publishing Co., 1873).

14 David Tyack, *The One Best System of Education: A History of American Urban Education* (Cambridge, MA: Harvard University Press, 1974), 177–181.

15 William A. Bullough, *Cities and Schools in the Gilded Age: The Evolution of an Urban Institution* (Port Washington, NY: Kennikat Press, 1974), 15–18.

16 Ibid., 22–26.

17 Lawrence Cremin, *The Transformation of the School: Progressivism in American Education, 1876–1957* (New York: Vintage Books, 1961), vii–x.

100 Foundations of Education

18 Tyack, *One Best System,* 126–132ff. The terms "pedagogical progressives" and "administrative progressives" are borrowed from this source.

19 Jean-Jacques Rousseau, *The Émile of Jean Jacques Rousseau: Selections,* William Boyd, trans. and ed. (New York :Teachers College Press [1956] 1976); and Howard Ozmon and Samuel M. Craver, *Philosophical Foundations of Education,* 7th edn. (Columbus, O: Merrill Prentice Hall, 2003), 131–132.

20 Johann Heinrich Pestalozzi. *The Education of Man: Aphorisms* (New York: Greenwood Press, [1951] 1969); and Friedrich Froebel, *The Education of Man* (Clifton, NJ: A. M. Kelley, 1974).

21 Cremin, *The Transformation of the School,* 101–103, and 128–135.

22 John Dewey, *Democracy and Education: An Introduction to the Philosophy of Education* (New York: Macmillan, 1916), 100–102, and 130–145; Dewey, *Experience and Education,* Kappa Delta Pi Lecture Series (New York: Collier Books [1938] 1963), 43–44; and Dewey, *Moral Principles in Education,* with a New Preface by Sidney Hook (Carbondale, IL: Southern Illinois University Press, 1975), 2, 11–13.

23 Dewey, *Democracy and Education,* 414–418; and *Experience and Education,* 78–84.

24 David F. Labaree, "Progressivism, Schools and Schools of Education: An American Romance," *Pedagogica Historica,* vol. 41, nos. 1 and 2: 275–288 (February 2005). See also Labaree, *The Trouble with Ed Schools* (New Haven: Yale University Press, 2004).

25 Larry Cuban, "The Open Classroom," *Education Next,* vol. 4, no. 2 (Spring 2004), at http://educationnext.org/theopenclassroom/ (accessed on February 24, 2009).

26 Raymond E. Callahan, *Education and the Cult of Efficiency: A Study of the Social Forces that Have Shaped the Administration of the Public Schools* (Chicago: University of Chicago Press, 1962).

27 John T. Wahlquist, The Philosophy of American Education (New York: The Ronald Press, 1942), 56–70; and John Wild, "Education and Human Society: A Realistic View," in *Modern Philosophies and Education: The Fifty-Fourth yearbook of the National Society for the Study of Education, Part I,* Nelson B. Henry ed. (Chicago: University of Chicago Press, 1955), 17–56.

28 See Leonard Ayres, *Laggards in Our Schools: A Study of Retardation and Elimination in City Schools Systems* (New York: Russell Sage Foundation, Charities Publication Committee, 1909).

29 Ibid., 28–29, 39–40.

30 Welker, *The Teacher as Expert,* 7.

31 Tyack, *One Best System,* 142–147; and Parker and Parker, 171–179.

32 Ibid., 97–104.

33 Cronin, 44–52.

34 David Tyack and Larry Cuban, *Tinkering Toward Utopia: A Century of Public School Reform* (Cambridge: Harvard University Press, 1995); and Michael Engel, *The Struggle for Control of Public Education: Market Ideology and Democratic Values* (Philadelphia: Temple University Press, 2000).

35 Tyack and Cuban, 15–22, 44–47, 54–59, 134–140.

36 Michael Kirst, "A History of School Governance, in *Who's in Charge Here? The Tangled Web of School Governance and Policy,* Noel Epstein, ed. (Denver: Education Commission of the States, 2004), 20–24, 28–32, 36–37.

37 Noel Epstein, "Introduction: Who should be in charge of our Schools?" in *Who's in Charge Here?,* 2–3.

38 Nancy Beadie, "The Limits of Standardization and the Importance of Constituencies: Historical Tensions in the Relationship Between State Authority and Local Control," in *Balancing Local Control and State Responsibility for K-12 Education. 2000 Yearbook of the American Education Finance Association.* Neil Theobald and Betty Malen, eds. (Larchmont, NY: Eye on Education, 2000), 47–120.

39 Although the Court's *Brown* decision rested on the "equal protection" clause of the Fourteenth Amendment, and not on the Tenth Amendment, the idea of state responsibility was clearly a part of the Court's thinking. In reference to the right to "the opportunity of an education," the Court held, "Such an opportunity, where the state has undertaken to provide it, is a right which must be made

available to all on equal terms" (p. 493). See *Brown v. Board of Education Topeka* (1954), 347 U. S. 483, also at http://supct.law.cornell.edu/supct/search/display.html?terms=brown&url=/supct/html/historics/USSC_CR_0347_0483_ZO.html (accessed on February 2, 2010).

40 *Serrano v. Priest* (1971) 5 C3d 584, and at http://online.ceb.com/CalCases/C3/5C3d584.htm (accessed on February 2, 2010). See also *Serrano II* (1976) 18 Cal. 3d 728, for a later ruling.

41 *San Antonio Independent School District v. Rodriguez* (1973) 411 US 1, at http://supct.law.cornell.edu/supct/html/historics/USSC_CR_0411_0001_ZO.html (accessed on February 2, 2010).

42 James E. Ryan, "The Tenth Amendment and Other Paper Tigers: The Legal Boundaries of Education Governance," *Who's in Charge Here: The Tangled Web of School Governance and Policy*, Noel Epstein, ed. (Denver: Education Commission of the States, 2004), 42–74.

43 Michael Kirst, "Turning Points: A History of American School Governance," in *Who's in Charge Here?*, 14–15.

44 "Land Ordinance of 1785," at http://west.stanford.edu/cgi-bin/pager.php?id=49 (accessed on February 2, 2010).

45 "Transcript of the Morrill Act of 1862," at http://ourdocuments.gov/doc.php?flash=true&doc=33&page=transcript (accessed on February 2, 2010); and Scott Key, "Economics or Education: the Establishment of American Land-Grant Universities," *Journal of Higher Education*, vol. 67, no. 2: p 196(25) (March–April 1996).

46 "The National Vocational Education (Smith-Hughes) Act," at http://www.cals.ncsu.edu/agexed/sae/smithugh.html (accessed on February 2, 2010).

47 Serviceman's Readjustment Act ("G. I. Bill") of 1944, *United States Statutes At Large* 58 Stat. L. 284); Michael J. Bennett, *When Dreams Came True: The GI Bill and the Making of Modern America* (Washington, D.C: Brassey's, 1996); and Reginald Wilson, "The G.I. Bill and the Transformation of America," *National Forum*, vol. 75, no. 4: p20(3) (Fall 1995).

48 For a general overview of federal government powers, see the Constitution's Preamble: ". . . to form a more perfect Union, establish Justice, insure domestic Tranquility, provide for the common defense, promote the general Welfare, and secure the Blessings of Liberty." Other, more specific powers that have been applied to education are granted in the body of the document and in its amendments (such as the "equal protection of the laws" clause of Amendment XIV).

49 See, for example, Kenneth Finegold, Laura Wherry, and Stephanie Schardin, "Block Grants: Historical Overview and Lessons Learned," Urban Institute, No. A-63 in Series, "New Federalism: Issues and Options for States" (April 21, 2004), at http://www.urban.org/url.cfm?ID=310991 (accessed on February 2, 2010).

50 James A. Johnson et al., *An Introduction to the Foundations of American Education,* 12th edn (Boston: Allyn and Bacon, 2002), 176. The "egg crate" characterization probably dates back to John Philbrick's creation of a specially designed, age-graded school in Boston, Massachusetts, in 1848. See Tyack, *One Best* System, 44–45.

51 Kathleen Bennett deMarrais and Margaret D. LeCompte, *The Way Schools Work: A Sociological Analysis of Education* (White Plains, NY: Longman Publishers, 1995), 48–49.

52 "Denver Public Schools Director Districts," at http://planning.dpsk12.org/DistrictMaps/Director-Districts.pdf (accessed on January 28, 2010); Los Angeles Unified School District, at http://notebook.lausd.net/portal/page?_pageid=33,47493&_dad=ptl&_schema=PTL_EP (accessed on January 28, 2010); The Legal Aid Society, "Questions about the NYC school structure." http://www.legal-aid.org/selfhelp/education/structure/structure_ny_schools.html (accessed on January 28, 2010).

53 NYC Department of Education, "About us" at http://schools.nyc.gov/AboutUs/default.htm (accessed on January 28, 2010) and "Winooski School District," http://www.winooski.k12.vt.us/ (accessed on January 28, 2010).

54 For ethical tensions between "professionals" and "the public," see Kenneth Strike and Jonas F. Soltis, *The Ethics of Teaching,* 4th edn (New York: Teachers College, 2004), 94–114.

55 Education Commission of the States, *Effective School Governance: A Look at Today's Practice and Tomorrow's Promise*," at http://www.ecs.org/clearinghouse/13/20/1320.htm (accessed on January 28, 2010).

56 J.H. Snider, "The Superintendent as Scapegoat," *Education Week*, vol. 25, no. 18: 31, 40 (January 11, 2006).

57 James A. Johnson et al., 182.

58 Ibid., 177.

59 Ibid., 178.

60 Maike Philipsen, ed., *Parental Involvement in the Schools: Ideas that Work*, Hot Topics Series (Bloomington: Phi Delta Kappa, 1997), 3.

61 Forrest W. Parkay and Beverly Hardcastle Stanford, *Becoming a Teacher*, 5th edn (Boston: Allyn and Bacon, 2001), 182.

62 U.S. Department of Education, "No Child Left Behind Act of 2001," at http://www.ed.gov./nclb/overview/intro/execsumm.doc (accessed on January 28, 2010); and "Four Pillars of NCLB," at http://www.ed.gov/print/nclb/overview/intro/4pillars.html (accessed on January 28, 2010).

63 Mathis, 679–686 (May 2003).

64 Ibid., 680–682, 684–686.

65 Diane Ravitch, *The Death and Life of the Great American School System: How Testing and Choice are Undermining Education* (New York: Basic Books, 2010); Christine Lagana-Riordan and Jemel P. Aguilar, "What's Missing from No Child Left Behind? A Policy Analysis from a Social Work Perspective." *Children & Schools,* vol. 31, no. 3: 135–144 (July 2009); and Andrew Dean Ho, "The Problem with 'Proficiency': Limitations of Statistics and Policy under No Child Left Behind," *Educational Researcher,* vol. 37, no. 6: 351–360 (August/September 2008).

66 Jane Hannaway, "Accountability, Assessment, and Performance Issues: We've Come A Long Way . . . or Have We?" in *American Educational Governance on Trial: Change and Challenges*, 25; and deMarrais and LeCompte, 25–34, 49.

67 Ronald David Glass, "Left Behind Once Again: What's Luck Got to Do with Current Educational Policies and Practices?" in *Philosophy of Education*, Philosophy of Education Society (Urbana, Ill: University of Illinois at Urbana-Champaign: 2006), 354–363; and David P. Ericson, "Luck in the Educational System," in ibid., 364–366.

68 Linda Darling-Hammond. "President Obama and Education: The Possibilities for Dramatic improvements in Teaching and Learning," *Harvard Educational Review,* vol. 79, no. 2: 210–223 (Summer 2009); and U.S. Department of Education, Office of Planning, Evaluation and Policy Development, *ESEA Blueprint for Reform* (Washington, DC, March 2010), 8–11.

69 William J. Bailey, *Organizing* Schools (Lancaster PA: Technomic Publishing, 1997) 22, 49–108.

70 Seymour B. Sarason, *How Schools Might Be Governed and Why* (New York: Teachers College Press, 1997), 35–94.

71 Robert Nelson Reddick, "History, Myth, and the Politics of Educational Reform." *Educational Theory*, vol. 54, no. 1: 73–87 (February 2004). Not only was there no "golden age" of achievement in elementary and secondary education, but it did not exist in higher education either. See, for example, Harold T. Shapiro, *A Larger Sense of Purpose: Higher Education and Society* (Princeton, NJ: Princeton University Press, 2003), 41–44.

72 William J. Mathis, "No Child Left Behind: Costs and Benefits," *Phi Delta Kappan*, vol. 84, no. 9: 679–680 (May 2003). See also the National Center for Education Statistics (NCES), "National Assessment of Educational Progress (NAEP) Overview," at http://nces.ed.gov/nationsreportcard/about/#overview (accessed on October 31, 2010).

73 Gert J.J. Biesta, "Education, Accountability, and the Ethical Demand: Can the Democratic Potential of Accountability be Regained?" *Educational Theory*, vol. 54, no. 3: 233–250 (August 2004).

74 Michael A. Peters, "The New Prudentialism in Education: Actuarial Rationality and the Entrepreneurial Self," *Educational Theory*, vol. 55, no. 2: 135–136 (May 2005); and Catherine Needham,

"Citizen-Consumers: New Labour's Marketplace Democracy," working paper, *Catalyst* (April 2003), at http://editiondesign.com/catalyst/pubs/pub10a.html (accessed on October 24, 2010).

75 Michael Barzelay, The New Public Management: Improving Research and Policy Dialogue (Berkeley: University of California Press, 2001), xi–xii, 2–3, 9.

76 Lynn, Laurence E., Jr., *Public Management: Old and New* (New York: Taylor and Routledge, 2006), 107, 143–144.

77 Michael Mintrom, "Educational Governance and Democratic Practice," *Educational Policy*, vol., no. 5: 616–617, 639–640 (November 2001). See also Amy Gutmann, *Democratic Education* (Princeton, NJ: Princeton University Press, 1987).

78 Abe Feuerstein, "Elections, Voting, and Democracy in Local Schools District Governance," *Educational Policy*, vol. 16, no. 1: 29–35 (January and March 2002).

79 "Argentina," *The World Factbook*, at https://www.cia.gov/library/publications/the-world-factbook/geos/ar.html (accessed on March 5, 2009).

80 E. Mark Hanson, "Educational Change under Autocratic and Democratic Governments: The Case of Argentina," *Comparative Education,* vol. 32, no. 3: 303–317 (1996). For a treatment of the "disappeared ones," see "Refusing to Forget," PBS transcript (October 16, 1997), at http://www.pbs.org/newshour/bb/latin_america/july-dec97/argentina_10-16a.html (accessed on February 4, 2010).

81 Silvina Gvirtz, Curricular Reforms in Latin America with Special Emphasis on the Argentina Case, in *Comparative Education*, vol. 38, no. 4: 453–469 (2002); and Jorge M. Gorostiaga et al., "Secondary education in Argentina during the 1990s: The limits of a comprehensive reform effort," *Education Policy Analysis Archives*, vol. 11, no. 17 (May 29, 2003), at http://epaa.asu.edu/ojs/article/view-File/245/371 (accessed on February 4, 2010).

82 Marcela Mollis, "Argentine Higher Education in Transition," *International Higher Education* (Winter 2002), at http://www.bc.edu/bc_org/avp/soe/cihe/newsletter/News26/text013.htm; and Liz Reisberg, "Measuring Institutional Quality in Argentina: The Devil Is in the Details," International Higher Education, no. 52 (Summer 2008) at http://www.bc.edu/bc_org/avp/soe/cihe/newsletter/Number52/Number52.htm (both accessed on February 9, 2010). For an official list of Argentina's higher education institutions, see "Autoridades Universitarias," at http://www.me.gov.ar/spu/ Servicios/Autoridades_Universitarias/autoridades_universitarias.html (accessed on February 4, 2010).

83 For a brief English summary of the law, see "Argentina: National Education Law (2006)," Global Legal Information Network, at http://www.glin.gov/view.action?glinID=188274 (accessed on February 9, 2010); and Silvina Gvirtz, "Education in Argentina: past, present and future tendencies," (2007), 13–14, at http://cei.mrecic.gov.ar/seminarios/John%20Gage/argentinos/Gvirtz.pdf (accessed on February 5, 2010).

84 Jorge M. Gorostiaga Derqui, "Educational Decentralization policies in Argentina and Brazil: exploring new trends," *Journal of Education Policy*, vol. 16, no. 6: 575–578 (2001); and Sebastián Galiana and Ernesto Schargrodsky, "Evaluating the Impact of School Decentralization on Educational Policy," *Economía*, vol. 2, no. 2: 275–314 (Spring, 2002).

85 Derqui, 575–578; and Gvirtz, "Education in Argentina: past, present and future tendencies," 6–12, at http://cei.mrecic.gov.ar/seminarios/John%20Gage/argentinos/Gvirtz.pdf (accessed on February 5, 2010); and Luciana Díaz Frers, "Differences in Resource Endowments and the Impact on the Argentine Education System," in *Unity and Diversity: Learning from Each Other*, vol. 5, Policy Issues in Federalism: International Perspectives (New Delhi: Viva Books, 2008), 53–64, at http://www.forumfed.org/en/libdocs/IntConfFed07/IntConfFed-India-2007-Vol-5.pdf#page=65 (accessed on February 5, 2010).

86 Sebastián Lacunza, "Argentina: Mixed Marks for Educational System (2008)," Inter Press Service (IPS), at http://ipsnews.net/news.asp?idnews=40671 (accessed on February 3, 2010).

87 United Nations Educational, Scientific, and Cultural Organization, *Overcoming Inequality: Why Governance Matters*, EFA Global Monitoring Report (2009), 116, 117, 121, and 148, at http://unesdoc.unesco.org/images/0017/001776/177683e.pdf (accessed on February 10, 2010).

3

Social Class and Education

Chapter objectives

Readers should be able to:

- understand the concept of social class and varying viewpoints on it.
- appreciate the historical influence of social class on educational policy.
- analyze social class and its impact on educational opportunity and attainment.
- explore leading research studies on how social class shapes the realities of schooling.
- gain an understanding of major contemporary controversies over social class and education such as school funding and access.
- explore ethical and philosophical ramifications of social class in education.
- understand how social class in education plays out in a different national context.

Opening questions

1. What is social class and its importance in education, past and present?
2. How has social class affected access to and the quality of education over time?
3. How have views on social class shaped educational policy?
4. What is the relationship between educational attainment and social mobility?
5. How do people's attitudes about social class affect their views on education?
6. What can be learned about social class from international comparisons?

The issue

Education is a social process indelibly connected with the society that supports it. Social continuity between generations would not be possible without education, because a society's heritage (its ideas, values, and beliefs) is passed from one generation to the next through social processes that induct the young into that society. These processes are a big part of what is meant by the term *education,* which itself may be divided into two broad categories—informal and formal education. **Informal education** occurs as an incidental part of life, but it is highly significant nonetheless. For example, a child usually learns to speak its native language through the ordinary, everyday experiences encountered in family and community life. This is also how most children first learn basic values and social roles. In other words, one "inherits" a social heritage not through genetics but through the social and cultural processes that transmit that heritage.

Formal education, however, is consciously deliberate and it, too, plays a vitally important role in social continuity. It usually occurs in institutional settings where content, activities, and processes are purposefully arranged to achieve certain goals. For example, every child may enter school already possessing a language, but the school attempts to refine the child's use of language in more skillful ways. In formal education, one is deliberately taught about one's heritage in a more detailed, organized fashion than usually occurs informally, and learners are thereby introduced to studies that connect them with centuries of human history and cultures from around the world, all of which extend far beyond the informal experiences of most people.

Societies are both alike and different in how they provide education, and American society is no exception. American education includes features adapted from other societies, but it also has elements that make it unique. A characteristic of virtually all societies is how social class influences provisions for education as well as educational achievement and attainment. While Americans may not always identify themselves by class, and while American society may not have as fixed a class structure as some societies do, social class impacts how people see themselves and what opportunities they have, including educational opportunities.

For Further Reflection: In your own experience, has social class affected your educational opportunities and if so, how and why? Consider the even broader question of how social class might impact your future life.

Background

Social class is as old as history, if by class we mean a way of ranking the various strata of a society. For example, Plato described three ideal classes in ancient Greek society: the philosopher kings who provided leadership, the soldiers who provided protection, and the workers who produced goods and services. Plato envisioned a scheme of education for each class, but he wrote mostly about the education of the philosopher kings. Similarly, Aristotle saw three great divisions of society, the rich, the poor, and those in between, and he argued that education should be available to all members of society alike, provided they were free citizens.[1]

European traditions

By the Middle Ages, European society was generally organized into the nobility, the gentry, free peasants, and serfs. In the sixteenth century, a powerful merchant class also had emerged, along with a sizable expansion of trade and industry. By the seventeenth century, when England successfully planted colonies in North America, England itself was divided into the nobility at the top, followed by the gentry, the professional and merchant class, the yeomen and tenant farmers, and finally the largest class of all, the common people. Generally, these five classes were typical of other European societies as well, and they shaped the social assumptions of the policy makers who planned the colonies as well as the colonists who settled along the eastern shores of North America.[2]

It is estimated that in 1600 about 35 to 40 percent of Europeans were literate, that is, they could comprehend written material at least at a rudimentary level. In Europe, **literacy** was higher in urban than rural areas, and higher in northern than in southern Europe. It was highest among males from the urban upper classes, mainly because urban areas had the wealth and population to support schools, the upper classes could afford schooling, with males favored over females. Generally, literacy was associated with power, and access to education was mostly restricted to the powerful.[3] Such was the framework of educational assumptions the colonists brought with them, but in confronting New World conditions, those assumptions proved difficult to maintain.

Cross-Reference: See Chapter 6, Gender and Education, for more discussion of gender bias in education, pp. 257–306.

Class and education in colonial America

In Europe, the large extended family was the basic social institution, and for most people, the local community supplied what the family did not. The early colonists assumed this to be the general structure of social authority everywhere; however, colonial conditions demanded extensive labor, which reduced the time parents could spend with their children. Far removed from the familiar community networks of Europe, the colonists had to rely to a much larger extent on individualism and small self-sufficient families. In short, colonial conditions demanded a new kind of education.

Early colonial period

In 1607, the first permanent English colony was established at Jamestown, Virginia, and in 1621, the Virginia Company of London encouraged charitable contributions for the education and religious conversion of the native peoples. A college was to be erected at a place called Henrico Town, a settlement on the bluffs overlooking the James River (near present-day Richmond, Virginia), but an uprising by the Powhatan Confederacy, a group of tribes along the James River, ended the venture in March 1622.[4]

Cross-Reference: See Chapter 5, Ethnicity and Education, for an extended discussion of Native Americans and their views on education, pp. 207–256.

The Virginia colonists followed the English tradition that education was a responsibility of home and church, not government. When the Virginia House of Burgesses dealt with the plight of destitute children in the 1631–32 session, they chose religious instruction. In the 1642–43 session, legislation was enacted for the education of orphans in "the rudiments of learning," and in 1646 this was revised to include preparing destitute children "in honest and profitable trades and manufactures." A major intent was "to avoid sloth and idleness" by employing the children in the "public flax houses" to learn cloth making. Despite such legislative efforts, there is scant evidence that the laws had any great salutary effect on destitute children.[5]

To an inquiry in 1671, Virginia governor Sir William Berkeley replied that there were "no free schools nor printing" in Virginia, for learning brought "disobedience, heresy, and sects into the world" while printing "divulged them, and libels against the best government. God keep us from both!"[6] The attitude of Virginia's aristocratic leaders, at least as reflected by Governor Berkeley, was to do as little as possible.

For Further Reflection: To what extent does our society today continue to see schooling as a means to prevent "sloth and idleness" or, as more contemporary language would put it, "keep kids off the streets"? Should schools be used for that purpose? Do you think schools are effective in that regard?

Of all the measures to promote education in the early colonial period, none had the sweep of those in the Massachusetts Bay Colony. The first college founded in the English-speaking colonies was Harvard College in 1636. A large donation of money and books was made by "Mr. [John] Harvard (a godly Gentleman, and a lover of Learning, there living amongst us)." Others contributed lesser amounts "and the publique hand of the State added the rest." Still, despite the "publique hand," social class strongly influenced who gained access to Harvard College for generations to come.[7]

Perhaps the most inclusive educational action taken by Massachusetts was the Old Deluder Act of 1647, which required townships of more than "50 householders" to appoint a reading and writing teacher whose wages were to be paid "either by the parents and masters of such children, or by the inhabitants in general." Although the means of financing were vague and there was lax compliance with the law, the act helped establish a pattern across New England, such that by the late eighteenth and early nineteenth centuries that region had a higher literacy rate than either the middle or the southern colonies.[8]

Suggested Activity: Is religion still a widely recognized justification for literacy? Are there contemporary arguments supporting religion as an important reason for literacy education, and if so, what are they? What is your opinion on the issue?

For an in-depth discussion of religion and education, see Chapter 8, Religion and Education, pp. 355–410.

Late colonial period

Some observers date the beginnings of free public schools from the Old Deluder Act of 1647, but in fact it did not establish either free or universal public schools. The primary financial obligation still remained with parents, although it became common practice for some towns to give limited public support to their schools to lower tuition costs, and a few localities allowed very poor children to attend tuition-free. In these communities, at least some schooling was available to all classes, but whether a family was able to take advantage of it depended on that family's circumstances. Despite shortcomings, a network of schools developed in New England that ranged from elementary petty schools, to secondary grammar schools, to Harvard College.

In the southern colonies, legislation for education was intended to help paupers and orphans become employable adults, but lawmakers were mostly silent on the education of other classes. A notable exception was the founding of the College of William and Mary in Virginia in 1693, primarily intended to prepare candidates for the ministry. Generally, the southern assumption was that education should be provided by private means. A similar pattern was found in the middle colonies, which relied mainly on voluntary efforts, religious charity, and traditional forms of schooling. If New England took the lead in public support for schools, and if the middle and southern colonies relied on charitable and private approaches, it was still the case that in each region the schools served the requirements of a **hierarchically divided society**.[9]

Class and colonial education

The offspring of the gentry and the well-to-do upper middle class, particularly the sons, were usually educated in classical (Greek and Latin) literature and languages, with some attention to mathematics, rudimentary science, and a few other general subjects. Lower-middle-class youth, again mostly males, were likely to get basic education and then be apprenticed in skilled trades or businesses. Lower-class children received some religious instruction, and a few might receive some rudimentary reading instruction. Slaves got on-the-job training in agricultural and vocational skills, but it was rare for any slave to become literate.

During colonial times, not everyone went to school: Instruction might be provided in the home if a parent had both the knowledge and the time to do it, while wealthy families often had private tutors for their children. In the churches, most pastors provided religious education, and a few might include helping the children learn to read and perhaps even to write. In other words, many colonists were illiterate, some possessed a moderate degree of literacy, and a few were well educated.

> **Suggested Activity:** Interview a teacher or school counselor. Do they see a correlation between parents' social class and the tracking of their children? To what extent, in other words, does social class continue to influence the type and quality of education a student receives?

Where schools were available, the most common were the petty schools for young children that taught the **rudiments** of reading, writing, and arithmetic, usually with a strong religious emphasis. Typically, petty schools were located in substantial villages or towns and provided instruction in English. Most depended on tuition payments, but some received public funding as well. There were a few "free" schools for the very poor, institutions that relied on bequeaths, endowments, and other charitable contributions for support.

At the secondary level were the grammar schools, which taught Latin and Greek languages and literature along with other academic subjects. Coming late in the colonial period were the academies, secondary schools that offered a college-preparatory curriculum and a more practical curriculum as well. At the higher education level were the colleges, of which nine had been established by the time of the American Revolution, that offered studies leading to the bachelor of arts degree. In addition there was a variety of private, entrepreneurial forms of instruction, or private venture schools. For example, skilled tradesmen, ministers, physicians, lawyers, or others might give instruction in the evenings for a fee, teaching general subjects or their particular knowledge and skills to interested learners. With few exceptions in colonial times, educational opportunity was most available to those who could pay for it.[10]

Class and education from the early republic to the Civil War

In 1783, the Treaty of Paris officially ended the American Revolution, but the nation remained vulnerable. Numerous efforts were made to strengthen the new republic, a number of them motivated by the Enlightenment faith in progress as well as a homegrown faith in American destiny that energized so many of the revolutionary generation.

Benjamin Franklin and practical education

As the new American republic sought to gain its footing, the classical tradition of education remained strong, but there was also a growing desire for education more attuned to contemporary interests. As is usually the case, developments do not suddenly spring up in full maturity but have their roots in the past.

Benjamin Franklin (1706–90) was one of those Americans whose hopes for the future were emboldened by Enlightenment ideas of progress. While he lived most of his life during the colonial period, his views help illustrate some of the influences that impacted education in the early United States.

Born and reared in a large family in Boston, Franklin only received one year of formal schooling at the Boston Latin School. Apprenticed to an older brother to learn the printing trade, he not only proved to be a voracious reader but also a promising writer. After a dispute with his brother at the age of 15, Ben ran away to Philadelphia where he eventually made a name for himself as a master printer, a widely read author, and one of the most knowledgeable men of his day.

Despite the fact that he became very wealthy and gained international fame as a statesman and scientist, Franklin always viewed himself as a "leather apron" man, a tradesman and (he proudly stated) a printer. He strongly identified with "the middling sorts" of people who sought to build up the community with useful knowledge, a class-based point of view that helps explain his educational ideas.[11]

A critic of traditional education, Franklin once observed of Harvard College that, with all its classical languages and religious emphases, it produced graduates who could neither "dig for a living nor live by their wits," and who finished "as great Blockheads as ever, only more proud and self-conceited." Despite the popular image of Franklin as thoroughly utilitarian, however, broad social responsibility was at the top of his educational objectives. "*True merit*," he believed, consisted of "an *Inclination* join'd with an *Ability* to serve Mankind, one's Country, Friends, and Family," an ability "greatly increased by *true Learning*" and one that should be "the great *Aim* and *End* of all Learning."[12]

In 1749, Franklin advocated a new kind of secondary education designed to serve the interests of the rising American middle class, and from his efforts and those of his associates, the Philadelphia Academy emerged in 1751. Franklin maintained that the academy should help students enter "the several Professions for which they are intended." Others associated with the founding retained the classical curriculum at the academy, but Franklin's "practical studies" became an option, including such subjects as arithmetic, accounting, geometry, astronomy, logic, ethics, English, modern foreign languages, writing, speaking, history, gardening, and "mechanics" or practical physics.[13]

Shortly before the colonies declared independence from Britain, the school changed its name to the College of Philadelphia, and after the revolution it became the University of Pennsylvania. Still, as Franklin hoped it would, the idea of secondary schools with practical as well as classical studies appealed to the "middling" parts of society, and academies became the standard for American secondary schools until displaced by public high schools in the late nineteenth century.

For Further Reflection: What is the relationship between classical and practical studies today? Is the college-preparatory curriculum the modern equivalent of the traditional classical curriculum, and are current vocational/technical studies equivalent to what Franklin meant by "practical studies"? What does the American public expect its high school and college graduates to be able to do? To what extent are they class based, and do they "promote the well-being of society"?

In the nineteenth century, the United States metamorphosed from an agrarian into an industrialized nation, and the need for a more inclusive system of education that served students from all levels of society became a rallying cry for reformers. Various alternatives were put forward to educate more people: Charity schools, free schools, subscription schools, Sunday schools, and Lancastrian schools were all tried, but each had serious drawbacks, and none seemed to meet the goal of universal education.[14]

Public common schools

Although Massachusetts had a strong record in education from early colonial days, by the 1820s its schools had deteriorated. As industrialization spread, cities and towns around Massachusetts attracted both the rural poor and immigrants from Europe looking for work in the new factories. Among the results were overcrowded slums, unemployment, low wages, greedy industrialism, and increased crime and violence. People feared social disintegration, and a number of reformers rose up who embraced the idea of public, tax-supported common schools (as they were then called) for all children as the way to alleviate social conditions. These schools were intended to be socially inclusive and to widely distribute literacy, social unity, and sturdy "republican" values. From Massachusetts and surrounding states, the common school idea spread.

The most representative spokesman for common schools was Horace Mann of Massachusetts, who spoke and wrote eloquently about existing socioeconomic divisions. He noted that in European tradition, "men are divided into classes,—some to toil and earn, others to seize and enjoy," but in a free republic all are supposed "to have an equal chance for earning, and equal security in the enjoyment of what they earn." A new kind of feudalism lay in American industrialism's "vast and overshadowing private fortunes," one potentially "more oppressive and unrelenting than that of the Middle Ages." Massachusetts was "exposed, far beyond any other state in the Union, to the fatal extremes of overgrown wealth and desperate poverty," Mann argued, and he proclaimed that, "Nothing but Universal Education can counterwork this tendency to the domination of capital and the servility of labor." Indeed, it "would do more than all things else to obliterate factitious [class] distinctions in society."[15]

For Further Reflection: What are examples where education has, indeed, alleviated social and economic tensions? To what extent can education solve social problems? Does education truly provide each rising generation with "a brighter and more plentiful future"?

An indication of how the education/social-class relationship actually played out, however, may be seen in the example of St. Louis, Missouri. Between 1840 and 1880, St. Louis public schools grew from a few struggling common schools to a diversified school system of kindergartens, elementary schools, evening schools, high schools, and normal (or teacher-training) schools. The student body swelled from a mere 266 students in 1840 to 55,870 by 1880, with most of the growth coming during the 15 years after the end of the Civil War in 1865. For all this growth, however, many parents still allowed their children to drop out after only a few years of elementary school, despite the fact that free public education in St. Louis was available up through high school. Why? A major variable in how long students attended school was the occupations of the fathers. The majority of students attending the district elementary schools had fathers in skilled and unskilled occupations, but the majority of students continuing to high school and normal school had fathers in white collar, business, managerial, or professional occupations. As late as 1880, children with fathers in unskilled occupations comprised 27 percent of all district elementary students, but only 3 percent of the high school students, while children with fathers who were professionals made up only 3 percent of the elementary school but 13 percent of the high school population. The peak years of attendance for all children across all categories were between ages 7 through 13. This was prior to the establishment of child labor laws; consequently, after age 13, the dropout rate dramatically increased until, after age 16, only about 15 percent of all eligible children remained in school. Of students between the ages of 13 and 16 at least 80 percent of the children of professionals attended, while only 31.7 percent of the children of unskilled workers attended. In other words, the lower a child's socioeconomic class, the greater the possibility of dropping out and entering the workforce, usually in unskilled or semiskilled jobs. At that time, many children did not finish high school—particularly lower-class children who had to work to help support their families—but children of the higher occupational classes attended longer, and children of professionals were far more likely to complete high school. The length of time students attended usually reflected the socioeconomic values and outlooks of their families.[16]

Thus, almost a half century after Mann called public education the "great equalizer," cases such as St. Louis showed that it worked only imperfectly. Nevertheless, through the efforts of educational reformers and people's growing recognition that changing conditions called for better educational opportunities, the belief that education and social conditions were causally linked became an enduring part of the American outlook.

Such belief has been subject to criticism, however. For one thing, it seems doubtful that schools by themselves are capable of solving deep-seated socioeconomic conditions, and there is a danger in viewing the schools as a cure-all. Since schools are created and financed by society, when they venture too far from a society's preferences, their very existence might be called into question. For another, it is doubtful that any given set of curriculum plans and teaching strategies will affect the future exactly as their advocates claim. Obviously, schools do not and cannot exercise full control over society, because many influences help shape the directions a society takes. In their zeal, the common school reformers overemphasized the ability of education to ameliorate socioeconomic inequities, but perhaps subsequent experience has taught that other measures must be implemented and that education by itself is an "imperfect panacea."[17]

Be that as it may, the use of education to increase people's knowledge and to help them pursue desirable personal and social goals seems preferable to either doing nothing or resorting to authoritarian force to bring about social change. Experience seems to show, moreover, that schooling usually has a positive impact on people's futures and it usually results in individual and social good. Finally, many if not most Americans continue to believe that having good schools is one of the ways for their children to have brighter futures.

> **For Further Reflection:** It is a common assumption that family values determine how much education a child receives. Is this assumption valid? What causes the variations in how parents support the education of their children? What factual conditions support your conclusions?

Class and education in the late nineteenth and early twentieth centuries

It was probably not until the 1880s that socioeconomic class, more than any other form of inequality, so fully determined economic, social, and political power in the United States. People obviously experienced inequalities because of such factors as race, gender, and ethnicity, but class was perhaps the more powerful influence because it impacted so many people. This began to change after the end of World War II in 1945, as available jobs, higher take-home pay, affordable consumer goods, and increased educational opportunity all helped make more Americans consider themselves part of the middle class. For all that, social class continued to shape American social life as one of many forms of inequality.[18] The passage from a relatively high level of class consciousness in the Gilded Age of the late nineteenth century, or during the Depression of the 1930s, to the widespread growth of middle-class identity in the decades after World War II was accompanied by various developments reflected in the schools.

Education and social Darwinism

Social Darwinism is a term usually applied to the belief that, similar to Darwin's account of the evolution of biological species through natural selection over eons of time, human society itself is shaped by a no less intense struggle, one that British philosopher Herbert Spencer called the **survival of the fittest**. In other words, in the competition among people in the movement up and down the social strata, those who "survive" best, who enjoy riches and power and prestige, are deemed the "fittest." Thus, the term *social Darwinism* (although Darwin himself never made such a generalized application of his theory). Spencer also saw no need for state intervention to help the poor (or "unfit") through public housing or public education, because he believed it disrupted the "natural" evolutionary process of social survival. The poor who were truly "unfit" should be allowed to die out in the evolutionary process, making way for only the fit members of society to survive, reproduce, and evolve. Spencer's writings attracted an American following, possibly because his ideas seemed to describe the desperate nature of Gilded Age competition. Such "robber baron" industrialists as Andrew Carnegie and John D. Rockefeller were attracted to his ideas, perhaps because they saw Spencer explaining their competitive world of corporate industry and high finance (or as critics charged, because he helped them justify their own ruthless economic acquisitions). Spencer's ideas also seemed to appeal to those who feared social, political, and economic reform.[19]

In any event, social Darwinism bolstered the so-called **heredity thesis**, which claimed scientific backing for its view that heredity was the single most important factor determining human intelligence. The heredity thesis emerged at a time when science was rapidly gaining prestige, and by wrapping themselves in the cloak of "objective science," heredity advocates exerted an important influence over social and educational policies. However, as noted by critics at the time, there was no reason to believe that the lower classes were genetically weaker than the upper classes, mainly because environmental factors, not genes, made the difference. Some geneticists, weary of the exaggerated "scientific" claims, pointed out that biologically the future belonged to the members of a species that reproduced most successfully, and since the lower classes bore children in far greater numbers than the upper classes, then the lower classes were likely the more biologically fit. Still others doubted that intellectual traits were solely determined biologically, and they argued that intelligence was also conditioned by social and cultural influences experienced after birth.

Finally, some were convinced that biological inheritance, for all its importance, was not the sole determining factor in history and culture, because civilization is primarily the product of the human mind, not of biology per se. Increasingly, many scholars found social Darwinism to be unsatisfactory, and the weight of opinion came down on the view that, while important individual physical and mental characteristics might be biologically inherited, social characteristics were not. Moreover, it was highly unlikely that any society, past or present, could regulate human reproductive behavior so rigorously as to produce large-scale social classes, particularly when mating frequently occurs across class lines and when sexual behavior is so difficult to control with any degree of certainty.[20]

Nevertheless, some scholars were fascinated with the heredity thesis. For example, researchers in the field of intelligence testing, such as psychologists Lewis Terman, Robert Yerkes, Henry Goddard, Carl Brigham, and Madison Grant, were drawn to it. Some adherents raised alarms about what they believed was a decline in American intelligence due to the influx of "inferior," lower-class immigrants. Terman became disillusioned with this line of thinking, but others continued to support the use of intelligence tests for purposes of social control. Once again, criticism swelled in the scholarly community, and prominent thinkers disavowed the Spencerian version of heredity, which they believed was based on emotional appeals to class, race, and ethnic prejudice, not scientific inquiry. Unfortunately, many laws and policies had by then been put in place that fostered various classifications, groupings, and selection processes in schools and other institutions, including laws enacted in 27 states that allowed authorities to sterilize so-called mental defectives. Moreover, such laws remained in effect in some states until the 1970s.[21]

From rags to riches: the role of success literature

Throughout most of its history, American society has experienced boom-and-bust economic fluctuations that are often accompanied by growing extremes of wealth and poverty. Labor unrest, changes in how people earn a living, and ideological conflicts also usually accompany these fluctuations. In the boom-and-bust upheavals of the late nineteenth century, a new form of **success literature** emerged that appealed to those experiencing economic instability and social change, and its successors in the genre continued to be published up to the present. In truth, however, success literature has a long history in the United States, including Cotton Mather's sermons on the "Puritan work ethic" in the seventeenth century and Benjamin Franklin's "self-help" writings in the eighteenth. In the closing decades of the nineteenth century, however, the genre grew to include such widely popular developments as the Horatio Alger stories, "rags to riches" novels for juveniles. Success manuals for adults also sold well, some in tens of thousands and a few in hundreds of thousands of copies in what appeared to be an insatiable market between 1870 and 1910.[22]

Some of the authors were influenced by the view of social life as a competitive struggle for survival, but most of them rejected social Darwinist determinism; instead, they promoted hard work, frugality, dependability, character, and "true manhood" as the proper pathways to success. They shunned social revolution and advocated traditional values as the best way for people to fit themselves into the corporate industrial order and to make it work, at least in some small way, to their advantage. Although the literature helped legitimize the existing social order, most of the authors tried to encourage their disheartened readers, just as they also wanted economic returns for themselves from their writings.

The typical customer was neither rich nor well educated but of modest income and education aspiring to higher things. Most of the success literature authors characterized society as divided between the **haves and** the **have nots**, not between **capital and labor** as the socialists saw it; instead, success literature authors preferred to draw the line between the industrious and the lazy or the frugal person and the spendthrift wastrel. Some authors criticized the excesses of "greedy capitalism," but they consistently advocated hard work and individual effort as the best solutions. They emphasized one's place in the secular moral order because most of their writings viewed success not as gaining mere wealth or position but in becoming moral and virtuous.

Many authors of success literature upheld basic education but were wary of higher education because the "self-made man" must learn the ropes by hard work and struggle, not academic study. Besides, at a time when even a high school education was a luxury for most people, few of the readers of success literature could afford college. Instead, the virtues promoted by the literature were to be reliable workers, avoid greed, be democratic in social relations, and avoid immodest behavior. Thus, virtue was its own reward, spiritually and materially, and riches could (and should) be gained by the virtuous. Indeed, the projected goal of most success literature was not great wealth but middle-class respectability; it was a middle-class ideology of "self-made men" and middle-class status achieved by decent, law-abiding Americans who believed in progress and the new industrial order behind it. If economic struggle was a reality, so also was the fluid nature of the American class system, which encouraged aspirations to higher status. The message to readers was to avoid slipping backward, just as it consoled them if they did not achieve the projected "rags to riches" heights.[23]

Changes in work and the rise of vocational education

Prior to the 1880s, schools were seldom viewed as institutions directly involved in job preparation, although most everyone recognized the economic benefits of education. Still, many people doubted the value of education beyond the elementary grades, because by 1890 only 3.5 percent of 17-year-olds graduated from high schools. As the twentieth century dawned, reformers charged that traditional schools were irrelevant to the new economic realities, because they failed to teach skills necessary for occupational advancement and they ignored the needs of industrial society. From business, labor, agriculture, and education came reformers demanding that schools must de-emphasize traditional academic subjects and become vocationally oriented. They advanced the view that the main job of schools was to train the young for the world of work, and they achieved a great deal of success in their efforts.

A worrisome problem at the time was the rapid changes occurring in occupations across the economy. Large factories and mass production were rapidly displacing small operations run by independent craftsmen. Local enterprises were being overrun by large corporations seeking to control the production process from raw material extraction to manufacturing, distribution, advertising, and wholesaling and retailing. In 1850, a factory with 100 employees was considered large, but by 1909, Cambria Steel in Johnstown, Pennsylvania, had 20,000 employees, and the General Electric plant in Schenectady, New York, had 15,000; in 1913, Pullman employed 15,000 at its Chicago plant alone, and in 1916, Henry Ford had 33,000 workers at his Highland Park plant in Michigan. Centralized production begat specialization: old-time craftsmen knew the production process from start to finish, but corporate industrial workers increasingly occupied only specialized machine-tending jobs. For example, in earlier times a tailor made the entire garment; by 1906, coat manufacturing alone involved 39 specialized occupations, parts of each coat handled by up to 50 employees before completion.[24]

Skilled artisans once controlled the design and production of goods, but under the new system of mass production, such control disappeared. Routine mechanical work replaced skilled craftsmanship, and the old apprenticeship system that once trained skilled workers rapidly declined. Where skilled labor once required years of apprenticeship, it now took only a few weeks to learn deskilled, mechanized, assembly-line jobs. As artisan knowledge was driven from the shop floor, it was replaced not by equally knowledgeable managers but by a hierarchy of production managers based on wages, status, and authority. In 1900, there was on average about one shop foreman for every 89 workers; by 1930, the ratio had shifted to one manager for every 34 workers.[25]

> **For Further Reflection:** On the one hand, vocational education is seen as an opportunity to make school more relevant, on the other hand, it is criticized as mere training rather than true education. Where does the truth lie?

As the new breed of education reformers insisted, the central role of the schools now became one of integrating youth into the hierarchical occupational structures of corporate industrial society, and one of the major ways to accomplish this was through vocational education.

Where once it was the salvation of souls, then the making of useful citizens, or even the promotion of equal opportunity, the central goal of schools increasingly seemed to be preparing youth for the new corporate economy. To accomplish this, the schools also were expected to integrate immigrants into the workforce, reduce worker alienation, lessen the possibility of labor conflict, and increase job capabilities for poor and working-class youth. But if vocational education proponents saw their solution as scrapping an outmoded academic curriculum and replacing it with practical understandings and skills demanded by the corporate industrial order, the history of those reforms reveals that vocational education solved few problems. Poverty, unemployment, and inequality remained, mainly because their roots were in the larger social, political, and economic system, not in the educational system.[26]

As industrialization, urbanization, and population increased, traditional small businesses gave way to giant corporations and big business trusts. With all these changes there came a slackening in the traditional belief that individuals could get by solely through their own efforts. Growing numbers of Americans found themselves living in urban environments where opportunities were limited and horizons shortened.

To some observers, however, the problems ran deeper, with social class divisions a central part of the problem. For example, a study of city school boards in the 1920s found them dominated by the wealthier classes, with 76 percent of all members coming from the proprietorial (31 percent), professional (31 percent), and managerial (14 percent) occupations, while only 22 percent came from commercial (6 percent), clerical (6 percent), manual labor (8 percent), and agricultural service (2 percent) occupations (the remaining 2 percent were unknown). Overall, whether city, county, or state school boards, the dominant classes of society were in control. This was considered a desirable condition by some leading administrative experts who wanted "efficient" school boards composed of members successful in large business operations or professional practices. The problem with this view, however, was the formulation of school policies by an unrepresentative portion of society; and permitting them to establish educational policies for everyone else was problematic. A leading counterproposal was a system of control in which schools were not the subservient tools of powerful community interests,[27] but during the heady times of the Roaring Twenties, when risky speculation and careless financial investment were rampant, it was a proposal that largely went ignored.

Suggested Activity: Research the social class composition of school board members in your school district; compare and analyze the meaning of your findings with others.

Depression, war, and the rise of the middle class

There were signs of economic distress in some parts of the economy during the 1920s, but dire trouble became obvious after the stock market crashed on Black Tuesday, October 29, 1929. Americans had experienced economic depressions before but never on the scale of the **Great Depression** that lasted from 1929 to 1940. From 1929 to 1934, the Dow Jones average fell precipitously, but corporate after-tax profits declined from $8.6 billion to negative $2.7 billion, the gross national product went from $85.9 billion to $47 billion, and the official unemployment figure (no one knew the actual number) increased from 3.2 percent to a whopping 24.9 percent of the civilian workforce. Farm income fell 60 percent, and not only did crop markets fail, but drought, dust storms, and grasshopper and boll weevil infestations all wreaked havoc on agriculture. In truth, the Great Depression became "a great downward-sucking maelstrom of economic collapse."[28]

The economic meltdown affected not only corporations, banks, and small businesses but people's incomes and retirement savings, all of which threatened basic necessities for countless families. Failure in one economic field usually had a domino effect on others. For example, when automobile production fell to one-third of its pre-1929 level, it caused a 60 percent drop in demand for iron and steel. This, in turn, meant job layoffs in mining and steel production, which also impacted machine tool manufacturers who had to cut their production by two-thirds. Such a domino effect spilled over into other economic activities as well, such as residential and industrial construction, which fell more than 80 percent from its pre-1929 levels. Similarly, depression in the private sector eventually meant depression in the public sector, too, because the depressed economy meant depressed tax revenues, which forced state and local governments to cut both services and payrolls. Thus, school budgets suffered extreme cuts all across the nation, such that during the winter of the 1932–33 school year, for example, Chicago was unable to pay its teachers.[29]

As the deprivations of the Depression increased, disaffection mounted. Some observers looked for solutions in the corporate business world of capitalism so popular in the 1920s, and some looked to radical remedies in socialism, but over time it became clear that what suffering Americans most wanted was not capitalistic or socialistic theories but decent jobs to feed their families and pay the bills.[30]

A heightened sense of **class consciousness** emerged from the Depression years, but it generated no sustained assaults on existing institutions; instead, people demanded reforms that allowed them to exercise greater participation in institutions. A 1939 poll showed that workers understood their own practical economic circumstances, with more than half placing themselves in the lower income levels. When it came to social class identity, however, the overwhelming majority claimed they were middle class. In short, workers could accurately appraise their own economic circumstances, but they stubbornly held on to the American view of upward **social mobility** and the American Dream.[31]

The Depression and the schools

During the decade from 1930 to 1940, a declining birth rate meant fewer students enrolling in elementary schools, as indicated in Table 3.1. Yet high school enrollment increased as students in the school pipeline came of age, and the number of students graduating annually nearly doubled. Due to the circumstances, one might expect students to avoid schooling and seek jobs to help their troubled families, but jobs were difficult to find and schools offered some enticing benefits.

Some enticements came from New Deal programs under the administration of President Franklin Roosevelt. For example, the National Youth Administration (NYA) provided funds to schools for work-study opportunities for needy young people, 95 percent of whom came from families on relief. The amount was small (on average only about $5.41 per ten-hour work week) in school-related jobs such as cafeteria and laboratory helpers, clerical aides to teachers, and school grounds landscaping, but it helped keep many poor high school students and some college students in school. Another program was the Works Progress Administration (WPA), a mostly adult-related program to put unemployed professional and technical people to work to serve the public good as, for example, teachers, nurses, librarians, and artists. Its most direct contributions to public schools were its provisions for school health services, supplementary

Table 3.1 Some statistics on schools during the depression, comparing school years 1929–30 and 1939–40

Selected characteristics	1929–30 school year	1939–40 school year
Total U.S. Population	121,878,000	131,028,000
Total 5- to 17-year-olds	31,414,000	30,151,000
Total Elem. and Sec. Enrollment	25,678,000	25,434,000
Elementary Enrollment	21,279,000	18,833,000
Secondary Enrollment	4,399,000	6,601,000
High School Graduates	592,000	1,143,000
Average Daily Attendance	21,265,000	22,042,000
Total Instructional Staff	880,000	912,000
Total Revenues	$2,089,000,000	$2,261,000,000
Federal	7,000,000 (.04%)	40,000,000 (1.8%)
State	354,000,000 (16.9%)	684,000,000 (30.3%)
Local	1,728,000,000 (82.7%)	1,536,000,000 (68.0%)

Source: Adapted from "Table 32. Historical Summary of Public Elementary and Secondary School Statistics: Selected Years, 1869–70 through 2005–06," National Center for Education Statistics (NCES), *Digest of Education Statistics*, at http://nces.ed.gov/programs/digest/d08_032.asp (accessed on March 23, 2010).

teachers, and surplus food programs that provided hot lunches to needy school children.[32]

Despite New Deal programs and other efforts to restore economic health, social class divisions continued to take a toll. A study conducted of a midwestern town in the late 1930s provides insight on how social class impacted the lives of students at a local high school. In general, the study found that the social behavior of students was closely related to the class position of their families in the community. Socioeconomic status conditioned what curriculum students pursued (college prep, general, or vocational) and how students were steered toward a curriculum. Class also impacted how grades were assigned, with higher grades more often assigned to upper-class students and failing grades to lower-class students. A similar pattern was found in disciplinary practices, with detention and expulsion most often meted out to the lower classes. Overall, the study noted, "the class system is far more vital as a social force in our society than the American creed."[33]

Still, students struggled to put their own stamp on their experiences. Another study examined how students adapted to Depression-era conditions between 1930 and 1939. The school was a state-funded vocational high school located in a New England industrial city of 147,000 people, a sizeable portion of whom came from southern and eastern European backgrounds. The students were all white (about 24 percent were native-born white and about 76 percent were of recent or second-generation immigrant origins). The school offered programs in 15 skilled trades (such as auto repair, electrical work, machine trades, printing, and foundry work). The school maintained an annual enrollment of 750, but there were long waiting lists every year during the period studied. One might expect the students to feel forced by Depression-era conditions to attend a trade school, but most of them believed they consciously chose to enter a skilled trade because it offered better job possibilities and a more secure future. They did not expect to become wealthy, but they did expect to become competent and versatile in their chosen trades. Most saw themselves as American individualists choosing their own destinies by taking advantage of the best options available to them. At the same time, they understood their need for group identities provided by trade guilds and unions. They also had ethnic identities learned from parents, multiethnic understandings learned from schoolmates and friends, and American values learned from the public schools and community, all of which they believed put them in good standing if and when the economy recovered.[34]

As the Great Depression lingered, however, despite all efforts to roll it back, critics emerged who charged that educators and educational policy makers had become bogged down in inexcusable inaction. Sometimes called reconstructionists, these critics maintained that educators occupied strategic positions to help society break free from the Depression by teaching the young to question the status quo and preparing them to change society as adults. Traditionalists replied that educators and schools were ill equipped to ease the Depression, much less remake society. Reconstructionists countered that, while education was only a formative step, it was crucial: Schools might not change society immediately, but they could and should help the young learn the knowledge and critical-thinking skills needed to rationally scrutinize society, develop visions of future possibilities, and work to change society for the better. Educators should serve as examples by providing community leadership, demanding reforms and better public policies, or even pursuing important public offices to achieve the goals of change. Indeed, educators should work for a radical reconstruction of the larger society, and it should be widespread and thorough.[35] Thus, these and other calls for radical change were made and found sympathetic ears, but they did not achieve sufficient public support to effect major policy changes.

For Further Reflection: In your opinion, can schools truly rebuild the social order? Compare your ideas with those of fellow students and friends. What arguments carry the greater weight and why?

For Further Reflection: Some observers see the recession that began in 2007 as reflecting elements of the Great Depression, calling it the "Great Recession" because of those similarities. How are they similar, and how are they different? What parallels exist concerning present-day cutbacks in educational expenditures with those in the Depression? What were the long-term impacts then, and what might current reductions have on our future?

Rise of the middle class

World War II helped end the Depression by rejuvenating American economic capacities with wartime production, and it refocused attention away from economic worries to the global tragedies of a world at war. In 1944, in anticipation of the war's end, Congress passed the Servicemen's Readjustment Act of 1944, or what came to be popularly called the GI Bill of Rights. This legislation provided unprecedented levels of funding for millions of war veterans to pursue further education upon their return. For those who chose an approved option, the act provided monthly stipends of $65 for single veterans, $90 for those with dependents, and a maximum of $500 per year for books and tuition expenses. By the time the act ended in 1956, more than 2.2 million veterans had attended college, 3.5 million had gone to technical schools, and approximately 700,000 had received agricultural instruction on farms. Overall, the GI Bill expended approximately $14.5 billion on the education of veterans before it ended. It also stimulated an educational boom, with almost 500,000 university degrees awarded in the 1949–50 academic year alone (as compared to only 216,500 in 1939–40). The bill helped millions of veterans acquire the preparation needed to improve their economic standing and, hence, their social class status as well. Many veterans who took advantage of the GI Bill were the first in their families to pursue higher education. Many also expected their own offspring to gain even more, which helped boost the large increase in college attendance in the second half of the twentieth century. From a financial standpoint, the money was well spent, because what most veterans received under the GI Bill was far exceeded by the taxes they paid back into the federal treasury from their increased earnings over succeeding years.[36]

Despite such successes in the postwar years, however, the problem of class-related inequality in educational opportunity seemed to persist. A leading study in the early 1960s examined the relationship between the educational success of students and the socioeconomic status of their families. Among the findings were the following: Teacher-student ratios were higher in low-income neighborhoods than in other neighborhoods. In low-income high schools, the reading scores of tenth graders averaged at least 2.6 grade levels below the norm. For every scholarship awarded to lower income students, ten were awarded to higher-income students, with low-income students who most needed financial help getting it the least. In regard to virtually all the significant factors, higher-income students consistently seemed to be in better positions.[37]

In the 1960s, equal educational opportunity became a major policy quest. Presidents John F. Kennedy and Lyndon B. Johnson each sought to remedy existing inequalities through federal initiatives. The Johnson administration significantly increased federal aid to schools in poverty-impacted areas with the Elementary and Secondary Education Act (ESEA) of 1965, which was an important part of Johnson's **War on Poverty**. A former schoolteacher, Johnson believed a comprehensive effort was needed to use education to overcome poverty, and his administration launched such programs as Adult Basic Education (ABE) for illiterate adults, Head Start programs for poor preschool children, and financial aid for poor students seeking to go to college.[38]

The intent was to break the cycle of poverty by educating the poor to move out of it. Financial assistance was given to school districts and nonschool programs (such as Head Start and ABE) that served poverty impacted areas. It was assumed that strong correlations existed between poverty and educational underachievement and that poverty produced educationally deprived children in need of special assistance. The legislation was characterized by both flexibility and accountability: flexibility for states, school districts and educational programs to use the funds but with more accountability for educational results. This "flexibility and accountability" theme came to characterize subsequent federal education initiatives as well, including the 1991 America 2000 program of President George H. W. Bush, the Goals 2000 program of President William J. Clinton, and the 2002 No Child Left Behind program of President George W. Bush.[39]

Today, federal education funds can be found in every state, most school districts, and more than half the public schools. Yet Congress has not provided sufficient funds to serve all eligible children. Money seems to go to some schools outside poverty-impacted areas while a number of qualifying schools are left out. At the same time, some schools with high poverty rates do not qualify because they are located in areas that are not considered poverty impacted.[40] At present, it is not clear whether such issues will be effectively addressed or whether more adequate poverty-related funding will be forthcoming.

Social class in the late twentieth and early twenty-first centuries

Today, social class is an often misunderstood concept, one reason being that scholars seem stuck on concepts developed in the nineteenth century in regard to capitalist industrial societies. Two theories of class have played significant roles in this conceptual development—those of Karl Marx, who viewed the history of industrial capitalism as leading to increased exploitation of the working class, and of Max Weber, who saw class as one of the ways people relate to one another socially.

Marx was the more controversial, a revolutionary whose theory of historical materialism held that one must first understand the "material forces of production" (such as agriculture, industries, and trades,) before one can understand the "superstructure" of society (such as institutions, political authority, and the class system). Since scientific, technological, and industrial innovations emerge from the material forces, the superstructure must accommodate itself to them in order for social life to flourish; however, those who benefit from the existing superstructure usually try to thwart change, which results in people getting caught in conditions beyond their control. For example, the Industrial Revolution produced unprecedented levels of new wealth that could have helped create a better life for all, but powerful interests in the superstructure refused to relinquish their privileges. Instead, they used capitalist traditions of private property and monopolistic practices to control society while they also gathered the bulk of the new wealth to themselves.[41]

Where Marx was a revolutionary who saw the fundamental conflict of capitalist industrial society occurring between the haves (capitalistic owners-investors, or the bourgcoisie), and the have-nots (industrial workers, or the proletariat), Weber was an academic sociologist who recognized class conflict but also investigated education and its relationship to industrial society. He believed that industrialism and its organizational structures had produced a bureaucratized "rational" society. A main function of schools had become one of teaching particular "status cultures" to "insiders," whose status was reinforced, and "outsiders," whose status was restricted.[42]

Education and training had become identified with a system of special examinations to assess the training of experts to serve emerging bureaucracies. This system supposedly allowed individuals a chance to move up rather than remain in a particular class, but it also produced a privileged class whose degrees, certificates, and diplomas enabled them to monopolize society's advantageous positions. Weber understood that prestige based on education was nothing new, but where the educational ideal of traditional society was to produce "cultured" people, the educational ideal of industrial society was to produce bureaucratic "specialists."[43]

Among the important features of Weber's ideas was his insight into how mass schooling was being used to sort and select students for bureaucratized corporate society, bestowing social mobility on some while denying it to others. More recent sociological theory takes a diversified approach, seeking to explain how individual experience is shaped but not completely determined by larger social and cultural conditions. For example, French sociologist Pierre Bourdieu maintains that individual lives are akin to roles played in various social and cultural "fields," and an individual may be involved in several fields at once. For instance, a schoolteacher might not only be a school employee but also a church member, a little league coach, and a volunteer firefighter. Each of these "fields" has its own implicit and explicit rules and expectations, and together they form dynamic domains where individual participants are not entirely free agents but are at least partially defined by the expectations and roles inherent in each organization.[44]

Many contemporary thinkers view social class as not nearly so dependent on economic conflict between haves and have nots, as Marx assumed, or on specialist roles in bureaucratic structures, as Weber would have it; rather, as Bourdieu saw it, a person's status or class in various social and cultural fields is dependent on a combination of factors, including material possessions and "things;" social prestige and authority; and education, command of language, and "taste" in artistic and cultural matters. Thus, many criteria impact a person's status in a society, because it is influenced by a complex network of relations between individual agency and various social, economic, and political factors.[45] What educators need to understand is what roles education and schooling play in this process.

Of course, people have behaved along class lines throughout history, and while Marx may have been correct that capitalism created a greater sense of class consciousness, it seems clear that capitalism itself did not create social classes. Class consciousness historically arose from people's everyday experiences of subordination and exploitation long before industrial capitalism appeared on the scene. Thus, subordination and exploitation can be found throughout history, not only in economic relations but in many other kinds as well, including kinship, gender, politics, and religion.[46]

Nevertheless, economic factors are significant in any consideration of social class. Marxism viewed class as capitalist owners and proletarian workers, largely ignoring other classes or strata of society. Capitalism viewed classes along occupational lines (as managers, supervisors, skilled workers, and unskilled workers), but this ignored the fact that any occupational group could itself be stratified. Where owners once stood out as powerful individuals who both owned the means of production and exercised direct control over it, during the second half of the twentieth century, ownership was significantly institutionalized by such things as mutual funds, insurance funds, and retirement systems, with ownership becoming dispersed and largely hidden from public notice. Actual control over production processes impacting class consciousness was now wielded not by conspicuous owners themselves but by hired managers and specialists who worked on behalf of owners and/or stockholders. Of course, the major beneficiaries of such conditions were very wealthy individuals or institutions, and so the issue of inequalities of income and wealth continued into the twenty-first century.[47]

By the end of the twentieth century, some observers saw new forms of social stratification developing. For example, as class-based social hierarchies supposedly weakened, people's political behavior seemed less defined by occupational identities. As economic affluence increased after World War II, people appeared to assume that their basic needs would be met by the corporate welfare state, and many shifted their political attention away from economic issues to "lifestyle" issues. This new individualism reflected beliefs that social class no longer counted; now it was all about ability and education. As class structures became more complex and as class relations underwent significant changes, society seemed to be entering a new stage of historical development where much higher levels of education and work autonomy were needed.[48]

However, other observers called attention to the growing downward mobility of the American middle class, as witnessed by trends beginning in the 1970s and accelerating in the 1980s, 1990s and 2000s. While the middle-class share of wealth actually increased from 1950 to 1970, during the 1970s it began to decline. By the 1990s the middle-class share of the economic pie was decidedly shrunken. Several reasons were proffered for this, including higher costs of living, corporate downsizing, exportation of industrial jobs to low-wage foreign countries, and the erosion of people's retirement savings by corporate greed and dishonest financial practices. Paradoxically, at the same time many business leaders, politicians, and moralists were roundly criticizing the middle class for importing too much, not producing enough, not saving enough, and not valuing family life. However, such criticism was countered by the argument that most middle-class families bought imports because they were cheaper and they did not save much because, after meeting expenses, there was little left to save. In many families, both parents found it necessary to work outside the home, and if they spent less time with their children, it was not because they devalued family life but because economic demands left little time for it. If, by 2000, the middle class was more educated than ever before, it also had little intellectual energy or time left to protect its own interests or pursue remedies to its problems.[49]

From another perspective, as American society entered the twenty-first century, it confronted an era as filled with inequalities and exaggerated lifestyles as during the Gilded Age. Few Americans seemed aware of it, even though most of them experienced only modest income increases after 1970. Average annual salaries went from approximately \$32,522 in 1970 to only \$35,864 in 1998, a mere 10-percent increase (adjusted for inflation). During that same time, the average annual income of leading corporate executives moved from $1.3 million (or about 39 times the average income of American workers in 1970) to $37.5 million (or a whopping 1,000 times the average income of workers in 1998). This was far different from the income direction between 1945 and 1970, when the middle class grew and income gaps actually narrowed between ordinary Americans and the very rich. After 1970, however, the big winners were the very rich who experienced a massive transfer of wealth to themselves. In 1998, for example, the top 10 percent of American taxpayers had annual incomes of $81,000 or more and the top 1 percent had incomes of $230,000 and higher. The truly stark differences, however, accrued to the top 0.01 percent, where annual incomes ranged from a low of $3.6 million to an average of $17 million.[50]

Contemporary conditions

When asked about their social class background, most Americans proclaim to be middle class despite the existing gap between the rich and the poor. Class divisions are not diminishing, and the number of those at the extreme low end of the spectrum is growing. According to U.S. Census Bureau statistics, poverty actually increased between 2000 and 2008. In 2000, the poverty rate stood at 11.3 percent of the population, or 31.6 million people. By 2004, it stood at 12.7 percent (37.0 million), and by 2008 it had increased to 13.2 percent (39.8 million), the highest since 1997.[51]

At the same time, education maintains a rather persistent connection with social class in several ways. One that is often measured and discussed is the economic relationship between education and income. As indicated in Table 3.2, statistical data strongly suggest that the more educational attainment, the better one's earnings are. Of course, a certain degree of care is needed in interpreting the education-earnings relationship, because there are usually multiple factors involved in a person's socioeconomic status.

While statistics may depict class divisions in stark terms, Americans tend to avoid thinking of themselves along class lines, and class consciousness is relatively low. Feudalistic Europe is usually seen as the epitome of class stratification, while an essential part of the American Dream has long held that social class should not be the determining factor in an individual's pursuit of success. There is nothing particularly wrong with individuals refusing to let class origins determine their life chances, but the tendency of most Americans to see themselves as middle class means actual **class differences** are seldom challenged and, if addressed at all, are usually explained as natural occurrences

Table 3.2 Median annual earnings, full-time workers 25 years old and over, by highest level of educational attainment, 2008

Level of attainment	Male	Female	Average
Less than ninth grade	$24,260	$18,630	$21,445
Some high school	29,680	20,410	25,045
High school completion	39,010	28,380	33,695
Some college	45,820	32,630	39,225
Associate degree	50,150	36,760	43,450
Bachelor's degree	65,800	47,030	56,415
Master's degree	80,960	57,510	69,235
Professional degree	100,000	71,300	85,650
Doctor's degree	100,000	74,030	87,015
Average, all levels	$59,520	$42,964	$51,242

Source: Adapted from "Table 384. Median annual earnings of year-round, full-time workers 25 years and over, by highest level of educational attainment and sex: 1990 through 2008," National Center for Education Statistics (NCES), *Digest of Education Statistics*, 2009, at http://nces.ed.gov/programs/digest/09/tables/d09_384. asp (accessed on March 31, 2010).

in a society that assumes the capable always rise to the top. Compared to many other countries, the United States offers many opportunities for most people, but it is far from accurate to say that success (or lack thereof) is not influenced by socioeconomic class.

Individuals in the United States are not legally prevented from rising through society's ranks, but some people have greater opportunities than others, and class plays an important role in it. The circumstances of a child's birth, whether born into poverty or comfortable economic conditions, or born to educated or uneducated parents, has important ramifications for a child's life chances. There is considerable research affirming that parental social class contributes to a child's educational attainment that, in turn, contributes to the child's future attainments. Social class fundamentally conditions a person's options, or lack thereof. Furthermore, class impacts access to health care, child care, and numerous other services that affect the quality of life. Privilege tends to breed more privilege, which greatly improves opportunities and assistance should a privileged person encounter obstacles in life. Contrarily, poverty and material deprivation usually have a negative impact on people, limiting their access to adequate care, goods, services, and education.[52]

Out-of-school factors (OFSs) are often directly related to school success, and class is indicative of many of those OFSs (for example, low birth weight, inadequate medical care, food insecurity, environmental pollutants, family stress, and neighborhood characteristics), any and all of which can significantly affect the learning opportunities of children. Indeed, poverty exacts a strong toll on communities, neighborhoods, families, and, therefore, schools and children.[53] In short, socioeconomic conditions shape life chances, a factual condition that has received inadequate attention in several leading school reform movements in the closing decades of the twentieth century and the beginning of the twenty-first century, a time characterized by policy shifts from concerns about equality of educational opportunity to concerns about school achievement as measured by test scores.

It is difficult to capture a simple meaning of *social class* because it consists of many attributes. Class membership may be defined by income and financial assets, such as inherited wealth, property, and investments (or the lack thereof); it may also be defined by educational attainment and professional or occupational status. Class may be characterized by attributes difficult to measure, such as power, prestige, and tastes in style and language. People speak of "middle-class values" or "working-class neighborhoods," indicating that those who belong to a particular social class share not only material but also cultural characteristics. To identify solely with one particular social class could prove difficult because any given individual might belong to several categories at once. Raised in a middle-class family, for example, a person may achieve a high educational status, such as a Ph.D. in English, yet not be able to find full-time employment. Teaching as an adjunct college professor, she might make little more than minimum wage and actually earn less than many unskilled laborers, her low earnings forcing her into a poor standard of living. Another person may grow up in poverty and barely succeed in graduating from high school, but she may develop interests and skills in a growing economic field where she earns a good salary and enjoys a lifestyle that places her in the middle class.

In addition, class membership can change over the life span as people move in and out of poverty, earn degrees, obtain (or lose) jobs, experience the economic consequences of marriage and divorce, and generally feel the effects of changes as broad as the global economy and as personal as aging or illness.

For Further Reflection: Think about your own life and the people you know. How clear-cut are definitions of class? To what extent do people identify with a class? Based on your observations and understandings, why do they exhibit a class identity? Have any crossed class lines or changed their class identities?

It has been argued that the traditional classification of middle class or lower class no longer adequately describes the job structure in the United States. Rather, the emerging class structure consists of an inner ring of permanent skilled workers and an outer ring of semiskilled part-time workers without such benefits as health insurance, retirement funds, vacations, or sick leave. The two-tiered job structure is not confined to any one sector of the economy. In academia, for instance, tenured faculty constitute an inner core while those in the outer core of temporary and poorly paid adjunct professors are hired by the course, moving from one job to the next. The "new economy" is said to demand a more flexible workforce willing to work long hours and perform at a high level of productivity. This is supposed to make the economy more productive, but job security and fringe benefits have suffered greatly, with employees always subject to being laid off. One might think about the role of the schools and wonder whether or not schools should be expected to produce the "human bricks with which the global economy is being built."[54]

WEB: Suggested Reading 3.1.

In general, American society is neither quite as open nor as socially mobile as the traditional American Dream would suggest. While social class is not all-determining, it can exert lasting effects on educational opportunities and other aspects of life. Social class often strongly influences school funding, educational resources, quality of teachers, extracurricular options, postsecondary opportunities, and more.

Ever since the rise of the public school in the nineteenth century, there have been claims it could serve as the "great equalizer." In 1848, Horace Mann stated his belief that public education would "give each man the independence and the means by which he can resist the selfishness of other men. It does better than to disarm the poor of their hostility toward the rich: it prevents being poor."[55] The common schools, as they were then called, were intended to counteract the influence social class had in shaping individual lives. They were seen as essential instruments in providing a common set of experiences to help knit a diverse society together and provide better opportunities for everyone regardless of class background.

The notion of schools as equalizers can be found in other countries as well. A study comparing educational opportunities in 13 countries found that educational inequalities remained stable over time in most of the countries, despite expansions of the educational systems in all of them. While educational attainment rose at the primary and secondary levels, it did not expand at the same pace in higher education; instead, a "bottleneck" effect developed in which existing higher education institutions were unable to absorb the increasing number of applicants. Effective equalization occurred most effectively in Sweden and the Netherlands, two countries that made serious efforts to equalize general socioeconomic conditions before expanding their educational systems. This suggests that economic equalization must precede educational equalization, at least for the latter to have good chances for success.[56]

> **For Further Reflection:** What types of economic reforms would it take to reduce the effects of class divisions and alleviate the most detrimental effects of poverty and economic deprivation?

School funding

According to National Education Association (NEA) statistics, state funds accounted for the bulk of school financial support between the 1999–2000 through 2009–2010 school years, ranging between 45.6 and 50.0 percent of total funding. During the same time period, local funding increased slightly from 43.1 percent to 44.1 percent, and federal funding increased from 7.1 percent to 10.2 percent.[57] However, local funding remains a significant source in the funding formula, and since it depends heavily on property taxes for revenues, wealthy communities are able to generate far more funds for their schools than are poor communities, a phenomenon that neither state nor federal funds have effectively equalized.

> **Suggested Activity:** Obtain statistics about your local school district and research the funding sources. Compare and contrast your findings with the data provided in this source.

One of the most widely cited works dealing with inequities in school funding is Jonathan Kozol's *Savage Inequalities,* an indictment of public education's funding structure circa 1991. Among the school systems studied was East St. Louis, Illinois, whose public schools were in disrepair and lacked essential resources, reflecting the grim poverty of the larger community. One school was evacuated because of sewage flooding, while another's sports facilities lacked "almost everything," including goalposts on the football field. East St. Louis High School's science labs were 30 to 50 years outdated, the heating system did not work correctly, supplies and texts were scarce, and teachers often had to pay for materials out of their own pockets. Overall, Kozol captured the deteriorating conditions of poor schools across the country and compared them with schools in wealthier communities. Wealthy communities had large numbers of class offerings, enjoyed sophisticated facilities such as greenhouses and swimming pools, and made use of services to perfect their music and athletic skills. Legal challenges to the funding inequities remained largely ineffective in altering systems marred by "savage inequalities." A central conclusion was that many inequalities are built into school systems by their dependence on property taxes as their main source of local funding.[58]

It has also been observed that school finance policy choices at all levels—federal, state, and district—systematically disadvantage the most needy students. An example is the so-called state expenditure factor in the funding formula of Title I of the Elementary and Secondary Education Act. Although the act was intended to help equalize funding when it was enacted in 1965, the funding formula now results in unequal federal aid allocated to poor children because high-spending states receive more Title I money per student than low-spending ones. For instance, during the 2003–04 school year, Maryland received 51 percent more Title I aid than Arkansas, even though Arkansas had more poor children. Various recommendations to remedy the funding gap include: an increased role of the federal government in school finance, federal compensation to offset the differing capacities of various states to support education, and spurring states toward greater efforts in those cases where low spending is due to low effort rather than low fiscal capacity.[59]

At the state level, furthermore, the most impoverished districts often receive fewer resources than the least impoverished districts, resulting in funding gaps of more than $1,000 per child in some states. This is particularly disturbing because the education of students growing up in poverty actually costs more since they usually have greater needs for increased instructional time and well-prepared educators. A prominent recommendation to close the funding gap is for states to reduce their reliance on local property taxes, assume more state responsibility for education funding, and target more funds specifically for the education of low-income students.[60]

At the district level the trend continues. In states where a significant portion of teacher pay is provided by local funds, and in the poorer districts, teachers tend to be paid less. In addition, poor districts have fewer unrestricted funds they can direct to their poorest schools. Recommendations to address the problems include: more transparent accounting practices that better reveal existing inequalities; adoption of "weighted" student funding, which means the allocation of funds in proportion to student needs; and changes in teacher compensation in order to more equitably distribute teacher talent and experience.[61]

> **For Further Reflection:** Some people say, "Throwing money at the public schools is not going to improve their quality." Others counter, "We have never tried it. So, how do we know?" What do you think? How central is adequate financial support to address shortcomings in public education?

Social class and school choice

The debate about **school choice** has not only been waged for years, it can also be difficult to follow. The issue is infused with strong ideological positions, a lack of reliable data on the effectiveness of school choice, and some confusing terminology. One question is whether school choice should be confined only to public schools or broadened to include private and "faith-based" religious schools. It is the latter option that has sparked most controversy because it could mean drastic changes in the legal and financial underpinnings of both private and public schools.

Supporters of school choice argue that it will revive antiquated, bureaucratic public school systems through healthy competition and thus greater efficiency. It would empower parents and students by providing choices, and it would free educators from worrisome state regulations, encouraging them to become more entrepreneurial in their search for innovative ways to educate. Advocates also argue that choice would equalize education by providing new alternatives to low-income families who, in the existing system, are the ones most relegated to low-quality public schools, unable to afford what wealthier families take for granted, the opportunity to choose a high-quality private school education for their children.

School choice and vouchers

Some choice advocates embrace the idea of **vouchers**, that is, parents or guardians dissatisfied with their local public schools would be able to apply for one voucher per child per year, with funds for the voucher drawn from tax monies allocated for public education. A variety of voucher plans have been floated, but the idea works along these lines: Under a voucher plan, applicants who met whatever qualifications the granting educational authorities might set would then be able to "cash" the voucher at a school of their choice to "purchase" a year of schooling for their child. Some advocates want vouchers restricted to public schools within districts, others want them extended to public schools across districts, while others want them opened to include nonpublic schools as well. Generally, advocates believe that some form of genuine school choice would be possible. We cannot expect parents whose children currently attend inadequate public schools to wait until those schools are reformed and improved, they say; instead, governments at the city, state, or federal levels should provide scholarships to needy families to send their children to either a public, independent, or religious school of their choice. One suggestion is for vouchers similar to Pell grants, currently available in higher education, made available to elementary and secondary students.[62]

In contrast, opponents warn that school choice exercised through vouchers would be, in the final analysis, little more than tax-paid supplements for wealthier patrons, because only the wealthier families would be able to supplement their vouchers to exercise genuine choice among a variety of schools, including those that might charge considerably more than a voucher alone would pay. The tuition fees at some expensive private schools exceeded $30,000 per student during the 2009–10 school year.[63]

Besides, poor parents and many middle-class parents as well would still have their choices limited to what they could afford, even with vouchers. To give an example, suppose a voucher plan of $5,000 per child (which probably exceeds most proposed or existing voucher plans) was put into effect allowing participants to apply their vouchers to private schools. As competitive markets actually operate, the more successful private schools would be able to charge whatever the market will bear. Under the circumstances, suppose also that the average cost of nearby, good-quality private schools was around $10,000 per year (many of them charge far more). Few poor families could afford the additional $5,000 needed to send even one child to such private schools, much less two or more children. Not many middle-class families could afford it either. Clearly, under such voucher plans, the majority of the population would have their choices confined to second- or third-tier private schools. Under such conditions the gap between the rich and the poor might actually increase, and rather than equalizing educational opportunity, school choice could lead to further stratification and inequality.

School choice programs in operation

Programs involving school choice have been implemented in several states, and a few are examined below. For example, in Milwaukee, Wisconsin, low-income public school students may receive vouchers for private schooling, a program that since 1998 includes religious schools as well. For the 2009–2010 school year, 177 schools were registered with the Wisconsin Department of Public Instruction to accept students through the Milwaukee Parental Choice Program (MPCP), with a student enrollment in September 2009 of 21,062. The program has generated some controversy, with its effectiveness a central topic of discussion. Based on a study of graduation rates over a five-year period, results suggested that low-income students in the MPCP were more likely to graduate from high school than their public school counterparts. However, in another study comparing state test scores, little difference was found between voucher students and public school students in Milwaukee. It has also been argued that taxpayers in Wisconsin are being overcharged to pay for Milwaukee's private school voucher program, effectively diverting resources better spent on public education.[64]

Beginning in 1997, an interesting experiment was conducted in New York City. The privately funded School Choice Scholarship Foundation randomly allotted 1,300 scholarships of $1,400 each to low-income families, with annual renewals available over a four-year period. The scholarships could be applied to the cost of any private school, and baseline data on student test performance and family background was collected prior to the allotment so that comparisons could be made with data collected at the end of the period. Comparisons were also made between "scholarship families" and "control families." Overall, private school attendance did not seem to make a difference on standardized test scores except for the scores of African American students, which showed a marked improvement. In addition, the research found that parents rated the private schools as more orderly than public schools and they reported fewer problems such as tardiness, missing classes, fighting, cheating, or racial conflicts. In comparison with control students, scholarship students more often reported that they got along with teachers and were proud of their school. They were also asked to do more homework than in public schools, and their parents were more involved in school than their public school counterparts.[65]

Such results have to be taken with caution, because it remains unclear what systemic impact, if any, widespread school choice programs might have. For instance, what will happen if vouchers become common and private schools face a massive increase in demand? Will private school costs increase to meet market demands? Similarly, if voucher costs are taken out of public school funding, what will happen to public schools and the students who remain in them? In other words, how viable is school choice as a tool to achieve equal educational opportunity and to counterbalance the negative effects that class background has on the quality of schooling a student receives? These questions are far from being answered.[66]

Some proponents of vouchers argue that marketplace competition with private schools will spur public school improvements in order for the public districts to compete, but how and to what extent will vouchers actually spur effective reforms in public school systems? For example, while the Milwaukee voucher program is one of the oldest, it does not seem to have affected school reform on a large scale, and Milwaukee's public schools continue to struggle. In order for this program to systematically do so, it has been suggested to replace charity vouchers with universal vouchers, include more families, and provide vouchers of sufficient value to create a genuine free market.[67]

Considering the New York program, it seems fair to ask what kind of private school experience could a $1,400 grant actually buy in New York City in the spring of 1997. According to data from the New York State Education Department, New York City provided a per-pupil public school expenditure of approximately $9,700 during the 1996–97 school year. Even if there were successful private schools operating on less than that (and a good number of them surely spent far more), the question must be asked: How many truly poor families, with only a grant of $1,400 per child, could raise the additional funds necessary to make up the difference? It seems clear that the actual cost of schooling a child in a private school would have far exceeded $1,400, and this casts doubt on what the experiment supposedly demonstrated. Indeed, follow-up research on the New York program showed that only 53 percent of those who were offered the scholarship program actually used it to attend a private school for three years, and almost half of those parents who declined a scholarship did so because they could not afford the added tuition and expenses not covered by the voucher.[68]

As critics point out, a central problem with vouchers is that they supposedly rely on market forces, but it seems that market forces seldom if ever work in favor of the poor. In a market economy, people buy what they can afford, not what they might truly want or choose. Simply put, to use the word *choice* to describe such conditions seems grossly misleading.[69]

Charter schools

Another option frequently advanced as a way to provide school choice is the idea of charter schools. There were about 5,000 charter schools in the 2008–2009 school year, and all but ten states had enacted charter school legislation. Charter schools are publicly funded schools run by a group of educators, parents, and community members who secure a lawful charter to operate a public school. There is a great deal of variation from state to state, and charters may be issued by local school boards, state school boards, or other designated legal bodies, depending on individual state law. A charter allows the group to run the school more or less independently (again depending on the laws a state may have).[70]

Advocates of charter schools see them as providing flexibility to educators, parents, and citizens to provide the kind of education a particular group of students needs and to be grounded in the community they serve. For example, former U.S. secretary of education Margaret Spellings maintained that, free from many regulations that govern traditional public schools, charter schools demonstrate they can innovate with unique organizational structures and use new instructional strategies that would be difficult to apply in most public school systems.[71]

Critics argue that charter schools are, in many respects, as unsatisfactory as vouchers because they take tax money away from regular public schools that so desperately need it. In addition, where charter schools are targeted for a specific group, they tend to operate in an exclusive manner. Advocates reply that charter schools are still *public* schools and are not exempt from public control in the way private schools are. Rather than being exclusive, many charter schools attempt to target the special needs of particular groups, but outside the centralized bureaucratic control of public school systems.

An interesting viewpoint is that the real crisis in education is not caused, as some critics would have it, by failing public schools and low test scores; instead, the actual problem is our loss of a sense of responsibility for community and for decency in personal relationships. In part, this is due to schools having grown too big and anonymous to provide the nurturing environment students need. We need smaller, locally controlled schools that encourage frequent interactions between students and adults. In short, we need "public schools of choice," including public charter schools, if they are properly structured and operated. The answer from this perspective is more participatory public educational institutions characterized by cultural norms and expectations different from large schools.[72]

Suggested Activity: Conduct a "mini-ethnography," keeping notes and making observations for a week concerning how much time children (those of siblings, neighbors, or your own) spend in actual, face-to-face interaction with adults, rather than in peer groups merely supervised by an adult.

A central question is how the system can be changed so that everyone can benefit from school choice. Choice proponents will probably gain greater public support when they can develop realistic ways to send every child to a high-quality school of choice without leaving anybody behind. Until then, critics of school choice will probably argue that rather than dismantling public school systems, the nation's energies and resources would be better spent on strengthening them.

Tracking and ability grouping

Social class not only influences funding and overall school quality but also many within-school experiences students have. Two curriculum approaches that involve social class are **tracking** and **ability grouping**. Tracking is a traditional practice in secondary education of assessing students and separating them into particular curriculum programs such as general, vocational-technical, and college preparatory. Placement decisions usually involved grades, test scores, teacher recommendations, and school counseling among other factors, but it has became clear to some observers that one of the most prominent factors was the social class, race, gender, and/or ethnic origin of students. After legal restrictions were placed on tracking, the practice fell out of favor, but vestiges of it are retained in the practice of ability grouping.

A leading factor that changed curriculum tracking in the United States was the district court decision in *Hobson v. Hansen* (1967), which ordered the Washington, D.C., public school system to abolish its tracking system. The court held that the tracking system and its use of intelligence quotient (IQ) test scores as a primary basis for placements was racially and socioeconomically biased against students in violation of the equal protection of the laws, a decision that discouraged traditional tracking programs nationwide.[73]

However, *Hobson* did not end tracking altogether, with ability grouping soon replacing it, although the latter was applied to specific courses rather than curriculum programs. The end result was still a differentiated curriculum within academic courses (for example, basic math, general math, advanced math, and honors math courses), but one more implicit than the previous tracking system, one that continues to have profound effects on students today.[74]

Children sometimes experience ability grouping as early as pre-school and kindergarten levels. In the early elementary grades, students are typically grouped by ability for reading and math instruction, but as they proceed up the grade levels they are increasingly placed in coures associated with such labels as advanced, general, or remedial. As critics see it, this kind of sorting is nothing more than tracking by another name, and it is deeply flawed. Some even describe it as "the new IQism," because it reflects similarities with the pseudoscientific claims of social Darwinism and certain aspects of the testing movement of the late nineteenth and early twentieth centuries.[75]

Cross-Reference: For a discussion of how tracking also relates to race and ethnicity in education, see Chapter 5, Race and the Education of African Americans, pp. 155–207 and Chapter 6, Ethnicity and Education, pp. 208–256.

For Further Reflection: Think back to your own days of elementary and secondary schooling. Were you tracked? In what ways? What effects did tracking seem to have on you and your peers? Did it impact your social life, such as what friends you had and what peer group you identified with? Did tracking motivate you to achieve at a higher academic level, or did it create resentment against academic achievement?

One effect of tracking is that students in higher-level courses tend to be taught with pedagogically superior methods and materials; they develop more positive attitudes toward themselves and toward school, and they are more likely to be positively received by the wider society. Social class continues to play a role in this kind of tracking because students from advantaged family backgrounds almost always receive the best placements. In addition, middle-class parents are more prone than lower-class parents to intervene on behalf of their children to influence decisions about their children's placement in advanced courses. These parents also tend to have considerable educational experience themselves, and they know how to navigate school systems and obtain information about courses beneficial for their children's future, a form of status and influence that most lower-class parents may lack. In other words, social class has an educational impact that advantages some people and disadvantages others.[76]

Opponents of tracking argue that even if educational policy makers are well intentioned and assume that ability grouping is beneficial for students, the practice is nothing more than an unquestioned habit, a tradition with harmful consequences. Contrary to the assumption that tracking helps students learn better in homogeneous groups, opponents bring evidence that most advanced students are not held back by mixed classrooms, and slower students actually learn better in mixed classrooms. There are research findings indicating that tracking deflates the self-esteem of lower-track students while inflating it in the upper tracks. The behavior of lower-track students tends to be influenced by their placement: They participate less in extracurricular activities, drop out in higher numbers, and experience more alienation from school than their upper-track peers. A leading study of 25 schools found that upper-track students were exposed to a higher quality of knowledge (they read works of literature while lower-track students worked with reading kits); their teachers spent more time on instruction in the classroom (instead of discipline or social activities); they perceived their teachers to be more concerned about them (and less punitive than teachers in lower-track classes), and they reported more positive peer relationships than did lower-track students. Tracking results in stigmatizing labels such as slow, basic, remedial, or fast, bright, and honors. Labeling, however, often leads to self-fulfilling prophecies with students placed in lower tracks tending to find it difficult to free themselves from the label and escape the track. Tracking also tends to separate students along socioeconomic lines as well as racial and ethnic lines. In sum, poor and minority students are over-represented in the lower tracks and underrepresented in the higher tracks, lower-class students seem to be negatively affected by tracking, and tracking seriously interferes with achieving equality of educational opportunity.[77]

While tracking and ability grouping have negative features, detracking may pose its own challenges. It has been argued that detracking may sacrifice opportunities for high achievers who benefit from tracking. Detracking also raises the question of whether high-quality instruction can be provided in mixed-ability classes. Not all studies find fault with ability grouping and tracking, and generalizations that are too sweeping should be avoided.[78]

There are studies showing support for tracking among teachers, parents, and students, especially since the practice is less rigid than in the past. A frequent claim is that heterogeneous classes are more difficult to teach and, again, tend to hold back talented students while leaving behind the struggling ones. Still, divided opinion about tracking does exist among parents, educators, and the general public, and despite the efforts to detrack the schools, evidence indicates that while some school systems have stopped it, others continue to use it. Perhaps what most accounts for the differences are the community environments of the schools. Urban and rural schools are more likely to detrack than suburban schools, but tracking or detracking are complex matters influenced by institutional, technical, organizational, and political factors. Parents often play a critical role when decisions about tracking policies are made, their support or opposition often making the difference in what policy is adopted.[79]

Some researchers argue that resistance to detracking is one way in which upper- and middle-class parents help create educational advantages for their children. One study of ten socioeconomically mixed schools undergoing detracking reforms concluded that "elite" parents tended to oppose detracking for fear that it could undermine their children's relative advantages. They based their resistance on labels, on the "symbolic mixing of high deserving and low deserving" students, rather than on information about the results in detracked classrooms. They were convinced that their children's placements in advanced programs were a result of merit or the children's academic achievement, not their privileged social class status or the fact that the placements were often a result of parental pressure and influence. Because of the resources (including tax monies) that elite parents brought to the system, they seemed to take for granted that their children were entitled to better educational opportunities than others. In addition, they used several strategies to undermine detracking efforts, including: threatening to pull their children out of public schools should educators alter the existing talented and gifted programs, co-opting educational administrators, and receiving special privileges in return for allowing small degrees of detracking to take place in the schools.[80]

The issue of tracking is far from resolved. It goes to the heart of discussions about how deeply embedded class-based practices persist in the schools, what roles people play in such processes, and how some educational practices continue to exist because they serve certain interests. At the same time, change is initiated and sustained only through people's actions. How to better understand this interplay of people's actions and school programs and practices, and how to make it work for good education, ought to be continuing quests for educators.

International comparison: India

India is located in southern Asia and is bordered by Pakistan in the northwest, China in the north, Nepal in the northeast, and Bangladesh in the east. India features an extensive coastline washed in the southwest by the Arabian Sea and in the southeast by the Bay of Bengal. Its geographical area measures about one-third the size of the United States, but with a population estimated at 1,156,897,766 (July 2009), it is the second most populous country in the world (only China has a larger population). India is a federal republic subdivided into 28 states and 7 union territories, with New Delhi as its capital. The people of India are divided ethnically into Indo-Aryans (72 percent), Dravidians (25 percent), Mongoloids (3 percent), and others. While Hindi is the national language and the primary spoken language of 41 percent of the people, there are 14 other official languages. English remains important for national, political, and commercial communication. The average life expectancy in India is 66 years; the infant mortality rate is estimated to be about 5 percent (50.78 deaths per 1,000 live births).[81]

The Indus Valley civilization is one of the oldest in the world, dating back at least 5,000 years. About 1500 B.C., Aryan tribes invaded and merged with earlier inhabitants, creating the classical Indian culture. In the eighth century, Arab incursions began, followed by Turkish incursions in the twelfth century, while European traders made their incursion in the late fifteenth century. The British colonized India until nonviolent resistance led by Mohandas Gandhi and Jawaharlal Nehru led to independence in 1947. Because of conflicts between Hindu and Moslem inhabitants, the subcontinent was divided into India and Pakistan, the former a secular state, the latter Muslim. East Pakistan became the separate nation of Bangladesh in 1971. Major problems for India today include a continuing dispute with Pakistan over Kashmir, overpopulation, poverty, environmental deterioration, and ethnic and religious conflict. The economy consists of traditional village farming, modern agriculture, handicrafts, modern industries and technology.[82]

Social stratification in India

Two terms are central in descriptions of social stratification in India: social class and caste. The term *social class* refers to socioeconomic stratification, while *caste* refers to social differentiation based on religious ideas. There is little agreement among scholars on the relationship between social class and caste, but clearly they are not one and the same, and people who belong to the same caste may well belong to different classes. In other words, there is no precise correlation between socioeconomic classes and religion-based castes.[83]

Class and India's educational system

The Indian school system is based on 12 years of primary and secondary education. Higher education offers three levels, culminating in a bachelor's, master's, or doctoral degree. Indian higher education is quite expansive and is one of the largest higher education systems in the world. It is also heavily subsidized and has produced many successful academics, but many of its highly skilled graduates emigrate to Great Britain or the United States, producing what is described as a massive "brain drain." According to India's 2001 census, 65.4 percent of the people are literate,[84] and while higher education is well developed, India's primary education lags behind, underfunded and plagued by high dropout and non-attendance rates. In addition, there is endemic absenteeism of teachers, as well as corruption and a lack of accountability. Private education claims to function more efficiently, but because private schools charge relatively high fees, such education is largely reserved for those with the financial means to pay for it. Thus, socioeconomic class determines to a considerable extent what educational opportunities are available.

One issue that clearly illustrates how social class impacts educational opportunity in India is that of compulsory education, because primary education is not compulsory. Indeed, the states are permitted by national law to enforce compulsory education if they so choose. However, it should be noted that India, a geographically large country with an immense population, faces obstacles to the introduction of compulsory education that many other nations do not face. For one thing, widespread compulsory education requires resources that India, a poor country, seems to lack. In addition, many lower-income parents would be deprived of the money generated by their children's labor on the farm or in the shop, if those children were compelled to attend school. While most parents are willing to make sacrifices for the sake of their children's future, poverty-stricken parents may simply not be able to afford it. One solution is broad and general economic growth that will generate widespread job opportunities, and the prospect of increased income and a better future will perhaps make it possible for more parents to demand and support compulsory primary education. Without such growth, the cost of sending children to school is perceived as too high and cannot be supported by the poor.[85]

Thus, social class influences Indian schooling in dramatic ways, not merely by determining the quality of education a person receives but whether an education is received at all. A longitudinal study of an Indian town found that educational change over the three prior decades was particularly significant for middle- and upper-status daughters who by and large surpassed their mothers in terms of educational attainment. However, for lower-class students—both females and males—little educational improvement was made. Poor families were either unable to see the benefits of education or simply could not afford to send their children to school when they were needed to perform chores at home. The great majority of lower-class sons and daughters became low-wage employees just like their parents.[86]

Historically, an illustrative example of how social class affected some individuals at the expense of others had to do with the use of the English language. English usage among Indians was limited in British colonial India, mainly because only the Indian aristocracy had access to it. They were able to acquire English in missionary and European-run schools that charged high tuition and only admitted a limited number of Indian children. English became a symbol of elite status and sophistication in Indian society, a status awarded only to those Indians who supported British colonial rule and were wealthy enough to afford the schooling. While English became a badge of the Indian upper classes, vernacular languages were the mark of the middle and lower classes. Social class divisions were not created by English usage, but such divisions were certainly reinforced by the selective acquisition of English by privileged groups in India.[87]

Summary and conclusions

As difficult as it may be to define the concept of social class, both historical and contemporary analysis show that social class impacts educational policy and practice. Of all the things that divide and separate people within a society, social class may be the most pervasive. It complicates education in many ways, from equal access and attainment all the way to individual success and failure in the educational process.

During American colonial times, access to education was usually connected to one's class status; that is, it was primarily the wealthier classes that received any extensive formal education. Nevertheless, there were trends and developments that encouraged a broadening of educational opportunity, including the education of the common people. One such example was the religious notion that the salvation of the soul was to a significant degree dependent on one's ability to read the Scriptures, which helped spur the founding of schools in the early colonial period. A more secular influence was the fact that the vast majority of the settlers were common people who came to the United States in hopes of improving the circumstances of their lives, and education was seen as one way of helping achieve this. Finally, a growing sense of distinctly American identity and self-reliance contributed even further to the notion that education ought to be more widely available and not be restricted to only the elite.

In the nineteenth century these ideas were further developed, and many people came to see public schools as the "great equalizer," and there was a sizable expansion of schools to more and more people. By the late nineteenth and early twentieth centuries, however, reformers pushed education as a servant of industrial expansion and they built large urban educational systems modeled along the lines of the modern corporation. Some policy makers, perhaps influenced by claims that existing social inequities resulted from natural competition and the survival of the fittest, saw no need to expand education or expend many resources on those from the lower classes. Others, enamored with a testing movement that promised to "scientifically" sort and track students into the vocational and academic curriculum programs they were most suited for, saw such differentiation as a more "efficient" way to run schools; however, the end results usually reflected the social class conditions of students more than their actual abilities or goals. Repelled by the excesses of urban industrial society, still other reformers called for using education to democratize industrial society and to make it more humane and livable. Economic setbacks such as the Great Depression aggravated class differences, but it also renewed calls for education as a means of social betterment. The expansion of educational opportunity in higher education following World War II helped further democratize access to a greater extent than ever before. It could be argued that, despite some detours and setbacks, the twentieth century witnessed the expansion of educational opportunity from the elementary to the secondary and higher-education levels, which all contributed significantly to the growth of the American middle class.

By the beginning of the twenty-first century, however, it appeared that the middle class was losing ground, and critics feared that American society was becoming characterized once more by a growing gap between the rich and the poor. The gap can be seen in unequal funding and in practices such as tracking and ability grouping, but school "choice" schemes such as vouchers promise to widen it further. Many contemporary policies and practices seem to be undermining past educational advances achieved through arduous efforts over the years.

For example, the current system of local school funding is marred by inequities, one reason being it depends on taxes on local wealth and property, which determines how much funding can be generated. Efforts have been made to equalize funding among localities by injecting more state and federal monies into poor districts. The War on Poverty during the 1960s increased federal monies to poverty-impacted areas in an attempt to reduce socio-economic inequities. Despite such efforts, the results have been mixed, one reason being poorly enforced programs over the long term. Perhaps reform of educational institutions alone is not enough to change socioeconomic conditions without some fundamental changes also being made in other, more powerful social, economic, and political institutions.

Recent educational reforms include the controversial school choice movement. Proponents argue that choice, particularly when exercised with school vouchers, will help bridge the gap between the wealthy and the poor. Critics argue that vouchers will not enable poor families to send their children to good private schools because, in fact, the actual voucher plans put into operation could not pay the costs of existing public schools, much less high-quality private schools. In short, the question of how school choice programs in operation thus far can possibly ameliorate class-based differences in educational opportunity remains doubtful.

Controversy also swirls around the issues of tracking and ability grouping. While most research on the issue indicates that tracking and ability grouping do not benefit the majority of students, these practices nevertheless continue in many school systems. Efforts to detrack the schools are typically met with resistance by the parents of students in the higher tracks, who appear to be the ones most benefiting from tracking. Social class lines also become pronounced because middle- and upper-class students are disproportionately represented in the higher tracks.

In conclusion, social class continues to impact provisions for education in the United States, although many reforms and expansions of schooling opportunities over the years have been instituted. Indeed, class continues to affect educational opportunity in many countries, despite the differences and variations between and among them. The long-term American hope that education might alleviate if not overcome the effects of social class has not been without some success, but the struggle is far from over. Social class continues to impact the life chances of Americans, including their educational chances.

Vocabulary

ability grouping
capital and labor
class consciousness
class differences
formal education
Great Depression
haves and have nots
heredity thesis
hierarchically divided society
informal education
literacy
rudiments
school choice
social Darwinism
social mobility
success literature
survival of the fittest
tracking
vouchers
War on Poverty

Notes

1   Plato, *The Republic*, W. H. D. Rouse, trans. (New York: Mentor Books, The New American Library, 1956), Books II, III, and IV; and Aristotle, *The Politics*, T. A. Sinclair, trans. (London: Penguin Books, 1981), Book IV, Chapter xi; Book VII, chapter xvi, xv, and xvii.

2   Lewis A. Coser, "Class," in *Dictionary of the History of Ideas: Studies of Selected Pivotal Ideas*, vol. 1 (New York: Charles Scribner's Sons, 1968, 1971), 441b–449b; and Maurice Ashley, *England in the Seventeenth Century, 1603–1714*, 3rd edn (Baltimore, MD: Penguin Books, 1962), 12–25.

3 Carl F. Kaestle et al., *Literacy in the United States: Readers and Reading since 1880* (New Haven: Yale University Press, 1991), 3–4, 13–18.

4 "A Colonizing Company Sponsors Educational Fund-Raising [Entry for November 21, 1621]," in *The Educating of Americans: A Documentary History*, Daniel Calhoun, ed. (Boston: Houghton Mifflin, 1969), 16, hereafter referred to as "Calhoun;" and Lawrence A. Cremin, *American Education: The Colonial Experience, 1607–1783* (New York: Harper and Row, 1970), 11–13.

5 "Piety for Virginia Households [Laws of Virginia, Feb. 1631–2]," in Calhoun, 17; "Protection for Public Wards [Laws of Virginia, March 1642–43]," in *Educational Ideas in America: A Documentary History*, S. Alexander Rippa, ed. (New York: David McKay Co., Inc., 1969), 17, hereafter referred to as "Rippa;" "Enforcement of Pious Teaching [*Laws of Virginia*, March 1645–6]" and "Labor for Poor Children [*Laws of Virginia*, October 1646]," in Calhoun, 18.

6 Sir William Berkeley, "A Governor of Virginia Takes Pleasure in Colonial Backwardness [from 'Answers to Inquiries from the Lords Commissioner of Foreign Plantations (1671)]," in Calhoun, 76.

7 "New England's First Fruits [1643]," in *American Higher Education: A Documentary History*, vol. 1, Richard Hofstadter and Wilson Smith, eds (Chicago: University of Chicago Press, 1961), 5–6.

8 "The Massachusetts School Law of 1647," in Rippa, 162; and William J. Gilmore, "Elementary Literacy on the Eve of the Industrial Revolution: Trends in Rural New England" (Worchester, MA: American Antiquarian Society, 1982), 87–178.

9 Rush Welter, *Popular Education and Democratic Thought in America* (New York: Columbia University Press, 1962), 12, 18–21.

10 Lawrence Cremin, *American Education: The Colonial Experience, 1607–1783* (New York: Harper Torchbooks, 1970), 167–224, 400–407, and 499–506; Merle Curti, *The Social Ideas of American Educators, With a New Chapter on the Last Twenty-Five Years* (Totowa, NJ: Littlefield, Adams and Company, 1968), 3–10; and Bernard Bailyn, *Education in the Forming of American Society: Needs and Opportunities for Study* (Chapel Hill: University of North Carolina Press, 1960), 20–21, 41–44.

11 Walter Isaacson, *Benjamin Franklin: An American Life* (New York: Simon and Schuster, 2003).

12 Benjamin Franklin, "Silence Dogood, No. 4 on the Higher Learning," in *Benjamin Franklin on Education*, John Hardin Best, ed., Classics in Education, No. 14 (New York: Teachers College Press, 1962), 38; and Benjamin Franklin, "Proposals Relating to the Education of Youth in Pensilvania [1749]," in Rippa, 108.

13 Franklin, "Proposals Relating to the Education of Youth in Pensilvania [1749]," in Rippa, 105, 106, 108; and "The Idea of the English School, Sketch'd out for the Consideration of the Trustees of the Philadelphia Academy [1751]," in *Benjamin Franklin on Education*, 150. See also Benjamin Franklin, *Educational Views of Benjamin Franklin*, Thomas Woody, ed. (New York: McGraw-Hill, 1931). See also Cremin, *American Education: The Colonial Experience, 1607–1783*, 376–378.

14 See, for example, Stanley William Rothstein, *Schooling the Poor: A Social Inquiry into the American Educational Experience* (Westport, CT: Bergin and Garvey, 1994), 1–9.

15 Horace Mann, "Twelfth Annual Report [1848]," in *The Republic and the School: Horace Mann on the Education of Free Men*, Lawrence A. Cremin, ed., Classics in Education, No. 1 (New York: Teachers College Press, 1957), 84–87. For biographies of Mann, see Jonathan Messerli, *Horace Mann: A Biography* (New York: Alfred A. Knopf, 1972); and Robert B. Downs, *Horace Mann: Champion of Public Schools* (New York: Twayne Publishers, 1974).

16 Selwyn K. Troen, "Popular Education in Nineteenth-Century St. Louis," *The Social History of American Education*, B. Edward McClellan and William J. Reese, eds (Urbana: University of Illinois Press, 1988), 119–136.

17 Henry J. Perkinson, *The Imperfect Panacea: American Faith in Education*, 4th edn (Boston: McGraw-Hill, 1995. See also Michael B. Katz, *Class, Bureaucracy, and Schools* (New York: Praeger Publishers, 1971). For a critical treatment of early twentieth century reforms, see Clarence J. Karier, Paul C.

Violas, and Joel Spring, *Roots of Crisis: American Education in the Twentieth Century* (Chicago: Rand McNally, 1973).

18 Ronald Schultz, "A Class Society? The Nature of Inequality in Early America," in *Inequality in Early America*, Carla Gardena Patina and Sharon V. Slinger, eds (Hanover, NH: University Press of New England, 1999), 216.

19 Richard Hofstadter, *Social Darwinism in American Thought*, revd. edn (Boston: Beacon Press, 1955), 35–50.

20 Carl N. Degler, *Search of Human Nature: The Decline and Revival of Darwinism in American Social Thought* (New York: Oxford University Press, 1991), 79, 128–129, 145–148.

21 Ibid., 50–51, 150–151; and Peter Quinn, "Race Cleansing in America," *American Heritage*, vol. 54, no. 1: 34–43 (February/March 2003).

22 Judy Hilkey, *Character is Capital: Success Manuals and Manhood in Gilded Age America* (Chapel Hill: University of North Carolina Press, 1997), 2–7. This book is also electronically available.

23 Ibid., 25–27, 90, 107, and 137–138.

24 Harvey Kantor, "Vocationalism in American Education: The Economic and Political Context, 1880–1930," in *Work, Youth, and Schooling*, 14–18.

25 Ibid., 16–21.

26 Harvey Kantor and David Tyack, "Introduction: Historical Perspectives on Vocationalism in American Education," in *Work, Youth, and Schooling: Historical Perspectives on Vocationalism in American Education*, Harvey Kantor and David Tyack, eds (Stanford: Stanford University Press, 1982), 1–3.

27 George Sylvester Counts, *The Social Composition of Boards of Education*. American Education: Its Men, Ideas, and Institutions, Lawrence Cremin, ed. (Reprint, New York: Arno Press [1927] 1969), 66ff, 78–80, 83–85, 90–91.

28 David Tyack, Robert Lowe, and Elisabeth Hansot, *Public Schools in Hard Times: The Great Depression and Recent Years* (Cambridge, MA: Harvard University Press, 1984), 3–7, 10–14.

29 David M. Kennedy, *Freedom from Fear: The American People in Depression and War, 1929-1945*. The Oxford History of the United States, vol. 9, C. Vann Woodward, gen. ed. (New York: Oxford University Press, 1999), 163

30 Tyack, Lowe, and Hansot, 6–17.

31 Kennedy, 322.

32 Tyack, Hansot, and Lowe, 122–132.

33 August B. Hollingshead, *Elmtown's Youth: The Impact of Social Classes on Adolescents* (New York: John Wiley and Sons, Inc., Science Editions, 1961), 452.

34 Ivan Greenberg, "Vocational Education, Work Culture, and the Children of European Immigrants during the 1930s," in *Inequity in Education: A Historical Perspective*, Debra Myers and Burke Miller, eds (Lanham, MD: Lexington Books, 2009), 147–158.

35 George Sylvester Counts, *Dare the Schools Build a New Social Order?* (New York: Arno Press, 1969). See also Tyack, Lowe, and Hansot, 18–27.

36 James T. Patterson, *Grand Expectations: The United States, 1945-1974*, vol. 10, The Oxford History of the United States, C. Vann Woodward, gen. ed. (New York: Oxford University Press, Inc., 1996), 68–69.

37 Patricia Cayo Sexton, *Education and Income: Inequalities of Opportunity in Our Public Schools* (New York: Viking Press, 1964), 114, 120, 124, 157, and 159.

38 John F. Jennings, "Title I: Its Legislative History and Its Promise," in *Title I: Compensatory Education at the Crossroads*, Geoffrey D. Borman et al., eds (Mahwah, N.J.: Lawrence Erlbaum Associates: 2001), 2–5.

39 Ibid., 6–21.

40 Erik W. Robelin, "Off Target? Political Considerations Cause Title I to Bypass Many Needy Schools," *Education Week*, vol. xxi, no. 1: 1, 45–47 (September 5, 2001).

41 For a synopsis of Marxism and education, see Howard A. Ozmon and Samuel M. Craver, *Philosophical Foundations of Education*, 7th edn (Upper Saddle River, NJ: Pearson Education, 2003), 307–312, 317–318, and 320–323.

42 Jeanne H. Ballantine, *The Sociology of Education: A Systematic Analysis*, 4th edn (Upper Saddle River, NJ: Prentice Hall, 1997), 9.

43 Max Weber, "The 'Rationalization' of Education and Training," *The Structure of Schooling: Readings in the Sociology of Education*, Richard Arum and Irenee R. Beattie, eds (Mountain View, CA: Mayfield Publishing Company, 2000), 16–19.

44 Chelen Mahar, Richard Harker and Chris Wilkes, *An Introduction to the Work of Pierre Bourdieu: The Practice of Theory* (New York: St. Martin's Press, 1990) 6–11.

45 Ibid. 7, 13, 14.

46 Schultz, 203–208.

47 Richard Scase, *Class*. Concepts in Social Thought (Minneapolis: University of Minnesota Press, 1992), 2–3, 33–34, and 41.

48 Terry Nichols Clark and Seymour Martin Lipset, "Are Social Classes Dying?" in *The Breakdown of Class Politics: A Debate on Post Industrial Stratification* (Washington, DC: Woodrow Wilson Center Press, 2001), 39–54; and Erik Olin Wright, *Class Counts: Comparative Studies in Class Analysis* (New York: Cambridge University Press, 1997), 18–19, 73, 101, 110–111.

49 Frederick R. Strobel, *Upward Dreams, Downward Mobility: The Economic Decline of the American Middle Class* (Lanham, MD: Rowman and Littlefield, 1993).

50 Paul Krugman, "For Richer: How the Permissive Capitalism of the Boom Destroyed American Equality," *New York Times Magazine* (October 20, 2002), 62(10).

51 U.S. Census Bureau, "Poverty: 2008 Highlights," at http://www.census.gov/hhes/www/poverty/poverty08/pov08hi.html (accessed on March 3, 2010)."

52 See, for example, Wendy Johnson, Caroline E. Brett and Ian J. Deary. "The Pivotal Role of Education in the Association between Ability and Social Class Attainment: A Look Across Three Generations," *Intelligence*, vol. 38, no. 1: 55–65 (January–February, 2010); and Maike Ingrid Philipsen. "The Problem of Poverty: Shifting the Attention to the Non-Poor," in *Late to Class: Social Class and Schooling in the New Economy*, Jane A. Van Galen and George W. Noblit, eds (Albany: State University of New York Press, 2007), 269.

53 David C. Berliner, *Poverty and Potential: Out-of-School Factors and School Success*. Boulder: Education and the Public Interest Center & Education Policy Research Unit. http://epicpolicy.org/publication/poverty-and-potential (accessed on March 16, 2010); and Sue Books, *Poverty and Schooling in the U.S.: Contexts and Consequences* (Mahwah, NJ: Lawrence Erlbaum Associates, 2004), 134.

54 Martin Packer, *Changing Classes: School Reform and the New Economy* (Cambridge, UK: Cambridge University Press, 2001), 278–279.

55 Horace Mann, "Twelfth Annual Report [1848]," in *The Republic and the School: Horace Mann on the Education of Free Men*, Lawrence A. Cremin, ed., Classics in Education, No. 1 (New York: Teachers College Press, 1957), 84–87.

56 Hans-Peter Blossfeld, Yossi Shavitt, *Persistent Inequality* (Westview Press, 1993).

57 National Education Association, *Rankings & Estimates: Rankings of the States 2009 and Estimates of School Statistics 2010*. NEA Research (December, 2009), 81, at http://www.nea.org/assets/docs/010rankings.pdf (accessed on May 8, 2011).

58 Jonathan Kozol, *Savage Inequalities: Children in America's Schools* (New York: Crown Publishers, 1991).

59 Goodwin Liu. "How the Federal Government Makes Rich States Richer." in The Education Trust, *Funding Gaps 2006*, 2–4, at http://www.edtrust.org/sites/edtrust.org/files/publications/files/ FundingGap2006.pdf (accessed on March 14, 2010).

60 Ross Wiener and Eli Pristoop, "How States Shortchange the Districts That Need the Most Help," in The Education Trust. *Funding Gaps 2006*, 5–9, at http://www.edtrust.org/sites/edtrust.org/files/publications/files/FundingGap2006.pdf (accessed on March 14, 2010).

61 Marguerite Roza, "How Districts Shortchange Low-income and Minority Students," in The Education Trust. *Funding Gaps 2006*, 9–12, at http://www.edtrust.org/sites/edtrust.org/files/publications/files/FundingGap2006.pdf (accessed on March 14, 2010).

62 Diane Ravitch, "Somebody's Children: Educational Opportunity for All American Children," in *New Schools for a New Century: The Redesign of Urban Education*, Diane Ravitch and Joseph P. Viteritti, eds (New Haven: Yale University Press, 1997), 251–273. Please note that Ravitch has since changed her mind. See Chapter 2, note 66.

63 For example, 2009–2010 tuition fees at Phillips Academy at Andover, Massachusetts, were $31,100.00 per day student and $39,900.00 per boarding student. See "Admission & Financial Aid," at http://www.andover.edu/Admission/TuitionAndFinancialAid/Pages/TuitionFees.aspx (accessed on March 12, 2010). Of course, the school has scholarship programs and fee waivers for needy students, but it is also highly selective in admissions.

64 Elizabeth Burmeister, State Superintendent, "News Release," State of Wisconsin Department of Public Instruction (March 13, 2009), at http://dpl.wl.gov/els/pdf/dpl2009_27.pdf (accessed on March 16, 2010); State of Wisconsin Department of Public Instruction, "MPCP Facts and Figures for 2009–2010 as of November 2009," *Milwaukee Parental Choice Program (MPCP)*, at http://dpi.wi.gov/sms/choice/html (accessed on March 16, 2010); John Robert Warren. "Graduation Rates For Choice and Public School Students in Milwaukee, 2003–2007," (May 2008), at http://www.schoolchoicewi.org/currdev/detail.cfm?id=271 (accessed on March 30, 2010); Catherine Gewertz, "Project on Milwaukee Vouchers Shares Baseline Findings," *Education Week*, vol. 27, no. 26: 6 (March 5, 2008); and Patrick J. Wolf. "The Comprehensive Longitudinal Evaluation of the Milwaukee Parental Choice Program: Summary of Baseline Reports," *SCDP Milwaukee Evaluation Report # 1* (February 2008), at http://www.uark.edu/ua/der/SCDP/Milwaukee_Eval/Report_1.pdf (accessed on March 16, 2010).

65 Mathematica Policy Research, Inc., "School Choice in New York after Three Years: An Evaluation of the School Choice Scholarships Program: Final Report" (February 19, 2002), vii–ix, at http://www.mathematica-mpr.com/publications/PDFs/nycfull.pdf (accessed on March 30, 2010).

66 Paul E. Peterson, David E. Myers, William G. Howell, Daniel P. Mayer, "The Effects of School Choice in New York City," in *Earning and Learning: How Schools Matter*, Susan E. Mayer and Paul E. Peterson, editors (Washington, DC: Brookings Institution Press, 1999), 317–339.

67 George A. Clowes, "With the Right Design, Vouchers Can Reform Public Schools: Lessons from the Milwaukee Parental Choice Program," *Journal of School Choice*, vol. 2, no. 4: 367–391 (November 2008).

68 "1996–97 Wealth, Expenditure, and Aid Data, Ranked by Expenditure per Pupil," http://www.oms.nysed.gov/faru/Primer/primer_pgiv.htm (accessed on March 30, 2010). New York City public schools were not the most expensive in New York State, which had an average per pupil expenditure of $9,658 in 1996–97. See National Center for Education Statistics (NCES), *Digest of Educational Statistics, 2002*, at http://nces.ed.gov/programs/digest/d02/dt168.asp (accessed on March 30, 2010); and Mathematica, ix.

69 Interview of Amy Wilkins, "School Colors: The Racial Politics of Public Education," *The Nation*, June 5, 2000, p. 14.

70 National Alliance for Public Charter Schools, *Public Charter School Dashboard*, at http://www.publiccharters.org/dashboard/schools/page/overview/year/2010 (accessed on March 21, 2010); and National Alliance for Public Charter Schools, *Public Charter School Dashboard*, at http://www.publiccharters.org/dashboard/schools/page/overview/year/2009 (accessed on March 21, 2010).

71 Margaret Spellings, Secretary U.S. Department of Education, U.S. Department of Education, "Making Charter School Facilities More Affordable: State-driven Policy Approaches," at http://www2.ed.gov/admins/comm/choice/charterfacilities/charterfacilities.pdf (accessed on March 21, 2010).

72 Deborah Meier, "Educating a Democracy," in *Will Standards Save Public Education?* Deborah Meier, ed. (Boston: Beacon Press, 2000), 3–31.

73 *Hobson v Hansen*, 269 F. Supp. 401 (D.D.C. 1967); and Beatrice A. Moulton, "Hobson v. Hansen: The De Facto Limits on Judicial Power," *Stanford Law Review*, vol. 20, no. 6: 1249, 1256–1258, 1262, and 1266 (June, 1968).

74 For background on continuing legal implications for tracking/ability grouping, see Richard S. Vacca, "Ability Grouping and Student Assignment: Legal and Policy Issues 2005–2006," *Education Law Newsletter*, Commonwealth Educational Policy Institute, at http://www.cepionline.org/newsletter/2005–2006/2005_Dec_Ability_Grouping.html (accessed on March 31, 2010).

75 Jeannie Oakes, *Keeping Track: How Schools Structure Inequality* (New Haven: Yale University Press, 1985); Kathleen Bennett deMarrais and Margaret D. LeCompte, *The Ways Schools Work: A Sociological Analysis*. 2nd Edition. (White Plains, NY: Longman, 1995); and David Gillborn and Deborah Youdell, "The New IQism: Intelligence, 'Ability' and the Rationing of Education," in *Sociology of Education Today*, Jack Demaine, ed. (New York: Palgrave, 2001), 65–99.

76 Samuel Roundfield Lucas, *Tracking Inequality: Stratification and Mobility in American High Schools* (New York: Teachers College Press, 1999); and Ellen Brantlinger, *Dividing Classes* (New York: Routledge, 2003).

77 Oakes, *Keeping Track*.

78 Adam Gamoran, "Classroom Organization and Instructional Quality," in *Can Unlike Students Learn Together? Grade Retention, Tracking, and Grouping*, Herbert J. Wahlberg et al., eds (Greenwich, CO: Information Age Publishing, 2004), 141–155; and James A. Kulik, "Grouping, Tracking, and De-tracking: Conclusions from Experimental, Correlational, and Ethnographic Research," in *Can Unlike Students Learn Together?* 157–182.

79 Tom Loveless, *The Tracking Wars: State Reform Meets School Policy* (Washington, DC: Brookings Institution Press, 1999), 1–2, 55, 65, 79, and 86.

80 Amy Stuart Wells and Irena Serna, "The Politics of Culture: Understanding Local Political Resistance in Racially Mixed Schools," *Harvard Educational Review*, vol. 66 no. 1 (Spring 1996), 93–118.

81 "India," *The World Factbook*, at https://www.cia.gov/cia/publications/factbook/geos/in.html (accessed on March 21, 2010).

82 Ibid.

83 Edwin D. Driver and Aloo E. Driver, *Social Class in Urban India: Essays on Cognitions and Structures* (Leiden, The Netherlands: E.J. Brill, 1987), 5–6.

84 Vimala Ramachandran, Introduction, in *Gender and Social Equity in Primary Education: Hierarchies of Access*, Vimala Ramachandran, ed. (London: Sage Publications, 2004), 19.

85 V.N. Balasubramanyam, *Conversations with Indian Economists* (New York: Palgrave, 2001), 15–18.

86 Susan C. Seymor, *Women, Family, and Child Care in India: A World in Transition* (Cambridge: Cambridge University Press, 1999), 180–181.

87 Tariq Rahman, "The Language of the Salariat," in *The Post-Colonial State and Social Transformation in India and Pakistan*, S.M. Naseem and Khalid Nadvi, eds (Oxford: Oxford University Press, 2002), 97–128, 106–108.

Race and the Education of African Americans

Chapter contents

Chapter objectives

- To better understand the origins of the term *race* and how its meaning has changed over time.
- To explore the impact of race on educational institutions, laws, policies, and practices, both historically and at present.
- To analyze major historical eras related to race and education (slavery, Jim Crow, and segregation and desegregation).
- To explore significant philosophical views on the educational implications of race.
- To better understand how leading problems in education are related to social constructs of race.
- To analyze contemporary reform movements addressing race and educational opportunity.
- To compare how the concept of race influences education in another country.

Opening questions

1. Why does the concept of race continue to demand attention in discussions of contemporary education?
2. How and why has the meaning of the term *race* changed over time?
3. What were some of the major historical developments associated with race and education?
4. What court cases and policy developments most influenced how race shaped America's schools over time?
5. What are some leading reform efforts addressing inequalities related to race?
6. What can be learned from international comparison about the significance of race?

The issue

Although it is only one of many influences impacting the lives of people across the centuries, **race** continues to have significance. In fact, race has been called an "American obsession."[1] Historically, race played an important role in defining who had access to education, and inequalities stemming from that history helped launch major social movements, such as the civil rights movement and the desegregation of public schools in the second half of the twentieth century.

The English word *race,* when used as a term to categorize people, has counterparts in several other languages (Spanish, Portuguese, Italian, French, German, and Dutch, to name a few). As a by-product of European colonial expansion into North America, however, slavery was established and supported by a rigid racial ideology. This is not to say that enslavement and racism were exclusively American phenomena, because throughout history people have formed communities, clans, tribes, and nations, and these kinds of group identities have figured in exploitation and violence. For example, history reflects many "us versus them" conflicts, such as the long-lasting enmity between the Greeks and Persians in ancient times, or the Rwandan clash of Tutsi against Hutu in recent times. However, none were based on a concept of race as it came to be defined during the era of American slavery.

Today there is scholarly opinion that it was not until the European expansion into the Western Hemisphere that a concept of race was developed to differentiate between masters and slaves. Prior to this, differentiation usually occurred along such lines as religion, ethnicity, geography, and tribal or national identities, not on race conceptualized as an innate biological condition associated with skin color. If the term *race* was used at all, it was usually used in a nationalistic sense, such as "the Spanish race" or "the French race." During early colonial expansion, European colonizers tended to view non-Europeans (such as

Africans or Native Americans) as "heathen savages," but by the eighteenth century a concept of race had developed that assumed the inherent superiority of "white" people over "colored" people, which provided ideological support for the permanent enslavement of people of color for generations.

Slavery was abolished in the United States in 1865, and state laws requiring racially segregated schools were struck down in 1954, but race continues to impact society and education in various ways. Since the mid-twentieth century, race has been a significant factor in most reforms to increase educational opportunity for all, but race continues to affect people's educational opportunities, and it needs to be understood for how it consequently affects all people's lives.

For further reflection: How do racial identities affect you and your friends and acquaintances? How do racial identities get shaped, and what causal factors in the larger society influence such developments? To what extent are those identities socially based, and to what extent are they matters of individual choice? What impact, if any, has this had on your education?

Background

Introduction

Although its exact origins are murky, the race concept has played a significant role in American education, and its origins can be traced back to the era of slavery. Almost four centuries have passed since the first Africans arrived in 1619 at the English colony of Jamestown in Virginia; at the time, race and slavery were not directly connected because the colonials did not equate the two in quite the way they would later.[2]

Although it may seem that racial prejudice afflicts all nations at some point in time, there are historians who maintain that prior to the sixteenth century there was nothing specifically racist in Western societies, but by the late seventeenth and early eighteenth centuries race became a major basis for differentiating human groups. At the same time, there are geneticists who state that the concept of race has no scientific validity in explaining how humans become distributed around the globe in groups that appear to be different, and there is a growing body of genetic evidence indicating that all modern human chromosomes contain genetic markers originating in eastern Africa with a female about 150,000 years ago and a male about 59,000 years ago, whose descendants gradually migrated around the globe to produce the wide variety of peoples we see today. In light of this evidence, the concept of race as discrete human groups originating independently of each other simply makes no sense.[3]

As the notion of race developed in American history, it concerned physical characteristics such as skin color and other observable attributes. These, in turn, left an indelible imprint on American history, even though slavery was abolished by the Thirteenth Amendment in 1865. In 1903, W. E. B. Du Bois predicted that the problem of the twentieth century would be "the color line," but it seems to have carried over into the twenty-first century as well. Despite considerable progress, the concept of race continues to be a source of anxiety in society and its educational institutions.[4]

The education of African Americans during slavery

During the first half of the nineteenth century two contradictory views about education existed in American society: One was that the inextricable relationship between a democratic society and an educated citizenry should be preserved, and the other was that the education of slaves somehow posed a threat to the peace and prosperity of organized society. At a time when free public schools were appearing in the northern United States, restrictive laws making it a crime to teach slaves to read and write were appearing in the southern states.[5]

Despite slavery's powerful grip on southern society, it exhibited some profound contradictions that are informative. Since masters had a free hand in how they treated their slaves, some chose to educate as many as they deemed necessary to conduct their affairs, such as in bookkeeping and other trades that required certain levels of literacy and numeracy. In addition, the children of masters often played school with their slave playmates, teaching what they were taught, and those who were sent off to boarding schools and colleges often took personal servants who might assist them in studies or wait for them outside classrooms where they could hear what transpired inside. Slaves who experienced such things might also share their knowledge with fellow slaves, but the odds against most slaves acquiring any formal education were huge. The majority of slaves experienced lives of unremitting toil and illiteracy, but this does not mean they placed no value on education. On the contrary, most were eager to have what was denied them, for they saw education as one of the chief benchmarks of freedom and equality.[6]

There were only a few educated black people who received recognition and acceptance during slavery times. One was John Chavis, a free man who led an extraordinary life as a soldier during the American Revolution, an ordained Presbyterian minister, and a respected teacher who taught both white and free black students in Raleigh, North Carolina. The record of his early life is not clear, and his childhood educational experience is unknown, but as a young man he was a private student of John Witherspoon, president of the College of New Jersey (later Princeton University). After Witherspoon's death in 1794, Chavis became a student at Liberty Hall Academy (which later became Washington and Lee University) in Lexington, Virginia. A devout Presbyterian, Chavis became a licensed minister in the Lexington Presbytery in 1800, received official certification of his free status in 1802, and was assigned to the Orange Presbytery near Raleigh, North Carolina, to serve as a circuit missionary to both blacks and whites in 1809. Because his salary was meager, Chavis found it necessary to open a school where he taught both white and free black students. His work was of such quality that he and his school became widely respected. Following the 1831 slave revolt led by Nat Turner (also an educated black man), laws restricting the education of blacks were tightened across the South, but Chavis remained an active educator until his death in 1838. During his life, Chavis taught many students, and while his impact on his black students is unknown, among his white students were a future U.S. senator and governors of North Carolina and New Mexico.[7]

Growth of schools for black people after the Civil War

The Union victory over the Confederacy in 1865 toppled the "slavocracy" regimes of the southern states. In relatively quick fashion, the Constitution of the United States had three important amendments added: the Thirteenth Amendment, which abolished slavery (1865); the Fourteenth, which provided the rights of citizenship and **equal protection of the laws** to all persons born or naturalized in the United States (1868); and the Fifteenth, which declared that citizenship rights could not be denied or abridged because of race, color, or previous condition of servitude (1870). Despite the Union victory and the constitutional amendments, however, at the time most black Americans continued to exist as a distinct underclass in which race was the distinguishing factor.

After the war, Congress enacted a series of laws called **Reconstruction**, which lasted from 1865 to 1877, when the last Union troops were withdrawn from the southern states. During Reconstruction, African Americans made some significant political and educational gains, such as elective and appointive offices in government and the admission of black children in relatively high numbers into public schools. They also played important roles in establishing statewide systems of public schools across the South. During that time, black people neither achieved full equality with whites nor did all white people readily accept the changes; nevertheless, some progress was made.

Freedmen's Bureau

One important agency of change was the **Freedmen's Bureau** (officially called the Bureau of Freedmen, Refugees, and Abandoned Lands), which proved to be one of the most important educational developments during Reconstruction. The bureau was established by Congress on March 3, 1865, just a few weeks before Lee's surrender at Appomattox Courthouse on April 9 and Lincoln's assassination on April 15, 1865. Originally intended to last only one year, the bureau was extended until 1870, when most of its major functions ended. Its general responsibilities included care for the millions of freed slaves and the administration of lands either abandoned by Confederates or seized or otherwise accumulated by Union forces. Among other things, it distributed food to the former slaves, regulated their labor contracts, ensured justice for them in legal matters, and encouraged the development of their churches. Yet its most significant and long-lasting work was the founding and/or support of numerous schools for black people.[8] Two obstacles for the Freedmen's Bureau were: It was obviously intended to be of short duration, and it had resources to get schools started, but it had no authority for their long-term operations and eventually had to turn them over to other agencies.

Northern missionary societies

Among the important private agencies that helped the Freedmen's Bureau were the **northern missionary societies**, the most prominent being the American Missionary Association, the American Baptist Home Mission Society, and the Freedmen's Aid Society of the Methodist Episcopal Church. Certainly the missionary societies provided crucial funds, supplied many of the teachers, and extended moral and political support at critical points, but they were also astonished to find that while the ex-slaves accepted aid and were grateful for the help, they were also staunchly committed to establishing and controlling schools of their own.[9]

Black people and statewide public school systems in the South

The important value black people placed on education was demonstrated when they established schools in areas liberated by Union forces during the war, and after the war's end they opened many additional schools across the South. In fact, when the Freedmen's Bureau and the northern missionary societies became active in the areas under Union control in the South, they often worked with schools already started by black people. As Reconstruction advanced, blacks gained seats in state legislatures and appointments to public boards and administrative posts from which they were a significant force for public education. A major outcome for both black and white people was the establishment of statewide public school systems across the South during Reconstruction.[10]

Before the Civil War, slavery stunted virtually every social institution in the South, black or white; nevertheless, there were the beginnings of fledgling common school systems in some southern states, notably in North Carolina. These efforts ended with the war, however, and afterwards there was strong resentment among many whites over the economic ruin from warfare, occupation by federal troops, and the sweeping social changes brought about by the abolition of slavery. Most white southerners favored public schools but not racially mixed schools, and this presented a major obstacle for the pro–public school forces, both black and white.

Despite some opposition, public schools were eventually established in all the southern states. Virginia, for example, saw its first statewide system of public schools come into existence under a Reconstruction government in 1870. William Ruffner, a native white Virginian, became the superintendant, and in his first year alone (he served for 12 years), more than 2,900 public schools were founded, with 3,000 teachers instructing more than 130,000 pupils (with 37.6 percent of eligible white children and 23.4 percent of eligible black children actually enrolled). A long-time advocate of public education, Ruffner championed free public schools for both white and black children, but he believed racially mixed schools would mean the loss of crucial white support. Although he faced opposition and had to fight off efforts by state officials to divert education funds to other causes, by the time Ruffner left office in 1882, Virginia had a system of public schools that would endure.[11]

Black people were staunch supporters of the new schools, but after Reconstruction ended, black schools faced some major hurdles. For example, the main sources of employment for most ex-slaves in the rural South were the plantations and large farms, and many employers opposed education for the ex-slaves and their children because, it was claimed, education gave black people unrealistic ambitions and ruined them as field hands. Some employers actually fired employees whose children attended school. As southern whites regained control of state governments after Reconstruction, black schools became grossly underfunded, enrollments fell, and black people faced increasing restrictions on their recently gained freedoms.[12]

The New South

The southern economy began to stir in the late 1880s and early 1890s, and a more positive mentality emerged. In part, this was due to the **New South** ideology, an outlook composed of northern-style industrial capitalism and social reform along with a reaffirmation of white political power. Aristocratic rural interests had dominated politics in the Old South, but now it was a growing urban middle class and emerging industrial interests that were ascendant. Calls to industrialize and prosper were broadcast from lectern, pulpit, and editorial page, and perhaps the best-known advocate from the latter venue was Henry Grady, editor of the *Atlanta Constitution*, who tirelessly promoted a vision of an industrialized, wealthy *new* South.[13]

Change did not occur overnight, but it did happen gradually by eroding old habits and presenting attractive new lifestyles. Consider, for example, how the abolition of slavery produced new incentives: Economic interests formerly beholden to a slave-based economy now had to look elsewhere for profits. This encouraged investments in railroad construction, agricultural improvements, factories, and the growth of business and industry. Economic improvement encouraged greater tax outlays for public services such as education. Unfortunately, New South efforts became twisted by the race question. For example, once white power was re-established in North Carolina, exclusionists wanted to stop funding black schools altogether, while accommodationists argued that black as well as white children must be educated for the state to progress. As accommodationists saw it, the proper question was not whether black schools should be supported but how and by whom. The accommodationists won, but at the price of unequally funded, segregated schools.[14] Similar developments could be seen across the South and in many border states as well.

The era of Jim Crow

The return of white rule after 1877 brought a new type of leadership that opposed Old South agrarianism and embraced industrial development and urban growth; nevertheless, old ways of thinking did not completely disappear. In the 1880s, a level of prosperity emerged that promised better funding for education, but it was short-circuited by an economic recession and the increasingly restrictive racist politics in the 1890s that gave rise to the phenomenon called *Jim Crow*, a rather odd term used to denote the harsh laws, policies, and attitudes of a white supremacy that redefined the place of black people in the late nineteenth and early twentieth centuries.[15]

Not all southern whites opposed the equal protection of the laws and full rights of citizenship for black people, but resentments fueled by the war and its aftermath made such developments difficult for many other southern whites to accept. There were those who tried to encourage acceptance, such as Lewis Blair, a successful Richmond merchant from an aristocratic Virginia family. In an 1889 book titled *The Prosperity of the South Dependent upon the Elevation of the Negro*, Blair favored black equality as an economic necessity for the prosperity of all. The South must eradicate ignorance among both blacks and whites in order to develop the intelligent labor supply needed for economic growth. White fear of racially mixed schools must be dropped or else genuine prosperity would remain beyond the South's grasp. As it turned out, Blair's words proved prophetic, but he faced such social ostracism from his peers that he recanted and embraced a more orthodox view. Advocates could also be found in other states, such as Robert Flournoy in Mississippi, but their examples were few, and the scornful intimidation they received from their own social circles helped Jim Crow tighten its grip.[16]

Racial segregation required by law

It should be noted that up to the 1880s, racial **segregation** was not usually required by law, although it was commonly practiced in many places. Black people were certainly never socially or legally equal to white people in the Old South, but they shared many accommodations and conveyances in close proximity to one another. Even after the war, both white and black patrons often used the same public transportation facilities, such as passenger trains and streetcars. Prior to 1885, no southern state legally required racially segregated railway facilities, but from 1887 to 1891, at least eight states enacted such laws. During the Jim Crow era, racial segregation that was formerly nonexistent or simply a matter of custom now became required by law. As the new public school systems got under way, they became racially segregated in all the former Confederate states and in some of the border states as well.[17]

WEB: Suggested Reading 4.1.

Jim Crow from a national perspective

With its ruling in **Plessy v. Ferguson (1896)**, the U.S. Supreme Court gave Constitutional approval for state laws requiring racial segregation, if the separate accommodations were equal. *Plessy v. Ferguson* involved a black passenger named Homer Plessy who took a seat on a white railway car in Louisiana, a state with a law requiring whites and blacks to use separate cars. Plessy was arrested and convicted for refusing to leave the white car, and when he appealed it, the Louisiana courts upheld the state's law. Plessy then appealed to the U.S. Supreme Court, and the court's majority opinion (delivered by Justice Henry B. Brown) held that while both blacks and whites were equal under the law, the Constitution was powerless to make them socially equal. Moreover, the court rejected Plessy's claim that he was denied "equal protection" under the Fourteenth Amendment because Louisiana law required that separate passenger facilities must be equal, and Plessy had accommodations on the black car equal to those on the white car; therefore, the separate facilities did not violate the equal protection clause of the amendment. The court did not use the exact wording of **separate but equal**, but the decision was quickly interpreted to mean just that. The one lonely dissent was made by Justice John Marshal Harlan, who pointed out that while Louisiana claimed its law applied alike to white and black citizens, everyone knew the intent of the law was to exclude black people from the white passenger cars, not the reverse. Harlan warned that the court's decision would only arouse racial tensions and encourage similar laws by other states seeking to skirt the requirements of the Constitution.[18]

Jim Crow attitudes not only gained support in the South but also in other areas of the country where public institutions and services were racially segregated. In effect, *Plessy* provided constitutional cover for legalized racial segregation, having perhaps its greatest impact in those states wishing to erect **dual school systems**, one for blacks and one for whites. Under "separate but equal" laws, racially segregated schools were indeed separate, but they were never equal in terms of funding, resources, or public opinion.

The education of black Americans after slavery

If knowledge is power, as seventeenth-century English philosopher Francis Bacon maintained, then black Americans had reason to strive for education, for they wanted the benefits of the knowledge and power so long denied them. Once the fetters of slavery were removed, most black Americans optimistically embraced the hope that education would actually be the great equalizer of society. There were disagreements, however, over what kind of education should be available and to what effect. Perhaps this is nowhere better illustrated than in the views of **Booker T. Washington** and **W. E. B. Du Bois**, two prominent educators who, each in his own way, struggled in difficult times to shape the condition of African Americans through education.

Booker T. Washington

His full name was Booker Taliafero Washington, and he was born a slave sometime in the spring of 1856 on an upland farm in Franklin County, Virginia.

His mother, Jane, was a caring mother and the cook for the owners; Booker never knew his father and took the name *Washington* from his stepfather, Washington Ferguson. After gaining freedom in 1865, the family moved to Malden, West Virginia, where they eked out a living in the nearby salt furnaces and coal mines.[19]

Around 1866, Washington's formal education began on a part-time basis at a small school for black children, but he also took a job as a house servant for the mine owner, General Lewis Ruffner, and his wife, Viola. Viola Ruffner took a special interest in Washington and introduced him to the literature, manners, and lifestyle of upper- middle-class gentility. Perhaps the most important educational influence on Washington, however, was **Samuel Chapman Armstrong**, the founder of **Hampton Institute** in Virginia. The Institute strongly reflected Armstrong's paternalistic belief that black people needed **industrial education**, by which he meant an education in the virtues of industriousness, thrift, and self-sufficiency, as much if not more than academic and technical/industrial understanding. In other words, black people must earn respect by possessing good character, owning property, educating their children, living down prejudice, cultivating peaceful relations with all, and understanding the need to "be patient—thank God and take courage."[20] Students worked on the institute's farm and in its shops to gain vocational training but also to help the institute become economically self-sufficient and to earn money for themselves to remain in school. The trades included agriculture, sewing, printing, carpentry and masonry, accounting, shoemaking, domestic service, and similar pursuits. Academic subjects included writing, grammar, history, geography, government, and moral philosophy. Students also engaged in intellectual discussions, with oratory and debate (at which Washington became particularly adept).

In October 1872, Washington was admitted to Hampton Institute. An apt pupil, he completed Hampton's program in three years and went back to Malden to teach school. In 1879, he returned to Hampton as a postgraduate student and teacher. In 1881, Armstrong recommended him to Alabama officials who were searching for someone to become the principal of a "normal school for colored teachers." Washington was promptly hired as head of **Tuskegee Institute** (now Tuskegee University), a position he maintained until his death in 1915, and from which he gained widespread fame as a black educator and leader.

Washington's genius resided in organization and implementation. State funding for Tuskegee Institute was woefully inadequate, and by necessity Washington had to raise private funding, a task at which he became quite skillful. When the Institute opened in 1881, he was the only teacher, but by 1894 there were 54 faculty members, 712 students, 2,200 acres of land, and 42 buildings. By 1900, Tuskegee's curriculum included not only teacher preparation but also agriculture, mechanics and trades, domestic science, nursing, music, and even Bible training. Not a traditional liberal arts school, Tuskegee required all students to take courses in both the academic and industrial departments to fully complete its programs.[21]

Washington's embrace of industrial education was also based on his own experience and on how he interpreted the conditions confronted by southern black people at the time. White supremacists sought to control blacks through restrictive laws, low-paying jobs, and social intimidation, while most blacks expected education to help lift them out of their unrelenting poverty and toil. Washington was convinced that hard work and economic uplift would help black people survive in the South's social system, and he was astonished to find that most black parents wanted their children to be taught "the book" instead of industrious labor. Washington emphasized that there was a big difference between being worked as slaves and working for themselves as free people, because the latter brought dignity and benefit, not servility. As he saw it, the most immediate goal for black people should be economic self-sufficiency, that is, to own their own homes, farms, and businesses and to achieve personal respect and moral standing in their communities.[22]

Under Washington's leadership as both an educator and fundraiser, Tuskegee Institute prospered. Indeed, his fundraising success enabled him quietly to aid other black efforts, such as newspapers and legal challenges to Jim Crow laws. With his pleasing personality and tireless capacity for work, Washington assuaged white fears while building Tuskegee into arguably the most influential black institution of the time, but his pathway was precarious. He was dedicated to the advancement of black people, but he had to avoid antagonizing a white power structure that could close Tuskegee at any time. As Washington saw it, insistence on social and political equality only served to inflame white reaction, so black people needed to delay agitation and focus instead on their own economic uplift through diligent work and through educational development in such institutions as Tuskegee.[23]

Washington publicly laid out his ideas in an important speech before a gathering of powerful white northern and southern industrialists and a few black guests at the Atlanta Cotton Exposition in 1895. He strove to be conciliatory but insistent: He asked his black listeners to "Cast down your buckets where you are" in the South, where they could find sustenance if they "put brains and skill in the common occupations of life." He asked his white listeners to cast down their buckets as well, "among my people, helping and encouraging them . . . to education of head, hand, and heart." If both black and white people worked together for common goals, it would benefit all. Then in a dramatic gesture, he raised high his open hand with fingers spread wide and then slowly drew them together as he said: "In all things that are purely social we can be as separate as the fingers, yet one as the hand in all things essential to mutual progress." In the standing ovation that followed, the thrust of his next sentence seemed lost: "There is no defense or security for any of us except in the highest intelligence and development of all."[24]

Washington's performance was widely acclaimed, and he won converts to his cause in the centers of power. He became a trusted advisor to President Theodore Roosevelt on black appointments and issues, and he seemed even more at ease in the company of powerful northern industrialist-philanthropists. However, some black leaders eventually came to call his speech the **Atlanta Compromise** and to view Washington himself as a hindrance to black advancement.[25]

As criticism mounted, Washington defended his advocacy of black people staying in the South because, he believed, that was where the problem most needed attention. He scathingly called his black critics "the Intellectuals," whom he thought wrongly assumed that industrial education was merely a concession to the white South. He argued instead that black people needed something more practical and positive than simply to be reminded of their sufferings. His critics would not be stilled, however, and the Atlanta speech continued to haunt both Washington and his followers. As one of his biographers notes, after Atlanta, whenever Washington tried to promote equal justice for blacks, white opposition pushed him back to his Atlanta stance.[26]

For Further Reflection: Throughout much of human history, the upper portion of society received a formal academic education, while the lower classes, if they received anything more than on-the-job training, got some sort of vocational training. What was Washington's rationale for "industrial education"? Were his objectives primarily vocational, or did he have additional objectives? If politics is "the art of the possible," was Washington simply trying to get what was possible for his people under very trying political conditions, or was he being too cautious and conservative?

William Edward Burghardt Du Bois

No Washington critic stands out more clearly than W. E. B. Du Bois, who was born on February 23, 1868, in Great Barrington, Massachusetts. His childhood playmates were mostly white, and along with them he attended the local public schools where he was a high achiever. In 1885, he entered Fisk University in Nashville, Tennessee, and upon completion of their program in 1888, he taught briefly in a nearby rural school where he directly observed the grinding poverty so many black people endured in the rural South. That same year he was admitted to Harvard University, where he received a BA in 1890, an MA in 1891, and a PhD in 1895. After teaching at several colleges, Du Bois became a professor at Atlanta University, where his sociological studies established his reputation as a scholar and where he gained widespread recognition as a leading black intellectual. He was one of the co-founders of the **National Association for the Advancement of Colored People (NAACP)** in 1910 and served for many years as the editor of *The Crisis*, its official publication. He became increasingly radical and joined the Communist Party, receiving the Lenin Peace Prize in 1959. He moved to Ghana, became a citizen in 1963, and died shortly thereafter at age 95.[27]

Although Du Bois grew more radical in his later years, his philosophical outlook had certain constants: cultural pluralism, pan-Africanism, racial solidarity, and collective economic improvement. During his conflict with Booker T. Washington, he consistently argued three democratic principles: the right to vote, civic equality, and the right to educational opportunity. After Washington's Atlanta speech, Du Bois was not at first a critic. At the time, he wrote Washington that the speech was "a word fitly spoken," but as Du Bois later explained, although he originally thought Washington's position offered good prospects, his hopes were dashed as Jim Crowism submerged black people into a legally segregated, subordinate class.[28]

The Washington-Du Bois Debate

According to Du Bois, he opposed Washington not for his industrial education model, but his specific views on black higher education and his failure to push the importance of equality and voting rights. Although their disagreement was not simply "vocational versus liberal education," it still revolved around their contending views on education. Washington argued that blacks needed practical skills for economic progress; Du Bois did not disagree with skills and progress, but he strongly advocated higher liberal education for the able few, the so-called **Talented Tenth**, to provide much-needed black leaders. Washington, too, recognized a place for higher liberal education (he sent his own children to liberal arts colleges), but he still insisted that industrial education should be black people's main focus. In the final analysis, perhaps the disagreement between Washington and Du Bois came from their competition for the allegiance of better educated black people, each hoping to draw that segment into his version of higher education in order to develop what each saw as the leadership needed to guide African Americans into the future.[29]

Du Bois also feared that Washington was steering wealthy philanthropists away from supporting liberal higher education for black people in favor of the

Hampton-Tuskegee type of institution. As Du Bois put it, their differences ultimately came down to contending views of effective leadership: "While my leadership was a matter of writing and teaching, the Washington leadership became a matter of organization and money."[30] In the eyes of critics, Washington's operation was the **Tuskegee Machine**, and Washington himself was "the Wizard" for his powers of persuasion among the rich and powerful. According to Du Bois, the Tuskegee Machine arose because political leaders, industrialist-philanthropists, scholars, and black office seekers sought Washington's advice, and his support or opposition could be decisive. Du Bois suspected that financial aid from northern industrialists was proffered mainly in hopes of cultivating cheap, nonunion black labor as a hedge against prounion white labor in the South. Such donors did not want liberally educated black college graduates who could raise troublesome questions about race, labor, and wages.[31]

> **Suggested Activities:** Peruse a biographical work on Booker T. Washington (recommended: Louis Harlan, *Booker T. Washington*. 2 volumes. New York: Oxford University Press, 1972, 1983), and look up what was meant by the Tuskegee Machine and the support/opposition to it in the black community. Make a brief report to class on the leading factors involved.

From another perspective, however, perhaps self-interest motivated the efforts of Du Bois and other critical black scholars because they needed funds from rich philanthropists to support their own institutions and research projects. Although the evidence is scant, Washington might have discouraged philanthropic support for Du Bois, because he clearly believed Du Bois was too radical and outspoken. Outside funding was scarce for black liberal arts colleges, while Tuskegee Institute enjoyed relative prosperity from philanthropic largesse. In any event, Du Bois recognized that technical schools produced artisans that society sorely needed, but his heart lay with colleges and universities that valued the liberal arts and sciences and that cultivated the kind of cultural knowledge he believed was indispensable for producing leaders with "quick minds and pure hearts."[32]

Du Bois's belief that the Talented Tenth would extend democracy and promote racial solidarity was, in effect, a "trickle-down" approach. As time passed, however, it became increasingly clear to him that in the competitive economic climate of the time, graduates of the black liberal arts colleges behaved little differently from their white counterparts in advancing their own self interests. He became disillusioned with the Talented Tenth idea and, by 1938, was calling for "the perfection of the Negro elementary school" as the essential issue deserving attention. Although he never repudiated his belief in the value of liberal higher education, by the 1950s he expressed disappointment with black intellectuals and maintained that true leaders must come from intelligent members of the black working class.[33]

> **Suggested Activities:** Consult sources on Du Bois that explain his view of the Talented Tenth and how he became disillusioned with it (a recommended work is *W. E. B. Du Bois: Writings*, Nathan Huggins, ed., New York: The Library of America, 1986). Consider making a brief report to class on the basic issues of the Talented Tenth as far as Du Bois was concerned, both early on and later in his life.

In sum, both Washington and Du Bois were strong advocates of educational opportunity and full citizenship rights for black people, but each came from a different perspective and with a different timetable in mind. On the one hand, Washington's aim was long term, but perhaps he compromised too much with the white power structure when it came to the enjoyment of those rights. On the other hand, Du Bois wanted more immediate change, but he put his faith in developing black intellectuals, a plan that failed to exert the socially conscious leadership he envisioned. Both men championed the right to educational opportunity, and each in his own way saw education as a producer of good citizens and as a social equalizer. In the end, both men had their hopes frustrated by the harsh conditions of their times.

> **For Further Reflection:** Compare and contrast Washington and Du Bois. Was one more realistic and far sighted than the other? Why or why not? Were the differences between the two men solely based on principle, or was it also based on "self-interests" related to their personal preferences concerning what kind of higher education was best for African Americans? Do you think either man "won" the debate, considering how things actually turned out? Justify your position with evidence and argument.

"Separate but equal" segregated schools

Under the separate but equal slogan, all the southern states and some of the border states passed laws requiring racially segregated public schools. The schools were never equal, particularly in regard to the inequities in school funding and its effects on educational achievement and attainment.

Early twentieth-century southern school reform

In the early 1900s, a public school reform movement swept the South. The genesis for reform came from a combination of factors. One was the northern industrialist-philanthropists who invested in southern education because they believed widespread education would hasten southern economic development, which would serve their own economic interests as well. The more visible force, however, was the number of southern educator-reformers who were impatient with existing conditions. Filled with New South visions of progress, they wanted to expand educational opportunity throughout the South and bring prosperity and social stability to the region. With the support of influential southern political leaders and with advice and funding from important industrialist-philanthropists, the reformers launched a series of Conferences for Education in the South between 1898 and 1914. In these conferences, education and its connections to economic development were highlighted, as also were the issues of white control and black dependency. One of the positive things to come out of the conferences was state-level educational reforms and better popular support for public schools. There also emerged two private but powerful advisory boards of education: the General Education Board and the Southern Education Board. The General Education Board was composed of industrialist-philanthropists who provided seed money for reform; the Southern Education Board was composed of New South educators who vigorously spread the gospel of school reform and economic progress. The southern states now embraced public education for all, but under white control with white schools receiving the greater share of resources and black schools the lesser.[34]

Philanthropic support

The impact of the Conferences for Education in the South helped stimulate industrialist- philanthropists to provide funds to enhance their views on what was best for southern education, and for most of them the model of choice was Booker T. Washington's version of industrial education, particularly when it came to the education of black youth. The General Education Board was created in 1902, with John D. Rockefeller the chief force behind it. By 1929 Rockefeller himself had contributed more than $129 million to it. This board not only served as an umbrella for Rockefeller and several other philanthropists, but it hired agents who went across the South to help existing schools and to create new ones that reflected its interest in spreading industrial education. The General Education Board's umbrella functions exercised strong influence over much of the philanthropy that flowed to black schools.[35]

Among the philanthropic funds, some of which coordinated their activities with the General Education Board, were the Anna T. Jeanes Fund, the Phelps-Stokes Fund, the Peabody Education Fund, the Julius Rosenwald Fund, and the John F. Slater Fund.[36] Probably the three most important were the Peabody, Jeanes, and Rosenwald funds.

The Peabody Education Fund was founded in 1867, the first large education foundation in the United States. It was established by George Peabody, an American of modest origins who became wealthy in banking. A strong believer in the importance of education, he established the Education Fund, which provided challenge grants to the southern states to encourage them to invest in the education of poor children, both black and white. Peabody money was also used to develop teacher preparation programs as well.[37]

Anna T. Jeanes was a wealthy, devout Quaker who established a fund in 1907 called the Fund for Rudimentary Schools for Southern Negroes. The signal work of the Jeanes Fund was its support of Jeanes Supervisors (or teachers), most of whom were black women chosen because they were also active leaders in their communities. Virginia Randolph of Henrico County, Virginia, was appointed in 1908 as the first Jeanes teacher, and her energetic work quickly established the model for others. Using the industrial education model, Jeanes teachers lived and taught in rural black communities to help make their schools central to community life. Jeanes teachers taught both academic and practical subjects to promote self-reliance and knowledge of practical capabilities needed in daily life.[38]

Suggested Activity: View five short videos of interviews, two with historians and three with former Jeanes teachers, at "Jeanes Teachers—the Next Needed Thing," http://www.southerned.org/1932_7.asp?ref=sef (accessed on April 24, 2010).

Julius T. Rosenwald gained his wealth as an executive at Sears, Roebuck and Company. Inspired by Booker T. Washington and his philanthropic supporters, Rosenwald became devoted to enhancing the education of black children. Established in 1917, the Rosenwald Fund primarily aided the construction of schools and libraries across the South, although it also provided some aid to teacher preparation and higher education as well. The fund's most important work was building schools, and before it ended in 1932, at least 5,137 schools had been built with fund assistance, and more than one-fourth of all black schoolchildren in the South attended Rosenwald schools.[39]

Despite the difficulties they faced, black people did make some educational advances. For example, in 1900 only 22 percent of black children aged five to nine attended elementary schools, but by 1940 at least 66 percent attended. In addition, where once there were insufficient facilities for students who wanted to attend, by 1935 there were sufficient buildings to accommodate the majority.[40] Still, black schools and teachers were woefully underfunded in comparison with their white counterparts, even with help from philanthropists, and black citizens were forced by necessity to devise various plans to supplement their schools.

The issue of double taxation

In the early 1900s, a popular myth circulated among whites that blacks paid so little in taxes that the costs of their schools largely fell on white taxpayers. Common-sense observations seemed to give credence to the myth: Black people had less property, fewer businesses, and less money to spend than whites; therefore, they obviously paid less taxes. This myth encouraged many white taxpayers to support reduced funding for black schools. Tired of what he believed was unfair and inaccurate gossip, Charles L. Coon, a white educator and member of the Southern Education Board, conducted a study of North Carolina's school tax collections and allocations for the 1905–06 school year. He found that black schools actually received less state funding than what was collected from black taxpayers for schools. In addition, it was later determined that, from 1900 to 1920, every southern state increased its tax appropriations for new white schools but almost none for new black schools.[41]

Under such conditions, black citizens had to develop private ways of financing their schools. This is what is meant by **double taxation**, for not only did black people pay their lawful taxes, and not only were they denied their legitimate share of school funds, but they had to "tax" themselves again through their own private contributions and efforts. The Rosenwald Fund helped allay some of this burden through challenge grants, but black citizens themselves had to provide the greater proportion through cash contributions and donations of labor, building materials, and land. For example, in 1920 the black citizens of Cleveland County, Arkansas, were determined to build a new schoolhouse for their children, but they could only raise a small amount of cash. Undeterred, they persuaded some owners of woodland properties to donate pine timber, which was felled by volunteer laborers. Another citizen donated his labor and the use of his sawmill to cut the logs into lumber, while still another contributed a small piece of land on which to erect the school. Once the materials were ready, volunteers provided the labor to raise the new two-room schoolhouse, all the while expending less than $400 in cash. For another example, in Jones County, Texas, black citizens developed a plan in which they pledged 300 days of labor, either through volunteer labor on construction of the new building or through donations from wages earned by work for hire. The proceeds of their efforts were placed in the county school board's building fund. In such manner, the black citizens of Jones County got a new schoolhouse valued at approximately $10,000.[42]

Black and white educational expenditures compared

These kinds of conditions continued until midcentury. Per pupil expenditures in the South in 1945 were twice as high for white children as for black children, and four times as much was invested for the construction and upkeep of white schools as for black schools. Salaries for white teachers were 30 percent higher than for black teachers, and only a fraction of the transportation cost spent on white children was spent on black children. In addition, the levels of illiteracy and school dropouts were much higher among blacks than whites, and black school attendance lagged behind that of whites. The differences were perhaps even greater at the college level: In those states requiring racially segregated institutions in 1947, $86 million was spent on white colleges and only $5 million on black colleges; no higher education institution in the South made it possible for blacks to pursue the PhD degree; only two medical schools served black students, while 29 served whites; and there was only one accredited law school for blacks, while there were 40 for whites.[43]

It would be a mistake, however, to conclude that during segregation times white schools in the South were awash in funds while only the black schools suffered. Virtually all public schools in the southern states were poorly funded in comparison to most states outside the South. Both white and black schools suffered from want of adequate resources, but black schools clearly suffered much more, demonstrating how unequal "separate but equal" truly was.

School desegregation

With the passage of time, it became clear to many observers that "separate but equal" only produced unequal schools. Such inequities were the central concern of the NAACP's legal team in its initial efforts to overturn *Plessy v. Ferguson*. At first they thought that if white authorities were legally forced to equalize school spending, then the expense would be so great that authorities would desegregate the schools out of economic necessity. However, as NACCP lawyer Oliver Hill put it, when authorities increased funding, what black people actually got were "little-better segregated schools" that "were new, but they were never equal." Faced with this reality, the NAACP legal team decided to push for total **desegregation**, a risky tactic because, "Jim Crow would be more deeply entrenched than ever if we lost, but it was a gamble we had to take."[44]

> **Suggested Activities:** View a copy of the video recording *The Road to Brown: The Untold Story of the Man Who Killed Jim Crow* (San Francisco: California Newsreel, 1990) [approximately 45 minutes]. Consider recommending it be viewed by your classmates by preparing a brief oral report on key features for their consideration. Suggestion: Provide more details on why the NAACP lawyers, under Charles Hamilton Houston's direction, decided to launch a direct attack on the Jim Crow legal underpinnings of racially segregated schools and why it was a gamble worth taking.

The Brown *decision*

The NAACP launched an all-out effort to end segregation, and they chose to challenge the constitutionality of racially segregated public schools. Prior lawsuits had slowly chipped away at *Plessy*, with lower-court rulings that pushed states to provide more equitable facilities for black and white alike. None of those rulings were definitive, but their constitutional implications helped NAACP lawyers build a better legal foundation for the landmark U.S. Supreme Court case ***Brown v. the Board of Education* (1954)**. A central player in the strategy was **Charles Hamilton Houston**, who was instrumental in bringing about several legal victories prior to *Brown*, but it was Houston's student and future supreme court justice **Thurgood Marshall** who actually argued the case before the court.

Linda Brown, the lead plaintiff in the case, sued for access to a nearby white school rather than having to cross railroad tracks and walk to a distant black school. Her case was consolidated with three similar cases from other states, all involving black children who, because of their race, were denied admission to their nearest local public school. The argument was that segregated schooling was not and could not be equal, and it denied students the equal protection of the laws as guaranteed by the Constitution's Fourteenth Amendment. In a unanimous (9-0) decision, the Supreme Court concluded that, ". . . in the field of public education the doctrine of 'separate but equal' has no place. . . . Therefore, we hold that the plaintiffs . . . are . . . deprived of the equal protection of the laws guaranteed by the Fourteenth Amendment."[45]

It took almost six decades (from 1896 to 1954) for *Plessy* to be overturned. What *Brown* actually ended was **de jure segregation**, or segregation required by law, and it was a mortal blow to Jim Crow laws across the South and elsewhere. However, the decision did not address **de facto segregation**, or segregation by nonlegal means (such as housing patterns). It also failed to state how soon desegregation should begin, and it provided no guidance on legally acceptable desegregation measures. Thus, on May 31, 1955, the Court reconvened to consider implementation measures (sometimes called ***Brown II***), but it only said that school desegregation must occur with **all deliberate speed**. Providing no deadlines or guidance for state and local school authorities, the court simply made federal district courts responsible for implementation.[46]

Resistance to Brown

One result was that some school districts desegregated soon afterward, while others delayed (or "deliberated") as long as possible. Some whites accepted the decision and tried to adapt, but others angrily resisted or took their children out of public schools and sent them to private ones. Political leaders in Virginia launched a campaign of **massive resistance** to circumvent *Brown* with state legislation to close any public schools that desegregated, but this tactic proved short-lived when Virginia's own supreme court of appeals declared the legislation in violation of the Virginia constitution, which required the state to provide free public schools.[47]

Perhaps the most extreme resistance came in 1959, in Prince Edward County, Virginia, in response to demands from black citizen for equitable, desegregated public schools. County officials simply closed the county public school system. A private school system for white children was soon in operation, but when it was suggested that blacks should undertake a similar approach, they reiterated their goal of a public school system open to everyone on an equal basis. The county's public schools remained closed for five years, forcing some black parents to move elsewhere or else send their children to relatives or friends in other school districts. Many parents lacked resources for such options and were forced to see their children go without schooling. Some locals and friendly outsiders tried to organize alternative schools in local churches, but these proved inadequate. The cynical closure of county schools by local officials meant lost years of schooling for many children, displacement of families that moved to educate their children elsewhere, separation of families that sent their children to other school districts, and helpless frustration for families without such resources.[48] While other southern communities experienced upheavals over *Brown*, none closed their schools for such an extended time as Prince Edward County.

School desegregation continued to face determined resistance in many other locales, however, and New Orleans is a case in point. This historic Louisiana city chose to begin its desegregation effort with four six-year-old black girls enrolled in two white elementary schools in the city's Ninth Ward, at that time a racially mixed but still predominantly white working-class area. The two schools were McDonough 19 School and William Frantz School, and both were desegregated on November 14, 1960 (McDonough 19 received three black children, and Frantz received one). At both schools, the girls were accompanied by their parents and by federal marshals, but they were met by noisy white demonstrators spewing verbal abuse and threats, with numerous TV cameras and news reporters on hand. By the end of the first day, few white children remained in either school because many white parents, alarmed over the safety of their children and what they saw, took their children out of the schools. Over the next few days, white parents who kept their children in school faced such pressures from the community that they withdrew their children as well. This boycott soon reduced the total school population at McDonough 19 to the principal, the secretary, the custodian, 18 teachers, and the three black children until the end of the term. At Frantz School, the circumstances slightly differed, with the student body reduced to the one black girl and a handful of white students varying between three to ten students per day for the remainder of the term.[49]

> **Suggested Activities:** Interview some older members of your own community who can remember the *Brown* decision and the attempts to follow or thwart its requirements. Ask what they thought about community reactions at the time and what they think now. Try to determine what differences, if any, exist between their two responses, and if so, what determined the difference. In your final analysis, consider desegregation's successes and failures in light of today, and assess whether or not society is better as a result.

Desegregation and its implementation

Events in Prince Edward County, Virginia, and New Orleans, Louisiana, were extreme, but they provide a glimpse of how the concept of race impacted people's lives during desegregation. Fortunately, it is difficult for raw human emotions to remain forever on edge, although periodic eruptions continued to occur where desegregation became a hot issue.

Freedom of choice

The *Brown II* doctrine of "all deliberate speed" was used by some local and state authorities to try numerous delaying tactics. Consider, for instance, the tactic called freedom of choice. On the surface, who could be against free choice, and what could be more democratic and fair? As events unfolded, however, it became clear that little free choice or democratic fairness was intended.

Virtually the only applicants under freedom of choice were black parents trying to transfer their children into better-funded and equipped schools, which almost invariably were white schools. Parents or guardians had to apply for transfers at designated board or committee offices usually staffed by personnel carefully chosen to discourage or intimidate applicants. Application forms were complicated and subject to rejection for the slightest error, with only a few error-free applications being approved. Transfers were kept to a mere trickle as officials, who claimed good faith compliance, were actually engaging in **passive resistance** (the use of tokenism and delay tactics). Such blatant practices almost guaranteed the issue would be appealed to the Supreme Court, as it was in *Green v. County School Board of New Kent County, Virginia* (1968), in which the court found that county's plan unacceptable.[50] It was a decision that effectively halted freedom of choice as a credible tool for desegregation.

Busing

In *Swann v. Charlotte-Mecklenburg Board of Education* (1972), the Supreme Court ruled that constructing new schools in more strategic locations, rearranging attendance zones, and using transportation capacities such as busing could be effective tools of desegregation, if carefully monitored by federal district courts for constitutional requirements and if the actions effectively dismantled racially segregated school systems.[51]

Whether the court intended it or not, busing soon became a remedy of choice for federal district courts. Not only did it have Supreme Court approval, but school buses were already on hand and school officials were long experienced in administering their operation. In addition, the ubiquitous yellow school bus was a familiar sight, and advocates hoped it would be an acceptable and efficient tool to help achieve desegregated schools. As district courts began issuing busing orders, however, public reaction in some instances reached the emotional levels following the 1954 *Brown* decision. Nevertheless, federal district courts kept busing as a legitimate tool in desegregation by transporting students from one part of a school district to another in order to achieve better racial balances within each school.[52]

Desegregation controversy was not limited to the South, however, for it soon erupted in other regions as well. In Boston, Massachusetts, increasing unrest over racial inequities in school funding came to the boiling point. Despite a 1965 state law that required racially balanced schools, the Boston School Committee refused to take effective action, which resulted in a NAACP lawsuit in 1971. Matters dragged along until 1974, when the federal district court ordered the Boston school system to remedy its racial imbalances, including the use of busing. Confrontations erupted in Boston similar to those in the South, including displays of simmering racism, public demonstrations, violent incidents, school boycotts, and white flight that left an increasingly black student population in the public schools. In 1973, 60 percent of the student population was white, but by 1987 only 26 percent was white.[53]

Some results

Busing helped desegregate schools in many communities, but the efficacy of cross- district busing came under increasing scrutiny. In part, this was due to the re-emergence of political conservatism at the national level in the 1980s, with school desegregation not among its priorities. It was also due to changing demographics, with racial minorities becoming concentrated in urban areas as the white middle class relocated to suburbia. By the end of the 1980s, court-ordered busing was being abandoned by federal district courts, sometimes by the same judges who ordered it in the early 1970s.[54]

Where many communities came to stand on desegregation can be seen in developments in Mississippi. With its Education Reform Act of 1982, Mississippi provided a large increase in school funding, a pay raise for teachers, and a reinstatement of compulsory education (which the state had abolished after the *Brown* decision of 1954). As the twenty-first century drew near, aspects of the past still lingered, but outside the delta and the urban areas with large concentrations of minorities, most of Mississippi's small towns and rural districts operated schools attended by both black and white children.[55]

Nevertheless, racial controversy continued to pop up around the nation over issues such as resegregation, hiring practices, test scores, the clustering of white children in certain classes, and funding inequities, but these were tame as compared to the confrontations over *Brown* or busing. In other words, and allowing for unique circumstances, schools in one place were experiencing approximately what schools in many other places were experiencing: some successes here and there, some continuing problems with roots in the past, and some new challenges to face.

Contemporary conditions

Race is a **social construct** that may help or hinder a person's chances in a society. A socially divisive notion of race continues to stalk American society, but many scholars have pointed out that the race concept itself has little useful meaning in either biological or sociological classifications. A closer look at current racial classification (such as Caucasian, African, or Asian) reveals that even characteristics such as skin pigmentation and similar physical features are becoming increasingly useless markers of group membership. For example, some Latino Americans are darker than some African Americans, and the range of external "racial" features can be as significant within racial groups as among them. Moreover, with today's worldwide transportation networks and the relative ease of human migration, mixed ancestry has become fairly common, and it may become the norm in the future. Exacting classifications of race in a scientific sense is impossible.[56]

Suggested Activity: View and discuss the videos *Race: The Power of an Illusion*, Episodes 1–3, produced by California Newsreel, 2003.

Race and socialization

How is it that such a loose concept as race ends up defining so much of our lives? The reason is both simple and complex: Our daily experiences are fundamentally shaped by race as a social construct. The issue should be particularly important for American educators who, by and large, remain predominantly white, even as more nonwhite and interracial children enter the schools. Educators need to consider what they convey about the nature of racial realities to their students, whose own experiences of race may differ significantly from those of educators.[57]

Racism may be defined as the belief that race is a primary determinant of basic human characteristics and capabilities and that one or more races have inherent superiorities over other races. Racism involves prejudices that one group holds against another, and it most frequently exists in social systems where advantages and disadvantages are based on race. A society is racist precisely to the extent that it provides systemic and prevailing advantages for one group over another, such as access to better schools, housing, jobs, health care, financial security, and social status. People who enjoy advantages may fervently defend them, even when they themselves do not personally affirm racist beliefs or openly exhibit racist attitudes.[58]

In order to better understand race in the United States, it is necessary to consider the issue of whiteness, white privilege, and how white racial identities are constructed. It has been observed that many white people seem to think racial identity is something other people have, but people of color learn early in life that they occupy a minority status. In this sense, thinking of oneself only as an individual is a legacy of the privileged status of whiteness. Such status may also reflect American values about rugged individualism and meritocracy, that is, if one is successful, it must be because one deserves it. Understanding racism as part of a social system that gives whites advantages and people of color disadvantages may help us comprehend why, in a society where racial identity can be life defining, black people tend to find their essential support among other black people.[59]

Concerning how racial identities are formed, children are not born black or white in any original, inborn sense of perception; instead, children are socialized into racial identities at the same time they learn other sociocultural traits and values (such as what it means to be rich or poor, Christian or Jewish). As children undergo the process of socialization, along the way they also learn racial terms and labels or experience **racialization** to such an extent that almost all of them come to accept prescribed racial identities.[60]

Racialization occurs in ongoing individual and group experiences where race and various ways of categorizing it are given importance, and these experiences tend to reinforce racial beliefs and categories found in education and other spheres of life. It may be difficult for many white people to understand what racialization means for black people because most whites rarely if ever face the kinds of racial discrimination that many blacks experience on a frequent basis.[61]

> **For Further Reflection:** To what extent are whites able to understand race and its consequences for nonwhites? Is there a way to facilitate such understanding? Is racism confined to whites, or do members of other groups exhibit it as well? What can each person do as an individual to help create better understanding and tolerance between and among groups?

Race and social status

Race continues to influence the distribution of societal goods and privileges, and in statistically significant ways blacks are worse off than whites. Generally speaking, whites have more wealth than blacks, and rich whites have more wealth than rich blacks. Not all black people are poor, of course, but according to U.S. Census Bureau statistics in 2007, the percentage of black people below the poverty line was higher (24.5 percent) than for whites (10.5 percent), although numerically speaking there were more poor whites (approximately

21.5 million) than poor blacks (approximately 9.2 million). Also, the median income of white households ($64,427) was significantly higher than of black households ($40,143). In addition, in 2009 it was reported that 35 percent of black children lived in poor families as compared to 11 percent of white children.[62]

Beyond such statistics lay what philosopher Cornel West calls "the murky waters of despair and dread" and "the eclipse of hope."[63] Depressing statistics are one thing, but it is quite another to experience the hopelessness and lack of regard for human life that some black people experience in daily life. When people are denied a fair share of societal goods and privileges, they often experience despair. When they also carry a disproportionate burden of social problems over an extended period of time, they lose hope and come to place little value on themselves or on others.

De facto segregation and its educational consequences

Despite all the rhetoric and change brought by past reforms, American society remains divided along racial lines. To be sure, there has been change, but as statistics indicate, society continues to experience worrisome racial segregation, both residential (where we live) and institutional (where we work or go to school). Despite the legal victory over state-imposed segregation in *Brown v. Board of Education*, full-scale desegregation has yet to be achieved, particularly in large urban centers where no white children are found in many public schools. Racial segregation continues to impact American education, but too few Americans seem concerned about its effects or seek new policies to address its institutional roots. It appears that too many Americans think of racial segregation as part of a distant past, with lingering pockets of segregation due to insufficient time for civil rights laws to take full effect. Such outlooks stand in sharp contrast to the serious consequences of segregation, which include concentrations of poverty, welfare dependency, family deterioration, and educational failure.[64]

Educational attainment and achievement

Race not only affects economic opportunity but educational opportunity as well. African Americans have used public schools to their advantage and their **educational attainment** rates have improved since the 1954 *Brown* decision; however, dropout rates remain significantly higher for black students than for white: In 2007, for example, the dropout rate for native-born black students was 12 percent, and for native-born white students it was 6 percent.[65] These percentages are national figures, and one must understand that dropout rates vary from one locality to another and tend to be low in wealthy school districts and high in poor districts. Where poor minority students are concentrated in inner-city schools, the majority of students often fail to complete high school.

Although there has been improvement over time, racial discrepancies in educational achievement continue to occur. According to the national assessment of educational progress (NAEP), reading score gaps, for example, have changed little during recent years, with no significant changes in racial/ethnic reading gaps since 2007. Explanations for such continuing achievement gaps are numerous, and one is that children from disadvantaged backgrounds tend to have fewer positive interactions with parents, neighborhoods, and schools than their advantaged peers, which may account for some of the differences.[66]

Over the last decades, the educational attainment gap between whites and blacks concerning high school completion rates has narrowed. It remained relatively steady in terms of some college attendance but has widened in regard to completion of undergraduate degrees.[67]

Educational attainment is crucial in many ways. Generally, the higher the level of educational attainment, the better the job opportunities and earnings. In addition, a strong correlation exists between lack of educational attainment and poverty. For instance, most children in low-income families have parents without any college education and, over the past two decades, the percentage of children in low-income families increased from 66 percent to 75 percent when parents had less than a high school diploma.[68]

There are other ways that educational attainment affects children's lives. Greater educational attainment of parents not only improves the living standards and quality of life of the family but the children's academic preparation as well. Parents with higher educational attainment are more likely to read to their children than parents with lower attainment. Children who are read to at an early age are more likely to be better prepared academically than children who are not read to. African Americans, in general, report less frequent reading to children by family members.[69]

Thus, education-specific indicators continue to show significant gaps between blacks and whites in the contemporary United States. While these gaps are narrowing in some respects, in others they remain and are too significant to be ignored. Numerous theories exist about the gaps, and they need to be examined, explained, and addressed at the policy, institutional, and individual levels.

Brown *revisited*

Prior to desegregation, most black educators usually had access to all teaching and administrative opportunities in the schools of their own communities, but desegregation curtailed careers for many black educators. For example, blacks lost 31,000 teaching jobs when their schools were closed or consolidated with white schools. Black teachers also faced nonrenewal of contracts more often than whites. If they did not lose their jobs, black educators were frequently reassigned to other functions not of their choosing, as when principals of former all-black schools were reassigned as assistants to white principals. Such developments restricted many black educators from cultivating academic achievement among black students as they once had.[70]

Other studies have reached similar conclusions. One example is a study of a black rural high school in operation from 1934 until 1969 that found that dedicated teachers and principals worked in close cooperation with their community, while parents were intimately involved in the school and supported it both financially and morally. The study provides insights for educators today about how black communities of the past met the needs of schoolchildren with good schools that were excellent in important ways and cannot simply be dismissed as inferior.[71]

Another study examined a small black community's response to the closing of its school in the wake of desegregation. Community members bemoaned the loss of an important source of cultural identity, and while they were keenly aware of the second-rate facilities and resources of black schools in the segregated South, they sincerely trusted their teachers as professionals who cared about the children, imparted values shared by the community, and kept in close contact with parents about student progress. The teachers made regular home visits and encouraged parents to reinforce the norms taught at school, while the school was perceived as a haven where students were prepared to live as best as they could in a segregated society. This trust was lost as the school closed and students were bused out to other schools to meet desegregation requirements. Students then had teachers who often lacked the traditional personal and social missions involved in "uplifting the race." Perhaps many subsequent educational problems (such as high dropout rates, self-defeating behaviors, and alienation) may be at least partially explained by the loss of such cultural supports.[72]

Unintended consequences of *Brown*

A leading purpose of *Brown* was to ensure that children would no longer be required by law to attend racially segregated schools. A second purpose, to extend the equal protection of the laws, proved more difficult to fulfill. After all the struggle to desegregate the schools, in many locales a new type of dual education system developed that consisted of private schools for predominantly white affluent citizens and public schools for predominantly poor blacks and whites.[73] One might argue that a division of public and private schools existed ever since public schools appeared, but the older pattern was based primarily on socioeconomic class lines. Certainly the new type of division included class lines, but race was now central because white flight from desegregation was a leading stimulus behind it. Moreover, while *Brown* provided important legal precedents to overcome educational inequalities based on race, the decision was implemented in ways that seemed to exact a high price for any gains accruing to the black community.[74]

In his study of school desegregation in Richmond, Virginia, historian Robert Pratt describes how citywide busing after *Brown* failed because whites not only protested forced busing but most of them transferred their children from public to private schools or moved from the city to adjacent and predominantly white counties for their children to attend public schools. Soon, busing in Richmond did little more than transport black children from their neighborhood schools across town to another school with predominantly black students attending. Cross-town busing was finally abandoned in 1986, ironically by the same federal district judge who first ordered it back in 1970. As did many other cities, Richmond witnessed the development of the new dual system of private schools for the children of affluent citizens (along with white flight to suburban public schools) and urban public schools for predominantly poor blacks and whites.[75]

Resegregation

What happened in Richmond reflected similar developments in most urban school systems around the country. This was **resegregation**, the process of formerly desegregated schools undergoing demographic changes in student bodies that resulted in a predominance of racial and ethnic minorities. The resegregation of schools noticeably increased during the 1980s and 1990s as a series of court and legislative decisions weakened prior desegregation efforts. The process of resegregation increased nationwide for both African Americans and Latinos in what has been called "double segregation," that is, segregation from affluent white and other middle-class students. As the example of Richmond shows, the South became relatively desegregated as a result of court orders, federal legislation, and their implementation, but its urban school systems resegregated due to white flight and other forms of affluent resistance. A consequence is that the nation's urban children may at present be more segregated in racially unequal schools than they were only a couple decades ago, although probably not at the level of legally enforced racial segregation prior to *Brown*. Furthermore, at the federal level no major national desegregation policies have been implemented since the 1980s, and this includes the No Child Left Behind (NCLB) legislation of 2001.[76]

It can be argued that some progress was made, but racial desegregation was never achieved in any fulsome sense of the term, and the equalization of educational opportunity along racial and other lines continues to be a challenge for the present and foreseeable future. The problem is complex, and the goal of providing equal educational opportunities for all children, regardless of race, is more comprehensive than desegregation. Given that many African American students continue to attend largely segregated and under-resourced schools, increased efforts must be made to improve the quality of those schools. At the same time, it also must be recognized that some minority schools are excellent examples of "communally bonded" schools that successfully educate children in close cooperation with families and communities. In addition, mere attendance in a racially diverse or predominantly white school does not guarantee successful educational experiences for black children.[77]

Suggested Activity: Read up on the Civil Rights Project, which began at Harvard University in 1996 as a multidisciplinary research and policy think tank and as a clearinghouse for intellectual resources for academics, policy makers, civil rights advocates and journalists, among others. Education reform and related efforts are central to its mission. In 2007, it was moved to the University of California at Los Angeles and renamed as the Civil Rights Project/ Proyecto Derechos Civiles. Its website is http://www.civilrightsproject.ucla.edu/ (accessed on April 20, 2010).

Continuing issues

Even when black and white children attend schools together, inhouse segregation (sometimes called clustering) may occur. Predominantly black or white classrooms often result from such practices as tracking a disproportionately higher number of white children into high-ability classes and a disproportionately higher number of black children into remedial and special education classes. For example, in North Carolina—where a relatively strong level of desegregation had occurred—resegregation has increased both between schools and within individual schools. This does not necessarily mean a marked decrease in racial tolerance but rather a waning of judicial oversight and a tendency among school officials not to use race in making school assignments.[78]

A combination of factors may lead students to segregate themselves on the basis of race. Adolescents who play and study together as young children might move into separate worlds as they grow older, one white and one black. In the racially and economically mixed community of the South Orange-Maplewood district of New Jersey, when children reach sixth grade they begin to drift apart along racial lines and to develop a separate racial consciousness.

Such developments are not unique to New Jersey but reflect a national trend that is fueled by such practices as ability grouping, which tends to become more intense around sixth grade and which separates students and sends them on different academic paths. In addition, high-achieving black students may be perceived by their peers as "acting white," while lower-achieving students are "acting black." Similarly, black honors students may be seen as "white black kids," and black students with mostly white friends may be called "Oreos." In addition, in mixed black-white classes, students report that in group work where students are able to choose, the tendency is to join groups according to race. Students also talk about a "drift" from interracial friendships to only hanging with members of their own race. Cultures begin to coexist rather than mix. Black students talk about discrimination they experience from teachers, while white students feel intimidated when they are in the process of becoming a minority in school. Both white and black students seem to be sharing less with one another, academically and culturally.[79]

> **For Further Reflection:** Reflect on your own school experience, past and present. Did (or do) students segregate themselves by race, and if so, why and how did (do) they act this way? What is your theory of why this happens? What can be (or should be) done about it?

Younger children tend to mix much more easily, which can be observed on playgrounds of racially mixed elementary schools where black and white children freely play with one another and sit at the same tables. Several explanations have been suggested for why this seems to change by middle school. For one thing, it is there that pubescence begins to occur, often accompanied by a search for personal identity. For another, black students are more likely than white students to include racial or ethnic explorations as they seek identity. Finally, black youth tend to think about themselves in terms of race and ethnicity because the rest of society seems to think of them in those terms too. As black children grow older, they enter the encounter stage of identity, often precipitated by experiences of racism and conditions that force them to struggle with a racial identity. For example, adolescents may observe that tracking and ability grouping in schools reflect racial and ethnic identities. Black girls may perceive that they do not fit white mainstream beauty standards, while black boys learn that the wider society often associates black males with violence and crime. As a coping mechanism, many black youngsters may disengage from old associations and seek support among new people of similar identities.[80]

Suggested Activities: Interview several friends or acquaintances about their perceptions of the impact of race today. Some possible questions are: "Does race really matter today?" and "Why do various forms of racial segregation continue to exist?" Analyze the responses to see what patterns are shown and what similarities and differences occur among respondents. Why do you think you got the results you did?

As a result of such experiences, African American students may develop an **oppositional culture** in schools by emphasizing forms of behavior different from the dominant culture. For instance, getting good grades is sometimes construed as "acting white," which can be interpreted as a negative image to be opposed. One explanation why such oppositional outlooks develop is found in the concept of **involuntary minorities**, that is, minority groups who have experienced a castelike status, such as African Americans whose ancestors were brought against their will to the New World as slaves, and Native Americans who were conquered and their lands colonized. Such involuntary minorities differ from voluntary minorities who came here by choice in search of economic, political, or religious opportunities or to flee oppression. Voluntary minorities are much more likely to accept a temporary second-rate status because they have opportunities to prove themselves worthy and to work their way up through society. However, involuntary minorities have a long history of oppression and exploitation and little experiential evidence showing that hard work will lead to success or remove discrimination; consequently, members of involuntary minorities, especially during their adolescence, are likely to develop oppositional cultures.[81]

In *Makes Me Wanna Holler*, Nathan McCall provides an autobiographical account of growing up as a black child in the South. Caught up in the construction of an oppositional culture, he and his peers realized that, despite all the rhetoric about equal opportunity and the rewards of hard work, generations of their forebears had been denied equality. They witnessed their own parents work hard yet never achieve the same standing as their white counterparts. As a result, these adolescents gave up on the system and developed oppositional behavior that resisted the expectations of both school and society. Academic achievement was scorned, and peer pressure was exerted on those who strove to excel. McCall and his peers set their own rules, including definitions of "respect" that could easily become deadly if violated.[82]

There are numerous factors behind such developments as resegregation and its attendant problems. One of them is how courts of law since the 1980s seem to have drifted away from their earlier efforts to enforce the *Brown* (1954) ruling to uphold equal educational opportunity as impacted by race. A recent indication of this drift can be seen in the decision of the U.S. Supreme Court in *Parents Involved in Community Schools v. Seattle School District No. 1 et al.* (2007). The case involved appeals from Seattle, Washington, and Jefferson County, Kentucky. Both public school systems had pupil assignment plans to ensure desired levels of racial balance in the schools. Seattle was never under court order to desegregate its schools, but it voluntarily adopted a classification system of either white or nonwhite to allocate attendance slots in its public high schools. Jefferson County, Kentucky, was previously under court order, but the order was dissolved in 2000 after the federal district court found it to be free of its segregated past. In 2001, Jefferson County voluntarily adopted a plan classifying pupils as black or other to decide attendance assignments among its elementary schools. Both the Seattle and the Jefferson County systems maintained that their policies were essential to meet requirements of law and to maintain appropriate racial diversity. Suit was brought against Seattle by an organization called Parents Involved in Community Schools and against Jefferson County, Kentucky, by Crystal D. Meredith on behalf of her son, Joshua. In both cases, the essential question was whether assigning children to different schools on the basis of race violated the equal protection clause of the Fourteenth Amendment. In Seattle the district court upheld the school district, and the ninth circuit court affirmed it. In Jefferson County the district court ruled that the school district had a compelling interest to maintain racial diversity, and the sixth circuit court affirmed this as well.[83]

The U.S. Supreme Court heard the appeals in 2006 and issued its decision on June 28, 2007. In a 5-to-4 split decision, the majority opinion was delivered by Chief Justice John Roberts, who held that whenever government distributes benefits or burdens on the basis of racial classifications, such actions must have strict scrutiny, and the school districts must show that their use of racial classifications is "narrowly tailored" to serve a "compelling" government interest, such as the need to remedy the effects of past discrimination. This was not applicable in *Parents v. Seattle,* because Seattle was never under court order to desegregate, and Jefferson County's prior court order had been dissolved. Another government interest would be to achieve student body diversity for its educational and pedagogical value, but neither Seattle nor Jefferson County made this a central part of their appeals. Seattle's classification scheme was simply white and non-white, while Jefferson's was black and other, both of which were anchored in "each district's specific racial demographics" rather than "any pedagogic concept of diversity." The opinion concluded that, "The way to stop discrimination on the basis of race is to stop discriminating on the basis of race."[84] The majority opinion reversed the decisions of each circuit court and remanded (or sent back) the cases to those courts for further deliberations.

In his dissenting opinion, however, Justice Stephen Breyer maintained that the two plans resembled many others adopted over the past 50 years to further the kind of racially integrated education promised by *Brown*. Indeed, the court not only "required, permitted, and encouraged" such plans, it also found them to be of "compelling" public interest. In sum, the majority opinion paid "inadequate attention" to past opinions; it not only reversed course but reached "the wrong conclusion" and erected new "legal rules that will obstruct efforts by state and local governments to deal effectively with the growing resegregation of public schools."[85]

Although *Parents v. Seattle* does not reach the forceful level of the unanimous (9-0) *Brown* decision of 1954, it provides a glance into an apparent doctrinal or ideological shift at even the highest court in the land, a shift that could have a heavy impact on educational policy in the future. It is necessary to keep in mind, however, that shifts in one direction or another have occurred in the past and will likely reoccur in the future as well.

Hope and renewal: reform efforts

Changing the conditions that give rise to such phenomena as resegregation and oppositional identities is a task of major proportions. Reform proposals range from relatively small steps that educators can implement in individual classrooms to system-wide and national reform agendas. Several help students seek mutual understanding and better tolerance levels, while others look at institutional frameworks and modes of financial support.

Race and culturally relevant education

Several approaches have been developed to ease cultural tensions involved in the education of immigrants and members of ethnic minorities, and they can also help with educational issues related to race. For example, multicultural education attempts to change schools through a variety of approaches, one of which is the use of curriculum materials that use not only Eurocentric but also racially diverse contributions to society. The goal is to encourage students to adopt a sense of pride and ownership of their respective cultural heritages. The curriculum should also help learners understand that some views of knowledge have been influenced by a racist past that might alienate students who identify with racial minorities. One major goal is to reduce racial prejudice in both schools and communities by helping students become aware of and resistant to contemporary racism and by encouraging them to question such views encountered in their own lives. An important pedagogical corollary is enabling teachers to adapt their instructional practices to fit the needs of students from racially diverse groups.[86]

Not only does culturally relevant education concern itself with the formal aspects of schooling but also with the informal or hidden curriculum. This includes attitudes, beliefs, and values that are not part of the official school program but are nevertheless transmitted to students informally, often unintentionally or covertly, through various socialization processes. Racist attitudes and beliefs filter through to students, perhaps from school programs and long-held educational beliefs and traditions but also from sources outside the schools, such as the entertainment industry, other mass media, and even family and community environments. Such influences inevitably affect how students think and act. Consider, for example, how sources in the larger society transmit notions about black and white mannerisms, musical preferences, clothing, and peer associations, and consider also how these are internalized by students and enforced by their peers. Culturally sensitive education attempts to address how students view themselves and the world, and it seeks not only to transform how race is treated in schools but to help students become positive agents of change in the larger society as well.[87]

> **Cross-Reference:** For a more extended discussion of multicultural education that includes ethnic differences other than race, see Chapter 5, Ethnicity and Education, pp. 208–256.

More specifically, the concept of culturally relevant teaching focuses on classroom practices designed to bridge the gap between white and black achievement. It proposes that teachers should avoid the "color blind" approach, which is often confused with fairness; instead, teachers should acknowledge students' racial identities, recognize that they are not all the same, and understand that fairness means acknowledging relevant differences. For example, traditionalists tend to see knowledge as something to be passed from teacher to student, while culturally relevant teaching sees knowledge as something for students to re-create, share, and critically analyze in the learning process. While traditional teaching often tilted toward routine, regimentation, and competition among students, culturally relevant teaching attempts to structure the social relations of the classroom in a familylike manner that emphasizes students cooperating and achieving shared goals of academic and cultural experience.

Successful teachers will go beyond the boundaries of their classrooms and reach out for parental and community involvement in delivering the curriculum, with emphasis on active student participation. Teachers also need to be aware of the political dimensions of teaching and see themselves as engaged with their students in efforts to bring about desirable changes in themselves and their communities.[88]

Standards, testing, and accountability

One of the major aims of the No Child Left Behind (NCLB) legislation of 2002 was to close the achievement gaps among students. Based on the principles of accountability, transparency, and choice, NCLB was supposed to catalyze change and raise student achievement nationwide.[89] Yet even NCLB proponents report that the achievement gap between white and black students (as measured by NAEP scores) actually increased after the introduction of NCLB accountability measures.[90]

Some critics state that Americans have now become so enamored with high-stakes testing that it is having undesirable consequences, particularly for segregated inner-city schools where an authoritarian emphasis on test scores is prevalent. They claim that NCLB squelches critical thinking, and its emphasis on punitive accountability measures serves to drive creative teachers away from the schools that most need them. In addition, NCLB makes impossible-to-achieve demands on the nation's schools that serve poor and minority students.[91]

Cross-Reference: For a more detailed discussion of "No Child Left Behind" (NCLB), see Chapter 2, School Governance and Control, pp. 54–103.

Afrocentric education and separate schooling

A concept of how to improve schooling for black children that has generated discussion and controversy is Afrocentric education. According to advocates, **Afrocentrism** means emphasizing African ideals in any analysis of African culture and behavior. Afrocentrism takes issue with social critics who view nihilism (loss of values and hope) as one of the major problems facing the African American community; rather, Afrocentric education attempts to lift up the values of the black community to counter media images of blacks as pathologically valueless, destructive, and violent when what has been lost is cultural centeredness. African Americans live in a "borrowed space" which they need to reclaim and define in their own terms in order to achieve the kind of transformation necessary for full participation in a multicultural society.[92]

A major goal of Afrocentric education is to infuse the African legacy into social and political change. It is concerned with Africans and people of African origins speaking for themselves rather than having their experiences analyzed only from a Western or Eurocentric view. It emphasizes "other ways of knowing" than just the accepted concepts of Western thought; instead, Afrocentric thinkers link knowledge with cosmology, society, religion, medicine, and tradition to arrive at "intellectual wholeness." An Afrocentric view of literature and orature (oral traditions and stories) differs from the Western view because the Afrocentric writer or speaker seeks peace, balance, and harmony among disparate views. As advocates see it, African Americans need to be understood in terms of African history, and Africans must be posited as subjects rather than objects of human history. In order to do this, Western cultural and scientific paradigms need to be questioned as the only true or valid approaches to any kind of study.[93]

Afrocentric education involves an African-centered pedagogy that recognizes the place of indigenous languages and fosters individual ties and services to family, community, nation, race, and world. It promotes social relationships and attitudes toward the world based on a positive, self-sufficient future for one's people without denying other peoples' worthiness and right to self-determination. This pedagogical approach fosters both cultural continuity and critical consciousness, a major goal of which is to help black American students overcome the "double consciousness" described by W. E. B. Du Bois, that is, black people having to view themselves as individuals and as stereotyped images projected by others. The pedagogy focuses on African American cultural conventions, speech patterns, storytelling schemas, and traditions of play in order to teach literacy, numeracy, and other subjects more effectively. Children's ways of thinking and knowing are used as cognitive scaffolding to provide a structural basis for teaching.[94]

The Afrocentric idea has met with criticism. Opponents argue that Afrocentric theories are based on faulty reasoning and that Afrocentrists circulate misinformation. One example is the claim that Socrates was an ancient African and that Greek philosophy was actually stolen from Egypt. According to critics, the reason Afrocentric interpretations of history are not taken seriously is that Afrocentrists see history as lacking objectivity and as widely open to self-serving interpretations by different nations and ethnic groups.[95]

Another criticism is that Afrocentric proponents are sometimes not qualified scholars in the fields in which they advance their theories. They tend to get entangled in contradictions when they simultaneously denounce Western civilization and attempt to take credit for it. A real danger of Afrocentrism, as its critics see it, is that its claim of insight into "black reality" and its race centered-ness in actuality promote a racial chauvinism that only widens the chasm between the races in the United States and parallels white racism in its claims to racial superiority.[96]

Educating black males

Both popular media and research literature frequently depict African American men as lacking in education, economic prowess, and social standing, portrayals that have become stereotypes. While many black males are successful in both school and society, as a group they experience a disproportionate rate of school failure, special education placement, and school suspension. To address these problems, several school reform efforts have been proposed specifically for black males. One includes many of the same suggestions made by Afrocentrists: Effective teachers of African American males form productive relationships with their students, expressing a special alliance through kinship-like terms or metaphors. They search for ways to motivate students based on the belief that effort, not ability, leads to success. This includes linking curriculum content to student interests outside school. In this view, effective teachers seek to build a classroom community among students and concern themselves with the whole student, helping each to become a good person. They teach and model personal values and use rituals and routines to reinforce those values. It is also maintained by some observers that African American males seem to prefer strict and caring teachers who not only give them support but also demand the best from them.[97]

Another approach consists in alternative schools and educational programs that are designed specifically to serve black males. Some plans call for all-male schools, others for school-wide programs in existing coeducation schools, still others for single classrooms within a school, pullout programs, before- and after-school programs, and mentoring and tutoring programs. The common themes in these programs are that they seek to build identity and self-esteem, teach academic values and skills, strengthen parent and community involve-ment, help students make the transition to manhood, and provide safe havens for black male children.

Currently, there are only a few all-male schools in operation. Examples are the Malcolm X African-Centered Academy and Marcus Garvey African-Centered Academy in Detroit, Michigan. The criticism of this approach is that such schools discriminate on the basis of race and gender—they admit only black male children. Such an approach seems to presume that the problems of black male children stem from female and nonblack children rather than the adult world with all of its customs, traditions, and controlling power over children. In addition, because they are Afrocentric in design, such schools are subject to the same criticisms directed against Afrocentrism in general. These schools have also been under legal attack for discrimination against females, but while some of the schools have admitted girls, their enrollment is nevertheless about 90 percent male.[98]

WEB: Suggested Reading 4.2.

Currently, many black youth repeatedly experience what amounts to a daily array of injustices, such as substandard schools, various forms of violence, and troubles with law enforcement. To counter such destructive forces and help youngsters become involved in civic life, a community-based approach designed to restore hope has surfaced in some urban environments. It is called radical healing and involves black youth challenging injustice and marginalization in constructive ways.

Based on the legacy of black radical activism of the 1960s and 1970s, radical healing seeks to provide young African Americans with opportunities to engage in caring relationships with adults and one another, make community connections, and build political consciousness and cultural identity. It involves post–civil rights activist organizations such as the Malcolm X Grassroots Movement that have come into existence, and the aim is to help these efforts and build activism among young black people using hip-hop culture, poetry, and film. Ultimately, the goal is not merely to provide young people with information about desired behaviors (such as stop smoking, stop being violent, and go to school) but to enable them to make productive choices, promote their interests, imagine a better life, and act on such visions.[99]

International comparison: South Africa

Framed by the South Atlantic Ocean and the Indian Ocean, the Republic of South Africa is located in the southernmost part of the continent of Africa. To the north it borders Botswana, Mozambique, Namibia, and Zimbabwe, while it completely surrounds Lesotho and almost surrounds Swaziland. Its population consists of approximately 49.1 million people, with an excessive mortality rate due to AIDS. Seventy-nine percent of all South Africans are black African, 9.6 percent white, 8.9 percent colored (mixed race), and 2.5 percent Indian/Asian. South Africa is a republic subdivided into nine provinces, with Pretoria as its capital. The first Dutch colonists came to the Cape of Good Hope (the southern tip of South Africa) in 1652, followed by the French Huguenots. In 1806, the British seized the Cape of Good Hope, causing the Dutch settlers (Boers) to migrate farther north. The second half of the nineteenth century saw the discovery of gold and diamonds, leading to wealth for some, increased immigration, and subjugation of native people. The Boers felt threatened by the non-Dutch-speaking immigrants, however, culminating in the Boer War (1899–1902), which ended in British victory. In 1910, what was called the Union of South Africa began to be run under a system of apartheid or legalized racial separation. During the 1990s, apartheid was politically dismantled and black majority rule established. Then-president Nelson Mandela signed the new constitution on December 10, 1996, and it went into effect on February 3, 1997. With plentiful natural resources and with some strong economic institutions, South Africa has a growing economy; nevertheless, it is plagued by high unemployment and leftover economic problems stemming from apartheid, notably the poverty and lack of opportunity for the most disadvantaged people, almost all of whom are black. Approximately 50 percent of the population lives below the poverty line.[100]

Race and education in South Africa

During precolonial times, the first systems of education in South Africa were informal in nature, meaning children were trained by families and tribes in what they needed to know in order to thrive and maintain their cultures. These systems were replaced by Christian schools instituted by the Dutch settlers and other European colonials. The primary purpose of colonial education directed at the indigenous African population was to teach the Dutch language for their easier conversion to Christianity. Such education was based on the Eurocentric assumption that the natives were primitive and in dire need of civilization as seen through European eyes. Such colonial thinking was steeped in racial viewpoints that demonized Africans and defined them as savages.[101]

After 1903, the educational system that had always been racially segregated in practice (de facto) was now segregated by law as well (de jure). It is interesting to note that, prior to the passage of Education Act No. 25 in 1907, pupils who were colored (of mixed race), while housed in separate schools from whites, were nevertheless educated in similar ways to white pupils because they were seen as racially closer to whites than blacks. After 1907, no distinctions were to be recognized between colored and native African pupils. They were all considered nonwhite in the system of apartheid. In effect, South African education was used by the white power structure to secure the continuous control and exploitation of the nonwhite population. The Bantu Education Act of 1953, for example, made provisions for white farm owners to act as managers of the schools serving black children, thus enabling them to close schools at will and disrupt black children's education whenever they were needed as laborers. White schools were well funded, while black schools had inadequate facilities, materials, and teachers. The result was undereducated black people who were prepared mainly for menial labor and economic exploitation. They were forced to seek out less skilled jobs and, in comparison to whites, grossly underpaid. Worsening educational conditions and poor employment opportunities for black high school graduates led to increasing civic unrest among the black population from the mid 1970s well into the 1980s. For example, in the 1976 student uprising in Soweto Township near Johannesburg, students demanded reform of the black schools. Not only in education but in other important sectors of South African society, a determined uprising against apartheid was occurring.[102]

From the mid-1980s, South African apartheid disintegrated, aided not only by internal resistance but also by internationally imposed economic sanctions. Nelson Mandela emerged victoriously in 1994 from the nation's first democratic elections, and political power was assumed by the black majority. Since then, the South African educational system has undergone significant change, although dramatic challenges continue, many of them residual effects from the system of apartheid. Given that the vast majority of the black population continues to live in poverty, for example, what type of school reform would be fair? Color blindness may sound appealing in a country where skin color was all that mattered for such a long time, but it may not be fair to ignore color now and deny the black population certain advantages they may need to catch up with whites and be able to compete more equitably. Today, South Africa sees itself as a multiracial democracy that has made great progress toward achieving better equality in educational institutions, school funding, and an outcomes-based curriculum, but opportunities to attend all schools, including high-quality schools that were formerly reserved for whites, can only be realized by urban black families wealthy enough to cover the fees and transportation costs involved. Likewise, black students still lag behind their white counterparts on measures of educational success.[103] In short, while de jure apartheid was abolished in South Africa, its legacy still remains to be more fully overcome.

> **For Further Reflection:** In both countries, South Africa and the United States, racial segregation is part of the recent past. What similarities and differences do you see between the two countries when it comes to how race continues to shape them?

> WEB: Suggested Reading 4.3.

Summary and conclusions

The problem of race in school and society has proved difficult to solve, and a great deal of time and energy has been devoted to it, as both the historical and contemporary records show. Some people today apparently think that enough has been done, but issues related to race continue to raise public concerns. There are divisions within existing society that relate to ethnicity, socioeconomic class, gender, and other stratifications, but none seem to pose quite the difficulties that race does.

Part of the problem faced by American society is that racial categorizations and racialization are rooted in the nation's unique history of slavery, particularly the way racism developed as a supporting ideology for it. Race was an important condition for white superiority and black inferiority, and one of its long-term legacies was racial segregation.

African Americans made some important advances after the Civil War, particularly in public education during Reconstruction, aided by the Freedmen's Bureau and northern missionary societies. A major factor was the desire of the freed people to educate themselves and their children for a new life of freedom. As the New South recovered from the war and became more industrialized and urbanized, new possibilities seemed ascendant, but the era of Jim Crow segregation brought white supremacy laws, black suppression, and segregated public institutions, conditions that endured for decades to come.

Following the model of industrial education established at the Hampton Institute in Virginia, Booker T. Washington attempted to make it the model of choice for the education of African Americans and their children. Emphasizing the values of industriousness, hard work, and economic goals over the acquisition of knowledge or social and political power, Washington made Tuskegee Institute the center for his policies, but his efforts to advance the cause of black people were severely hampered by Jim Crowism, and his attempts to appease the power structure, his Atlanta Compromise, came to haunt his efforts. W. E. B. Du Bois struggled with Washington over the direction education should take, particularly in the value of liberal higher education and the development of black intellectual leaders who would push for voting rights, civic equality, and educational opportunity for all.

In 1896, Jim Crow was bolstered by the Supreme Court's "separate but equal" doctrine in *Plessy v. Ferguson*. Segregated (but never equal) schools became legal and social fixtures until *Brown v. the Board of Education* in 1954, a case spearheaded by the NAACP that struck down state laws requiring racially segregated schools, while segregation caused by housing patterns and other socioeconomic conditions remained. Some education reformers then advocated programs (such as multicultural education and Afrocentric education) to better integrate black people and culture into the American mainstream. However, rapid change seemed elusive, and conditions continued to exist that stymied social and cultural integration.

Other countries grapple with the issues related to race as well, but while there are similarities with the American experience, there are distinct differences too. South Africa was troubled by a legalized system of segregation (apartheid) until recently and is still struggling to overcome its racist past. While recent and far-reaching educational reforms have occurred in South Africa, rooting out racial inequalities in education has proven very difficult.

One difficulty in addressing contemporary problems arising from race is that the magnitude of the problem often seems insurmountable. However, improvements have been made over time, more often than not in small incremental steps rather than dramatic leaps. The problem of race was centuries in the making, and it is unlikely to be solved in short order. Education alone cannot solve the remaining problems of race, but it can help if the lines of free inquiry and public debate are kept open. In other words, educational efforts to address lingering racial issues are not hopeless, but they will take commitment, patience, and broad societal support.

Vocabulary

Afrocentrism
all deliberate speed

Armstrong, Samuel Chapman
Atlanta Compromise
Brown v. the Board of Education (1954)
Brown II
de facto segregation
de jure segregation
desegregation
double taxation
Du Bois, W. E. B.
educational attainment
equal protection of the laws
dual school systems
Freedmen's Bureau
Hampton Institute
Houston, Charles Hamilton
industrial education
involuntary minorities
Jim Crow
Marshall, Thurgood
massive resistance
National Association for the Advancement of Colored People (NAACP)
New South
northern missionary societies
oppositional culture
passive resistance
Plessy v. Ferguson (1896)
race
racialization
racism
Reconstruction
resegregation
segregation
separate but equal
social construct
Talented Tenth
Tuskegee Institute
Tuskegee Machine
Washington, Booker T.

Notes

1 Studs Terkel, *Race* (New York: The New Press, 1992).

2 Audrey Smedley, *Race in North America* (Boulder, CO: Westview Press, 1999); and Theodore W. Allen, *The Invention of Whiteness* (New York: Verso, 1997).

3 Frederick Douglass, "The Color Line," 567, Electronic Text Center, University of Virginia Library, at http://etext.virginia.edu/toc/modeng/public/DouColo.html (accessed on April 12, 2010); Dante Puzzo, "Racism and the Western Traditions," *Journal of the History of Western Ideas* 15, no. 4 (October–December, 1964), 579; Smedley, 17, 39; and Spencer Wells, *The Journey of Man: A Genetic Odyssey* (New York: Random House, 2002), 30–33, 53–55. The authors wish to express appreciation to Professor Dirk Philipsen, a historian at Virginia State University, for his suggestions concerning this topic.

4 W. E. B. Du Bois, *The Souls of Black Folk* (Boston: Bedford Books, 1997), 45; Howard Winant, *Racial Conditions: Politics, Theory, Comparisons* (Minneapolis: University of Minnesota Press, 1994), 22.

5 James D. Anderson, *The Education of Blacks in the South, 1860–1935* (Chapel Hill: The University of North Carolina Press, 1988), 1–2.

6 Carter G. Woodson, *The Education of the Negro Prior to 1861* (Washington, DC: Associated Publishers, 1919). See particularly Chapter 4 (70–92) and Chapter IX (205–228); and Anderson, 4–7.

7 Woodson, *The Education of the Negro Prior to 1861*, 115–117; Woodson, *The Negro in Our History*, 5th edn (Washington, DC: Associated Publishers, 1928), 159–160; Theodore Carter Delaney, Jr., "Founder's Day Lecture," Washington and Lee University, January 19, 2001, at http://home.wlu.edu/~delaneyt/Chavis.htm (accessed on April 13, 2010); and "John Chavis," Ligon History Project, at http://www.ncsu.edu/ligon/about/history/chavis.htm (accessed on April 13, 2010).

8 "About the Bureau," The Valley of the Shadow, at http://valley.lib.virginia.edu/VoS/fbureau/aboutbureau.html (accessed on April 23, 2010).

9 Anderson, 5–6, 11–12; "The American Missionary Association," at http://northbysouth.kenyon.edu/1998/edu/charleston/ama.htm (accessed on April 14, 2010); H. L. Morehouse, "The Work of the American Baptist Home Mission Society for the Negroes of the United States," at http://www.reformedreader.org/history/pius/chapter12c.htm (accessed on April 13, 2010); and Jay S. Stowell, "Methodist Adventures in Negro Education [1922]," at http://docsouth.unc.edu/church/stowell/stowell.html (accessed on April 13, 2010).

10 Anderson, 5–7.

11 J. L. Blair Buck, *The Development of Public Schools in Virginia, 1607–1952* (Richmond: Commonwealth of Virginia, State Board of Education, 1952), 65–93.

12 Anderson, 23, 285.

13 Henry Grady, *The New South and Other Addresses*, Edna H. L. Turpin, ed. (New York: Haskell House Publishers, [1904] 1969), 37; "Henry W. Grady sells the 'New South,'" at http://historymatters.gmu.edu/d/5745/ (accessed on April 13, 2010); and C. Vann Woodward, *Origins of the New South, 1877–1913*, vol. 9 of *A History of the South*, Wendell Holmes Stephenson and E. Merton Coulter, eds (Boston Rouge: Louisiana State University Press and the Littlefield Fund for Southern History of the University of Texas, 1951), 105–106;

14 James Leloudis, *Schooling the New South: Pedagogy, Self, and Society in North Carolina, 1880–1920* (Chapel Hill: University of North Carolina Press, 1996), 17–23, 177–181.

15 The origin of the term *Jim Crow* is obscure, but it may have originated with a stereotyped image arising from "Negro minstrels" in which white actors in "black face" depicted a ragged comic figure who danced with a hopping step called the Jim Crow. See C. Vann Woodward, *The Strange Career of Jim Crow*, 3rd edn (New York: Oxford University Press, 1974); and Ronald L. F. Davis, "Creating Jim Crow: In-Depth Essay," at http://www.jimcrowhistory.org/history/creating2.htm (accessed on April 13, 2010), and Susan Falck, "Jim Crow Legislation Overview," at http://www.jimcrowhistory.org/resources/lessonplans/hs_es_jim_crow_laws.htm (accessed on April 12, 2010).

16 Lewis Harvey Blair, *The Prosperity of the South Dependent Upon the Elevation of the Negro (1889)*, C. Vann Woodward, ed. (Boston: Little, Brown and Company, 1964), 122–151; Charles C. Bolton, *The Hardest Deal of All: The Battle for School Integration in Mississippi, 1870–1980* (Jackson: University Press of Mississippi, 2005), 5–6; and Robert W. Flournoy to Thaddeus Stevens, (20 November 1865), at http://www.sewanee.edu/faculty/Willis/Civil_War/documents/FlournoyStevens.html (accessed 7 April 2011).

17 Woodward, *Origins of the New South, 1877–1913*, 211–212, 350–368.

18 Justice Henry Billings Brown, "Opinion," Plessy v. Ferguson, 163 U.S. 537 (1896), at http://supct.law.cornell.edu/supct/html/historics/USSC_CR_0163_0537_ZO.html (accessed on April 13, 2010); and Justice John Marshal Harlan, "Dissent," at http://supct.law.cornell.edu/supct/html/historics/USSC_CR_0163_0537_ZD.html (accessed on April 13, 2010).

19 Considerable reliance was made on two sources of biographical material on Booker T. Washington: Washington's autobiography, *Up from Slavery* (New York: Penguin Books, 1986), and the two-volume biography by Louis R. Harlan, *Booker T. Washington: The Making of a Black Leader, 1856–1901* (New York: Oxford University Press, 1972), and *Booker T. Washington: The Wizard of Tuskegee, 1901–1915* (New York: Oxford University Press, 1983).

20 From Samuel C. Armstrong, "Editorial," *Southern Workman*, 6 (February, 1877), 10, as quoted in Harlan, *Booker T. Washington: The Making of a Black Leader, 1856–1901*, 74.

21 Booker T. Washington, *The Story of My Life and Work*, in *The Autobiographical Writings*, in *The Booker T. Washington Papers*, vol. 1, Louis R. Harlan and John W. Blassingame, eds (Urbana: University of Illinois, 1972), 172–178.

22 Booker T. Washington and W. E. B. Du Bois, *The Negro in the South: His Economic Progress in Relation to His Moral and Religious Development* (New York: The Citadel Press, 1970), 46–49, hereafter cited as *The Negro in the South*.

23 Anderson, 5–6, 71–75, and 101–107.

24 *The Negro in the South*, 159. Washington used the "cast down your bucket" metaphor in a story of a storm-battered ship off the coast of South America, in distress because of broken masts and exhausted drinking water. When asking a passing ship to share some drinking water, the reply came back, "Cast down your bucket where you are!" Unbeknownst to the startled crew, their stricken ship was drifting through the outflow of fresh water from the distant mouth of the Amazon River.

25 *The Negro in the South*, 115–116.

26 Ibid., 125; "Extracts from My Larger Education, 1911," in *The Booker T. Washington Papers*, vol. 1, 424, 427–429; and Harlan, *Booker T. Washington: The Making of a Black Leader, 1856–1901*, 229.

27 Manning Marable, *W. E. B. Du Bois: Black Radical Democrat* (Boston: Twayne Publishers, 1986). See also Du Bois, *The Autobiography of W. E. B. Du Bois: A Soliloquy on Viewing My Life from the Last Decade of Its First Century*, Herbert Aptheker, ed. (New York: International Publishers, 1968).

28 Marable, 43, 51; and Du Bois, *The Autobiography*, 209.

29 Anderson, 104.

30 Du Bois, *The Autobiography*, 236–237.

31 Ibid., 223.

32 Du Bois, "The Talented Tenth [1903]," in *W. E. B. Du Bois: Writings*, selections and notes by Nathan Huggins (New York: The Library of America, 1986), 842, 847.

33 Du Bois, "The Revelation of Saint Orgne [1938]," in *W. E. B. Du Bois: Writings*, 1052–1053; and Marable, 195–196.

34 Anderson, 82–86.

35 Ibid., 86, 130, 137, 153, and 247.

36 "Explanation of Database Topics and Organizations: Philanthropic Funds," Jackson Davis Collection of African American Educational Photographs, Small Special Collections Library, University of

Virginia Library at http://www2.lib.virginia.edu/small/collections/jdavis/about/topic.html (accessed on April 12, 2010).

37 Anderson, 245–46, 280; African American Registry, "The Peabody Fund Established," at http://www.aaregistry.com/african_american_history/1776/The_Peabody_Fund_established (accessed on April 13, 2010); and Peabody Institute—Peabody Archives, "George Peabody," at http://www.peabody.jhu.edu/1972 (accessed on April 13, 2010).

38 Anderson, 86, 137, and 153; and Valinda Littlefield. "Jeancs Teachers History, Goals and Duties, The Homemakers Clubs, Rosenwald Schools, Health Care Contribution," at http://education. state-university.com/pages/2135/Jeanes-Teachers.html (accessed on April 24, 2010). See also "Virginia E. Randolph," at http://www.co.henrico.va.us/about-henrico/history/virginia-e—randolph/ (accessed on April 24, 2010).

39 Anderson, 79; and Beverly Jones, "Rosenwald Schools," *The New Georgia Encyclopedia*, at http://www.georgiaencyclopedia.org/nge/ArticlePrintable.jsp?id=h-1113 (accessed on April 14, 2010).

40 Ibid., 179–181.

41 Ibid., 54–56.

42 Ibid., 168, 170–171.

43 Richard Kluger, *Simple Justice* (New York: Vintage Books, 1977), 256–257.

44 Robert Pratt, *The Color of their Skin: Education and Race in Richmond, Virginia 1954–1989* (Charlottesville: University Press of Virginia, 1992), 17.

45 *Brown v. Board of Education of Topeka, Kansas*, 347 U.S.483, 98L.Ed. 873, 74 S.Ct. 686 (1954), at http://supreme.justia.com/us/347/483/case.html (accessed on April 14, 2010).

46 *Brown v. Board of Education of Topeka*, 349 U.S. 294 (1955), at http://supreme.justia.com/us/349/294/case.html (accessed on April 14, 2010). In particular, see pp. 300, 301.

47 Pratt, 11.

48 Vonita White Foster and Gerald Anthony Foster, *Silent Trumpets of Justice: Integration's Failure in Prince Edward County* (Hampton, VA: U.B. & U.S. Communication Systems, 1993), 3.

49 Liva Baker, *Second Battle of New Orleans: The Hundred-Year Struggle to Integrate the Schools* (New York: Harper Collins, 1996), 377–80, 395–96, 401–02, 411, and 420–21; and Alan Wieder, *Race and Education: Narrative Essays, Oral Histories, and Documentary Photography*, Studies in Postmodern Theory of Education, vol. 47 (New York: Peter Land, 1997), 82, 83–87, and 109–110.

50 *Green v. County School Board of New Kent County* (1968), 391 U.S. 430, at http://supct.law.cornell.edu/supct/html/historics/USSC_CR_0391_0430_ZO.html (accessed on April 14, 2010).

51 *Swann v. Charlotte-Mecklenburg Board of Education* (1971), 402 U.S. 1, at http://supct.law.cornell.edu/supct/html/historics/USSC_CR_0402_0001_ZO.html (accessed on April 14, 2010).

52 Howard Ozmon and Sam Craver, *Busing: A Moral Issue* (Bloomington, IN: Phi Delta Kappa Educational Foundation, 1972).

53 Sheehan, 73–94, 138, 193–95, 246–256; and Joseph Watras, *Politics, Race, and Schools: Racial Integration, 1954–1994*, Studies in Education/Politics, Mark B. Ginsburg, ed. (New York: Garland Publishing, Inc., 1997), 17–24.

54 Pratt, 108–109.

55 Charles C. Bolton, *The Hardest Deal of All: The Battle over School Desegregation in Mississippi, 1870–1980* (Jackson: University Press of Mississippi, 2005).

56 W. E. B. Du Bois, "Races," *The Crisis*, vol. 2, no. 4: 157–158 (August 1911) at http://books.google.com/books?id=AFoEAAAAMBAJ&printsec=frontcover&lr=#v=onepage&q&f=true (accessed on 30 October 2010); Kwame Anthony Appiah, "The Uncompleted Argument: Du Bois and the Illusion of Race," in Naomi Zack et al., *Race, Class, Gender, and Sexuality: The Big Questions* (Malden, MA: Blackwell Publishers, 1998), 40; and Wells, *The Journey of Man: A Genetic Odyssey*.

57 Cornel West, *Race Matters* (Boston: Beacon Press, 1993); and Christopher Knaus, *Race, Racism and Multiraciality in American Education* (Bethesda: Academic Press, 2006), 21.

58 Knaus, 21.

59 Amanda E. Lewis, *Race in the Schoolyard* (New Brunswick: Rutgers University Press, 2003) 12; and Beverly Daniel Tatum, *Why Are All the Black Kids Sitting Together in the Cafeteria* (New York: Basic Books, 1997), 102–103.

60 Tatum, 102–103.

61 Judith Blau, *Race in the Schools: Perpetuating White Dominance?* (Boulder, CO: Lynne Rienner, 2003), 205. See also Michael Omni and Howard Winant, *Racial Formations in the United States* (New York: Routledge and Kegan Paul, 1986).

62 Stephen Small, "The Contours of Racialization: Structures, Representations and Resistance in the United States" in *Race, Identity, and Citizenship: A Reader*, R. D. Torrs et al., eds (Malden, MA: Blackwell Publishers, 1999), 47–64; "Table 695, People Below Poverty Level and Below 125 Percent of Poverty Level by Race and Hispanic Origin: 1980 to 2007," *Statistical Abstract of the United States* (2010), at http://www.census.gov/compendia/statab/2010/tables/10s0695.pdf (04-20–2010), "Table 681, Money Income of Families—Median Income by Race and Hispanic Origin in Current and Constant (2007) Dollars: 1990 to 2007," at http://www.census.gov/compendia/statab/2010/tables/10s0681.pdf (accessed on April 20, 2010); Vanessa R. Wight and Michelle Chau, "Basic Facts About Low-income Children," National Center for Children in Poverty, at http://www.nccp.org/publications/pub_892.html (accessed on April 20, 2010).

63 West, 12.

64 Jonathan Kozol, *The Shame of the Nation: The Restoration of Apartheid Schooling in America* (New York: Crown Publishers, 2005), 10; and Douglas S. Massey and Nancy A. Denton, *American Apartheid: Segregation and the Making of the Underclass* (Cambridge, MA: Harvard University Press, 1993), 1–2.

65 Faustine Jones-Wilson, "The State of African-American Education," in *Going to School: The African-American Experience* (Albany: State University of New York Press, 1990); and "Status Dropout Rates by Race/Ethnicity" (Figure 20-1), National Center for Educational Statistics, U.S. Department of Education, at http://nces.ed.gov/programs/coe/2009/charts/chart20.asp?popup= true (accessed on April 20, 2010).

66 The Nation's Report Card, Reading 2009, at http://nationsreportcard.gov/reading_2009/reading_2009_report/ (accessed on April 20, 2010); and Stephen J. Caldas and Carl L. Bankston III, *Forced to Fail: The Paradox of School Desegregation* (Westport, CO: Praeger, 2005), 195–198.

67 Office of Educational Research and Improvement, National Center for Education Statistics, U.S. Department of Education, *Indicator of the Month: Educational Attainment*, at http://nces.ed.gov/pubs2000/2000010.pdf (accessed on April 20, 2010).

68 Ayana Douglas-Hall and Michelle Chau, "Parents' Low Education Leads to Low Income, Despite Full-Time Employment," National Center for Children in Poverty, at http://www.nccp.org/publications/pub_786.html (accessed on May 10, 2010).

69 Donald Joseph Yarosz and William Steven Barnett, "Who Reads to Young Children: Identifying Predictors of Family Reading Activities," in *Reading Psychology*, vol. 22, 22, 67–81 (2001), at http://nieer.org/resources/research/WhoReads.pdf (accessed on April 20, 2010).

70 Nancy Levi Arnez, "Desegregation of Public Schools: A Discriminatory Process." *Journal of Afro-American Issues*, vol. 4, no. 2: 274–282 (Spring 1976); and Michele Foster, "The Politics of Race: Through the Eyes of African-American Teachers," *Journal of Education*, vol. 172, no. 3: 123–141 (1990).

71 Vanessa Siddle Walker, *Their Highest Potential—An African American School Community in the Segregated South* (Chapel Hill: The University of North Carolina Press, 1996).

72 Maike Philipsen, *Race and the Cultural Consequences of a School Closing* (Cresskill, NJ: Hampton Press, 1999).

73 See, for example, what happened in Richmond, Virginia, in Pratt, 108–109.

74 Maike Philipsen, "The Second Promise of Brown," *The Urban Review*, vol. 26, no. 4: 257–272 (December 1994).

75 Pratt, 108–109.

76 Gary Orfield and Chungmei Lee, *Historic Reversals, Accelerating Resegregation, and the Need for New Integration Strategies*, A Report of the Civil Rights Project, UCLA, August 2007, 5–8, at http://www.civilrightsproject.ucla.edu/research/deseg/reversals_reseg_need.pdf (accessed on April 20, 2010). See also Gary Orfield and Chungmei Lee, "Segregation 50 Years after *Brown*: A Metropolitan Change," in *Beyond Silenced Voices: Class, Race, and Gender in United States Schools*, rev. edn, Lois Weis and Michelle Fine, eds (Albany: State University of New York Press, 2005), 17–20.

77 Jerome E. Morris, *Troubling the Waters: Fulfilling the Promise of Quality Public Schooling for Black Children* (New York: Teachers College Press: 2009), 139–145.

78 Charles T. Clotfelter, Helen F. Ladd, and Jacob L. Vigdor, "Classroom-Level Segregation and Resegregation in North Carolina," in *School Resegregation: Must the South Turn Back?* John Charles Boger and Gary Orfield, eds (Chapel Hill: The University of North Carolina Press, 2005), 70–86.

79 Tamar Lewin, "Growing Up, Growing Apart: Fast Friends Try to Resist the Pressure to Divide by Race," *The New York Times* (June 25, 2000), at http://www.nytimes.com/2000/06/25/us/growing-up-growing-apart.html (accessed May 10, 2010).

80 Tatum, 52–74.

81 Signithia Fordham and John Ogbu, "Black Students' School Success: Coping with the Burden of 'Acting White,'" *The Urban Review*, vol. 18, no. 3: 176–206 (1986); and John Ogbu, "Variability in Minority School Performance: A Problem in Search of An Explanation," *Anthropology and Education Quarterly*, vol. 18, no. 4: 312–335 (December 1987).

82 Nathan McCall, *Makes Me Wanna Holler: A Young Black Man in America* (New York: Random House, 1994).

83 "Syllabus," *Parents Involved in Community Schools v. Seattle School District No. 1* (551 U. S.____ [2007]), at http://www.law.cornell.edu/supct/pdf/05-908P.ZS (accessed on April 20, 2010).

84 Opinion of Chief Justice John G. Roberts, Jr., in *Parents Involved in Community Schools v. Seattle School District No. 1* (551 U. S. ___ [2007]), at http://www.law.cornell.edu/supct/pdf/05-908P.ZO (accessed on April 20, 2010), 11–15, 40–41.

85 Dissent of Justice Stephen G. Breyer in *Parents Involved in Community Schools v. Seattle School District No. 1*, at http://www.law.cornell.edu/supct/pdf/05-908P.ZD1 (accessed May 13, 2010). See also Nicole Love, "Parents Involved in Community Schools V. Seattle School District No. 1: the Application of Strict Scrutiny to Race-conscious Student Assignment Policies in K–12 Public Schools," *Boston College Third World Law Journal*, vol. 29, no. 1: 115–149 (Winter 2009).

86 James A. Banks, *Cultural Diversity and Education*, 5th edn (Boston: Pearson, 2006), 5.

87 James A. Banks, "Multicultural Education: Characteristics and Goals," in *Multicultural Education: Issues and Perspectives*, 6th edn, James A. Banks and Cherry A. M. Banks, eds. (Hoboken, NJ: Wiley, 2007), 1–31; and Sonia Nieto, "School Reform and Student Achievement: A Multicultural Perspective," in ibid., 387–407.

88 Gloria Ladson-Billings, *The Dreamkeepers: Successful Teachers of African American Children* (San Francisco: Jossey-Bass, 1994).

89 John E. Chubb (ed.), *Within Our Reach: How America Can Educate Every Child* (Lanham, MD: Rowman & Littlefield Publishers: 2005), ix.

90 Eric A. Hanushek, "Impacts and Implications of State Accountability Systems," in *Within Our Reach*, 101–102.

91 Paul Street, *Segregated Schools: Educational Apartheid in Post-Civil Rights America* (New York: Routledge, 2005), 177.

92 Molefi Kete Asante, *The Afrocentric Idea* (Philadelphia: Temple University Press, 1998).

93 Asante, 20, 179.

94 Haki Madhubuti and Safisha Madhubuti, *African-Centered Education: Its Value, Importance, and Necessity in the Development of Black Children* (Chicago: Third World Press, 1994), 21–23.

95 Mary Lefkowitz, *Not Out of Africa: How Afrocentrism Became an Excuse to Teach Myth as History* (New York: Basic Books, 1997).

96 D'Souza, 364–381.

97 Edmund W. Gordon, "Foreword," in *African American Males in School and Society: Practices and Policies for Effective Education*, Vernon C. Polite and James Earl Davis, eds (New York: Teachers College Press, 1999), ix.; Vernon C. Polite and James Earl Davis, "Introduction," in *African American Males in School and Society*; and Michele Foster and Tryphenia B. Peele, "Teaching Black Males: Lessons from the Experts," in Polite and Davis, 8–19.

98 "Malcolm X Academy," http://www.detroit.k12.mi.us/schools/school/384 (accessed on May 13, 2010); "Garvey Academy," at http://www.detroit.k12.mi.us/schools/school/313 (accessed May 5, 2010); and Ronnie Hopkins, *Educating Black Males: Critical Lessons in Schooling, Community, and Power* (Albany: State University of New York Press, 1997).

99 Shawn A. Ginwright, *Black Youth Rising: Activism & Radical Healing in Urban America* (New York: Teachers College Press, 2010), 144–147.

100 "South Africa," *The World Factbook*, at https://www.cia.gov/library/publications/the-world-factbook/geos/sf.html (accessed on October 30, 2010).

101 Ali A. Abdi, *Culture, Education, and Development in South Africa* (Westport, CT: Bergin & Garvey, 2002), 1–7.

102 Ibid., 23–69. For background on schools and political struggle in South Africa prior to 1988, see Simphiwe A. Hlatshwayo, *Education and Independence: Education in South Africa, 1658–1988* (Westport, CT: Greenwood Press, 2000), 69–101.

103 Edward B. Fiske and Helen F. Ladd, *Elusive Equity: Education Reform in Post-Apartheid South Africa* (Washington, DC: Brookings Institution Press, 2004), 1–2, 5–10, 232–234.

5

Ethnicity and Education

Chapter objectives

- To explore the meaning and usage of such terms as *ethnicity, pluralism,* and *assimilation.*
- To clarify the significance of ethnicity in shaping educational institutions, laws, policies, and practices.
- To show the variety of challenges faced by selected groups.
- To describe the educational experiences of various ethnic groups.
- To analyze the controversial nature of school reform efforts such as bilingual and multicultural education.
- To compare immigrant policies and experiences with another country.

Opening questions

1. Why does ethnicity matter in today's educational institutions?
2. What roles have assimilation and Americanization played in American education past and present?
3. What effect does ethnicity have on schooling and education?
4. How do the backgrounds and experiences of different ethnic groups impact American education?
5. Why are bilingual and multicultural education controversial, and how does the controversy relate to differing understandings of the good society?
6. What reforms have been attempted to improve the educational experience of immigrant and ethnic minorities?
7. What can be learned by comparing and contrasting the significance of ethnicity in the United States with another country?

The issue

Immigrants and their descendants have helped make the United States a nation of diverse cultural backgrounds, national origins, and ethnic identities. It is often called a "nation of immigrants" in both a past and present sense. This may even apply to the Native Americans, too, for there is growing archaeological evidence that their ancestors probably came in several successive waves, perhaps not only from Asia, but possibly other points of origin as well. Thus, when European explorers arrived there were already a variety of indigenous peoples in place.

The United States has also often been called a "melting pot of nations." Exactly when this metaphor originated is uncertain, but a popular play titled *The Melting Pot*, written by Israel Zangwill in 1908, certainly helped spread it. Two central characters in the play are Vera Revendal, a genteel social worker in an urban settlement house, and David Quixano, a local musician providing an evening's musical entertainment for the house's immigrant clientele. David tells Vera of his own immigrant experience as a Russian Jew. In an emotionally charged passage that audiences seemed to love, David describes America as "God's crucible," a "great Melting-pot" where immigrants from around the world are melted down and recast. They come from various national origins, languages, and histories: "But you won't be long like that, brothers, for these are the fires of God you've come to," a seething pot that mingles "East and West, and North and South, the palm and the pine, the pole and the equator, the crescent and the cross," a place where people from "all races and nations" may have hope in the future.[1]

The melting pot metaphor stuck in the popular imagination, but it proves less accurate than might first be assumed. Immigration is surrounded by insecurities and contentiousness today, and so it was in Zangwill's day. For illustration, the issue may be divided into two broad perspectives. On the one hand were those who valued cultural unity. They believed that immigrants from northern and western Europe would better fit American society and that access should be limited to the preferred kinds of people. On the other hand were those who valued cultural diversity. They believed immigrants added valuable economic and cultural perspectives and should be allowed to contribute to the development of American society.

Today similar tensions are present, found not only in political wrangling about immigration and border security but also in arguments over the most appropriate ways to educate the newcomers. Such tensions are difficult to ease, but it is helpful to remember that they have surfaced in one way or another with each new wave of immigrants. What both the unity and the diversity sides seem to forget is that society is always changed, if only slightly, by what each immigrant group adds, just as immigrants are changed by giving up some things and gaining others in the process of becoming Americans.[2]

Schools reflect the society that creates and supports them; hence, the unity-diversity tension is found in schools, too, evident in such current issues as whether the languages immigrant children bring with them should be recognized in school programs or whether the children should be immersed in English-only instruction.

Since the beginning of public school systems in the nineteenth century, one of their assumed obligations was **assimilation**, or fitting immigrant children as quickly as possible into American lifestyles and common values. By the early twentieth century, this process came to be called **Americanization**, or educating immigrant children to shed their parents' cultures and embrace American ways. There are those who continue to believe a top priority of the schools should be the rapid assimilation of newcomers to protect national unity from perceived internal and external threats. There are also those who champion more deliberative educational approaches that respect differences and allow cultural diversity.

An important ingredient of this continuing tension is the matter of **ethnicity**, or characteristics connected with national, racial, linguistic, religious, or other cultural origins. In raw numbers, the United States is now undergoing the greatest immigrant wave in its history, and ethnic diversity is not only a demographic fact but also a heated political issue. Such conditions directly impact the schools, and educators need to be as knowledgeable as possible about them.

Cross–Reference: For a discussion of race and education see Chapter 4, Race and the Education of African Americans, pp. 155–207.

For Further Reflection: How do ethnic identities affect your own life and the lives of your friends and acquaintances? How are such identities shaped, and what factors in the larger society influence them? How are those identities historically and socially based, or how are they matters of individual choice? What impact, if any, does ethnicity have on your education?

Background

Diversity has been and continues to be a fact in American education. In order to get a better grasp of that diversity, the following sections examine representative samples of the ethnic spectrum and their educational experiences, including Native Americans and Polish, Italian, Chinese, and Mexican immigrants.

American Indian education before "discovery"

When Christopher Columbus arrived in 1492, he called the native peoples Indians, erroneously believing he had reached India, and the name stuck. As scientific inquiry into American Indian origins developed, evidence indicated that they migrated from Asia across the Bering Strait, a land bridge, approximately 10,000 years ago, but recent findings suggest a human presence as early as 25,000 years ago. Some scholars maintain that a variety of prehistoric peoples penetrated the Americas, not only from Asia and the regions of the Pacific but perhaps Europe and Africa too.[3]

Today, most Americans probably think of their early history as the "discovery" of the New World, seldom considering how the arrival of Europeans brought a "new world" to American Indians too. Not only were they confronted by invaders seeking land, but they also faced diseases to which they lacked immunity, new technology on which they became dependent, and missionaries who wanted to convert them. This started American Indians on a painful historic journey of decline and revival.[4]

No one knows exactly how many indigenous people were present in 1492, but their population clearly shrank to a historic low in the 1890s, from which many feared they could not recover. A century later, however, the 1990 census reported approximately 1,937,000 American Indians in at least 556 recognized tribal entities, with names that reach across time: Apache, Cherokee, Cheyenne, Choctaw, Iroquois, Navaho, Seminole, Sioux, and Shoshone, to name a few. In 2000, the Census Bureau combined the population count of both the American Indian and "Alaska Native" into one population category of American Indian/Alaska Native (AI/AN), which then stood at approximately 2.66 million persons. By 2008, the AI/AN population estimate was approximately 3.1 million.[5]

Prior to the arrival of Europeans, the young learned their tribe's way of life from their elders, from tribal lore and legends, and from observation and participation in daily life. A glimpse into this process may be seen in the oral traditions of the Catawbas, a small tribe in the Catawba River valley along the border of the Carolinas. The Catawbas believed that stories developed children's minds and showed them how to live. Oral traditions were passed down the generations, with stories about tribal adventures, trials, and triumphs and with children taken to old town sites, battlefields, and other locales to drive home the lessons. There were also stories about nature and the spirit world: how the chipmunk got its stripes and the robin its red breast, what caused storms or cured disease, or what pleased or displeased the spirit world. From divining the meaning of a falling star to making pottery, such education helped youngsters learn the Catawba world.[6]

Another glimpse was provided in 1879 by Chief Joseph of the Nez Perce tribe in western Idaho. Traditions were passed from parent to child since time immemorial, laws that taught the young to treat others as they were treated, never be the first to break a bargain, always speak the truth, and never take another's belongings without paying. They were taught that the Great Spirit sees and hears everything and that people are given the spiritual homes they deserve.[7]

Storytelling continues to this day to transmit societal information, norms, and values. Think about your family and its traditions. What role do stories play? What, if any, do they play in schools? How could educators capitalize even more creatively on the educational values of stories?

WEB: Suggested Reading 5.1.

Education after "discovery": some examples

The Cherokees were a large, powerful tribe in the Appalachian highlands stretching from Georgia to Kentucky. Christian missionaries came among the Cherokees in the early 1800s, and one of their most important outposts was the Brainerd Mission in Tennessee, established in 1817. Among its goals was saving souls and "civilizing" the Cherokees through education. Such efforts were encouraged by the U.S. government and also the Cherokee Council, but traditional Cherokees rejected being "civilized" at the cost of losing their traditions.[8]

Around 1820, a Cherokee named **Sequoyah** introduced a syllabet that enabled the Cherokees to write and read their own language, and its use spread rapidly. By 1830, one missionary felt confident enough to report that, while some Cherokees could read and write English, a "large majority between childhood and middle age" could read and write Cherokee. Nevertheless, the state of Georgia took steps to drive the Cherokees from their homeland to the designated Indian Territory in Oklahoma. Georgia's acts were appealed to the U.S. Supreme Court, which ruled that the Cherokees held their lands legally and Georgia had no right to remove them. Despite the court's decision, under the direction of President Andrew Jackson, the Cherokees were forcibly removed to the Oklahoma Territory in 1838, a death-dealing travesty known as the Trail of Tears.[9] Needless to say, this was a setback to educational efforts.

Textbox: Sequoyah

According to contemporaneous accounts by white observers, when Sequoyah (1770?–1843) first encountered printed English books, he became convinced that a writing system was possible for the Cherokees as well. Uneducated by Euro-American standards, Sequoyah developed a system of 86 abstract symbols representing the syllabic sounds of the Cherokee language (technically, a syllabet rather than an alphabet). Skeptics have asked how a supposedly illiterate individual could develop a sophisticated writing system, and some respondents claim the Cherokees had a written language long before whites arrived, confined to a small and secretive group of tribal scribes of which Sequoyah became a member. However, no hard evidence has been produced, and none of Sequoyah's own writings survive to provide his version of the syllabet's origins. The following facts are well documented, however: In 1821 the Cherokee Council (the Cherokee governing body) officially adopted the writing system Sequoyah provided, and its use can be seen in the Cherokee translation of the Bible in 1825, a Cherokee constitution in 1827, and the newspaper *Cherokee Phoenix*, which began publication in 1828. Today, the Cherokee people hold Sequoyah in high regard, and his syllabet occupies an honored position in Cherokee cultural and educational traditions. Furthermore, his statue in the the U.S. Capitol and the giant redwood tree named after him (the sequoia) serve to commemorate his work.

Sources: Margaret Bender, *Signs of Cherokee Culture: Sequoyah's Syllabary in Eastern Cherokee Life* (Chapel Hill: The University of North Carolina Press, 2002), 25–36; Grant Foreman, *Sequoyah* (Norman; University of Oklahoma Press, 1938). See also "Sequoyah (ca. 1770–ca. 1840)," The New Georgia Encyclopedia, at http://www.georgiaencyclopedia.org/nge/Article.jsp?id=h-618 (accessed on October 13, 2010).

Cherokee society became divided between "mixed bloods," who accepted Christianity and schooling (about 25 percent of the population), and "full bloods" (about 75 percent of the population), who stuck to traditional tribal ways. Among the missionaries sent to the Cherokee homeland was the father-son team of Evan and John B. Jones, who sympathized with the traditionalists and went with the tribe to Oklahoma in 1838. When the Cherokee Council established a public school system in 1841, the Joneses championed bilingual education, but it was not until 1866 that the younger Jones was authorized to write bilingual textbooks; thus, the Cherokees developed the first bilingual and bicultural school system in the United States. By the end of the nineteenth century, most Cherokees were better educated than many white Oklahoma neighbors. The Cherokee school system remained in operation until tribal control dissolved with the creation of the state of Oklahoma in 1907, at which time Cherokee children began attending that new state's public schools.[10]

Education and culture brokers

Educated American Indians often served as "culture brokers" between their tribes and the Euro-Americans. Although the schools could alienate students from their tribal cultures, both whites and Indians needed interpreters and mediators to communicate effectively with one another. Some whites thought the Indians needed education to be "civilized," but many Indians had their own views about white people's education. In 1744, Benjamin Franklin recorded the reactions of several chieftains to what some of their young men learned at the College of William and Mary: Upon returning home after years of schooling, the graduates could no longer run swiftly, live in the woods, or hunt and kill deer; in the eyes of the chiefs, they were no good as advisors, hunters, or warriors and, in effect, were "good for nothing." However, a Catawba named John Nettles successfully completed William and Mary in the early 1770s, and upon returning to South Carolina, he helped Catawba leaders in their dealings with whites and also translated for whites who negotiated with Catawbas. Similarly, Cherokee students at the Brainerd Mission in Tennessee defended Cherokee traditions before their white teachers, but they also expressed affection for their teachers and believed they did important work for the Cherokee people.[11]

> **For Further Reflection:** Many people serve as culture brokers at some point in their lives. An example is the introduction of a friend to one's own family and the negotiation of differences, however subtle, between the friend's and the family's cultural conventions. Think of examples in your life. What can be learned for the world of schooling? Are schools culture brokers of some sort? If so, how? How do your own experiences with cultural brokerage inform your future professional practice in which you may have to function as the culture broker for students and society at large?

National policy and American Indian education

Where education was a part of national policy concerning American Indians, it was viewed as a way to **acculturate** them to Euro-American ways. By the late nineteenth century, the dominant government policy for Indian education was akin to the Americanization of foreign immigrants, the aim being greater cultural unity. In 1880, the U.S. Board of Indian Commissioners stated that life as "savage wanderers" was untenable, and American Indian children must attend common schools and industrial schools.[12] Some policy makers wanted Indian children to attend regular public schools, but on large western reservations with sparse populations, long travel distances, and poor economic conditions, regular public schools were not close by. Besides, even where the children lived near public schools, they were usually denied access by state and local authorities, not simply because their education was a federal responsibility but also because of white prejudice against them.

For a considerable period, the U.S. government viewed American Indian tribes as separate but dependent nations. Between 1794 and 1871, the government negotiated more than 400 treaties with various tribes, and at least 120 had educational provisions. At first, the federal government allowed Christian missionaries to provide educational services through small grants from the Civilization Fund established by Congress in 1819. With the Indian Appropriation Act of 1871, however, all treaty making with the tribes ended, and thereafter the government assumed direct responsibility for American Indian education.[13]

By the late nineteenth century, American Indians were under extreme duress from warfare, disease, and destitution; they seemed to be a vanishing people. Thomas J. Morgan, commissioner of the Bureau of Indian Affairs (BIA), argued that while the Indians must conform to national interests, they must also have a proper education. Unfortunately, many parents would not send their children to BIA schools, and Thomas took this to mean "a new generation of savages" unless the children were attracted to the schools with kindness where possible but compulsion when necessary, including the withholding of rations and the use of the U.S. military to get the children into BIA schools.[14]

The schools

By the beginning of the twentieth century, there were at least five kinds of schools for American Indian children: off-reservation boarding schools, on-reservation boarding schools, on-reservation day schools, public schools, and traditional missionary schools. On-reservation boarding schools and day schools produced the least resentment, while the most notorious were the BIA's **off-reservation boarding schools**. In 1879, Richard Henry Pratt established the first one in Carlisle, Pennsylvania, to isolate students from tribal influences and "to educate the Indian out of them." Using the Carlisle model, the BIA established boarding schools in the Oklahoma Territory in 1887. Children were taken from their families and tribal communities, sent to distant boarding schools with students from other tribes and traditions, and permitted to go home only for brief vacations. Once a child entered the school, Americanization started with baths, haircuts, uniforms, military discipline, English names, and English-only language enforcement. Rigid rules, strict discipline, and homesick students produced runaways and resentful parents.[15]

However, the boarding schools sometimes inadvertently perpetuated tribal identities. For example, Kiowa leaders and parents encouraged school attendance at the Rainy Mountain Boarding School in Oklahoma, even though they resented heavy-handed policies and practices. Kiowa usage was strictly forbidden, but former students recalled speaking it in private and away from school. They learned English, and many later found jobs in the white economy;

nevertheless, they retained a strong sense of Kiowa identity. In such cases, boarding schools could not erase Indian identities because the abilities of the children to adapt were underestimated.[16]

Underfunded schools meant inadequate food and the use of student labor to supplement meager budgets, with students not properly educated for either their native cultures or the white world. By 1920, the results seemed abundantly clear: A combination of unrealistic education and disease, malnutrition, short life expectancy, and white encroachments on tribal lands all produced bleak prospects for the American Indian people.[17]

Early twentieth-century education reforms

By the 1920s, a new breed of reformers sought to change the poor conditions of American Indian schools; consequently, Congress increased funds for BIA schools and also subsidized public school systems that enrolled Indian students. With the Indian Citizenship Act in 1924, Congress also finally extended to American Indians the full rights of U.S. citizens. By 1930, the BIA reported that approximately 90 percent of the children were enrolled in the schools, but poor health, malnutrition, an unsuitable curriculum, and an average attainment of only fifth grade continued to plague the schools.[18]

In the 1930s, reforms by both the Hoover and Roosevelt administrations brought changes, such as reservation community schools, **cross-cultural education** in both tribal and outside cultures, Indian art and culture in the schools, and better Indian access to and federal funding for public schools that accepted Indian students. Unfortunately, the economic realities of the Great Depression hampered those reforms, and World War II brought them to a standstill.[19]

During the war, American Indians provided valuable military service to the country, and some policy makers wanted to give them greater independence as American citizens. Afterward, however, the onset of the Cold War drew public focus onto international affairs, and the BIA fell back on the Americanization track, with vocational education and job-training programs to move people off reservations into urban job markets. That policy weakened the previous reforms, and movement off the reservations threatened tribal cultures and properties. In the 1960s, a new generation of activist leaders arose, aided by such organizations as the National Congress of American Indians (NCAI) and the American Indian Movement (AIM), and they helped redirect Indian education through the remainder of the twentieth century.[20]

An era of self-determination?

It could be said that the historic goal of all American Indian tribes was freedom to determine their own fates. In the late 1960s and the early 1970s there was growing recognition of ethnic minorities, and a developing body of scholarly research on American Indian history and culture documented the failed government policies and the diminution of tribal cultures. In 1969, the U.S. Senate issued the Kennedy Report, a scathing indictment of coercive governmental and educational policies, calling them a "national disgrace."[21]

Congress passed the Indian Education Act of 1972 with funds stipulated for community-based schools and bilingual and culturally relevant curriculum materials, and the **Indian Self-Determination and Education Assistance Act of 1975** allowed the BIA to make contracts with tribal governments to run their own schools, giving them greater control over curriculum, instruction, and school management, but again high dropout rates, low achievement levels, and inadequate funding continued to be problems. In short, the trends that emerged in the closing decades of the twentieth century were promising, but their full effectiveness remained to be seen.[22]

Immigrant waves to the United States

The history of immigration to the United States may be divided into phases or waves. The first wave included a variety of western European immigrants who arrived in the seventeenth and eighteenth centuries, among whom the English language soon became dominant. In the first half of the nineteenth century, a second wave was mainly composed of Irish and German immigrants. Following the Civil War, a third wave of immigrants (lasting roughly from the 1870s to the 1920s) came from southern and eastern Europe, most of whom settled in the cities. World War I interrupted the flow, but in the mid-1920s Congress imposed country-by-country quotas on immigration, which slowed it to a trickle. In the 1960s, however, reforms eliminated the quotas and helped set the stage for the fourth wave of immigration, which is—numerically speaking—the largest yet and which is still occurring, mostly from countries in Latin America and Asia.

Historic immigration patterns

The phenomenon of these "rolling waves" of newcomers has been called "the greatest migration in history." A huge burden was placed on social institutions, particularly the schools, to make a united people out of many diverse peoples— or what is meant by the motto *e pluribus unum* (out of many, one). In being transplanted from their homelands to the United States, many immigrants encountered for the first time a sense of their own distinctiveness (as Irish or Italians, for example) in a new land where the cultural assumptions of their homelands were not self-evident.[23]

Progressive reform and immigration

In the late nineteenth and early twentieth centuries, many progressive education reformers saw public schools as instruments to bring about important social changes. Among the beliefs many progressives held was that education helped produce equality and that all children should be schooled to become productive citizens. In facing the problem of massive immigration, however, progressive educational reformers were split between **pluralists** and **nativists**.

The pluralists valued ethnic differences, and most wanted to avoid "denationalizing" immigrant children too quickly or in any total sense. They preferred an education that respected **cultural pluralism** while also preparing every child to become a functioning member of society. The problem with pluralist reformers, some critics charge, is that they failed to deal constructively with cultural differences and, instead, put their faith in economic remedies, the workings of the "melting pot," and slogans about the merits of cultural pluralism.[24]

On the contrary, nativists insisted on rapid Americanization or even the outright exclusion of "undesirable" immigrants. For example, Elwood Cubberley, a professor of education at Stanford University in the early 1900s, saw the newcomers as "a very different type." Rather than the familiar immigrants from northern and western Europe, they were now from southern and eastern Europe and the Middle East (Italian, Pole, Bohemian, Slovak, Austrian, Bulgarian, Bosnian, Russian Jew, Syrian, Turk, and Armenian), peoples who were, according to Cubberley, "largely illiterate, docile, [and] lacking in initiative," with almost no "Anglo-Saxon conception of righteousness, liberty, law, order, public decency, and government."[25] At that time, many Americans were only a generation or two away from being immigrants themselves, but the sheer numbers and diverse origins of the newcomers, combined with determined and highly vocal critics, all produced fuel for fear and prejudice.

Generally speaking, most reformers wanted education to provide cultural harmony, social mobility, and economic utility to deal with the massive industrialization, urbanization, and immigration from the late nineteenth through the mid-twentieth centuries. Both native-born and newcomer alike faced major stresses, including an increased need for greater literacy and knowledge, but hard pressed by massive economic change and population growth, most reformers did not fully comprehend either the forces of change or the plight of the immigrants. The remedies they put in place helped establish patterns of response that persist to the present time. For illustration, the following sections examine some representative aspects of those patterns as experienced by four major immigrant groups: Polish, Italian, Chinese, and Mexican.

Polish immigrants

By far, the bulk of Polish immigration to the United States came between the 1880s and 1920s with the newly arrived settling mostly in the urban areas of the Northeast. During the nineteenth century, Poland was occupied by three different powers—Germany, Russia, and Austria. In the German-occupied sector, children had access to better schools than in the other two sectors; however, after German chancellor Otto von Bismarck imposed state control over the Roman Catholic Church of Poland in 1871, the schools began reflecting anti-Catholic and anti-Polish views, which helped push the initial wave of Polish immigrants to the United States, followed by subsequent waves from the other two sectors. When Polish immigrants arrived, American free public schools appealed to them because most of them were poor. Most of them were also devout Roman Catholics; therefore, existing Catholic **parochial schools** previously established by Irish and German immigrants also proved a popular choice. Of course, not all Polish immigrants were of a single mind about either education or religion. Some Poles were secularists, some were Jews, but most were Catholics; some enthusiasts even claimed that one must be Catholic to be truly Polish. After Catholic leaders encouraged Polish immigrants to attend existing parochial schools and to start building their own as well, most of them chose the parochial school option.[26]

> **For Further Reflection and Cross-Reference:** Should tax monies be used to support parochial schools? See Chapter 8, Religion and Education, particularly the section "The Separation of Church and State," pp. 370–374.

Almost all Polish immigrants maintained strong affinities for Polish traditions, but this did not keep them from eventually developing loyalty to the United States. As their schools developed, they reflected an almost exclusive emphasis on the Polish language and culture, even to the point of reprinting old textbooks from Poland. With the passage of time, however, curriculum materials were developed specifically for Polish American schools, and American values came to be emphasized, even when students continued to be taught in Polish. When societal pressures emerged for the Poles to become more Americanized, such as government concerns about Polish immigrant loyalty to the Allied cause during World War I, the Polish nationalism expressed in their curriculum materials was toned down. By the 1930s, English usage increased in both verbal instruction and printed materials, although Polish continued to be used for religious instruction. By the 1940s, English was becoming the standard language in Polish schools and communities, but a strong sense of ethnicity still flourished.[27]

Eventually the strong Polish identity declined, and the pressures came not only from the outside. The Catholic Church served a variety of immigrant groups, and church leaders decided they had to build an American rather than an Irish, Italian, or Polish American Catholic Church. In 1916, there were more than 1,200 Catholic "national" parishes in the United States, with some using a particular immigrant group's native language exclusively or else using English only occasionally. In 1918, however, the papacy stopped the creation of new national parishes, except in special cases. In addition, the maintenance of a strong Polish identity suffered because the Polish American community never founded its own higher education institutions, as the Irish did with Notre Dame University or the Jews with Brandeis University. Thus, with fewer institutional structures to cultivate Polish identity, it receded over time.[28]

For a variety of reasons, Polish immigrants had lower educational attainment and achievement levels than other immigrant groups. Even as late as the 1970s, second- or third-generation Polish descendants still did not achieve the levels of other comparable groups. This was complicated by a tradition going back to the Polish peasantry that family needs took precedence over individual needs. Perhaps the most significant factor in low educational attainment, however, was low wages. Most Polish immigrant families lived in poor economic circumstances, and many parents pulled their children out of school to work and support family economic needs. Of course, few parents viewed their children as mere economic assets, and some children voluntarily quit school to help their families, but prior to 1940 the preoccupation of most Polish families was adequate income, not social mobility or self-improvement through education. If a wage-earning parent suffered incapacitation or death, it drastically affected family circumstances and often meant a child's schooling was abruptly terminated in favor of a job. Poor health and diet also affected Polish children's abilities to profit from school. Many Polish children went to school without adequate breakfasts, and some refused to attend when they lacked adequate shoes or clothing. Thus, while cultural traditions played a role, economic factors impacted the educational attainment and achievement of Polish immigrant children.[29]

For Further Reflection: How do economic circumstances affect the education of children today, nationally and internationally? Can schools make a difference, and if so, how? Or are changing economic conditions the responsibility of the larger society?

Italian immigrants

The great influx of Italian immigrants occurred from the 1880s to the 1920s, when more than 4.5 million people came to the United States. Most came from southern Italy, from the regions of Abruzzi, Calabria, Campania, and the island of Sicily. They were overwhelmingly of rural origin, and a long history of poverty and exploitation conditioned them to value family, blood kin, and the local village above all else. Many Italian immigrants intended to return home after "making it" in the United States, and several hundred thousand actually returned to their native land in the early 1900s. This fed negative attitudes about "ungrateful" Italian immigrants, but most Italian immigrants came to stay.[30]

In their new homeland, Italian immigrants faced an industrial society that was unfamiliar to them, a formerly rural people now living in urban areas and working in mechanized industries. Often exploited by their own *padrones* (labor bosses) and confronted with a strange and hostile social environment, many held tightly to the old ways by keeping to their families in close-knit ethnic neighborhoods where they found support and could protect their children from unwanted assimilation. For such reasons, an Italian enclave (or Little Italy, as it was often called) sprang up in many American cities.[31]

> **For Further Reflection:** How important is family to educational success? What are some of the various ways that family impacted the educational attainment of immigrant children?

However, where Polish immigrants clung to their Catholic parish schools, the Italians did not because most of the parents preferred public schools. Since the majority of Italian immigrants were from the rural peasantry who identified with their local villages, they had little or no identity with the central church hierarchy in Rome, perhaps because it was run by the upper class that had long oppressed them; they might respect distant church leaders, but they identified church and religion with their local priest, who was usually one of them. Therefore, in the United States the pleas of the church hierarchy for Italian parish schools yielded far less response than among Polish immigrants.[32]

American tradition holds that free public schools enabled most immigrant children to enter adult society, with at least some achieving wealth and success. Numerous immigrants left testimonials to the availability of free public education and how the American faith in education brought hope and meaning to the immigrant world of privation and want. In recent years, however, this tradition has been questioned. Revisionist critics maintain that public schools were instruments designed to control immigrants, not free them. Rather than being avenues to equality and upward mobility, the schools were compulsory, bureaucratic, class biased, and racist.[33]

The Italian immigrant experience provides a good source of material to test such views. There is evidence that the schools probably did control more than liberate, but while assimilation was slow, it was also relentless and came from a number of influences in addition to schools. Many second- and third-generation Italians eventually moved out of the old neighborhoods and into the larger society as bankers, merchants, manufacturers, builders, and members of the learned professions, all of which was aided by formal education. Italian immigrants did not exhibit the nationalistic identity with their origins as the Poles did, but they nevertheless took great pride in Italian culture, particularly its art and music, and they maintained close affinity with those sources of pride.[34] Today, ethnic Italian identity is still present, but most descendants of Italian immigrants perceive themselves as part and parcel of mainstream American society. Indeed, Italian Americans are found at every level of American society, including governors' offices and the U.S. Congress, to name but two.

For Further Reflection: In your opinion, are schools more prone to control immigrant students today or to serve as empowering forces? Justify your position.

Chinese immigrants

In 2008, approximately 13.5 million people of Asian origin resided in the United States. People of Chinese origin made up the largest proportion, but while Chinese immigrants might share many things in common, they are also diverse. In the nineteenth century, many of the first Chinese immigrants to the United States came primarily from Canton Province in China. Since then, others have not only come from mainland China but also from Hong Kong, Taiwan, the Philippines, and other countries to which Chinese people migrated historically.[35] Thus, people considered Chinese Americans may actually differ in significant ways, not only in terms of social class or educational background but national origin as well. What they share in common is an ethnic Chinese identity.

WEB: Suggested Reading 5.2.

An important Chinese educational tradition dates back to Confucius (551–479 B.C.E.), an educator-philosopher who was born poor but became influential and widely known for his teachings on ethics and ancient Chinese ideals. Confucius eventually rose to high government office where he attempted to reform a corrupt system. After his death, disciples spread his teachings to such an extent that the Confucian tradition of great respect for education became an important force in Chinese life.[36]

A related tradition was the Chinese examination system, established by the Han Dynasty (202 B.C.E. to 220 C.E.), which lasted until 1905. Originally intended to help select competent government officials, the examination system became corrupt, with high test scores up for sale and high offices awarded to a favored few, while the great majority of Chinese people remained poor and illiterate. Comprehensive education for all children was not realized in China until the second half of the twentieth century.[37]

Despite long-held Chinese traditions that placed high value on education and learning, when significant numbers of Chinese began immigrating to the United States in the mid-nineteenth century, they were prohibited from becoming naturalized citizens or owning land because of prejudices about their national/racial origins. Congress passed the Chinese Exclusion Act in 1882 and the Oriental Exclusion Act in 1924 to sharply curtail immigration from China and other Asian countries. Such attitudes also sometimes led to Chinese children being barred from schools. For example, in the 1880s Chinese students were refused admission to the San Francisco public schools, and the parents of Mamie Tape took the issue to court in *Tape v. Hurley* (**1885**). The California State Supreme Court ruled that Chinese children could not be excluded from public schools, but the San Francisco school board evaded the court's decision by establishing the segregated Oriental Public School. The school grew in enrollment but employed few Chinese or bilingual teachers. Although the school proved ineffective in teaching English, students were forbidden to speak their native language in the school or on the playground.[38]

WEB: Suggested Reading 5.3.

Chinese immigrants also often faced prejudice from the larger society, such as discrimination in employment. It was not until the 1940s and World War II that employment barriers began falling for Chinese Americans. In addition, the civil rights movement of the 1950s and 1960s benefited Chinese Americans as well as other minority groups. The **Immigration Act of 1965** abolished the national-origin quota system, although immigrants with desirable skills or with relatives who were permanent residents or U.S. citizens continued to receive favorable treatment. Stemming in large part from the U.S. involvement in the Vietnam War, the Indochinese Refugee Resettlement Act of 1975 and the Refugee Act of 1980 further liberalized immigration laws, permitting the entry of close to one million additional Southeast Asian refugees.[39]

While Chinese immigrants historically came from the lower echelons of their societies, a significant number of the more recent immigrants have been relatively well educated or became so after arriving in the United States, which made it easier for them to enter the American middle class. Still, a number of Chinese immigrants continue to come from the working class, and they usually find only low-paying jobs that restrict where they can live or the extent to which they can educate their children.

One problem for Chinese immigrant students was the lack of attention to their language needs in schools. In *Lau v. Nichols* **(1974)**, however, the U.S. Supreme Court ruled that the failure of San Francisco schools to provide English-language instruction to Chinese American students denied them a meaningful education and violated the Civil Rights Act of 1964. The court did not impose a remedy, but it recognized that teaching the students English as a second language was one option and teaching them in Chinese was another. Whatever the remedy chosen, the court ruled, it was the board of education's responsibility to "apply its expertise" and "rectify the situation." The *Lau* decision also encouraged the passage of the **Equal Educational Opportunity Act of 1974**, which supported bilingual education programs in public schools.[40]

Mexican immigrants

In 2008, the population of both native and foreign-born Hispanic residents in the United States stood at approximately 46.8 million people, of whom approximately 28.9 million were native born and more than 17.8 million were foreign born. Of the total number of Hispanics, approximately 30.7 million were of Mexican origin. Prior to the 1990s, most Mexican Americans resided in the Southwest, but today they are the fastest-growing group throughout the country. This growth has been driven by an internal **secondary migration**, because most Mexican immigrants initially establish themselves in the Southwest and then migrate to other locales.[41]

However, the story of Mexican Americans began much earlier. When the war between the United States and the Republic of Mexico ended with the Treaty of Guadalupe-Hidalgo in 1848, Mexico not only had to accept the U.S. annexation of Texas but it also had to cede California, Arizona, New Mexico, Nevada, Colorado, Utah, and part of Wyoming to the United States. Mexicans who remained in the newly acquired territory had to decide whether to maintain their Mexican citizenship or become American citizens. Most chose the latter, thus becoming the first Mexican Americans. The treaty also obligated the United States to protect its new citizens' rights, such as ensuring the retention of their language, religion, customs, and property claims; however, many of them saw their status reduced rather than enhanced.[42]

The descendants of these first Mexican Americans would eventually be joined by many others in search of jobs and economic improvement during the early twentieth century. Most were unskilled laborers, but some were members of the middle class fleeing the Mexican Revolution of 1910. Generally, **stereotyping** and prejudice made it difficult for Mexican Americans to move up socially and economically, as illustrated by the Dillingham Commission Report of 1911, which stated that, "Because of their strong attachment to their native land, low intelligence, illiteracy, [and] migratory life . . . the Mexican . . . is less desirable as a citizen than as a laborer." Mexican immigrants were exploited as cheap labor in the factories and fields, but during the Great Depression of the 1930s they were often viewed as unfair competition to native-born American laborers. The federal government deported Mexican workers in the 1930s to free up jobs for unemployed American workers, but when production increased during World War II, the government once again recruited Mexican agricultural workers as short-term emergency labor. This "bracero program" actually continued until 1964 and involved a sizable labor pool, but American growers controlled workers' wages and prevented them from organizing to improve working conditions. When the bracero program ended, however, the migration of Mexican job seekers did not. Some of them resided in Mexico and daily commuted to work in the United States on work permits called green cards. Others were migrant farmworkers who legally entered the United States on short-term work permits during harvest seasons. Still others crossed the border illegally. Most border crossers probably intended to return to Mexico, but for various reasons many remained and settled. In short, both authorized and unauthorized immigrants came and continue to come into the United States from south of the border.[43]

The power of names and perceptions

Immigrants and their descendants from Mexico and countries to the south are considered part of the **Hispanic** or **Latino** community, yet some prefer terms such as *Spanish American, Mexican American, Chicano,* or *Chicana*. Identification with one term rather than another may be significant because names can have historical meaning or political connotations. *Hispanic* and *Latino* are sometimes controversial terms; some prefer Latino and criticize Hispanic as carrying racist implications. Others prefer Hispanic because it signifies users of the Spanish language, and *Hispanic* is the term used by the U.S. government in its official documents. Native-born Spanish-speaking inhabitants of the southwestern United States may prefer Hispanic, while immigrants and their descendants from Mexico and Central America may prefer Latino. Perhaps general terminology should be rejected in favor of specific terminology that accurately differentiates between American minority groups and immigrants and refugees. Minority groups would include people of Mexican descent and people of Puerto Rican descent as designations, for example, while immigrants and refugees would include Cuban immigrants, Central American refugees, or South American immigrants.

Hispanics or Latinos often experience difficulties with the fluctuating identities created by labels. They may be perceived as black, nonwhite, white, other race, Spanish, mixed, Afro-Latino, or white Hispanic.

Sources: Martha E. Gimenez, "Latino/Hispanic—Who Needs a Name? The Case Against a Standardized Terminology," in *Latinos and Education: A Critical Reader*, Antonia Darder et al., eds. (New York/London: Routledge, 1997), 226; Clara E. Rodríguez, *Changing Race: Latinos, the Census, and the History of Ethnicity in the United States*. (New York: New York University Press), 3–6.

For Further Reflection: It is potentially misleading to make generalizations involving large numbers of people; however, academic disciplines such as sociology and anthropology are dependent on research-based generalizations intended to capture significant group characteristics. Without such generalizations, the social sciences could not exist, and many social phenomena might be perceived as coincidental and go unexamined. Think about this dilemma. How can one make sense of society without generalizations? How does one avoid the trap of inappropriate generalizations?

Suggested Activity: Many countries recruit foreign workers in times of labor shortages but tend to view these individuals as parasitic once the shortage has lifted. Read about so-called guest workers in Germany, for example. Consider how such foreign labor policies come about and what implications those policies might have for the workers' families, in particular their children.

In many respects, the history of Mexican American schooling during the first half of the twentieth century was one of segregation. In the past, most Mexican American children were placed in segregated classrooms or schools, similar to what African American children experienced, but the segregation Mexican Americans faced was more often based on language and cultural differences than physical attributes. A common stereotype was that people of Mexican origin tended to be lazy, violent, uncultured, uninterested in education, and generally not worthy of full assimilation into American society. Although segregated education was deemed by some to be in the best interest of Mexican American children so they could overcome perceived linguistic and cultural deficiencies, one consequence was an extraordinarily high dropout rate. For example, during the 1930s there were few Mexican American students attending California high schools, and those who did were often tracked into vocational education programs, boys for manual labor and girls for domestic work. **Culturally biased testing** bolstered the tracking system, with test scores used to justify placement decisions. A disproportionate number of Mexican American students were thus separated from their non-Mexican peers and denied equal access to academic programs, particularly the children of migrant farmworkers who, following the cycle of harvests, could not remain in a given school very long. They had to attend schools operating on shortened days and terms, or they were simply denied access on the claim that their frequent moves created problems for the schools. Sometimes school boards collaborated with local agricultural and business interests to ensure availability of sufficient hands during harvests. Mexican migrant workers were seen as a "necessary nuisance" because their labor was needed. They were also easily exploited as cheap labor and, if considered at all, the children's education was a secondary concern.[44]

For Mexican Americans who were a permanent part of the American population, policy makers embraced an Americanization approach. This was based on the assumption that Mexican American communities, if left unchanged, would destabilize the larger society, and schools were seen as crucial to stabilization. In the southwestern United States, the Americanization of Mexican Americans was particularly emphasized because of their significant numbers and because policy makers assumed that their cultural backgrounds were inferior and in need of "cultural illumination." As the Los Angeles superintendent of schools put it in 1923, "if we Americanize them, we can live with them." In 1939, an Arizona principal stated that more time was needed to educate Mexican American students because they would steal and vandalize if they did not "catch the idea of respect for human values and personalities." Such views reflected a common sentiment of the time that "the American way" was the only right way. Colleges and universities instituted courses to prepare teachers to deal with the special problems that children of Mexican origin were thought to have. Teachers were to encourage the children to substitute "desirable" traits for "undesirable" ones, such as the use of English, not Spanish, in school. In effect, the policy was to replace Mexican culture with the norms and values of the larger Anglo American society.[45]

Suggested Activity: How should the education of minorities be accomplished, and is there a difference in the needs of immigrants and existing minorities? Investigate the courses in your own program of study. What assumptions are made about immigrant and minority cultures in comparison to mainstream American culture? Are prospective educators being prepared to continue the Americanization tradition with groups considered different? If so, what should be done? What do you propose as the most appropriate model of educating immigrant and other minority students?

Suggested Activity: Interview a practicing educator (a teacher, counselor, or an administrator) who has experience instructing immigrant and minority students. What philosophical views does this person have about those experiences and the value of exploring different cultures in the curriculum?

Organizations such as the League of United Latin American Citizens (LULAC) and the American GI Forum (AGIF) helped combat the rising discrimination against Mexican Americans. In education, lawsuits were brought not only against segregated schools but also against tracking and ability grouping practices that denied equal educational opportunity. Many participants hoped that the 1946 court decision in *Mendez v. Westminster School District* (1946) would end legal school segregation for Mexican American students in California, but the court decision was circumvented by local school districts that used such evasive practices as school choice plans and the classification of students by ability.[46]

The situation was aggravated by some of the arguments advanced by LULAC and AGIF that Mexican Americans were, if not Caucasian, then at least "other white." Local school districts used the other white argument to "desegregate" the schools simply by mixing African American and Mexican American students, claiming they had desegregated the schools while they also still maintained exclusive schools in white neighborhoods. In the 1960s and 70s, however, the Mexican American "other white" argument changed to the "equal protection of the laws" strategy so successfully used by African Americans in their desegregation cases. Thus, in *Cisneros v. Corpus Christi Independent School District* (1972), the California court ruled that Mexican Americans were an identifiable ethnic minority group. The 1954 *Brown* decision, with its legal obligation to desegregate African American students, was now applied to Mexican Americans as well. In **Keyes v. School District No. 1, Denver, Colorado (1973)**, the U.S. Supreme Court held that Hispanic students in Denver experienced difficulties similar to African American students because both faced educational inequalities when compared to the majority of white students. Moreover, since Denver school authorities historically manipulated policies and rules in order to have racially and ethnically segregated schools, the entire school district must be desegregated. Despite these important legal successes, however, desegregation proceeded slowly for Mexican Americans, with de facto segregation actually increasing in some locales between the 1960s and 1980s. Overall, desegregation efforts made by Mexican Americans and others helped change old patterns of educational discrimination, but equal educational opportunity for Mexican American students still remained elusive.[47]

Suggested Activity: Changes in deeply ingrained behavior and institutional structures do not come easily. If existing conditions serve powerful interests, then reform encounters resistance, as history amply illustrates. Examine the literature for evidence of immigrants succeeding, and an example of an immigrant group that saw its efforts thwarted. Evaluate scholarly explanations for success and failure. What lessons can be drawn from your analyses?

Suggested Activity: Research the history of your ancestors coming to the United States. What ethnic groups are parts of your heritage? When did they come to the United States and under what conditions? What was their reception, and what assistance as well as barriers did they encounter? How did subsequent generations experience schooling and education?

Contemporary conditions

The connection of ethnicity and education is an enduring one in the United States, one that changes with each new group of arrivals but which also retains some familiar features. At present, ethnicity continues to be both an educational concern and an important learning tool.

American Indians have long struggled to gain some semblance of control over their own education, and they have made some progress. Tribes now exercise much more control over education on the reservations, and progress has been made in preserving tribal cultures and languages, but too many members continue to suffer from poor economic conditions, poor health, and inadequate educational opportunity.

In addition, Americans have often had ambivalent feelings about every new wave of immigrants. Just as John Quincy Adams advised the immigrants of his day to become Americans and to "'cast off the European skin, never to resume it,'"[48] so, too, do many Americans today expect immigrants from Latin America, Asia, or elsewhere to cast off (or at least subdue) their cultural practices and identifications and take on enough American identity to enter mainstream culture. The problem is that many if not most immigrants—past and present—come not simply to shed cultural origins but to flee political tyranny, religious persecution, and economic want or to pursue some dream they believe is more likely to happen in the United States.[49] The nation may be a collection of immigrants, but many present-day descendants of immigrants seem impatient with newcomers and expect them to change quickly or else go back where they came from. Despite a sometimes less-than-friendly reception, immigrants continue to arrive. With a global economy and a transnational migration of workers in pursuit of jobs, there is also a growth of international education and a transnational migration of students pursuing educational opportunities from one nation to the next, which signals that the relationship between migration and education may become increasingly significant on a global scale.[50]

National education policy and contemporary American Indian education

Today, there is much more tribal control of school operations and curriculum, as seen in the growth of curriculum materials devoted to cultural traditions and languages, as well as bilingual and bicultural materials and programs, but these developments have also been hampered by the standards movement, high-stakes testing, and No Child Left Behind legislation. While increased tribal control has become accepted national policy, however, it is well to remember past examples of American Indian education being affected by changing political winds.[51]

Federal government presence continues through the Bureau of Indian Affairs (BIA) and its Bureau of Indian Education (BIE). In the 2007–08 school year, the BIE funded 184 elementary and secondary schools located on 64 reservations in

24 states. Of these 184 schools, 59 were operated by the BIE, and the remaining 125 were operated by tribes under BIE contracts and grants. In 2009, the BIE also funded 26 tribal colleges and universities and directly operated two of them, the Haskell Indian Nations University in Lawrence, Kansas, and the Southwest Indian Polytechnic Institute in Albuquerque, New Mexico.

Today, the majority of American Indian students no longer live on reservations, and most now attend local public schools; however, many still attend either BIE or tribally operated schools. In addition, some reservations are still so remote and sparsely settled as to make day schools unfeasible, so students must still attend boarding schools. As late as 2006, the BIE operated seven off-reservation boarding schools and 14 "peripheral" dormitories for reservation students attending the nearest public schools.[52]

The No Child Left Behind (NCLB) Act of 2002 called for greater accountability of schools, including American Indian schools. There is support for accountability but lingering concern about obstacles for American Indian students in remote, economically strapped communities. Not only has inadequate funding been a perennial problem, but also high dropout rates, substance abuse, poor health and housing, and high unemployment, all of which adversely affect the capacity of the children to learn and the schools to meet their needs.[53]

The National Indian Education Association (NIEA) conducted hearings on NCLB, concerned that culturally appropriate education developed in previous years might be sacrificed by the emphasis on standardized test scores and test-related instructional approaches. Association members did not want to diminish the self-determination role of tribal governments and American Indian communities to shape the education of their children.[54]

A national study of American Indian/Alaska Native (AI/AN) education was conducted in 2007, and it found that the reading and math performance of fourth- and eighth-grade (AI/AN) students was lower than other grade-level peers. Yet, it also revealed that AI/AN students in public schools scored higher than peers in BIE schools, while fourth-grade AI/AN students in city schools scored higher than African American and Hispanic peers. It is interesting to note that AI/AN fourth graders in Oklahoma and Minnesota and AI/AN eighth graders in Oklahoma and Oregon scored higher than all AI/AN peers in other states around the nation.[55]

Contemporary immigration and educational issues

In some respects, historic patterns of immigrant experience continue, even as national and cultural origins have undergone significant changes. As in the past, newcomers tend to be concentrated in central cities, have larger families, experience higher unemployment, and have less formal education than the general population. Generally speaking, immigrants from Asia and Europe usually have more education than those from Latin America. Also, the longer foreign-born persons reside in the United States, the more likely they are to become naturalized citizens. According to the U.S. Census Bureau report in 2000, there were 28.4 million foreign-born residents, and almost 40 percent of them entered the country after 1990, a mere decade. Of those who arrived before 1970, more than 80 percent had citizenship by 2000; in comparison, less than 9 percent who arrived after 1990 had acquired citizenship, a percentage rate that had not significantly changed by 2008.[56]

The fastest-growing portion of children in the United States is from immigrant families. Furthermore, the number of immigrants has increased in almost all states, with more than 80 percent from Latin America and Asia. In comparison to peers, children from immigrant families are more likely to live in poverty and underachieve academically, and a majority speak a language other than English at home. While one-fifth of all children living in poor families had immigrant parents in 1990, it is projected that one-third will have immigrant parents by 2015. Ethnic minority and culturally, linguistically diverse children are also overrepresented in special education services, a phenomenon that has been a controversial issue for decades.[57]

American society is undergoing the largest wave of immigration in its history, and the current foreign-born population is—numerically speaking—twice as large as the former historic peak in 1910. This condition creates issues, such as immigration's impact on economic opportunities. Critics point to the number of recent immigrants lacking a high school education (about 40 percent), which can exert a downward pressure on wages that, in turn, depresses the earnings of the poorest 11 percent of native-born workers. Low wages mean higher profits for employers, but low-wage workers suffer the most because they have less to start with. Another criticism is that large-scale immigration puts costly pressures on social institutions such as schools. For example, student populations shifted from white to nonwhite majorities in California's large urban school districts in the 1980s. Immigrants of childbearing age had birth rates exceeding those of native-born residents, and growing numbers of students came from 140 different language backgrounds other than English. As tensions increased, various proposals were floated, such as denying the children of undocumented immigrants the right to attend public schools because, critics alleged, their parents paid few taxes while the children created high public education expenditures. Rumors also circulated that immigrants came to California to get welfare handouts (despite abundant evidence that most came for jobs).[58] Such tensions began surfacing in other communities as well.

Between 1820 and 2008, more than 74 million people of foreign birth obtained legal permanent resident status in the United States. More than half (or 39.5 million) of these immigrants came from Europe (including 8.3 million from Germany, 5.4 million from Italy, 5.4 million from the United Kingdom, and 4.7 million from Ireland). Out of a total U.S. population of almost 92 million in 1910, for example, approximately 13.5 million were of foreign birth, with more than 11.8 million from Europe alone. In more recent times, immigrant origins have been more diverse. As indicated in Table 5.1, by 2007, out of a total population of approximately 301.6 million people, 38 million legal residents were of foreign birth, with the two largest portions from Asia (9.7 million) and Latin America (almost 20.4 million, of which 11.7 million were from Mexico alone).[59]

Added to this was the scope of unauthorized (or undocumented) residents of foreign birth, which was a controversial issue in the 2008 presidential election. Although unauthorized immigration itself was not new, the size of it was, just as its details were more complex than appeared at first glance. Some immigrants actually entered the country with proper documents but remained after the documents expired and, therefore, became unauthorized residents. Others entered the country without documents (or illegally), and if not apprehended and returned, they also became unauthorized residents. No one knows the exact number, but the Office of Immigration Statistics estimated in January 2008 that there were approximately 11.6 million unauthorized immigrants in the United States, with the main sources being Mexico, El Salvador, Guatemala, Honduras, and the Philippines.[60]

Table 5.1 Resident population of the United States by selected world region and/or country of birth, 2007

United States Total Population	301,621,159
Native-Born	263,561,465
Foreign-Born	38,059,555
Africa	1,419,317
The Americas	21,248,337
Latin America	20,409,676
Mexico	11,738,537
Asia	10,184,906
China	1,930,202
Europe	4,990,294
Italy	417,511
Poland	484,777
Oceania	216,701

Source: Adapted from "Select Population Groups," Country of Birth, American FactFinder, U.S. Census Bureau, at http://factfinder.census.gov/servlet/IPCharIterationServlet?_ts=259275806730 (accessed on May 1, 2009).

In order to shed light on issues surrounding immigration's educational dimensions, it is helpful to examine recent developments regarding ethnicity and education, viewing them from the perspective of selected ethnic groups whose experiences often differ. Chinese immigrants, for example, are more likely to achieve some type of postsecondary education comparable to native-born students, but Hispanic immigrants are less likely.[61] The following sections illuminate some of these issues.

Academic achievement and Mexican Americans

Mexican American students generally have encountered obstacles in educational achievement and attainment, although there are numerous exceptions. Still, the lack of school success among Mexican American students, as compared with their white peers, remains a stubbornly persistent problem.[62]

Academic difficulties of any group are seldom due to one factor alone but to several, such as individual and family problems and issues related to unequal funding, curriculum tracking, and other grouping practices. There is research suggesting that some Latino students do well in the classroom while others of similar background do not. One factor, for example, might be the role of the family, because parents who provide a quiet, orderly home environment and appropriate discipline, who teach responsibility, self-control, and the value of education are probably more likely to have higher achieving children than those who do not.[63]

Other research paints a different picture. For example, most policies seem to focus on such factors as English language fluency and bilingual education, rather than the problem of underachievement. Such policies run the risk of trying to mold different cultures to fit dominant paradigms. Typical programs designed to increase parental involvement are generally based on American middle-class values of success, but Mexican parents may define parental roles and the success of their children differently from dominant views. For example, good parenting may not be defined as rearing children to obtain high status jobs or advanced degrees; rather, emphasis may be placed on becoming virtuous, hardworking, and dutiful to the extended family. For many Mexican parents, the child's academic work is perceived as the teachers' domain, and school expectations that parents should help children academically may remain unmet. Teachers may be concerned about an immigrant parent not teaching the five-year-old son his ABCs, when Mexican tradition is to help young children learn syllabic sounds (such as "ba" [bah] and "be" [bay]), not the names of letters. Also, in Mexican homes family needs may be valued over individual needs, and parents may be reluctant to divert attention from family events to a child's school project. This does not mean American schools should stop teaching the alphabet or requiring school projects; rather, educators need to understand Mexican American cultural values, and Mexican American parents need to understand how American schools work in order for their children's school experiences to be more fulfilling.[64]

For Further Reflection: In much of the industrialized world, independence and individualism are highly valued, but many people's well-being and identity are deeply connected to family and kinfolk.

1. How should we design schools and other institutions to accommodate both individual independence and group identity, rather than forcing a choice one way or the other? How can we make educational institutions more sensitive to cultural differences and responsive to the needs of different ethnic groups?
2. Are there some practices or attitudes immigrants often try to retain that are self-defeating and should be given up? How are judgments about what is worth preserving and what is in need of change to be made? Does this decision-making power belong to groups or to institutions?

WEB: Suggested Reading 5.4.

Some observers used to believe that the academic difficulties of most immigrant students, not only Mexican Americans, existed because their cultural backgrounds were so different as to limit their school success. Others suggested that a combination of factors, such as minority status, low income, and inadequate school financing might be the more significant factors. While such things as language differences might be major problems, they can be less important to educational achievement and attainment than inadequate educational resources.[65]

Cultural tensions and Chinese American education

Until recently, there was little national discussion about the education of Asian American students, but the impact of Asian immigration on American society has changed this. Issues of language and cultural differences, academic performance, curriculum content and school violence are among the leading topics, but for a long time, Asian Americans have been perceived as the **model minority** of high achievers experiencing few difficulties compared to other minority students. This stereotype masks the educational challenges faced by many Asian American students.[66]

WEB: Suggested Reading 5.5.

For Further Reflection: Is it a compliment to be considered a "model"? How may "positive" stereotypes become oppressive? What impact, if any, does this have on the schools?

Contrary to the stereotype, the cultural and linguistic differences between foreign-born immigrant students of Asian origin and native-born American students can be so pronounced that immigrant students often face nearly impossible obstacles. For example, some traditional Chinese views on education can conflict with American views. American teachers generally see education as an interactive process, with emphasis on problem solving, creativity, and critical thinking, while Chinese immigrants may see education as a formal process of factual retention, lots of homework, and strict obedience to teacher-directed instruction. Traditional Chinese parents may prefer formal classrooms, teacher authority, and obedience to rules instead of student participation and interchange. These kinds of parental expectations can pose problems for students by bringing them into conflict with the expectations of their teachers, but the problem is intensified if the cultural differences of parents and students are misinterpreted as cultural deficiencies.[67]

There is also research indicating that Chinese American students might encounter difficulties from **marginality**, **bicultural identity**, and **multiple perspectives**. Marginality, or feeling on the outer edge of society, results from trying to maintain Chinese family traditions while also trying to assimilate into the dominant culture without much success. Similarly, bicultural identity can be enriching but can also lead to a type of double consciousness in which an individual has a foot in both Chinese and American cultures, without finding a secure identity in either. Some students may also develop multiple perspectives, such as a person reared in a traditional Chinese family in San Diego, California, who is also influenced by the Hispanic culture in nearby Mexico, and who becomes fluent in Chinese, Spanish, and English. Indeed, these are perspectives many Americans highly value, but for immigrant children with parents dedicated to preserving the cultural roots and traditions of their country of origin, multiple perspectives may present difficulties that teachers need to understand.[68]

WEB: Suggested Reading 5.6.

Suggested Activity: Discuss with others the concepts of marginality, bicultural identity, and multiple perspectives. In what ways, if any, can you relate to them? Have you experienced any of them, and if so, what did they mean for you?

Language constitutes one of the cultural factors that Chinese immigrants may experience differently from other immigrant groups. There are five major Chinese languages: Han, Manchu, Mongol, Muhammadan, and Tibetan. Han is what the rest of the world refers to as Chinese and is spoken by approximately 94 percent of the population, but it also has many dialects, the most important of which is Mandarin, the official language of modern China. Since the 1960s, the majority of Chinese immigrants speak at least some Mandarin, but learning **English as a second language (ESL)** is complicated by the major differences between Chinese languages and the English language, particularly concerning grammar, speech, and writing. Chinese tends to be monosyllabic, with different tones put on a syllable to create meanings; English is polysyllabic with emphasis on individual word sounds and meanings. For example, English consonant sounds such as the *l* in *lice* or the *r* in *rice,* or consonant clusters such as *bl*ack or *spr*ay do not exist in Chinese and are extremely difficult for Chinese immigrant students to pronounce. There are syntactical or word order differences too. Mandarin can have several different words to describe a thing or concept, such as eight different words for *cousin,* depending on the type of cousin (elder male cousin on father's side or younger female cousin on mother's side, for example). In oral and written expression, an English essay starts with an introduction, then an extended analysis, and a final conclusion. Chinese writing usually takes a different approach. Rather than choosing essay topics on their own, Chinese students are more likely to defer to their teachers, considering it rude to take or defend a position without proper authorization.[69] Such possibilities should be understood by teachers in their teaching and expectations, particularly with recently arrived or very young students.

> **For Further Reflection:** Are you able to speak a second language? If not, interview someone who is. Consider the following questions: What does learning another language actually involve? What enablers and barriers confront the language learner? What are the implications for educators?

Bilingual education

Being able to communicate in more than one language can be a valuable asset, as is the ability to move between different cultures.[70] Over time, many immigrant students have achieved these ends to one degree or another, but for many others, education may become overshadowed by different concerns, such as the need to quit school for a job. An important effort to improve the success of immigrant students is bilingual education, or the use of two languages in instruction.

Bilingual education was originally started to help non-English speakers develop a command of English. The main idea was to begin instruction in a student's native language and gradually increase instruction in English until proficiency was achieved. A variety of approaches soon developed around this idea. One was to begin content instruction in the student's native language, provide instruction in English as a second language (ESL), and eventually transition to all-English instruction in the curriculum. Critics claimed this approach treated native languages as conditions to be overcome; instead, they promoted English as a second language while also preserving the student's native language. Another variation was **limited English proficiency (LEP)**, in which immigrant students would learn English as a second language while retaining their native languages for most instructional purposes.[71]

Both historically and at present, most immigrant students and their parents have faced difficulties in transitioning from one culture to another. It is often the case that immigrant parents speak little or no English, and some may even be illiterate in their native languages as well. Many also must work more than one job to provide for family economic necessities. Some fear they might shame their children because they do not speak English well or lack sufficient understanding of American ways. Immigrant parents may also experience a shift of authority from themselves to their children who learn English and American customs more rapidly and, as a result, become translators of the outside world for their parents.

Seattle, Washington, is a city that has made serious efforts to accommodate both immigrant children and their parents. A major port of entry on the west coast of the United States, Seattle has been an important point of arrival for many immigrants since the nation relaxed restrictions with the Immigration Act of 1965 and subsequent legislation. Seattle adopted bilingual education, and by the mid-1990s, a new curricular approach was undertaken that also included immigrant parents as active partners. A handbook in several languages was produced to explain the new curriculum, and numerous meetings of parents and educators were accompanied by language interpreters. By 1998, Seattle had approximately 46,000 students, of whom about 6,200 were immigrant children representing 75 different native languages and dialects. At the time, the most common foreign languages were Vietnamese, Chinese, Laotian, Spanish, Cambodian, Somali, Ethiopian, and Filipino. Most immigrant children were placed in initial bilingual education programs and then transferred to transitional bilingual programs for additional instruction. Economic conditions of immigrant families often compounded the children's educational difficulties, and among the measures used in some schools were Friday dinners for families, followed by a family reading hour and use of instructional assistants to translate notes from parents and to schedule subsequent calls or visits to parents who could not read.[72]

By 2009, the Seattle public schools had a Bilingual Student Services Program comprised of three options: (1) Bilingual Orientation Centers (BOCs) for students with the least knowledge of English to get them started in reading, speaking, and writing English, as well as to provide introduction to American culture in either an elementary or a secondary BOC; (2) English Language Learning (ELL) Centers in most Seattle public schools that provided either ELL or ESL programs, with instructional assistants as needed for native languages; and (3) placement of students proficient in English into regular classrooms. In addition, there was a Bilingual Family Center that provided numerous services, including interpreters at school meetings as well as internet sites where translations of school information and related documents could be accessed in Cambodian, Chinese, Ethiopian (Amharic, Oromo, and Tigrigna), Laotian, Somali, Spanish, Filipino (Tagalog), and Vietnamese. For other ethnic groups, there was the African American Academy (K–8), the American Indian Heritage Middle College at North Seattle Community College, and the federally sponsored Huchoosedah Indian Education Program.[73]

Controversy surrounding bilingual education
Bilingual education programs have encountered criticism since gaining popular appeal in the late 1960s and early 1970s. Some critics fear that bilingual education strengthens linguistic divisions that create national disunity along ethnic lines. They also maintain that English must be the accepted language of the United States, and non-English speaking students should be taught in full immersion,

English-only programs. Other critics fear that bilingualism serves social and political rather than educational goals. They charge that bilingual education was pushed by radical reformers in the 1960s, not as a temporary aid for non-English speaking students but as a way to preserve immigrant languages and cultures for political purposes. Thus, these critics argue that radicals took a useful teaching and learning technique and turned it into a political philosophy.

Advocates of bilingual education have used court decisions to advance their cause, such as the U.S. Supreme Court's *Lau v. Nichols* (1974) ruling, which held that the provision of English-only instruction to students who do not understand it is, in effect, a denial of meaningful education. The decision did not require a specific remedy, but critics claim radicals used the decision to push bilingual education. This resulted in millions of dollars spent on bilingual education, even though research results were inconclusive about its effectiveness. Critics also claim that advocates successfully pushed bilingual education as a civil right rather than an instructional approach, which riled critics because they believe those growing up in an English-speaking society are not helped if instruction is given in their non-English, native languages.[74]

Perhaps such criticism is at least partly responsible for three states (California, Arizona, and Massachusetts) passing laws that require English to be the primary language of instruction within their borders. The move was first joined in California, where state law allows some issues to be decided by statewide initiative and referendum votes. Proposition 227, which required English as the primary language of instruction, was passed by a 61 percent majority in June 1998. In November 2000, neighboring Arizona followed suit with a similar law. Both states allow parents to request bilingual education for their children, but the processes are cumbersome and may hinder its use.[75]

The most recent state to follow suit was Massachusetts, which passed an English-only law for its public schools in 2002, effective in fall 2003. Modeled after the California law, the Massachusetts law requires that all children in Massachusetts public schools "shall be taught English by being taught in English." The Gastón Institute for Latino Community Development and Public Policy at the University of Massachusetts, Boston, studied the effects of the law and found that the identification of LEP students actually declined between 2003 and 2006, as did enrollment in English learner (EL) classes specifically designed for English language development. Some students were placed in general education programs with little or no language support, while a larger number were enrolled in sheltered English immersion (SEI) classes (with simple English used to teach academic content, and native languages used only to answer a question or help a student complete a task). The dropout rate almost doubled as language services declined and as enrollments in SEI programs increased. A central conclusion was that the state should make better efforts to meet the language needs of its students.[76]

WEB: Suggested Reading 5.7.

Advocates of bilingual education maintain that the opposition supports the melting pot myth and disguises the actual difficulties immigrant students experience in English-only immersion. They also argue that opponents tend to ignore research evidence that supports bilingual education. Moreover, if opponents achieved their goal of monolingual, Anglocentric schools, it would leave rising generations poorly prepared for the multicultural future that current demographics indicate is likely to occur. Bilingual education tends to bring political ideologies to the surface, and contemporary debates are only current eruptions of longstanding political disagreements over how to view human diversity and provide equal educational opportunity. Thus, the question of how to teach language minorities and yield the best results is not simply about language but also about ethnic discrimination too. As bilingual advocates see it, then, to overcome discrimination, students need healthy senses of self-worth, including respect for their ethnic origins, in which native languages are essential.[77]

The Oyster-Adams bilingual school

In 1971, a Spanish and English dual-language curriculum was established at Oyster Elementary School in Washington, D.C. A bilingual immersion program, it assigned two teachers to each class, one using Spanish, the other English. The school soon gained a reputation for solid academic achievement, as measured by standardized tests, and achievement levels at or above grade level. Initiated mainly to meet the educational needs of Spanish-language children living in an English-language environment, today the student body is more diverse and draws from many neighborhoods, nationalities, cultures, and socioeconomic circumstances.

The Oyster program enjoys wide recognition as a successful bilingual model using linguistic and cultural differences as strengths rather than deficiencies. Started as a prekindergarten through sixth grade program, it has numerous applicants from within and outside the school's regular attendance zone. In 2007, Oyster Bilingual School became the Oyster-Adams Bilingual School when it added the seventh and eighth grades at a second campus (the former Adams Elementary School). Today, students are still taught the English and Spanish dual-language curriculum, and cultural and linguistic differences continue to be highly valued.

Sources: Oyster-Adams Bilingual School, at http://www.oysterbilingualschool.com/ (accessed on May 15, 2010); Rebecca D. Freeman, *Bilingual Education and Social Change* (Philadelphia: Multilingual Matters LTD, 1998).

WEB: Suggested Reading 5.8.

Multicultural education

Although **multicultural education** is a broad-based approach that includes more than ethnicity, it has been called an imperative in large part because America's ethnic diversity is increasing and larger numbers of students are entering the schools with little or no English background. Some advocates see multicultural education as a major reform of public education: It embraces the notion that all students, regardless of gender, social class, ethnicity, or other racial and cultural characteristics, ought to enjoy equal educational opportunities.[78]

Multicultural education entails several components. It integrates content based on various cultures rather than a single one. It also examines knowledge construction and how it is shaped by cultural assumptions, with a goal of improving critical-thinking abilities and reducing cultural biases and prejudices among students. It emphasizes an equitable pedagogy to meet the needs of diverse students, and it questions the sociocultural assumptions behind ability grouping, seeking to close achievement gaps and open better educator-student interactions. Finally, it encourages all those connected with learning—teachers, parents, and students—to be involved in appropriate ways.[79]

Cross-Reference: For a more detailed discussion of equal educational opportunity, see Chapter 7, Gender and Education, pp. 330–332.

WEB: Suggested Reading 5.9.

Controversy surrounding multicultural education

Some critics argue that multiculturalists, in their zeal to overturn the traditional Eurocentric curriculum, seem to reduce Western heritage to a list of Western crimes. When advocates energetically criticize Eurocentric cultures and dismiss Western history as inherently racist and oppressive, they need to keep in mind that their exercise of free speech and intellectual freedom are human rights championed by the Western tradition. Some zealous critics go so far as to charge that overly enthusiastic multiculturalists, in their distaste of assimilating immigrants, actually encourage cultural divisiveness to serve their own political goals. A less caustic criticism is that multiculturalism becomes a form of **cultural relativism** when it assumes that all cultures are inherently equal. At the same time, multicultural textbooks tend to celebrate the positive features of non-European cultures while ignoring the negative aspects. In this sense, traditional biases in Eurocentric texts are merely replaced by the new biases of multiculturalism.[80]

Cross-Reference: For related discussions, particularly on race and Afrocentrism, see Chapter 4, Race and Education, pp. 155–207.

Suggested Activity: Talk to a practicing classroom teacher about multicultural education. Does it exist in his or her school? What are the teacher's experiences with multicultural education, and what attitudes does he or she hold toward it?

The gulf between advocates and critics appears wide, but that is usually the nature of educational debates at the historic moments in which they occur. For all the smoke and thunder, perhaps such debates are a sign of health, because the ideas behind multiculturalism's critique of existing society—the right of individuals to self-determination, the value of human equality and autonomy, the illegitimacy of one group dominating another, the connection of reason and knowledge with personal biography and social history—all of these ideas emerged from within the Western tradition. It has been suggested that the true value of democratic education is found in its capacity to question and even subvert outworn traditions, while it also seeks to understand the past, challenge the present, and serve as a prod into the future.[81]

WEB: Suggested Reading 5.10.

International perspective: Switzerland

Switzerland is a landlocked nation located geographically in central Europe. It is largely a mountainous country (the Alps and Jura Mountains), bordered by France in the west, Italy in the south, Germany in the north, and Austria and Liechtenstein in the east. Its estimated population in July 2009 was approximately 7.6 million, about 70 percent of whom lived in urban areas. Densely populated and wealthy, Switzerland has technologically sophisticated industries, internationally known banks and insurance companies, extensive tourism, and a per capita gross domestic productivity (GDP) among the highest in the world.[82]

Switzerland's official name is Schweizerische Eidgenossenschaft (Latin: *Confoederatio Helvetia* [CH]), an expression of its historic cultural and linguistic diversity that came together in a complex federal system of government. Four major languages are spoken: German (63.7 percent), French (20.4 percent), Italian (6.5 percent) and Rumantsch (0.5 percent, a dialect spoken in parts of Switzerland and Italy). They are the four officially recognized languages used in legislation and official government documents and communications, but there are also other spoken languages, including Serbo-Croation (1.5 percent), Albanian (1.3 percent), Portuguese (1.2 percent), and English (1 percent). Also, numerous dialects of the four major languages are spoken in different regions of the country, with Rumantsch having five dialects itself.[83]

As a country, Switzerland dates back to 1291 when a group of Germanic forest communities formed a loose alliance or confederation. In 1848, Switzerland developed a strong constitutional federalist system with a central government and 26 autonomous cantons (comparable to states or provinces). Switzerland's diversity grows out of these coexisting cantons comprised of overlapping ethnic, religious, and linguistic communities. Most cantons are officially monolingual (either French, German, Italian, or Rumantsch), and one religion dominates each canton. Another source of diversity are immigrants and refugees, some as workers from such European countries as Italy, Spain, and Turkey and some from more diverse origins such as Africa, the Antilles, and other non-European countries as well.[84]

> **For Further Reflection:** Think about the sociopolitical significance of languages. How do languages influence the makeup of a society? Why do most people care very deeply about the preservation of their native language? How are language, tradition, and power related?

Immigration policy

Although it is culturally diverse, Switzerland has a history of tightly controlled immigration determined mainly by Swiss economic needs, cultural interests, and popular sentiments about "over-foreignization." After World War II, for instance, Switzerland enforced a rotation model of immigration in which the residency of foreign workers was strictly short term, and they were admitted or expelled according to economic needs. Foreign workers also faced deportation if they disturbed the public order in any way. While the number of foreign workers holding permanent residency has climbed steadily over time, at present citizenship is very difficult to obtain. It is a strict *jus sanguinis* (based on blood or family lineage) policy of citizenship, which means that even second- or third-generation immigrant offspring do not automatically become Swiss citizens. The process of obtaining citizenship is also expensive.[85]

Recently the Swiss government developed a selective new model of immigration due to several factors, among them the continuing need for highly qualified workers from abroad. Examples of specific components of the new policy include bilateral agreements implemented with the European Union in 2007 to eliminate restrictions on the free movement of persons between countries within the union, and the Foreigners Act of 2008 that makes it easier for highly skilled Europeans to migrate to Switzerland but more difficult for non-Europeans.[86]

Today, the percentage of immigrants varies by region (approximately 3 percent in rural areas versus 35 percent in Geneva), which helps explain why immigration and related educational policies also vary considerably. Nevertheless, Switzerland has increased its educational support of immigrant children. During the 2009–10 school year, for instance, Swiss schools offered native language and culture instruction in almost 40 different languages, reflecting the diversity of Swiss immigrant children.[87]

Multilingual education

Educational policy is largely the responsibility of the cantons, and therefore each decides the official language of the canton and the schools. One complex national issue in Swiss education concerns the teaching of languages, such as the teaching of a second language, the teaching of English as a foreign language, the teaching of dialects, and the teaching of immigrant children in both the dominant language of the canton and children's native tongues. This complexity results in a terminological jungle: for example, standard German is called different things in different places - foreign language, second language, half-foreign language, neighbor language, and partner language.[88]

All Swiss students are required to learn at least one additional language; this acquisition of another national language has been called "a prerogative and duty of the citizens of this multilingual state."[89] The choice of the second language depends on the canton in which the student resides. As a norm, students in German-speaking parts of the country learn French as a second language, French speakers learn German, Italian speakers either German or French, and Rumantsch speakers either German, French, or Italian. Given its linguistic diversity, Switzerland struggles to harmonize language instruction and to standardize such things as the timing to initiate second language instruction (usually after the fifth, sixth, or seventh grade). A specific controversy surrounds the teaching of English (*Sprachenstreit* or "language strife"), because it is not one of the four national languages, although internationally important. Another issue concerns teaching dialects in schools. For example, French-speaking Swiss may be suspicious of efforts to support German dialects in German-speaking schools because it might increase language barriers between the French- and German-speaking citizens. In French-speaking Geneva, educators are faced with the question of whether students ought to learn standard German or the spoken version, Swiss-German (*Switzerdeutsch*), as the second language. Controversy surrounds whether Swiss-German is a standard second language or merely a dialect that might limit students' abilities to communicate with fellow citizens.[90]

Despite its ethnic and linguistic diversity, Switzerland is sometimes described not as a multilingual country but as a country where several coexisting monolingual societies share a common federal government. For Switzerland, then, language instruction is a major issue in education because it not only involves communication but also cultural and ethnic traditions as well, and the schools are at the center of debate surrounding multilingualism.

Summary and conclusions

Ethnicity and cultural differences continue to be sources of conflict, just as they are also sources of creativity and innovation. Societal change is almost certain to affect educational institutions. The United States has undergone several significant demographic shifts over time, caused in part by changing immigration patterns. Prior to the late twentieth century, most immigrants came from Europe, but today it is Latin America and Asia that provide the majority of immigrants. The history of immigration has been marked by tension between assimilation and pluralism, unity and diversity. A continuing challenge is how best to integrate or ameliorate these contesting forces.

An obstacle for American Indians, historically and currently, is how to educate their children in the larger society while also preserving their own native languages and cultures. A long history of suppression, including the imposition of an education that suppressed their linguistic and cultural traditions, has made progress difficult. Forced assimilation began softening in the 1920s, and since the 1960s important legislative and policy changes moved toward greater self-determination in American Indian education. Yet the struggle continues as American Indians seek an educational approach that provides better equal educational opportunities for their children.

European immigrants encountered many challenges after they arrived. For example, the Poles struggled with poverty and low educational attainment, and while they sought to maintain their ethnic identity through parochial schools reflecting Polish traditions, their children's education was compromised by pressing economic needs. Italian immigrants from mostly rural backgrounds had to make some harsh adjustments as they entered American urban industrial society. Over time, both Poles and Italians assimilated and are today considered part of the majority culture, but in many respects they also maintain important ethnic traditions. Critics continue to debate whether schools should be instruments of liberation or instruments of social control to assimilate immigrants into existing society, but the fact remains that the United States truly was and is a "nation of immigrants," and while many immigrants found the transitions difficult, most ultimately succeeded.

For Further Reflection: In your opinion, how have schools sometimes been the "great equalizers of society," and how have they sometimes been instruments to mold people into upholding the existing social order?

Some immigrant groups have faced unique issues, such as Mexicans Americans who have a long history of second-class status, first in territorial annexation, then labor recruitment, and now the problem of documented or undocumented status. Long regarded a source of cheap labor, Mexican immigrants frequently were denied access to quality schooling, while many native-born Mexican Americans experienced segregated schooling and Americanization. As with other minorities, the civil rights movement in the mid-twentieth century benefited Mexican Americans, but the extent of school success continues to be a problem.

Chinese Americans form another part of the American story of variety. Initially confronted with racial prejudice, exclusion, and school segregation, in recent times Chinese Americans have been perceived as members of the "model minority." While many Chinese immigrants are academically successful, others are hampered by popular assumptions that Chinese immigrants always do well, in part because of their ethnic backgrounds. In actuality, cultural and linguistic challenges confront Asian students just as they do other immigrants.

Clear and accurate explanations of problems and their causes are hard to come by, but they are necessary for successful reform efforts. For example, advocates of bilingual and multicultural education see their programs as ways to promote both majority and minority cultures in education in ways that help bridge social and cultural divisions, while critics see such education approaches as threats to social unity and as devices that encourage ethnic tensions and erect new forms of internal dissension. At present, there seems to be little common ground between the contending sides, but American society has confronted such divisions before, and the hope is it will successfully ameliorate or resolve present divisions.

Switzerland, a linguistically diverse nation with more than one official language, provides an international comparison. It faces challenges from diversity similar to those in the United States, but it also differs in significant ways. Switzerland is a small country with four national languages, but the linguistic and cultural distinctions among the four remain distinct, even though many citizens are bi- or multilingual. Although Switzerland has stringent and carefully controlled immigration and citizenship policies, all Swiss students are required to study the dominant language of their canton and at least one additional language as well. Maintaining several official languages and a culturally diverse population takes constant effort to build a society characterized by respect for cultural traditions, tolerance, and appreciation of differences. Although different, both Switzerland and the United States are diverse and struggle to respect diversity and also find common ground, a challenge in which schools play vital roles.

Vocabulary

acculturate
Americanization
assimilation

bicultural identity
bilingual education
cross-cultural education
cultural pluralism
cultural relativism
culturally biased testing
English as a second language (ESL)
Equal Educational Opportunity Act of 1974
ethnicity
Hispanic
Immigration Act of 1965
Indian Self-Determination and Education Assistance Act of 1975
Keyes v. School District no. 1, Denver, Colorado (1973)
Latino
Lau v. Nichols (1974)
limited English proficiency (LEP)
marginality
model minority
multicultural education
nativists
off-reservation boarding schools
parochial schools
pluralists
secondary migration
Sequoyah
stereotyping
Tape v. Hurley (1885)

Notes

1 Israel Zangwill, *The Melting Pot* (New York: Macmillan, 1923).

2 Peter D. Salins, "Assimilation, American Style," *Reason Magazine*, vol. 28, no. 9: 20–27 (February 1, 1997), at http://www.reason.com/news/show/30150.html (accessed on May 26, 2010); and Desmond King, *The Liberty of Strangers: Making the American Nation* (New York: Oxford University Press, 2005), 3–24 and 167–176.

3 "Paleoamerican Origins," *Smithsonian Encyclopedia*, at http://www.si.edu/Encyclopedia_SI/nmnh/origin.htm (accessed on May 24, 2010); Daniel C. Schiffner, "The Current Debate about the Origins of Paleoindians in America," *Journal of Social History* (December 22, 2003), at http://www.thefreelibrary.com/_/print/PrintArticle.aspx?id=111897842 (accessed on May 24, 2010); and David Thomas, *Skull Wars: Kennewick Man, Archaeology, and the Battle for Native American Identity* (New York: Basic Books, 2000), xvii–xxiv, 125–132.

4 James H. Merrell, *The Indians' New World: Catawbas and Their Neighbors from European Contact through the Era of Removal* (Chapel Hill: University of North Carolina Press, 1989), viii–x.

5 U.S. Census Bureau, "Table 1. Top 25 American Indian Tribes for the United States: 1990 and 1980," at http://www.census.gov/population/socdemo/race/indian/ailang1.txt (accessed on May 25, 2010); and "Table 9. Resident Population by Race, Hispanic Origin, and Age: 2000 and 2008," *The 2010 Statistical Abstract*, at http://www.census.gov/prod/2009pubs/10statab/pop.pdf (accessed on May 25, 2010).

6 Merrell, 259–271; E. Fred Sanders and Thomas J. Blumer, "The Catawba Nation under Siege: A Troubled History of Tribal Sovereignty," in *Foundations of First People's Sovereignty: History, Education and Culture*, Ulrike Wiethaus, ed. (Washington, DC: Peter Lang, 2008), 97–122.

7 Chief Joseph, "Selection from a Speech Before Assembled Dignitaries in Washington, D. C., January 14, 1879," in *The Wisdom of the Great Chiefs: The Classic Speeches of Chief Red Jacket, Chief Joseph, and Chief Seattle*, Kent Nerburn, ed. (San Rafael, CA: New World Library, 1994), 19–20.

8 Joyce B. Phillips and Paul Gary Phillips, "Introduction," *The Brainerd Journal: A Mission to the Cherokees, 1817–1823*, Joyce B. Phillips and Paul Gary Phillips, eds (Lincoln: University of Nebraska Press, 1998), 1–5, 18–19.

9 Samuel A Worchester, Letter to William S. Coodey, March 15, 1830, *New Echota Letters: Contributions of Samuel A. Worcester to the Cherokee Phoenix*, Jack F. Kilpatrick and Anna G. Kilpatrick, eds (Dallas: Southern Methodist University Press, 1968), 77–80; and *Worchester v. Georgia* (1832) at http://supct.law.cornell.edu/supct/html/historics/USSC_CR_0031_0515_ZO.html (accessed on October 13, 2010).

10 William G. McLoughlin, "An Alternative Missionary Style: Evan Jones and John B. Jones among the Cherokees," in *Between Indian and White Worlds: The Cultural Brokers*, Margaret Connell Szasz, ed. (Norman: University of Oklahoma Press, 1994), 99–102, 104–109, 113, 116, 118–120; and Delores J. Huff, *To Live Heroically: Institutional Racism and American Indian Education* (Albany: State University of New York, 1997), 2–4.

11 Huff, xii–xiii, 1–2; Merrell, 240–242; Michael C. Coleman, "American Indian School Pupils as Cultural Brokers: Cherokee Girls at Brainerd Mission, 1828–1829," in *Between Indian and White Worlds: The Cultural Brokers*, 122–135.

12 Board of Indian Commissioners, "Indian Education," in *Americanizing the American Indians: Writings by "Friends of the Indian" 1880–1900*, Francis Paul Prucha, ed. (Cambridge, MA: Harvard University Press, 1973), 193–196.

13 U.S. Constitution, Article I, Section 8, and Article II, Section 2; and David E. Wright, III, Michael W. Hirlinger, and Robert E. England, *The Politics of Second Generation Discrimination in American Indian Education: Incidence, Explanation, and Mitigating Strategies* (Westport, CT: Bergin and Garvey, 1998), 7–8.

14 Thomas J. Morgan, "Compulsory Education," in *Americanizing the American Indians*, 252–256.

15 Thomas, 49–50, 53–63, and 101–112; Richard Henry Pratt, "The Advantages of Mingling Indians and Whites," in *Americanizing the American Indians*, 261, 266; and Sally J. McBeth, "The Primer and the Hoe," *Natural History*, vol. 93: 4–11 (August 1984).

16 Clyde Ellis, "Boarding School Life at the Kiowa-Comanche Agency, 1893–1920," *The Historian*, vol. 58, no. 4: 778–793 (Summer 1996).

17 Margaret Connell Szasz, *Education and the American Indian: The Road to Self Determination Since 1928*, 3rd edn (Albuquerque: University of New Mexico Press, 1999), 8–9, 12; and McBeth, 4–11.

18 Vine Deloria, Jr., and Clifford M. Lytle, *American Indians and American Justice* (Austin: University of Texas Press, 1983), 217–222, 240–244.

19 Lewis Meriam et al., *The Problem of Indian Administration* (Baltimore: Johns Hopkins University Press, 1928); Szasz, 3, 18–29, 60, 89, 91, 97, 101–105, and 189; and Deloria and Lytle, 92–102.

20 Guy B. Senese, *Self-Determination and the Social Education of Native Americans* (New York: Praeger, 1991), 3–7, 11, 16, 19–21, and 37; and Szasz, 113–114.

21 Szasz, 146, 150.

22 Ibid., 200; Senese, xi–xii, 183; and David Wilkins, "Indigenous Self-Determination: A Global Perspective," in *Foundations of First People's Sovereignty: History, Education and Culture*, Ulrike Wiethaus, ed. (New York: Peter Lang, 2008), 11–20.

23 David Tyack, *Turning Points in American Educational History*, David Tyack, ed. (Waltham, MA: Blaisdell Publishing Co., 1967), 228–229.

24 Oscar Handlin, "Education and the European Immigrant, 1820–1920," in *Immigrant America: European Ethnicity in the United States*, Timothy Walch, ed. (New York: Garland Publishing, Inc., 1994), 7–12.

25 Elwood P. Cubberley, *Public Education in the United States: A Study and Interpretation of American Educational History* (New York: Houghton Mifflin, 1919), 337–338.

26 William J. Galush, "What Should Janek Learn? Staffing and Curriculum in Polish American Parochial Schools, 1870–1940," *History of Education Quarterly*, vol. 40, no. 4: 395–400 (Winter 2000).

27 Ibid., 417.

28 Timothy Walch, "The Ethnic Dimension in American Catholic Parochial Education," *Immigrant America: European Ethnicity in the United States*, Timothy Walch, ed. (New York: Garland Publishing, Inc., 1994), 142; and Mark M. Krug, *The Melting of the Ethnics: Education of the Immigrants, 1880–1914* (Bloomington: Phi Delta Kappa Educational Foundation, 1976), 6–7, 49–51.

29 John Bodnar, "Schooling and the Slavic-American Family, 1900–1940," *American Education and the European Immigrant: 1840–1940*, Bernard Weiss, ed. (Urbana: University of Illinois Press, 1982), 78–81.

30 Krug, 23–25.

31 Ibid.

32 Walch, "The Ethnic Dimension in American Catholic Parochial Education," 142–146.

33 See, for example, Colin Greer, *The Great School Legend: A Revisionist Interpretation of American Public Education* (New York: Basic Books, 1972), and Michael Katz, *Class, Bureaucracy, and Schools: The Illusion of Educational Change* (New York: Praeger, 1971).

34 Salvatore J. LaGumina, "American Education and the Italian Immigrant Experience," *American Education and the European Immigrant: 1840–1940*, 61–72; and Krug, 25–28, 51–54.

35 "Table 6. Resident Population by Sex, Race, and Hispanic-Origin Status: 2000 to 2008," *2010 Statistical Abstract*, at http://www.census.gov/compendia/statab/2010/tables/10s0006.pdf (accessed on May 25, 2010); and Karen Humes and Jesse McKinnon, "The Asian and Pacific Islander Population in the United States: Population Characteristics," *Current Population Reports*, U.S. Census Bureau, Department of Commerce, Economics and Statistics Administration (March 1999).

36 Howard Ozmon and Samuel M. Craver, *Philosophical Foundations of Education* (Upper Saddle River, NJ: Merrill, Prentice Hall, 2003), 103–104.

37 Meyer Weinberg, *Asian-American Education: Historical background and Current Realities* (Mahwah, NJ: Lawrence Erlbaum Associates, 1997), 12–15.

38 Ibid., 17–20.

39 Ibid., 22–24; and Don T. Nakanishi, "Growth and Diversity: The Education of Asian/Pacific Americans," in *The Asian American Educational Experience: A Source Book for Teachers and Students*, Don T. Nakanishi and Tina Yamano Nishida, eds (New York: Routledge, 1995), xiii.

40 *Lau v. Nichols*, 414 U.S. 563 (1974), at http://supct.law.cornell.edu/supct/html/historics/USSC_CR_0414_0563_ZO.html (accessed on May 15, 2010). See also Weinberg, 24–28.

41 "Table 1. Hispanic Population, by Nativity: 2000 and 2008," Statistical Portrait of Hispanics in the United States, 2007, Pew Hispanic Center, at http://pewhispanic.org/files/factsheets/hispanics2008/Table%201.pdf (accessed on May 28, 2010); and "Table 6. Detailed Hispanic Origin: 2008," Statistical Portrait of Hispanics in the United States, 2007, Pew Hispanic Center, at http://pewhispanic.org/files/factsheets/hispanics2008/Table%206.pdf (accessed on May 28, 2010).

42 Julian Samora and Patricia Vandel-Simon, *A History of the Mexican-American People* (Notre Dame: University of Notre Dame Press, 1977), 6, 99–100.

43 Ruben Donato, *The Other Struggle for Equal Schools: Mexican Americans during the Civil Rights Era* (Albany: State University of New York Press, 1997), 37–40; Julian Samora and Patricia Vandel Simon, *Los Mojados: The Wetback Story* (Notre Dame: University of Notre Dame Press, 1971), 6–7, 17–19, and 149; and "Mexican Immigrant Labor History," at http://www.pbs.org/kpbs/theborder/history/timeline/17.html (accessed on May 15, 2010).

44 Donato, 12, 29–33.

45   Gilbert G. Gonzalez, "Culture, Language, and the Americanization of Mexican Children," in *Latinos and Education: A Critical Reader*, Antonia Darder, Rodolfo D. Torres, and Henry Gutíerrez, eds (New York: Routledge, 1997), 162–173.

46 Guadalupe Salinas, "Mexican-Americans and the Desegregation of Schools in the Southwest," in *Latino Language and Education: Communication and the Dream Deferred*, Antoinette Sedillo López, ed., vol. 5 (New York and London: Garland Publishing, Inc., 1995), 157; Guadalupe San Miguel, Jr. "Mexican American Organizations and the Changing Politics of School Desegregation in Texas, 1944 to 1980," in *Latino Language and Education*, 180–186.

47 *Cisneros v. Corpus Christi Independent School District*, 467 F.2d 142 (CA5 1972); and *Keyes v. School District No. 1, Denver, Colorado*, 413 US 189 (1973), at http://supct.law.cornell.edu/supct/html/historics/USSC_CR_0413_0189_ZO1.html (accessed on May 15, 2010); Richard R. Valencia, "The Plight of Chicano Students: An Overview of Schooling Conditions and Outcomes," in *Chicano School Failure and Success: Research and Policy Agendas for the 1990s*, Richard R. Valencia, ed. (London: The Falmer Press, 1991), 7; and San Miguel, 186–192.

48 As quoted in Arthur M. Schlesinger, Jr., *The Disuniting of America: Reflections on a Multicultural Society*, rev. and enl. ed. (New York: W.W. Norton and Co., Inc., 1998), 31.

49 Timothy Walch, "Introduction," *Immigrant America: European Ethnicity in the United States*, ix–xii; and Michael C. Charney et al., "Introduction," *Asian Migrants and Education: The Tension of Education in Immigrant Societies and among Migrant Groups*. Education in the Asia-Pacific Region Series, vol. 2 (Dordrecht, The Netherlands: Kluwer Academic Publishers, 2003), xvii.

50 Mary V. Alfred, "Transnational Migration, Social Capital and Lifelong Learning in the USA," *International Journal of Lifelong Education*, vol. 29, no. 2: 143–147 (March 2010).

51 K. Tsianina Lowawaima and Teresa L. McCarty, *To Remain an Indian: Lessons in Democracy from a Century of Native American Education* (New York: Teachers College Press, 2006), 91–93, 95–103, 117–132, 134–138, and 151–158.

52 See "Bureau of Indian Education," Bureau of Indian Affairs, U.S. Department of the Interior, at http://www.bia.gov/WhatWeDo/ServiceOverview/IndianEducation/index.htm (accessed on May 17, 2010); and Bureau of Indian Education, at http://enan.bia.edu/home.aspx (accessed on May 15, 2010).

53 "Indian Education," Hearing before the Committee of Indian Affairs, United States Senate, One Hundred Ninth Congress, June 16, 2005 (Washington, DC: U.S. Government Printing Office, 2005), 1, 13, 17, 20, 26, and 29, at http://www.gpo.gov/fdsys/pkg/CHRG-109shrg115/pdf/CHRG-109shrg115.pdf (accessed on May 17, 2010).

54 National Indian Education Association, *Preliminary Report on No Child Left Behind in Indian Country* (Washington, DC: National Indian Education Association, n.d.), at http://www.niea.org/sa/uploads/policyissues/29.23.NIEANCLBreport_final2.pdf (accessed on May 15, 2010).

55 *National Indian Education Study, 2007, PART I: Performance of American Indian and Alaska Native Students at Grades 4 and 8 on NAEP 2007 Reading and Mathematics Assessments*, at http://nces.ed.gov/nationsreportcard/pdf/studies/2008457_1.pdf (accessed on May 15, 2010), 22–23, and 58–59. For additional information, see *National Indian Education Study, 2007, PART II: The Educational Experiences of American Indian and Alaska Native Students in Grades 4 and 8, Statistical Analysis*, at http://nces.ed.gov/nationsreportcard/pdf/studies/2008458.pdf (accessed on May 15, 2010).

56 "The Foreign-Born Population in the United States: Population Characteristics, March 2000," at http://www.census.gov/prod/2000pubs/p20–534.pdf (accessed on May 15, 2010); and Table 2.6 Foreign Born Population by World Region of Birth, U.S. Citizenship Status, and Year of Entry, 2003, at http://www.census.gov/population/socdemo/foreign/ppl-174/tab02-06.pdf (accessed on May 15, 2010).

57 Michael Sadowski, ed., *Teaching Immigrant and Second-Language Students: Strategies for Success* (Cambridge, MA: Harvard Education Press, 2004), 1–2; Sue Books, *Poverty and Schooling in the U.S.: Contexts and Consequences* (Mahwah, NJ: Lawrence Erlbaum Associates, 2004), 53; and Robert L. Rhodes, Salvador Hector Ochoa and Samuel O. Ortiz, *Assessing Culturally and Linguistically Diverse Students: A Practical Guide.* The Guilford Practical Intervention in the Schools Series (New York: The Guilford Press, 2005), 15.

58 Steven A. Camarota, "Does Immigration Harm the Poor?" *The Public Interest* (Fall 1998), at http://www.cis.org/articles/1998/sacPublicInterest.html (accessed on May 15, 2010); John J. Miller, "The Politics of Permanent Immigration: How Pro-Immigration Forces Triumphed—and Why They're Likely to Keep Doing So," *Reason* (October 1998), at http://findarticles.com/p/articles/mi_m1568/is_n5_v30/ai_21141904 (accessed on May 15, 2010); and Ron Unz, "California and the End of White America," *Commentary* (November 1999) at http://www.onenation.org/9911/110199.html (accessed on May 15, 2010).

59 These population numbers were derived from the following sources: "Immigrants to U.S. by Country of Origin," *Infoplease*, Pearson Education 2000–2009, at http://www.infoplease.com/ipa/A0201398.html (accessed on May 15, 2010); "Table 2. Persons Obtaining Legal Permanent Resident Status by Region and Selected Country of Last Residence: Fiscal Years 1820 to 2008," *Yearbook of Immigration Statistics: 2008*, at http://www.dhs.gov/ximgtn/statistics/publications/LPR08.shtm (accessed on October 29, 2010); "Table 42. Foreign-Born Population—Selected Characteristics by Region of Origin: 2007," *Statistical Abstract of the United States*, at http://www.census.gov/compendia/statab/cats/population/nativeandforei gn-bornpopulations.html (accessed on October 29, 2010); and "Table 3. Foreign Born, by Region of Birth: 2000 and 2007," *Statistical Portrait of the Foreign-Born Population in the United States, 2007*, Pew Hispanic Center, at http://pewhispanic.org/files/factsheets/foreignborn2007/Table%203.pdf (accessed on October 29, 2010).

60 Michael Hoefer, Nancu Rrytina, and Bryan C. Baker, "Estimates of the Unauthorized Immigrant Population Residing in the United States: 2008," Office of Immigration Statistics, at http://www.dhs.gov/xlibrary/assets/statistics/publications/ois_ill_pe_2008.pdf (accessed on May 15, 2010).

61 Gabriella C. Gonzales, *Educational Attainment in Immigrant Families* (New York: LFB Scholarly Publishing, 2005), 101.

62 Richard R. Valencia, "The Plight of Chicano Students: An Overview of Schooling Conditions and Outcomes," in *Chicano School Failure and Success: Research and Policy Agendas for the 1990s*, Richard R. Valencia, ed. (London: The Falmer Press, 1991), 4–20.

63 William A. Sampson, *Black and Brown: Race, Ethnicity, and School Preparation* (Lanham, MD: Scarecrow Press, 2004).

64 Gualdalupe Valdés, *Con Respecto: Bridging the Distances between Culturally Diverse Families and Schools, An Ethnographic Portrait* (New York: Teachers College Press, 1996), 29, 160–205.

65 Ibid., 27.

66 Don T. Nakanishi, "Growth and Diversity: The Education of Asian/Pacific Americans," in *The Asian American Educational Experience: A Source Book for Teachers and Students,* Don Nakanishi and Tina Yamano Nishida, eds. (New York: Routledge, 1995), xi.

67 Yali Zou, "The Voice of a Chinese Immigrant in America: Reflections on Research and Self-Identity, in: *Immigrant Voices*, Enrique T. Trueba and Lilia I. Bartolomé, eds (Lanham: Rowman & Littlefield Publishers, 2000), 198; and Dan Wang, "Family-School Relations as Social Capital: Chinese Parents in the United States," *The School Community Journal*, vol. 18, no. 2: 142–143 (Fall/Winter 2008).

68 Li-Rong Lilly Cheng, "Socio-Cultural Adjustment of Chinese-American Students," in *Asian-American Education: Prospects and Challenges*, Clara C. Park and Marilyn Mei-Ying Chi, eds (Westport, CT: Bergin and Garvey, 1999), 10–17.

69 Marilyn Mei-Ying Chi, "Linguistic Perspective on the Education of the Chinese-American Students," in *Asian-American Education: Prospects and Challenges*, 18–39.

70 Terry Wrigley, *The Power to Learn: Stories and Success in the Education of Asian and Other Bilingual Pupils* (Sterling, VA: Trentham Books, 2000), 3.

71 Rebecca D. Freeman, *Bilingual Education and Social Change* (Philadelphia: Multilingual Matters, 1998), 4–6; "Bilingual Education," *Education Week* (January 24, 2001), at http://www.edweek.org/rc/issues/english-language-learners/ (accessed on May 15, 2010).

72 Diane Brockett, "Reaching Out to Immigrant Parents," *Education Digest* (April 1998).

73 See "Welcome to the Seattle Public Schools," at http://www.seattleschools.org/area/main/index.dxml; "Bilingual Student Services" at http://www.seattleschools.org/area/bilingual/index.dxml; "Bilingual Orientation Centers," at http://www.seattleschools.org/area/bilingual/bocs_intro.htm; English Language Learning Programs," at http://www.seattleschools.org/area/bilingual/ell_programs.htm; "Bilingual Family Center: Welcome!" at http://www.seattleschools.org/area/bfc/index.dxml (all accessed on May 15, 2010); and "Family Involvement in Seattle Public Schools: Highlights," at http://www.seattleschools.org/area/fam/highlight.dxml (accessed on June 5, 2009).

74 Diane Ravitch, "Politicization and the Schools: The Case of Bilingual Education," *Proceedings of the American Philosophical Society*, vol. 129, no. 2: 121–128 (June 1985).

75 Proposition 227, English Language in Public Schools. Initiative Statute, at http://primary98.sos.ca.gov/VoterGuide/Propositions/227text.htm (accessed on May 15, 2010); California Codes, Education Code, Section 305–306, at http://www.leginfo.ca.gov/cgi-bin/waisgate?WAISdocID=5809826097+14+0+0&WAISaction=retrieve (accessed on May 5, 2009); Mary Ann Zehr, "Arizona Grapples with Bilingual Ed. Changes," *Education Week* (January 24, 2001), at http://www.edweek.org/ew/articles/2001/01/24/19arizona.h20.html (accessed on May 15, 2010); and Sonia White Soltero, *Dual Language: Teaching and learning in Two Languages* (Boston: Pearson/Allyn and Bacon, 2004), 3.

76 *The General Laws of Massachusetts*, Part I. Administration of the Government, Title XII. Education, Chapter 71a. Transitional Bilingual Education, Section 4. English Language Education, at http://www.mass.gov/legis/laws/mgl/71a-4.htm (accessed on May 15, 2010); James Vasnis, "Boston Students Struggle with English-only Rule," *The Boston Globe*, April 7, 2009, A-1, at http://www.boston.com/news/education/k_12/articles/2009/04/07/boston_students_struggle_with_english_only_rule/ (accessed on May 15, 2010); and Rosann Tung et al., *English Learners in Boston Public Schools: Enrollment, Engagement and Academic Outcomes, AY2003-AY2006: Final Report,* The Mauricio Gastón Institute for Latino Community Development and Public Policy, University of Massachusetts, Boston, and the Center for Collaborative Education, Boston, April 2009, at http://www.gaston.umb.edu/articles/2009%20Final%20ELL%20Report_online.pdf (accessed on May 15, 2010).

77 Donaldo Macedo, "English Only: The Tongue-Tying of America," *Journal of Education*, vol. 173, no. 2: 9–20 (Spring 1991); Jim Cummins, "Foreword," in *Bilingual Education: From Compensatory to Quality Schooling*, María Estela Brisk, ed. (Mahwah, NJ: Lawrence Erlbaum Associates, 1998), vii–ix; and Eugene E. García, *Teaching and Learning in Two Languages: Bilingualism and Schooling in the United States* (New York: Teachers College Press, 2005),160–161.

78 James Banks, "Series Foreword," in Larry Cuban, *Frogs into Princes: Writings on School Reform* (New York: Teachers College Press, 2008), vii–x; and Carl A. Grant and Christine E. Sleeter, *Turning on Learning: Five Approaches on Multicultural Teaching Plans for Race, Class, Gender, and Disability.* 5th edn (San Francisco: Wiley, 2009), 177.

79 James Banks, "Multicultural Education: Characteristics and Goals," in *Multicultural Education: Issues and Perspectives*, 5th edn James A. Banks and Cherry A. McGee Banks, eds (San Francisco: John

Wiley & Sons, 2005), 3, 20–25; and Sonia Nieto,"School Reform and Student Achievement: A Multicultural Perspective," in *Multicultural Education: Issues and Perspectives*, 387–407.

80 See Schlesinger, *The Disuniting of America*; and Dinesh D'Souza. *The End of Racism: Principles for a Multiracial Society* (New York: The Free Press, 1995), 343, 350.

81 Benjamin Barber, *An Aristocracy of Everyone: The Politics of Education and the Future of America* (New York: Oxford University Press, 1992), 146–149, 191.

82 "Switzerland," *The World Factbook*, at https://www.cia.gov/library/publications/the-world-factbook/geos/sz.html#top (accessed on June 7, 2010).

83 Koordinationskommission für die Präsenz der Schweiz im Ausland, EDA, Bern, *Die Schweiz – Landschaft und Umwelt, Staat und Politik, Sozialstruktur, Wirtschaft, Erziehung und Bildung, Kultur* (Schweiz: COCO Switzerland, 1998); Charles L. Glenn, with Ester J. de Jong, *Educating Immigrant Children: Schools and Language Minorities in Twelve Nations* (New York: Garland, 1996), 128; and Kümmerly and Frey, *Schweizer Brevier* (Zollikofen-Bern: Geografischer Verlag, 1999), 26.

84 "Swiss History," swissworld, at http://www.swissworld.org/en/history/ (accessed on June 7, 2010); "Language Distribution," Swissworld, at http://www.swissworld.org/en/people/language/language_distribution/ (accessed on June 7, 2010); and Patrick R. Ireland, *The Policy Challenge of Ethnic Diversity: Immigrant Policies in France and Switzerland* (Cambridge, MA: Harvard University Press, 1994), 147.

85 Glenn and de Jong, 129; and Ireland, 148–152.

86 *European Commission, "Background information on migrant and minority populations, immigration and integration policies, etc."* http://mighealth.net/ch/index.php/1 (accessed July 28, 2010).

87 Schweizerische Konferenz der kantonalen Erziehungsdirektoren, Unterrichtsangebote, at http://www.ides.ch/dyn/13341.php (accessed on July 27, 2010).

88 Claudine Brohy and Anne-Lore Bregy, "Mehrsprachige und plurikulturelle Schulmodelle in der Schweiz oder: What's in a Name?" *Bulletin suisse de linguistique applique*, no. 67, 85–99 (1998), at http://www.eric.ed.gov/PDFS/ED422731.pdf (accessed on June 27, 2010).

89 Daniel Stotz. "Breaching the Peace: Struggles around Multilingualism in Switzerland." *Language Policy*, vol. 5, no. 2: 252 (June 2006).

90 Gunter M. Hega, *Consensus Democracy? Swiss Education Policy between Federalism and Subsidiarity* (New York: Peter Lang, 1999), 139; and Glenn and de Jong, 130.

6

Gender and Education

Chapter objectives

- To explain how gender relations are contextually defined and subject to change over time.
- To discuss the progress and challenges surrounding gender bias in education.
- To delineate the historical efforts to overcome inequalities in education based on gender.
- To analyze how gender continues to shape the status of the teaching profession.
- To explore how major theories of knowing, learning, and thinking reflect prevailing societal attitudes toward men and women.
- To clarify how children learn culturally constructed gender identities and gender roles.
- To develop better understanding of gender equality and conditions in educational institutions that perpetuate gender biases.
- To analyze societal constructions of femininity/masculinity and how these affect the educational achievement of both girls and boys.
- To critique reform efforts intended to eradicate gender bias in education.
- To explore the issue of gender in education by way of international comparison.

Opening questions

1. In what way is the concept of gender culturally defined, and what social forces lead to such definitional changes?
2. What historical developments have most affected gender equity and why?
3. How has the teaching profession been shaped by gender?
4. How does gender continue to affect theories of learning and knowing?
5. How does gender influence the socialization of the young?
6. How do educational institutions at the elementary and secondary levels reflect gender bias?
7. What efforts are being made to develop gender equity in schools, and how successful are these efforts?
8. What conclusions about gender issues in education can be drawn from international comparison?

The issue

Of all human relations, perhaps the one that has historically been most characterized by mystery and misunderstanding is the relation between males and females. Art and literature are devoted to it; great religions contain ideals and prescriptions regarding it; and major social institutions such as families have been organized around it. Just as race, ethnicity, and class invariably influence people's lives, so also does **gender**. Educational institutions shape gender relations and are also shaped by them. Images of what is appropriate for males and females have long impacted such things as admissions, student tracking, and curricular and extracurricular activities. Educators and students, furthermore, may consciously or unconsciously perpetuate **gender stereotypes** while also striving to create more equitable gender relations.

Much has changed in recent times in regard to gender, and some might argue that gender has ceased to be a problem in education; after all, dramatic improvements have been made in girls' and women's access to schools and educational programs, and such blatant practices as routinely scheduling girls in home economics and boys in shop classes have been reduced or eradicated. Much also has been done to encourage females in math, science, and other traditional male disciplines. In higher education, females have surpassed males in college admission and graduation rates.

However, such improvements do not mean **gender bias** has disappeared in education; rather, it has become more subtle and informal. For example, better educational opportunity has not necessarily meant that females reap the same occupational benefits as males. Although there have been improvements, the so-called glass ceiling continues to keep women underrepresented in the higher echelons of power and influence. In other words, it is not so much the formal obstacles to education that are of primary concern today but more subtle and informal obstacles that demarcate as effectively as the old ones did. Thus, while much has been done to improve gender equity, both female and male students need education that is appropriate for them, and the quest for equal educational opportunity, as far as gender is concerned, remains uncompleted.[1]

The meaning of the term gender arises from cultural conventions and institutional arrangements, and it differs from **sex**, or the biological attributes typically associated with egg, sperm, and reproduction of the species. As used here, gender is a sociocultural term based on ideas, concepts, or abstractions of what it means to be feminine or masculine, including how gender impacts such things as educational achievement, social status, and personal identity.

There is a long history of debate over gender relations and the conditions that prevent females from the same rights, educational opportunities, and control over their lives and bodies as males have. The debate has shifted over time from an emphasis on the more blatant to the more subtle forms of discrimination involving socialization patterns and deeply internalized assumptions about gender. Gender bias is a form of prejudice, which may be defined in its most general sense as thinking ill of others without sufficient warrant, an aversive or hostile attitude taken toward another person who belongs to a specific group and is therefore presumed to have the stereotypical qualities ascribed to that group.[2] Such a definition helps clarify what gender bias involves, that is, a person's gender serves as the group identity, and certain stereotyped characteristics are ascribed to that group, such as "all women are emotional" or "all men are violent," each of which is an ascription frequently applied to individuals because of their gender. The problem with ascriptions is that they are frequently based on faulty logic and are simply not true.

Gender bias does not necessarily involve hostile attitudes, however. The seemingly benevolent belief that women are naturally suited to take care of children, for instance, is not inherently hostile and is embraced by many women themselves. Such beliefs become prejudicial when based on unwarranted assumptions about individual persons solely on the basis of their gender that, when given credible social acceptance, serve to lock both women and men into narrowly defined roles. Instead of being innate features determined by biology, most gender-related behaviors are due to environmental conditioning and are just as socioculturally constructed as the gender stereotypes that accompany them.

Suggested Activity: When people discuss parental involvement in school, child care, summer camps, extracurricular activities, babysitters, and other issues relating to the care of their children, does the conversation involve both genders equally? How do you explain your observations?

Suggested Activity: Consider parents you know who have school-age children, are both working full time outside the home and are equally sharing child-rearing and domestic responsibilities. How many couples fit this description? Which parent usually takes care of most domestic duties? In your opinion, are traditional expectations the rule, or are the expectations changing?

Not all gender differentiation is meant to be harmful, but harm is often a result. Consider the loss to society caused by the casual belief that females are intellectually inferior to males. The resulting cost of undeveloped human talent is incalculable, not to mention the personal hardships experienced by individuals having to occupy an assigned, inferior status in social, political, and economic affairs. Similar harm results from males being forced into aggressive behavior because it is considered the "manly" thing to do. Perhaps the true problem of gender bias comes from forcing individuals to fit into the abstract cultural ideals of womanhood or manhood, ideals which few individuals possibly fit in all respects. While it may be important to maintain male and female distinctions in some aspects of life, it is also important to take care with how those distinctions are made and to what effect. Education has played a role in transmitting gender distinctions, but it also has been and continues to be a setting in which gender distinctions can be made more helpful and humane.

Background

Historically speaking, male dominance has been a feature of most cultures. Explanations for this include differences between males and females in such things as brain size, chromosomes and hormones, spinal curvature, physical strength, and genitalia and reproductive systems, but none satisfactorily explain the extent of gender-based social and cultural distinctions made over the course of history. One hypothesis is that women's inferior status did not evolve around physical or biological differences but around cultural ideals of womanhood.[3]

The colonial period

Despite obvious gender inequities during the colonial period of American history, women played an important role in domestic economic production and in social life. Men's work was located outdoors or related to external business pursuits, and women's was in child care, household industries, and community functions such as caring for the sick and taking in orphans. Although women held an inferior position in the power hierarchy, they met important social and economic needs crucial to society.[4]

Suggested Activity: Interview several family members or friends, and ask them to define or describe their understanding of womanhood and manhood today. Do their views differ from one another, and how do they compare to definitions that prevailed in earlier times?

Women also played an important educational role. In early colonial times, the family served as the basic educational institution, because formal schooling was not readily available in many communities. Few overt gender distinctions occurred in the earliest years, but by age five or six gender came into sharper focus in chores and work assignments. Boys dominated apprenticeship opportunities, although some girls were apprenticed too. Most literate parents promoted education for both male and female children for practical reasons and for religious purposes such as Bible reading. As colonial life became more settled, schools increasingly complemented family-based education. The number and types of schools grew until, by the early 1700s, there were at least four basic school types, including dame schools, reading and writing schools, Latin grammar schools, and colleges. Most teachers at the time were male, but dame schools were usually taught by women and concentrated on the rudiments for small boys and girls. The reading and writing schools, adapted along the lines of the petty schools of England, provided a more thorough grounding in the three Rs. Some women taught in these schools, and a fair number of girls attended as well, but as age increased and school type changed, males became dominant, both as teachers and as students. This was true in the Latin grammar schools, which provided secondary education and preparation for higher education, but particularly in the colleges, male domains concentrating on classical studies in the liberal arts as preparation for the professions and for leadership positions in society.[5]

From roughly 1750 to about 1820, some fundamental changes occurred. In 1776, the Declaration of Independence proclaimed that "all men are created equal," and many people apparently took the statement literally. Abigail Adams criticized women's absence from the declaration and implored her husband, John, to include women's rights in the deliberations of the Second Continental Congress in 1777. He raised the issue of women's voting rights but to no avail. Such an outcome was indicative of the times: Even Thomas Paine, the radical pamphleteer whose broadsides did so much to stir revolutionary fervor, had little effect when he also championed a political role for women. There were others who also advocated changes: In the eighteenth century, Benjamin Franklin thought females should be educated not only in basic literacy but also in foreign languages, business management, and accounting, and he professed respect for women's abilities in philosophical and scientific matters as well. Benjamin Rush urged that women should not only be educated in child rearing and home economics but also in the principles of liberty, government, patriotism, the liberal arts, and business management, points of view echoed by De Witt Clinton and Charles Burroughs in the nineteenth century as well.[6] Although few such advocates saw women taking on truly equal roles with men, they did reflect a slowly developing view that the better education of females was indispensable to the survival of organized society and cultural life.

> **Suggested Activity:** Look up a source of correspondence between Abigail Adams and her husband John Adams or read biographical treatments of the Adamses. What were their views on the education of females and the status of women?

The cult of true womanhood

A new image emerged for women during the early to middle decades of the nineteenth century, sometimes referred to as the **cult of true womanhood**. As reflected in images presented in books, popular religious literature, and women's magazines from 1820 to 1860, a new abstraction of womanhood—based on a view of woman as domestic, submissive, pliable, and pious—was lifted to such heights that "If anyone, male or female, dared to tamper with the complex of virtues which made up True Womanhood, he was damned immediately as an enemy of God, of civilization, and of the Republic;" moreover, the greatest responsibility for upholding the image belonged to the female, "to uphold the pillars of the temple with her frail white hand,"[7] a role presumably excluding women whose hands were not white.

The decades from 1820 to 1860 witnessed upheavals that fundamentally altered American society. Sometimes called the Era of the Common Man, this period generated great moral crusades to extend democratic citizenship rights, provide humane treatment of the mentally ill, abolish slavery, soften the impact of industrialization, and spread the development of public common schools. Major changes occurred in patterns of living and in the roles that men, women, and children occupied. Public elementary and secondary schools were established across the country during the nineteenth century, and females were to emerge in a paradoxical situation: They won many educational opportunities formerly reserved for males, and they gained access to all levels of schooling, but they still emerged with a distinctly inferior status.

The Industrial Revolution spread the factory system, and the economic role of most males was transformed from independent farmer or artisan to factory laborer working for someone else. Many products formerly handcrafted on farms or in small shops were now machine made in mass-production factories more cheaply than those made by hand. At the same time, industrialization also displaced many women from the traditional household or domestic economy, and they entered the industrial labor force in growing numbers as well. Children, too, were hired out to factories to supplement meager family incomes. Important aspects of industrialization were based on the cheap labor supply of the lower classes, and among the cheapest were the women and children.

For example, Samuel Slater, a nineteenth-century Rhode Island industrialist, recruited whole families to work in his textile factories. One man entered a contract with Slater for weekly wages on the following basis: $5.00 for himself, $2.33 for his sister, $2.00 for a 16-year-old son, $1.50 for a 13-year-old son, $1.25 for a 12-year-old daughter, and $.75 for an eight-year-old daughter.[8] Adult women were rarely if ever paid equal wages for equal work. As industrialists further simplified textile manufacturing and machine tending became the norm, women and children were increasingly hired, with women laborers soon outnumbering men in some light industries. Women's historic roles as managers of home economies and providers of community social services diminished under industrialization.

> **For Further Reflection:** What appears a relic of "the olden days" continues to this day, albeit to a lesser degree. Discrimination still exists in wage or salary discrepancies where women earn less than men. Why does this inequity continue? What needs to happen, in your opinion, in order for women to gain equal pay? How is education connected to this issue?

The cult of true womanhood celebrated an ideal of superior moral force that swept across the upper classes and influenced the lower as well, but only a few actual women could afford the projected lifestyle. Nevertheless, the message was touted from pulpit, lectern, newspaper, magazine, and novel: Woman's mission was not only to shape the social graces of husband and children but to spread the blessings of civilized domesticity to the distant corners of the nation. Indeed, many a rustic frontier town was "tamed" by women through family life, cultural events, benevolent societies, temperance crusades, reading circles, and schools, but the new model of womanhood took root most securely in urban areas where industrialization and modernization were driving forces.[9]

> **Suggested Activity:** Study images of women in the popular media today, particularly in magazines, television, movies, and on the internet. To what extent are women still portrayed as "soothers," "tamers" and "superior moral forces"? How are present-day images of femininity constructed, and how have they changed from older images? If so, what role has education played in those changes?

In contrast, laissez-faire capitalism encouraged reckless speculation and a boom- or-bust economy, which often caused unemployment and foreclosures that, in turn, bred crime, vice, and substance abuse. Thus, the nineteenth century witnessed the development of a set of counteracting values: Men were drawn away from family farms and neighborhood industries into the outer world of the competitive marketplace, while the education of the young was left more and more in the hands of women who were supposed to protect humane values in a world gone mad with material acquisition.[10] In short, the concepts of manhood and womanhood were once again set on conflicting courses, and they never achieved more than a precarious balance at best.

Women in the common school movement

The common school movement was supported by large numbers of women. Although the aim of providing tax-supported schools to every child fell short of the mark in some areas (such as black children being excluded in the slaveholding South), the movement provided many girls and boys throughout the nation with a chance to attend school. Men filled leadership roles in the movement, but great numbers of women were active on its behalf. People in the movement were convinced that the solutions to major social problems ultimately rested on education.[11]

A reflection of the "true womanhood" image found in the movement was the belief that female teachers would provide a superior morality, better social harmony, and a more civilizing kind of influence, a view that has also been called **sentimental womanhood**. This challenges the assumption that women's new status was due solely to economic change; rather, sentimental womanhood was anchored in traditional assumptions that man was governed by the head and woman by the heart, a concept that neatly fit emerging economic beliefs that men were naturally competitive, rational, and unemotional in the pursuit of economic gain, while women were inherently maternal, affectionate, and moral in pursuit of cultural and social uplift. It was thus but a small step for adherents of this view of womanhood to conclude that the answer to the social stresses of industrialization was the maternal instinct. If the essence of motherhood was teaching, then society would be more effectively saved if women's maternal influence dominated the schoolroom.[12]

Be that as it may, economic factors still influenced women's entry into the teaching profession. Many men left teaching because they could ill afford to ignore the economic opportunities open to them in the expanding industrial markets of the day. Furthermore, women entered teaching because of their need for paid work as much as maternal instinct. Teaching was one of the few respectable professions open to women at the time. Whether it was the cult of true womanhood, economic necessity, or free choice that led them to it, the fact remains that an increasing number of women became teachers. Where teaching was once mostly a job for men, by the mid-nineteenth century women were openly recruited to teach in the new common schools. The belief that women were better at working with children was shared by reformer Horace Mann, who was pleased to report in 1843 that over a five-year period male teachers in Massachusetts had increased by only 131, while women teachers increased by 691. He also noted that the average monthly pay for men was $32.22, and for women, $12.78. While he recognized the economy of hiring women teachers, Mann also bemoaned the effects poor salaries had on attracting and retaining the best of them. He complained that some wealthy women spent more on a single piece of clothing than devoted female teachers received in annual salaries. Throughout the 1840s and 1850s, female teachers were paid about one-third of what male teachers were paid; nevertheless, females continued to enter the profession in growing numbers.[13]

One of the pioneers of female education in the nineteenth century was Emma Hart Willard, who devised a plan for a secondary school that led to the founding in 1821 of the **Troy Female Seminary** in Troy, New York. Willard sought financial support from the New York legislature on the grounds that females deserved education as much as males, but an education designed specifically for their needs. Mirroring the notion of sentimental womanhood, Willard proclaimed that appropriate female education would enhance the prosperity of a nation dependent on the character of its citizens, the formation of which rested on mothers. How much better mothers could perform this vital task, she argued, if they were properly educated. The New York legislature rebuffed her request, but by 1850 the diligent Willard garnered sufficient private support to found Troy Female Seminary and to establish its good academic reputation in quick order. She also believed that women would make good teachers for the common schools because nature had designed them with the capacities of persuasion, softness, and patience to care for children. If properly trained, they would educate children better than men and more cheaply too. Furthermore, it would free up men otherwise engaged in teaching to go out and create new wealth for the nation in the many business and industrial occupations for which, she believed, women were not naturally suited.[14]

Other advocates of women's role in the new schools included Catherine Beecher and Mary Lyon. Beecher, who founded **Hartford Female Seminary** in 1823, a private girls' school in Connecticut, was a strong advocate of public schooling, **coeducation**, and teacher preparation. She also founded an organization called the National Board of Popular Education that, among other things, helped place young women in teaching positions in the public common schools. Beecher, too, was a believer in the socially redemptive power of women, that it was to mothers and teachers that society should look for those who could most effectively mold the character of each rising generation.[15]

Mary Lyon founded a school for women that was an equivalent in scholarly effort and liberal education to men's colleges when she opened **Mount Holyoke Female Seminary** (later Mount Holyoke College) in 1837. Her plans for the institution included an evangelical religious emphasis and a strong academic reputation, with a primary objective of preparing young women to be teachers. Like Willard and Beecher, Lyon spread the view of womanhood devoted to social and moral redemption, but she also believed that teaching was a sacred activity and that teachers should be paid no more than ministers or missionaries. Indeed, she gave half of her own salary to mission work, and she argued that the true rewards of teaching were spiritual, not material.[16] For all her earnest idealism, however, Lyon's views on teacher pay may have helped contribute to the poor economic status of the teaching profession.

WEB: Suggested Reading 6.1.

By 1890, the work of Willard, Beecher, Lyon et al., led to women holding a predominant numerical role in the teaching profession at the elementary level. Women's numbers in high school teaching increased as well. Public high schools grew rapidly after the 1870s, and like the common school, they embraced coeducation and admitted girls as well as boys on a tax-supported tuition-free basis. Eventually, women occupied roughly two out of every three teaching positions by the early 1900s. The greater number of women in the teaching profession helped open the doors of the colleges and universities, which by the early twentieth century surpassed the normal schools in the preparation of teachers. Oberlin College was the first to admit women on a coeducational basis as early as 1833, but after 1865, there was a vigorous growth of private women's colleges, such as Vassar (1865), Smith (1875), Wellesley (1875), and Bryn Mawr (1885), to name a few. These institutions rejected domestic studies for women and promoted a rigorous academic education on par with men's colleges. In addition, most of the new public colleges and state universities that opened in the late nineteenth and early twentieth centuries also admitted women students.[17]

Not only did opportunities for women expand in teaching but gradually in other learned professions as well. It may be reasonably argued that entry into the teaching profession helped women gain a foothold in other learned professions. In effect, teaching aided women in achieving new levels of occupational status.

Perhaps one of the more significant developments from 1870 to 1900 was the increasing attendance of girls in the American high school, an institution that changed from a relatively elite institution to an extension of common schooling as it displaced the academies and seminaries of the early nineteenth century. By 1900, girls represented 59 percent of all secondary school enrollments, by which time the public high school was also the dominant American secondary school. Despite some efforts to stem the tide of coeducation, girls and boys studied many of the same subjects together, and this higher level of curricular equality allowed many girls to develop a new sense of their abilities to compete with boys intellectually. Such experiences were important to the rising generations of women involved in reforms for the rights of women.[18]

One of the outgrowths of women's participation in the public school movement was their acquisition of knowledge and skills about the inner workings of social institutions. From 1860 to 1920, there was a growing conviction among women that they should enjoy all the rights of citizenship and become involved in all the proper spheres of organized society. Not to be discounted was the surge of women into the labor market, for while they were economically exploited, they also gained experience with independence and self-sufficiency outside the traditional bounds of home and marriage. The picture was far from rosy, however. For example, in 1860 women textile workers only earned about $3.00 for a 75-hour week, as opposed to about $5.00 for men. By 1900, the average female tobacco worker in Pittsburgh still only earned about $5.00 per week as compared to $10.00 for men, and male bakers earned up to $100.00 per month, while women bread packagers earned only about $22.00 per month. (By way of comparison, a subsistence wage for an individual was figured at $7.00 per week in 1906). Of course, women were not alone in being wage exploited, for most men did not earn much more than women, and children earned far less. Labor unions were not well organized at the time, and if employers wished to take economic advantage of employees, there was little or nothing employees could do about it.[19]

Once again, a new interpretation of the cult of true womanhood came into being, this time based on helping people learn to manage their lives better and to adjust to the demands of industrialized society. Perhaps the best known of these "housekeepers of society" was Jane Addams, who founded Hull House, a social settlement house in the slums of Chicago. The Hull House program was designed to help poor immigrants ease their way into the American social and industrial mainstream by teaching them sound practices in home economy, sanitation, and proper child care, among other things. Another reformer was

Crystal Eastman (1881–1928), a pacifist working in the settlement houses of New York. She was a leading advocate of voting rights for women and one of the founders of the American Civil Liberties Union. Another influential figure was Charlotte Perkins Gilman (1860–1935), who advocated that the motherly instinct of love and service should be directed outward to large-scale social problems rather than focused inward on the home. Still others were Susan B. Anthony (1820–1906), a teacher who became an acknowledged leader in the **temperance movement** (control or prohibition of alcoholic beverages) and in the **women's suffrage movement** (right to vote for women); and Carrie Chapman Catt (1859–1947), an Iowa school superintendent who became prominent in the women's suffrage movement. These and other women were so successful that by 1920, the Eighteenth Amendment prohibiting the manu-facture and sale of alcoholic beverages and the Nineteenth Amendment giving women the right to vote were added to the U.S. Constitution. Notwithstanding these steps forward for women, World War I put the country through a strenu-ous test, and afterward there was a strong desire to return to normalcy and a resultant faltering of the women's movement. For example, Carrie Catt tried to use the League of Women's Voters to get women more effectively involved in exercising their newly won right to vote, but she found that women did not vote any more intelligently than men. Crystal Eastman agitated for a home- and school-based education that freed children from gender stereotyping, but to no avail.[20]

> **Suggested Activity:** Read historical accounts of women's participation in such move-ments as the abolition of slavery and temperance. What roles did they play in these organizations and how did their participation mark a major change in the social and political fabric at the time?

Women's changing status

Yet another image of womanhood was emerging, one that in many respects is still present today. In part, it evolved from the 1920s imagery of woman as a frivolous, pleasure-seeking, hard-drinking, cigarette-smoking, jazz-loving flapper. Most women, of course, worked as hard as ever in the home or in the paid labor force, but the flapper image was pushed in song, the popular press, and the new medium of motion pictures. The image was also anchored in the materialism unleashed after the lean times of World War I. Advertisers bombarded the public with hard-sell messages on hairstyles, makeup, clothes, automobiles, cigarettes, and the entertainment industries. In truth, the new image repackaged the old view of woman as man's temptress, with no deep intellectual aspirations and no sense of social responsibility beyond self-adornment, catching a husband, and bearing children. The Great Depression of the 1930s helped stifle the flapper notion, but the image of **woman as sex symbol** was retained. In reality, women workers dealt with the Depression very much the same as men: they endured deprivation and took whatever work became available. Labor unions gained some recognition during Roosevelt's New Deal administration, but women were still paid less than men. In some cases, women could hardly get any paying jobs because of the persisting view that their role was homemaking while men's was bread winning. Generally, in schools the issue of girls and boys being educated in the values of shared power was ignored.

The Depression and World War II did not produce as many female leaders of national scope as the previous era; however, among the notables was Eleanor Roosevelt (1884–1962), who urged women to work for social change but who also believed that women should place family before career. Intellectuals such as anthropologist Margaret Mead (1901–1978) researched how cultural and educational practices brought about inequalities between males and females, but progress in transmitting such views to the wider society was slow. World War II took women out of the home and into the labor force as never before, but (as after the preceding war) there was a desire to return to domesticity and material consumption afterwards. Women, as the chief purchasers of household goods and services, again became targets of the hard sell, and the sexually alluring temptress image was marketed more vigorously than ever. In the 1950s, a new woman as sex symbol image, typified by such public personas as Marilyn Monroe, became firmly implanted. By the 1960s, the nation's former inhibitions against pornography slowly gave way, and by the 1970s, X-rated movies and slick pornographic magazines became common.

The sex symbol image did not go unchallenged, however, and numerous studies found that the professional ranks did not admit enough women, graduate schools did not encourage women to apply, and the public schools "programmed" girls to accept traditional roles. Feminist activists urged a more concerted effort, and the **National Organization of Women (NOW)** was formed in 1966 to promote initiatives such as equal employment, equalization of social security benefits, and equal educational opportunity. Although NOW challenged existing inequities, rapid change remained elusive. Conditions led to what was loosely termed the **women's liberation movement**, which helped focus public attention on the general status of females in society and on such specific issues of sexism and gender bias in schools and in educational materials. While the media may have exaggerated the impact of such developments, there were some concrete results: For one thing, in the closing decades of the twentieth century there was a vigorous scrutiny of education concerning how male and female roles were presented. Hundreds of studies examined curriculum materials, school rules and regulations, and the organizational and employment structures of school systems. The extent of actual improvement might be questioned, but the fact remains that from the 1960s on, increasing public attention was turned to the issue of gender bias in American society.[21]

For Further Reflection: Does the use of women as sex objects sell products? What "educational effect" does this have on children and young adults, and how does it impact the status of women? How does the image of woman as sex object in advertising affect children's thinking about femininity and masculinity? For example, does the Barbie doll phenomenon have anything to do with how girls come to view themselves?

Contemporary conditions

In the summer of 1991, federal appeals court judge Clarence Thomas was nominated to the U.S. Supreme Court. The initial issues involved how Thomas's legal philosophy might affect his interpretation of cases likely to come before the court, and after testimony before the Senate Judiciary Committee, it appeared that Thomas might be easily confirmed. In early October, however, a media bombshell exploded when Professor Anita Hill's confidential testimony in preliminary proceedings became public. Hill testified that Thomas subjected her to several instances of **sexual harassment** when she was one of his employees in the Department of Education and, later, in the Office of Economic Opportunity. On October 11, both Thomas and Hill appeared before the judiciary committee, with Thomas categorically denying the allegations and Hill insisting on the veracity of her testimony. The hearings revealed strong political and ideological positions, but perhaps the most significant point to emerge from the whole episode was the explosive nature of sexual harassment and gender bias, this time brushing against the U.S. Supreme Court. Although Thomas eventually became an associate justice on October 15, 1991, the controversy helped bring the impact of gender bias on the personal lives of people into sharp public focus.

In order to appreciate more fully how people come to possess outlooks about gender, it is necessary to examine several significant influences. If gender bias permeates institutions and social values, it must have avenues of expression by which the young are initiated into its beliefs. These include traditions about gender differences, the innumerable influences impinging on boys and girls as they grow up, and, of course, the schooling experience itself.

Notions about whether and how males and females differ have undergone significant changes. For centuries, the predominant belief was that the two sexes were fundamentally different in educational potential. During the second half of the twentieth century, however, as women gained more participation and power in social institutions, such assumptions came under intense scrutiny. By the end of the twentieth century, most Americans probably no longer believed that females were intellectually inferior or needed a separate kind of education. In education, the emphasis became one of enabling females to achieve the same standards of excellence as males but doing so under conditions conducive to their own styles of learning and knowing. Advocates argued that existing institutions were far from perfect, and rather than merely granting females their fair share in society as defined by males, institutional changes should be made that recognized and cultivated what females themselves had to offer. However, as recently as 2005, Harvard president Lawrence Summers made the explosive statement that natural differences between men and women may be one reason why fewer women succeed in math and science careers.[22] That remark may indicate how some assumptions about female intellectual inferiority are still alive in even the most renowned halls of academia, despite all the studies and reforms.

Gendered approaches to thinking and knowing

The early 1980s saw the publication of important studies on **women's ways of knowing** and moral reasoning that were previously missing from educational theory and practice. Traditional educational institutions were mostly designed for males, and when female learners were included, they were expected to fit into existing institutional frameworks. The new studies attempted to understand female perspectives and to incorporate them into educational institutions in ways to serve all students better. However, achieving such ends requires long-term efforts, because it is more difficult to make historic institutions gender sensitive than it is simply to admit females into them.

Human intelligence has always been a domain of interest to educators and psychologists alike. By the 1970s, studies were indicating that girls in their early years were generally more precocious than boys, learning to talk and to discern differences in objects at an earlier age. It was suggested that this precociousness might be due to myelinization (maturation of the myelin sheath that speeds nerve impulses), which occurs earlier in girls than boys. Boys, however, caught up later, and while girls excelled in such things as reading and writing by first grade, boys excelled in numbers, spatial concepts, and similar areas. In addition, as development continued, girls showed fewer extremes on the intelligence continuum than boys. By adolescence, males appeared to be more analytical and logical and tended to take more intellectual risks, while females appeared to be more attuned to emotion, more holistic in decision making, and more intuitive and comparative in their approach to problems. Some researchers attributed the differences to hormones, and others suggested a difference in the use of right- and left-brain hemispheres by males and females, but overall whether the differences were due to socialization or to innate sex differences or some combination of the two was not clear because researchers could not determine where innate sex differences ended and socialization or acculturation began. A tentative conclusion was that, since girls and boys faced different cultural expectations in learning how to behave as adults, each apparently developed mental attributes necessary to meet those expectations.[23]

Recent research indicates that boys are outperformed by girls in English and that girls are catching up with boys in mathematics and science. Perhaps such progress by girls in those fields is clear evidence that there are no clearly defined "girls" and "boys" subjects. Nevertheless, gender gaps continue to exist, and one explanation might lie in how both males and females view the various subjects and approach knowledge or learning. The gap in the reading motivation among elementary students, for instance, indicates that boys tend to value reading less than girls.[24]

Ways of knowing

Researchers examined different conceptions of knowledge and learning, seeking to understand how gender-related socialization led to gender-specific approaches in education. While it was important to comprehend that males and females might differ, it was just as important to study how approaches to learning and knowing were sanctioned and rewarded by society and what approaches were not. For example, as women gained full access to higher education, they frequently felt alienated, had difficulty asserting themselves with authority, and were not always fully respected for their research and scholarship. Although women made progress, they often encountered difficulties because of male-oriented academic conventions built into educational institutions and processes, including how human learning and knowing were evaluated. It seemed that such gendered frameworks did not value modes of thought that might be characteristic of females.

One of the pioneering researchers on gender issues is Mary Belenky, widely recognized for her work on women's ways of knowing. A metaphor women often use to capture their intellectual development is voice (such as "finding your voice"), which differs from the visual metaphors males tend to use, such as "seeing the light" when something becomes clear. Visual imagery implies seeing an object to properly know it, while speaking and listening imply face-to-face engagement between knower and object. Belenky and her associates found that women's ways of knowing include a variety of approaches: Some are referred to as subjectivist knowers relying on intuition and personal experience rather than logical analysis and abstraction, while others are deemed procedural knowers using systematic analysis to approach situations. Females reared in families lacking opportunities for open discussion tend to be silent, those reared to be independent tend toward an intuitive "inner voice," and those reared in caring and connected families tend to be procedural. Belenky and her associates concluded that educational institutions need to accommodate female ways of learning and knowing and to accept female students as knowers with functioning minds that bring prior knowledge and experience to the educational environment. Traditional higher education institutions used a doubting model of teaching that challenged students' prior beliefs, but many women students have been socialized into self-doubt and find the doubting of teaching unhelpful. Many older women students use "maternal thinking" based on individualized responses in rearing children, a mode of thought that differs from the replication and universal application model valued in academia. In addition, some women respond better to evaluation standards that are set collaboratively by students and teachers rather than by traditional academic authority. They prefer a "housewifery" model where people work and produce according to their own rhythms. Thus, women should be taught with a "connected" model where teachers act as "midwives" helping students "give birth" to ideas instead of the traditional "banking model" where teachers "deposit" knowledge and ideas into students' minds, from which students may later "draw."[25]

Of course, the metaphor of teachers as midwives of knowledge also has a long history of masculine application. The Greek philosopher Plato developed what is called the doctrine of reminiscence in which people do not create knowledge but discover it instead. Plato believed that human souls originally possessed true knowledge, but their earthly manifestation in a physical body and material world only corrupted and distorted that knowledge. This makes education (as defined by Plato) both necessary and difficult, for it must help people "remember" what they once "knew." Indeed, Plato's mentor, Socrates, actually spoke of himself as a midwife of knowledge who, through skillful questioning and dialectical discussion, helped his students (all males) give birth (or draw out) ideas from within their own minds. It seems clear that Plato did not intend the midwife metaphor to be strictly a female way of knowing, even if the term had a feminine connotation.[26]

> **For Further Reflection:** Do males and females truly differ in their ways of knowing and, if so, what are the ramifications for educational institutions? More specifically, think about your own recent class assignments and exercises. Were there differences in how the men and women in your class approached certain discussion questions? Did they use different ways of knowing in order to solve problems and make sense of material?

Ways of moral reasoning

Another pioneer is Carol Gilligan, who addressed the role of gender in moral reasoning. She maintains that psychological theorists long misunderstood how women think about moral issues, going back at least to Sigmund Freud who cast women as emotional and presumably less able to develop a strong sense of justice. Jean Piaget and Lawrence Kohlberg, two prominent developmental psychologists, continued that tradition in the twentieth century by implying that women's sense of justice is compromised. They believed their theories were based on universal standards; however, Gilligan maintains that their theories represent male conceptions of human developmental stages. For example, Kohlberg's "universal" stage theory was developed solely from male samples, which ignores the early childhood experiences of girls encouraged to embrace relationships and fear separation because they are of the same gender as their typical primary caregiver, the mother. Boys, being of different gender from their mothers, are reared to embrace individuation and separation and may feel threatened by the level of intimacy girls come to prefer. These experiences lead to significant differences between men and women, shaping not only the play of children but also the problem-solving strategies and moral reasoning of adults. Thus, women tend to be concerned about human relationships and connections that lead to different choices, while men are more concerned with individual achievement, autonomy, and justice. The assumption that female constructions of moral problems are inferior to male constructions has led stage theorists such as Kohlberg to conclude that women will have difficulty reaching the highest stage of moral development where people are concerned about rights, responsibilities, and individualism rather than care, connection, and relationships. Instead, Gilligan maintains that psychological theories should account for the developmental experiences of both genders, and psychological understanding of humanity would thereby be enriched.[27]

Gilligan's work is a powerful reminder that gender equality does not mean exact sameness. Both theory and practice should reflect the differences between females and males and how they approach things and choose courses of action. Gender differences should not be interpreted as deficiencies but as valuable approaches, each with its own merits.

For Further Reflection: A spontaneous reaction to gender stereotyping may be: "How terrible! Surely such behavior disappeared a long time ago. Women today are just as autonomous as men!" Have gender expectations become more open minded and balanced? Are male and female roles now rewarded equally? Compare predominantly female professions with predominantly male professions on such things as pay, status, and public esteem. What do your comparisons show? Are there examples that demonstrate the opposite, and if so, how do you explain them?

Suggested Activity: Daily routines are often powerful indicators of social reality. Study some gender-specific behaviors of friends and acquaintances and explain why those differences persist. Do people consider women or men to be better equipped to do certain things? Why?

WEB: Suggested Reading 6.2.

Justice and caring: a philosophical dichotomy?

Morality has a long tradition as a quest for justice, expressed in principles of what is good, right, and virtuous. Along similar lines, the search for truth, including moral truth, rests on the supposedly masculine foundations of reason, neutrality, and detachment. Feminists have questioned these assumptions, particularly the view that they are the only philosophically defensible ways of getting close to moral knowledge or truth; instead, feminists claim that the good may be defended just as well in terms of relationships and that moral truth may be pursued from the vantage point of personal experience. However, caution needs to be exercised when approaching the good and right from the standpoint of gender, because it seems simplistic to claim that men always think in principled, rationally detached fashion or that women always view the world through the lens of relationships and care. Such thinking is untenable because it assumes that caring men and principled women are contradictions in terms, and it locks moral thought into narrowly defined gender categories. Nel Noddings, who has been instrumental in developing an **ethics of care** in educational theory, maintains that care and justice are not mutually exclusive and may be applied at different points in a moral undertaking. Justice is an invaluable ethical goal when developing educational policy, and care needs to be a central goal when implementing policy. An example would be a justice-based policy to eliminate academic tracking, a practice that is often discriminatory and fraught with social class implications. If justice demands the abolition of tracking, an ethic of care demands that educators should avoid forcing all students into a one-size-fits-all curriculum that ignores individual talents, needs, and interests.[28]

However, justice and caring are not always easily compatible, as any teacher knows who has struggled with assigning grades. Grades are supposed to be just (or fair), accurately reflecting academic achievement or progress. At the same time, grading should also be used to encourage the student, a concern steeped in care. Because justice and care may sometimes conflict does not mean that they are inherently different or that one is superior to the other. Kenneth Strike argues that the tension between justice and care is rooted in the moral pluralism (or conflict in moral values) that is simply a part of contemporary society. In order to make the best choices when faced with difficult moral questions, one has to consider individual cases, seek reflective equilibrium between conflicting values, and settle on a reasonable course of action, such as a reasonable balance of justice and care.[29] It is clear that moral life is complex and that one is unlikely to achieve good moral reasoning by a simplistic "either justice or care" type of thinking. The point is that various ways of moral reasoning are significant resources in ethical decision making, and when used effectively should help inform educational theories and scholarly discourse to include all of humanity rather than one portion thereof.

Suggested Activity: Interview a teacher, counselor, or administrator about situations in which the ethic of care may have conflicted with the ethic of justice. How did the educator approach the dilemma? Share your findings with others in class.

Sex-role identities

That children are molded by socially defined sex roles before they get to school has long been noticed, but there has been a growing body of research illustrating how girls and boys face stereotyping from the moment of birth, such as blue clothing for boys and pink for girls. Adults react differently to boys and girls, giving boys rougher treatment and girls more gentle handling. Boys are envisioned as "future football players," while girls are "sweet and adorable." Toys such as rattles may be neutral for infants, but soon girls are given dolls and boys trucks, and boys in particular are discouraged from playing with girls' toys. A visit to any mainstream toy store demonstrates that most toys, games, and play devices continue to be clearly designed along gender lines. As found in a study of young children's playgroups, boys are more drawn to construction toys and tend to make vehicles, guns, or movable parts out of such things as Lego toys, while girls tend to gravitate to a "home" corner and to play social games, construct play objects different from boys, and prefer different types of books than boys. Exceptions certainly exist, as they always have, because girls or boys not only belong to gender groups but are, first and foremost, members of the human group. It is also true that some girls may like trucks and some boys may be drawn to the "home" corner in a childcare center. In other words, **intragender differences** exist, and researchers have increasingly given attention to differences within gender groups and recognized that neither boy nor girl aggregates are homogeneous. Nevertheless, gender differences matter, particularly when inequities occur between populations of girls and boys, and the differences cannot be easily explained by chance factors or individual preferences alone.[30]

Suggested Activity: Visit a toy store and consider how toys influence the formation of gender identities. Note details of what you observe, considering the types of toys, their colors and functions, and the gender messages they convey. Does playing with these toys socialize and perpetuate gender stereotypes in children? Why or why not?

For Further Reflection: A true story: A parent was looking for a mystery novel for her nine-year-old son. The owner of the bookstore asked her whether her son would consider reading an excellent mystery featuring a girl as protagonist. "Many boys refuse reading books in which girls are the main characters," the owner explained. Interpret the sales person's statement. Do you think it is generally true, and why or why not?

Not only toys and books, but also influences such as television, motion pictures, and computer programs and games might initiate children into a gendered world where men are portrayed as action oriented and women as adaptive. Thus, the adult world can present boys and girls with different role expectations, and children are shaped and molded into "appropriate" gender behaviors.

Attention to boys

While most recent scholarly attention on gender stereotyping has focused on the problems of girls, some researchers point out that boys also suffer from gender bias. This emphasis came primarily in the mid-1990s, due at least in part to the impression that many barriers to female equality had fallen and that females were gradually achieving a better level of equality in education. One may hear sentiments in these concerns that, while we have long been concerned with schools shortchanging girls, it is now time to worry about the boys, especially given the evidence that over a considerable period of time females scholastically outperform males. How, then, do we account for the poor school performance of boys? Explanations range from the lack of appropriate adult male role models to a **crisis of masculinity**, as women gain greater access to spheres of society previously reserved for men.

Part of what sparked concern about boys is related to young black males being disproportionately affected by crime, violence, unemployment, drug abuse, and incarceration. Some observers maintain that racism is responsible for the image of black men as criminal and deviant, all of which results in limits put on black male freedom of action, including restrictive school rules and legal measures. Attention has also focused on the problems of white males, particularly since the tragic killings and injuries committed at Columbine High School in Littleton, Colorado, on April 20, 1999, in which the two instigators were white, middle-class male students, alienated and unable to express their emotions in appropriate ways.[31]

Some critics characterize the recent concern about boys' underachievement as a kind of "globalized moral panic," instigated by alarmists. These critics group the alarmists into three viewpoints: the "pity the poor boys" argument of the so-called men's movement that portrays boys as suffering at the mercy of feminist teachers, unable to develop their masculinity; the "failing schools–failing boys" viewpoint that pushes higher standards and better school effectiveness; and the "which boys discourse" about lower-class boys who do poorly in some subjects as compared to girls. Rather than sounding alarms, we should seek to understand how versions of masculinity and femininity, historically and currently, have created problems for girls, boys, and educators.[32]

> **For Further Reflection:** Would you agree with the argument that we are facing a "globalized moral panic" about the underachievement of boys, or is this an exaggeration fueled by overzealous ideologues? What evidence is there of such a panic? What roles do popular media play in such "panics"?

Some view recent concerns about boys' underachievement as inappropriate because, from the late seventeenth to the late twentieth centuries, many boys underachieved and it was never considered to be a problem specific to boys. Male success was usually attributed to something within, such as a boy's intellect or personal drive, but failures were attributed to external factors such as pedagogy, texts, or teachers. For girls, the situation was the reverse, with failure interpreted as a shortcoming of intellect while success was due to external factors such as successful teaching methods. For example, in 1693 philosopher John Locke was concerned that boys failed to master Latin while girls easily mastered French. He did not think the differences were due to girls' intelligence but to the more successful methods used to teach French. Today, one suggestion is that boys might not perform well because of existing images of masculinity (such as the silent, manly hero always displaying emotional control), images without much communicative demonstration.[33]

Some studies address masculine peer pressure on lower-class boys and its detrimental effects on their academic achievement. One hypothesis is that such boys come to see school success as incompatible with masculinity, a factor also found among middle-class boys. There are exceptions among all socioeconomic backgrounds, of course, and while some boys reject educational achievement as traditionally unmanly, other use it to develop their male identities; nonetheless, a disproportionate percentage of male students reject academic achievement and engage in disruptive behavior that hinders achievement. Such patterns may persist because perceptions of masculinity have remained fairly constant, as risk-taking, wit, resistance, defiance, humor, and competitiveness are highly prized in males.[34]

These points have been raised before, however. In 1969, Patricia Sexton attributed many problems of boys to the aggressive quest for manhood in American society. At that time, about 70 percent of successful suicides were males, and boys outnumbered girls three to one in mental institutions for children. In addition, boys were more likely to be labeled mentally retarded, were more prone to be discipline problems in three out of four instances, had learning disabilities and behavior disorders three to ten times more than girls, died more often in accidents, suffered brain damage more at birth, had dyslexia by about five to one over girls, and experienced more speech disorders by about two to one. One conclusion was that boys were under more pressure from practically all quarters but had fewer emotional outlets than girls, while the institutions primarily responsible for rearing the young—the home and school—did not help boys achieve manhood easily. Dominated by women, these institutions kept boys in a feminized dependent status while external society expected males to be independent. Sexton maintained that the ultimate source of the problem lay in society's division into two spheres of power: the male sphere of science and technology, business and finance, and the military and politics and the female sphere revolving around school, home, family, church, and social services. Denied access to power, women released their creative impulses to shape human destiny through the only avenues open to them: institutions that shaped and molded individuals, with particular emphasis on husbands, sons, and male students who had opportunities that females lacked, providing feminine rather than masculine role models for young learners. Sexton concluded that the solution lay in allowing women access to power and release of their creative energies in all spheres of society.[35]

In this light, the recent criticism of a "globalized moral panic" over the plight of boys seems rather exaggerated. Sexton had found difficulties for boys decades earlier. In light of her evidence, it seems that concern for boys would be a humane response, not a moral panic. What is more important, however, is to understand how inherited and invented versions of femininity and masculinity continue to create problems for students, teachers, and society itself. Simply dismissing concerns about boys' underachievement on the grounds that they have always underachieved ignores the moral question of whether educators should be concerned if any student underachieves, regardless of gender, origin, or historical background. It seems the morally desirable argument is to educate every student as far as humanly possible, given the level of understanding, pedagogical knowledge, and resources available, that educational achievement problems associated with gender are not inherent to or created by either girls or boys but already reside in the adult world's social and cultural traditions and preferences.[36]

Suggested Activity: Interview three women who are members of a learned profession (such as education, business, health care, or law), and ask them about their experiences, as females, in their chosen fields. How does their level of competitiveness compare to that of their male colleagues, and has it changed during their lifetimes? Also, interview three men in similar fields on their views concerning the changing roles of females in their profession. Do the female and male views differ, and if so, how?

WEB: Suggested Reading 6.3.

Sexual identity

If gender is a social and cultural construction, then notions of male and female are defined by human beings in particular social and cultural contexts. When those contexts change, gender definitions are subject to change as well, as in the past when female teachers were not permitted to wear slacks or get married. Men are subject to prevailing images of masculinity too. For example, males who want to enter what are now considered predominantly female professions can face difficulties.[37] In short, culture definitely influences what gender means and what is considered acceptable male and female behavior.

WEB: Suggested Reading 6.4.

Not only do social and cultural conventions vary considerably when it comes to gender, but **sexual identity**, a concept related to gender, does as well. What is declared "normal" or "deviant" depends on the time period, who defines the terms, the ruling religious and ideological beliefs, and so forth. For example, **homosexuality** was present in ancient China and Japan, in Indo-European cultures such as ancient Greece, and later in Islamic countries. In some historical periods, homosexuality was treated harshly, as in the twentieth century when Nazi Germany incarcerated homosexuals or even put them to death. The idea that gay men are feminized and lesbians are masculinized is a cultural construct not universally shared. In ancient Greece, for instance, homosexual behavior was not always viewed as unmasculine for males or unfeminine for females. Moreover, ancient Greece accepted homosexual and/or bisexual behavior from such mythical figures as Zeus or Hercules, and historical personages as Alexander the Great. In some cultures, homosexual activity was expected of male teenagers and considered a necessity for the attainment of strength and virility.[38]

In the United States, beliefs about sexuality, including **heterosexuality** and **lesbian, gay, bisexual, and transgender (LGBT)** identities have varied by time and setting. Homosexuality, for instance, has been seen as a sin, a crime, an illness, or simply a difference. Newspapers such as The New York Times once censored the word homosexual, and many people considered the mere study of homosexuality a dubious activity. During the recent past, however, a number of scientific studies on homosexuality have been conducted, and some results suggest that homosexuality might be genetic or prenatal in nature.[39]

WEB: Suggested Reading 6.5.

In the contemporary United States, some people view diverse sexual identities as individual lifestyle choices in a diverse society; others view LGBT persons as deviants unwilling to "get a grip and become normal." The very concept of sexual identity may appear threatening when it is seen as a danger to society that undermines the moral fabric of "normalcy." Some individuals fear it so much that they resort to violence against members of the LGBT community. Much was accomplished by the civil rights movement of the 1950s and 1960s, but where social justice concerns equal rights for LGBT persons, there are still challenges to be met.

Although heterosexuality is generally seen as the norm, research indicates that clear distinctions between heterosexuals and homosexuals are difficult to maintain. Part of this is due to sexuality not being defined by two polar opposites called homosexuality and heterosexuality, but with a greater range of sexual feelings and behaviors. Beliefs continue to exist that sexuality is an either-or proposition and that people can choose or change their sexual orientation if they have the will to do so. As some observers insist, however, being gay or lesbian may not be a matter of choice; alternately, it may develop at an early age, despite individual efforts to deny or change behavior. Beliefs also exist that gay or lesbian persons are promiscuous, gravitate to particular occupations, and are easily identified. Such stereotypes have consequences, however, because they create psychological stresses for people subjected to them that may lead to depression, addictions, and even suicidal tendencies.[40]

One theory shaping discussions about gender and sexuality is so-called queer theory, which defines gender as "performances" rather than as biological sex; that is, it is not individuals who choose which gender they will be, but gender norms that are repeated, embodied, and performed through language and actions. Those performances are based on what is referred to as compulsive heterosexuality enforced by society through rewards for appropriate gender-related, heterosexual behaviors and through punishments for deviations from what is considered heteronormative sexual behavior. Examples in schools include assumptions that everyone is heterosexual (married characters in stories presumed to be male and female and little girls presumed to like playing princesses attracted to princes, for example). **Heteronormativity** is also found when parents are assumed to be a man and a woman, thus negating the fact that some children have LGBT parents, or when members of the LGBT community face discrimination in their personal and professional lives because of their sexual identities.[41]

Negative attitudes about members of the LGBT community affect social institutions in numerous ways. While researchers, educators, policy makers, and citizens seem willing to discuss issues concerning race, ethnicity, class, disability, and gender, an openness that helps inform the public, reluctance appears to arise over the issue of sexual identity. LGBT persons may not only experience continuing discrimination and alienation as a result, but also be silenced on an issue that needs public understanding. Statistics indicate that many adolescents who admit same-sex feelings, for instance, may be forced out of their homes and into the homeless teenager population. Schools may also be hostile environments where some students face homophobic harassment.[42] Because adolescents who may be LGBT usually suffer from stigmatization both in and out of school, they often try to hide their sexual identities. It is difficult to know the exact numbers, but it has been suggested that it ranges between 1 and 10 percent of all adolescents in the United States.[43]

Whatever the percentage, LGBT persons constitute an "invisible" minority who face stark choices, such as coming out and openly acknowledging their sexual identity, which can mean hostility from peers and communities, or else passing as straight to hide their sexuality, which itself can be demoralizing. Misunderstanding, prejudice, and hostility lead some to depression and self-destructive behaviors, not only because of their personal pain and confusion but also as a result of the hurtful rejection that often comes from peers and family. They need support in the schools from educators they can trust and programs to assist their educational and personal development.[44]

Suggested Activity: Youth suicide is an alarming problem. Nine percent of all youth currently report suicide attempts, and a significant number of them are gay and lesbian youth. Discuss with others why, despite these factors, schools seem to be hesitant to address the problem. For a reading on this problem, see David Campos, *Understanding Gay and Lesbian Youth: Lessons for Straight School Teachers, Counselors, and Administrators* (Lanham, MD: Rowman and Littlefield Education, 2005).

LGBT students often experience academic setbacks, and schools need to find better ways of addressing their needs. Suggestions include the improvement of educator attitudes toward LGBT persons, because all of these potential role models (teachers, counselors, and administrators) exert considerable influence and can have life-enhancing effects on their students. Some observers suggest that the issue of various sexualities ought to be included in the curriculum in some suitable fashion similar to other minority group studies. In addition, the National Education Association (NEA) recommends that school districts develop policies and programs for educating and counseling LGBT students.[45]

WEB: Suggested Reading 6.6.

Gender and elementary school

There have always been education critics, some of them alleging that schools contribute to various social ills rather than solve them. Such is the case with gender, particularly in the late twentieth and early twenty-first centuries when schools have been scrutinized as never before in regard to gender discrimination in curriculum materials, teaching practices, and educational policies. The single most influential school is probably the elementary school, because it touches virtually everyone and may even surpass family influence for some children. In many families today, both parents work outside the home, and this means a growing number of children are in school longer, particularly where after-school care is available. The elementary school spans those crucial years when children's basic moral values are learned and when gender identities that become significant in adulthood are established. The elementary school teaches the basic knowledge most people carry with them the rest of their lives. In many respects, then, the elementary school is still the *common* school, coming closest of all other school levels to serving the American ideal of equal educational opportunity.

WEB: Suggested Reading 6.7.

Definitions of gender roles

Despite the elementary school's historic role as a unifying and equalizing institution, it is by no means immune to gender bias. In the 1970s, critics charged that gender bias permeated the elementary school, not only in curriculum, but in **sex-segregated** activities, such as boys grouped for contact team sports, and girls grouped for home-oriented play activities. More subtle differentiations were found in separate boy and girl seating arrangements and lineups for marching to lunch or recess. Similarly, men occupied school leadership positions, while women occupied the lower ranks. In effect, children only had to observe school surroundings and role models to learn the gender stereotypes of the larger society.[46]

Since those days, curriculum materials generally have become more **gender sensitive**. In children's literature, female adventurers are more prominent, and males are sometimes depicted in domestic scenes. Simply altering male and female textual images is not enough, however, because the curriculum needs to show female contributions as well as male contributions in, for example, the study of history.[47] This means more than mere special observances or portions of textbooks on female contributions, but accurate treatment of the options and actions available to both males and females in any period of study.

WEB: Suggested Reading 6.8.

Suggested Activity: Form a research team with a few classmates and compare recently published elementary curriculum materials with sources published prior to 1970. Examine both sets for gender stereotyping. What do you find? Have changes been made? Discuss your findings in class. What are the implications of your research?

While much progress has been made at achieving gender equity at the elementary level, challenges persist. One area is science education where studies continue to show that elementary school males perform better than elementary school females on science achievement tests. Another area is reading where, conversely, boys continue to be less motivated than girls.[48]

Male elementary school teachers

Gender equity in school is not merely an issue of materials or curriculum but also of staffing. Children learn much about "men's work" and "women's work" through exposure to adult role models, of which teachers are among the more prevalent for children on a daily basis. Conventional beliefs that women are more naturally capable of nurturing young children or that men are more naturally capable of providing discipline are reinforced by economic practices that perpetuate gender-based divisions of labor. It is also frequently observed that traditional gender bias plays a role in discouraging men who might otherwise like to pursue a teaching career. Fewer men in the teaching profession limits children's educational exposure to adult male role models. In recent years, the percentage of male teachers has declined across all grade levels, a condition that has received a great deal of media attention, with descriptions ranging from "scarce" to "shrinking fast."[49]

That there has been a shortage of male teachers can be verified by the historical record. It needs pointing out, however, that male percentages have fluctuated over time, probably due to various developments. For example, in the 1869–70 school year the percentage of male teachers in public elementary and secondary school stood at 42.8 percent, but in 1919–20, the male teacher percentage was a mere 14.1 percent (probably due to the effects of World War I). The percentages remained relatively low over the next few decades (probably due to the Depression of the 1930s and World War II, 1941–45) until the 1950s.[50] As indicated by Table 6.1, the male percentage hovered between the low-to-mid-30-percent range from the 1960s until declining again in the 1990s.

However, male teachers have historically had a stronger numerical presence at the secondary level, with percentages for male elementary teachers much lower than the combined figures in Table 6.1 suggest. The percentage of male teachers at the elementary level is indicated in Table 6.2. Although the decline over the 14-year period was slightly less than 1 percent, whether further shrinkage will occur remains to be seen.

An obvious question is why there are so few males at the lower levels of schooling. Male elementary teachers may sometimes encounter unpleasant social conventions about doing women's work or have their masculinity and sexual motives questioned. Male teachers also may be expected to be stern disciplinarians and guardians of school safety. Such conditions can deter prospects from even considering an elementary teaching career, thereby short-circuiting

Table 6.1 Number and percentage of full-time male and female elementary and secondary teachers: selected years, spring 1961 through spring 2001

Number and percentage	1961	1966	1971	1976	1981	1986	1991	1996	2001
Number (in thousands)	1,408	1,710	2,055	2,196	2,185	2,206	2,398	2,164	2,979
Male Percentage	21.0	31.3	31.1	34.3	32.9	33.1	31.2	27.9	25.6
Female Percentage	68.7	68.9	65.7	67.1	66.9	68.8	72.1	74.4	79.0

Source: Adapted from National Center for Education Statistics (NCES), "Table 69. Selected Characteristics of Public School Teachers: Selected Years, Spring 1961 through Spring 2001," at http://nces.ed.gov/programs/digest/d09/tables/dt09_069.asp (accessed on August 3, 2010).

Table 6.2 Percentage of full-time male and female teachers by school type and level, during the 1993–94, 1999–2000, and 2007–08 school years

School year	Sex of teacher	Private schools	Public schools	Public elementary	Public secondary
1993–94	Male	31.4	31.9	16.1	47.7
	Female	68.6	68.1	83.9	52.3
1999–2000	Male	29.7	30.0	15.2	44.8
	Female	70.3	70.0	84.8	55.2
2007–08	Male	29.9	28.4	15.6	41.3
	Female	70.1	71.5	84.4	58.7

Sources: Adapted from National Center for Education Statistics (NCES), "Table 33–1a. Number and Percentage Distribution of Full-time Teachers, by School Level, School Type, and Selected Characteristics: School Years 1993–94, 1999–2000, and 2003–04," at http://nces.ed.gov/programs/coe/2007/section4/table.asp?tableID=719 (accessed on August 3, 2010); and "Table A-27–1. Number and Percentage Distribution of Full-time Teachers by School Level, Sector, and Selected Teacher Characteristics: School Years 1999–2000 and 2007–2008," at http://nces.ed.gov/programs/coe/2010/section4/table-tsp-1.asp (accessed on July 31, 2010).

recruitment efforts. In short, males who enter elementary teaching must be diligently constructive in working out what it takes to be an effective teacher of young children.[51]

There is research, however, that cautions against inflating expectations about increasing the proportion of male teachers, whether elementary or secondary. One study found considerable variation among boys, girls, and teachers in regard to the importance of gender in the teaching-learning process. Another study claims that male teachers provide stronger motivation for boys, and it was found that the effects of teacher gender did not vary substantially between boys or girls. Most variance in motivation occurred at the student level, with no teacher components showing up as significant.[52]

Another problem has been the number of teachers who leave elementary classrooms after only a few years of experience. A recent longitudinal study found that, when it came to people leaving the profession, men were more likely than women to stay, but more men left the classroom to take up other duties within the system. Perhaps male teachers were more readily promoted than female teachers, a longstanding source of contention among female members of the profession.[53]

Gender and secondary school

Studies conducted in the 1970s and 1980s generally found that harmful stereotyping occurred at the secondary level with gender-differentiated curricula and the channeling of female and male students into different experiences. More recent studies show a marked decrease in such overt gender discrimination, but gender equity still remains a goal to be achieved.

Peer culture and gender roles

Gender-related behavior in schools is shaped by adults, but also by peer culture. Student peer groups not only police one another and construct powerful peer cultures that shape, mediate, and limit behavior, but they also mediate images of masculinity and femininity. For example, a British study found that male secondary-school pupils continued to dominate both classroom space and teacher time, just as they had at the elementary level. Girls, on the other hand, constructed femininity around "mature" behavior, which often meant that they were more passive and abdicated power to boys.[54] Certainly there are exceptions to this, but gender-related behavior outside accepted norms runs the risk of strong peer disapproval.

One aspect where **peer culture** proves to be most powerful spans **notions of bodies, sexuality, and beauty**. Peer opinions matter for any student, male or female, and as children develop and encounter sexuality and eroticism, they also face peer pressures and feelings of shame related to gender roles, which may prove more difficult for girls than for boys. Male sexuality tends to be viewed as a natural force, but female sexuality is often treated as a cause for shame. Closely related are cultural images of bodies and beauty. Many adolescent girls fall victim to **eating disorders**, reinforced by media images and adolescent peer perceptions that beauty is equated with thinness. A study of middle school girls found such examples as a small group taking turns nibbling on one shared sandwich during lunchtime, discussing new diet strategies, and reassuring one another that they were appropriately thin.[55]

Peer-reinforced standards of appearance affect boys too. A common human experience is becoming aware of one's body, such as a small child's fascination with its toes. The body becomes an early source of identity for both girls and boys. It appears that the harmful influences projected on girls by prevailing cultural images of body are also impacting boys, particularly concerning the use of anabolic steroids. Reports indicate that it is not merely an American phenomenon but also a concern in other countries as well. Boys, in particular, have been found to use steroids to bulk up for competitive athletics and also to enhance muscular physical appearance.[56]

In a study of peer, school, and African American ideals of masculinity, it was found that peer groups are centrally important and serve varying functions for black adolescent males. A traditional view of African American masculinity is being "cool" and "tough" in a racist world of powerlessness and frustration. Such a peer group can serve as a refuge, but it can also be a source of alienation. Just as girls may find comfort among peers while also being simultaneously confined by them, young black males can find both self-esteem and frustration with peers. For example, a black high school student with a white girlfriend found that some peers accepted him, some rejected him, and others were jealous. In other words, peer pressures can vary by individual circumstances and by group cohort.[57]

For Further Reflection: Based on your own experience, describe how peer groups shape identities. Can you think of instances in your own life where the peer group shaped your gender identity and how you thought of yourself as a woman or man?

WEB: Suggested Reading 6.9.

Classrooms and courses

Although gender relations are rooted in traditions, they are not static. Evidence suggests that students today are more likely to perceive males and females as equally capable rather than seeing male achievement as the standard. In fact, girls may be perceived as the better students. Another change is that girls today tend to perceive future careers as higher priorities than previous generations. Girls now may be more self-confident and no longer worry that academic achievement is "unfeminine"; however, girls still view acting mature as proper feminine behavior in the classroom, indicating that they feel they must suppress their impulses in favor of care for others and domesticity.[58] In that sense, girls are preparing for a **double burden** many of them will carry as adults: They will be fully involved in occupations outside the home but still be primarily responsible for child rearing and housework.

Progress toward gender equity in education has been made, but some qualifications need to be noted. In science and mathematics, girls' achievement has strengthened considerably. Scores on math and science assessments are becoming comparable, and on average girls earn even more credits in math and science courses than boys do, in addition to graduating with a higher combined grade point average (GPA) in math and science courses than their male counterparts.[59]

Gaps continue to exist, however. Boys earn higher National Assessment of Educational Progress (NAEP) scores in math and science, for example, and while a larger number of all advanced placement (AP) test takers in 2009 were girls, in most areas related to science, technology, engineering, and math (STEM), more boys than girls took the tests. Of those taking the AP physics test in 2009, for instance, 38 percent were girls, and of those taking AP computer science, only 10 percent.[60]

WEB: Suggested Reading 6.10.

Many factors contribute to these persistent gaps, one of them being lingering stereotypical depictions of men and women in textbooks. One review of high school chemistry textbooks, for instance, found that most of them pictured men more than women by a large margin. Stereotypes do matter, however, and research indicates that female students have higher science comprehension after viewing counterstereotypical images (female scientists) than after viewing stereotypical depictions of scientists as male. The opposite is true for male students whose science comprehension is higher after exposure to stereotypical images than counterstereotypical ones.[61]

Extracurricular activities

In general, females are more likely than males to participate in music and other performing arts, academic clubs, school newspapers, yearbooks, or student government. In contrast, boys tend to be more likely to participate in athletics.[62]

School success and extracurricular activities are positively correlated, because students involved in sports, the band, school governance, clubs, and other activities tend to do better in school than those not involved. Sports commonly receive most attention, particularly boys' football and basketball, but for several decades girls' participation in athletics has increased while boys' participation rates remained constant. Sports have the potential to challenge gender stereotypes because, for example, female basketball or soccer players may not mesh with traditional views of feminine behavior. Athletics may also reinforce narrow gender roles, with some sports viewed as typically male and others as typically female. Dancing or figure skating for instance, are usually viewed as feminine activities in which participating boys risk ridicule, but football or baseball are viewed as masculine and ill suited for girls, who presumably lack physical toughness and endurance. Girls continue to report unfair treatment in sports, and they are negatively affected by too few female coaches. While considerable progress can be cited, the current situation illustrates that access and increased participation are not enough. That boys dominate sports and girls dominate literary extracurricular activities suggest that traditional gender views still have influence. The goal is not only to encourage more participation of girls in sports but also to broaden boys' involvement in areas dominated by girls. In order for gender equity to become a reality, both girls and boys must have equal acceptance and support of their abilities and interests.[63]

Career choices

Just as girls consider fewer career opportunities than boys, women tend to cluster in a small number of job categories and are over-represented in minimum wage categories. The upper echelons of most professions continue to be dominated by men, and while women's numbers have increased and continue to grow, gaps remain. Despite the increasing significance of the STEM disciplines for the nation's economy and growth, for instance, women still lag behind. They earn fewer computer and information science degrees, and are underrepresented in computer technology–related professions. In 2008, women accounted for only 25 percent of information technology or IT-related occupations in the U.S. workforce and received only 12 percent of the undergraduate degrees in computer and information science.[64]

The income gap between men and women has narrowed throughout the twentieth century, but women still earn less than men: In 2009, women's median earnings were 80.2 percent of men's earnings. These percentages varied significantly by state: For example, in Louisiana, women's median earnings were 65 percent of men's, but in the District of Columbia, women earned 96.5 percent of men's.[65] Such conditions are instances of **gender stratification**; they are found in both schools and workplaces, and there is a relationship between them.

Given current economic conditions, it is crucial for schools to prepare both females and males equally well in a wide range of capabilities. Continued gender stratification produces serious obstacles for students whose futures depend on a variety of understandings and skills. It is important for girls to develop technical know-how, just as it important for boys to develop communication skills. Since 1994, federally funded school-to-work programs have attempted to correct skewed occupational distributions by encouraging both male and female students to consider nontraditional careers. Schools can influence students' career choices, but schools alone cannot resolve all the gendered notions about careers and professions in the larger society.[66]

Sexual harassment

Although it has long been a factor in schools, workplaces, and other realms of life, it is not always exactly clear what sexual harassment is. It may be loosely defined as conduct that creates a hostile environment characterized by unwelcome verbal or physical behavior of a sexual nature that limits a student's ability to benefit from curricular programs or have equal educational opportunity. At the same time, it is possible for lines to get blurred between harmless play and sexual harassment, especially where adolescent experimentation is concerned. Helpful definitions of sexual harassment are needed for courts, policy makers, and educators to deal with it more effectively. The courts and the Office for Civil Rights of the U.S. Department of Education distinguish between two kinds of sexual harassment: "*quid pro quo* harassment" or sexual blackmail by an educator demanding sexual favors from subordinate students in return for favorable decisions or actions on their behalf; and hostile environment harassment, which includes verbal, nonverbal and physical conduct of a sexual nature displayed by an educator, employee, student, or third party. A broader concept is **gender violence**, or violence directed against people because of their gender, such as gender-based bullying or hazing rituals.[67]

In addition to the difficulty of defining sexual harassment, it is difficult to diagnose when it occurs. For example, students at middle and high school ages may not always feel free to confide in adults concerning experiences of sexual harassment. Yet, it can have profound effects on their lives. Sexual harassment may push students to study less, curtail participation, cut classes, or avoid school altogether in order to avoid or escape such harassment.[68]

Sexual harassment may not only affect a student's grades and self-esteem, but it may also result in serious complaints and even lawsuits for school systems. It can include opposite-sex, same-sex, student-to-student, and adult-to-student cases as well. Among leading court decisions involving sexually related cases is ***Franklin v. Gwinnett County Public Schools* (1992)**, in which student Christine Franklin reported sexual advances from a teacher on school grounds, but she was instructed by school administrators not to tell anyone. She sued for compensatory damages under Title IX of the Education Amendments of 1972 (now known as the Patsy T. Mink Equal Opportunity in Education Act). The case was appealed to the U.S. Supreme Court, which ruled that the school had discriminated against Franklin by not dealing with her complaint. It was also the first case of its kind where compensatory damages were awarded. However, in ***Gebser v. Lago Vista Independent School District* (1998)**, the Supreme Court ruled in favor of the school administration on grounds that the administration had no actual knowledge of the student-teacher sexual relationship. These two cases illustrate the extent to which school personnel are legally responsible for adult-to-student sexual harassment. As for student-to-student sexual harassment, the Supreme Court ruled in ***Davis v. Monroe County Board of Education* (1999)** that schools are liable if they are aware of the sexual harassment but do not stop it.[69]

Court involvement is only one way to deal with sexual harassment. Ideally, it should be handled at the school level, and there is a search for effective ways to prevent sexual harassment and sexual violence in schools. A variety of concerns are present, however: The increase in sexual harassment litigation contributes to an atmosphere of confusion, not only from fear of lawsuits but from hasty laws and regulations of questionable effectiveness. Also, misapplied charges of sexual harassment have muddied the waters, such as a frivolous complaint that a girl's skirt was sexually harassing a boy.[70] In the final analysis, physical safety and psychological well-being in schools must remain as central goals.

> WEB: Suggested Reading 6.11.

Single-sex education

Championed as a device to achieve gender equity and attacked as an anachronism standing in the way of equal educational opportunities, **single-sex education** is a controversial issue. Advocates of single-sex education for girls argue that public as well as private schools ought to provide girls with separate and safe learning environments. If boys dominate the classroom and receive more of the teacher's attention, the argument goes, schools ought to provide opportunities for girls to excel in their own ways. Single-sex education is seen not only as a remedy for problems faced by girls but also for boys as well, with male-only academies for African American boys being a leading example. The argument in support of all-boys schools resembles the argument made for girls: African American boys tend to underachieve in coeducational schools, and they need institutions that pay particular attention to their needs in order to thrive. Critics of single-sex education argue that such practices are forms of segregation and that both boys and girls will never learn to get along in life if they do not learn to do so in school.

The research is equally conflicting about what environment is best for students, single-sex or coed, and what role the teacher's gender plays in providing the best education. Under such conditions, it is usually possible to find evidence supporting most ideological positions held on the issue.[71]

At the K–12 level, single-sex education is an umbrella term for diverse approaches, including both single-sex classrooms and single-sex schools, which makes simple generalizations about this approach to education difficult. Widely accepted evidence that single-sex education works better than coeducation is scarce, and single-sex education in and of itself does not ensure good education (another term subject to variable meanings). Research provides positive results for some students in some settings, but long-term results are even less certain. Furthermore, single-sex education does not mean the absence of gender bias because gender stereotypes can be perpetuated almost anywhere, including in single-sex and coeducational settings.[72]

WEB: Suggested Reading 6.12.

WEB: Additional Information 6.1.:
GENDER AND HIGHER EDUCATION

International perspective: Australia

Located in the area of the globe called Oceania, Australia covers the world's smallest continent. Bisected by the Tropic of Cancer, it is bounded by the Timor and Arufura seas in the north, the Coral Sea in the east, the Pacific Ocean in the southeast, and the Indian Ocean in the west and southwest. Its nearest neighbors are Indonesia and New Guinea. Australia has a population of slightly more than 21.5 million people (July 2010 estimate), of which 92 percent are white, 7 percent are Asian, and 1 percent are Aboriginal and other. Most of the inhabitants live in the temperate coastal areas, while the large interior (or Outback) is arid and sparsely populated.[73]

Heavily influenced by British traditions, Australia's first schools were established in the late eighteenth century, and compulsory education came in the late nineteenth century. By 2009, approximately 65.85 percent of all pupils attended public schools, and approximately 34.15 percent attended private schools. In the past school-age children living in the remote Outback depended on educational radio broadcasts and correspondence courses, but a recent program seeks to provide Outback students with laptop computers loaded with various educational programming and, where possible, connection to the internet. One of the recent priorities of the government is what it calls its Education Revolution, which involves increased national spending to upgrade all Australian schools, including sufficient student computers.[74]

Australia has a federal system of government (national, state/territory, and local), with education a traditional state/territory government responsibility. Recently, national government funding has been added as well, including aid to private schools. Australia has six states and two territories, and while there are small variations among them, all have compulsory attendance between ages six and 16, all provide a noncompulsory preschool year (which almost all children attend), and all provide a compulsory preparatory (or kindergarten) year followed by 12 years of primary and secondary schooling. Students have the options to leave school at age 16, attend postsecondary technical and vocational education, or continue secondary education to successful completion and qualify for admission to a college or university.[75]

Gender and national educational policy

Two national reports significantly influenced Australian policy on gender and education. *Girls, School and Society* in 1975 called for maintaining the traditional curriculum but rooting out gender distortions and stereotypes. Although the distinct ways girls learn or the differences among them were not highlighted, the issue of gender in education was recognized as part of the larger national issue of women's status in Australia. A more far-reaching approach was taken in the *National Policy for the Education of Girls in Australian Schools* in 1987. It recognized that girls are not a singular homogeneous group, but they have varied educational needs that require supportive curricula and teaching practices.[76] Thus, by the late 1980s, Australian national educational policy was recognizing "women's ways of knowing" and differences among female learners, and it developed curricular programs better designed to meet girls' particularized needs.

According to critics, however, after all the attention to girls' learning needs, it was doubtful they were better educated to understand how Australia's social, political, and economic structures maintained the status quo. Furthermore, while policy was also directed at improving the academic education of females, the focus was mainly on subjects leading to careers for women in engineering, science, and technology, with little attention to the service sector where most females found employment. Finally, recognition of gender equity as a legitimate national educational policy indicated that Australia's national government was now more heavily invested in school operations that were once the sole responsibility of state governments, but schools and teachers were confronted with greater central regulation, and the freedom to engage in local pedagogical and curricular reforms was being curtailed.[77]

Gender in school and society

As in most countries, Australian society has a major influence on how gender roles are formed by institutional forces, such as the mass media, religion, sports, and employment, influences that affect children's gender identities as much or more than schools. "Gender agendas" are formed not only at the personal and school levels but also at societal levels that begin at birth with such influences as gender-specific play, toys, clothing, and media programs for children. Although gender is influenced by school curricula and teaching practices, the larger society has a profound impact on gender roles through parenting, domestic labor, earning a living, and class and ethnic identities as well. For example, males may generally have more power than females, but upper-class males and females have more power than lower-class males and females, just as males and females of a dominant ethnic group have more power than those of a minority group. Part of the solution lies in educational programs that help students understand genders as social constructions over which both individuals and groups might have some control. It also involves making changes in the adult world so that men become less defined by employment and women less defined by domesticity. In sum, schools cannot solve the problem alone, because the solution ultimately depends on changes in the larger society.[78]

Boys and gender in Australian education

Australia has a strong masculine tradition dating back to its pioneering days, the "bush" tradition of the camaraderie of sturdy, reliable "mates" that continues to have popular currency (such as the Crocodile Dundee character of movie fame). As the drive for equity in the education of females gained ground, reaction arose concerning the plight of boys and their need for attention. Some critics complained that the concern about boys was eclipsing gains made by girls, while others maintained that more public attention was needed on the actual gender problems both male and female children encountered in school and society. The resolution—as far as schools could provide it—seemed to be not "degendering" the curriculum but helping students better understand how gender roles are historically conditioned and are social and cultural constructions rather than inborn traits.[79]

The status of females in Australian education today

Among the key objectives has been to increase educational participation and transition into the workforce. There was an increase of "fully engaged" young people (either in full-time education or in full-time work) between 1999 and 2009, but 16 percent of 15- to 19-year-olds (224,000 people) were still not fully engaged by 2009. Of that 16 percent, more than half were not working or studying at all and the remainder were occupied only in part-time work, with males more likely to be classified as "unemployed" and females classified as "not in the labour force."[80]

In 2010, Australia was in the process of developing a national curriculum, a draft of which was released for public feedback on March 1. Although gender equity had lost prominence as an educational issue, the topic of gender retained a place in the draft of the new curriculum, particularly in the history curriculum, which included sections ranging from women's struggles for equality and full citizenship to the change in attitude toward birth control and contraception to the increased participation by females in education and workplaces.[81]

In 2008, there were 3,457,049 full-time and part-time students from "pre-year" through year 12 attending public and private schools. Of that total, there were 1,759,305 males and 1,697,744 females. That same year, the number of students enrolled by all providers of higher education institutions, both public and private, was 1,066,095, of which 477,252 were males (44.8 percent) and 599,843 were females (55.2 percent). Such statistics indicate that, while males continued to outnumber females in Australia's primary and secondary schools, females now outnumbered males in the colleges and universities by 10 percentage points,[82] a higher education trend that seemed to be occurring in many other countries as well.

Summary and conclusions

It is difficult to bring about immediate changes in institutions such as schools because the redirection of an institution (let alone a whole society) seldom proceeds in full-scale fashion. Progress toward gender equity has been made, but gender bias has not disappeared. Although biological sex is one factor in gender, it is not the same as gender (conceptualized as feminine or masculine), which comes out of sociocultural conventions and institutional arrangements. Thus, women's subordinate status did not arise from biology so much as from social and cultural ideas of womanhood or manhood and what it meant to be feminine or masculine.

Concerted efforts for social, political, and economic equity have mostly occurred in recent times. In the United States in the late eighteenth century, female education gained attention as indispensable to the new republic, and during nineteenth-century industrialization the education of girls was expanded, as was the role of women in social reform and in education, particularly as teachers in the new public common schools. By the end of the century, public schools embraced coeducation from elementary through high school, and by the early twentieth century, female students outnumbered male students in the schools.

The conviction that females should have citizenship rights and societal access on par with males gained ground, and by the end of the twentieth century, females actually gained numerical dominance in schools from kindergarten to higher education, and female participation in the labor market greatly expanded, although still hampered by pay and job discrimination. Nevertheless, by the twenty-first century more women participated in greater numbers in almost all social institutions and at all levels than ever before. In education, females were gaining academic standing equal to that of males, with greater recognition of women's ways of learning and knowing.

As barriers to gender equity in education were reduced, attention was also directed to boys, with growing recognition that gender bias affected both girls and boys. However, female achievement in math and science still lagged behind males, just as males lagged behind females in verbal and written achievement. For all the changes, gender inequities lingered in institutional structures, professional practices, and behavioral patterns. Some critics pushed single-sex schooling as a remedy to gender problems in education. Others countered that sex segregation did not address the sources of most gender problems, particularly sociocultural forces that transmit gender messages, often without people being aware of it.

At the high school level, females are still less likely than males to pursue such fields as math, science, and technology, and males continue to be underrepresented in the performing arts and literary activities. In higher education, males still outnumber females in certain studies and in the professoriate and administration. In careers, females continue to be over-represented in the lower-paying fields, while males continue to be better paid and to dominate most of the learned professions. The issue of sexual harassment, while much more prominent in public awareness, has not disappeared from either schools or workplaces.

Narrow images of masculinity and femininity also play roles in defining sexuality and sexual identities. The ways these issues are viewed have changed as well, but homosexuality and other sexual identities often meet hostile prejudice rather than tolerance and understanding in social institutions, including schools. Students facing such treatment often suffer from isolation and stigmatization and are even subjected to overt violence, while a cloak of silence remains in most schools concerning issues of sexuality.

It is evident that girls and boys are socialized into gender roles virtually from the moment of birth, and as they mature the roles are reinforced by many forces such as families, communities, and other societal and institutional settings, including schools. Although males and females possess so many characteristics in common, gender differences continue to matter in countries around the globe. Australia is an example of a country where concerted efforts have been made to increase gender equity in educational opportunities and experiences. It is a nation that seems to continue its efforts as its understanding of the issues also changes and develops, and one of the constants in that country's efforts is the awareness of education's role in achieving gender equity.

There is a continuing need to examine and correct the root causes for gender bias, particularly the educational roots. While some distinct gender differences must be recognized, all persons should have the best education possible—regardless of origin, condition, or gender—from the local community to the wider society.

Vocabulary

coeducation
crisis of masculinity
cult of true womanhood
***Davis v. Monroe County Board of Education* (1999)**
double burden
eating disorders
ethics of care
***Franklin v. Gwinnett County Public Schools* (1992)**
***Gebser v. Lago Vista Independent School District* (1998)**
gender
gender bias
gender sensitive
gender stereotypes
gender stratification
gender violence
Hartford Female Seminary
heteronormativity
heterosexuality
homosexuality
intra-gender differences
lesbian, bisexual, gay, and transgender (LBGT)

Notes

1 Jenny Shaw, *Education, Gender and Anxiety* (London: Taylor and Francis, Ltd., 1995), 1–3.

2 Gordon Allport, *The Nature of Prejudice* (Garden City, NY: Doubleday Anchor Books, 1954).

3 Mary P. Ryan, *Womanhood in America: From Colonial Times to the Present*, 2nd edn (New York: New Viewpoints, A Division of Franklin Watts, 1979).

4 Ibid., x–xii, xiv–xvii, 10, 14–16, 28–29.

5 See Lawrence A. Cremin, *American Education: The Colonial Experience, 1607–1783* (New York: Harper and Row, 1970).

6 Sochen, 73–80; and Merle Curti, *The Social Ideas of American Educators* (Totawa, NJ: Littlefield, Adams, and Company, 1968), 176.

7 Barbara Welter, "The Cult of True Womanhood," *American Quarterly*, vol. 18, no. 2, part 1: 152–153 (Summer, 1966).

8 Ryan, 53–54, and 82–85; and Lawrence Cremin, *American Education: The National Experience, 1783–1876* (New York: Harper and Row, 1980), 348–350.

9 Ryan, 98–101.

10 Ibid., 75–80; and Welter, 71–73.

11 Eleanor Wolf Thompson, *Education for Ladies, 1830–1860: Ideas on Education in Magazines for Women* (Morningside Heights, NY: King's Crown Press, 1947), 73–90.

12 Phillida Bunkle, "Sentimental Womanhood and Domestic Education, 1830–1870," *History of Education Quarterly*, vol. 14, no. 1: 3–30 (Spring 1974).

13 Michael Apple, "Teaching and `Women's Work': A Comparative Historical and Ideological Analysis," in *Expressions of Power in Education: Studies of Class, Gender and Race*, Center for Cross-cultural Education Lecture Series, vol. 3, Edgar B. Gumbert, ed. (Atlanta: Center for Cross-Cultural Education, 1984), 35, 38; and Robert E. Potter, *The Stream of American Education* (New York: American Book Company, 1967), 238–239.

14 Emma Hart Willard, "A Plan for Improving Female Education," in *Pioneers of Women's Education in the United States: Emma Willard, Catherine Beecher, Mary Lyon*, Willystine Goodsell, ed. (1931, reprint, New York: AMS Press, 1970), 58, 62, and 72.

15 Catherine Beecher, "Suggestions Respecting Improvements in Education," in *Pioneers of Women's Education*, 147; and Bunkle, 20.

16 Mary Lyon, "New England Female Seminary for Teachers," in *Pioneers of Women's Education*, 254; and Bunkle, 21–22.

17 Lynn D. Gordon, *Gender and Higher Education in the Progressive Era* (New Haven: Yale University Press, 1990), 13–51.

18 John L. Rury, *Education and Women's Work: Female Schooling and the Division of Labor in Urban America, 1870–1930* (Albany: State University of New York Press, 1991), 17–18, 35–48.

19 Ibid., 83, 120–124.

20 Ibid., 135–144.

21 Judith Stacey et al., eds, *And Jill Came Tumbling After: Sexism in American Education* (New York: Dell Publishing, 1974).

22 Marcia Bombardieri, "Summers' remarks on women draw fire," *The Boston Globe*, January 17, 2005, at http://www.boston.com/news/local/articles/2005/01/17/summers_remarks_on_women_draw_fire/ (accessed on May 22, 2009).

23 Jack Fincher, *Human Intelligence* (New York: G. P. Putnam's Sons, 1976).

24 Colin Noble and Wendy Bradford, *Getting It Right for Boys . . . and Girls* (New York: Routledge, 2000), 120; National Center for Education Statistics (NCES), *The Condition of Education 2007: Science Performance of Students in Grades 4, 8, and 12*, at http://nces.ed.gov/pubs2007/2007064.pdf (accessed on July 12, 2010); and Barbara A. Marinak and Linda B. Gambrell, "Reading Motivation: Exploring the Elementary Gender Gap," *Literacy Research and Instruction*, vol. 49, no. 2: 129–141 (2010).

25 Mary Field Belenky et al., *Women's Ways of Knowing: The Development of Self, Voice, and Mind* (New York: Basic Books, 1986).

26 Howard A. Ozmon and Samuel M. Craver, *Philosophical Foundations of Education*, 7th edn (Columbus, OH: Merrill, an imprint of Prentice Hall, 2003), 16.

27 Carol Gilligan, *In a Different Voice: Psychological Theory and Women's Development* (Cambridge, MA: Harvard University Press, 1982).

28 Nel Noddings. *Caring: A Feminine Approach to Ethics and Moral Education* (Berkeley: University of California Press, 1984); Nel Noddings, *The Challenge to Care in Schools: An Alternative Approach to Education* (New York: Teachers College Press, 1992); and Nel Noddings, "Introduction," in *Justice and Caring: The Search for Common Ground in Education*, Michael Katz, Nel Noddings, and Kenneth Strike, eds (New York: Teachers College Press, 1999), 1–2.

29 Kenneth Strike, "Justice, Caring, and Universality: In Defense of Moral Pluralism," in *Justice and Caring*, 21–26.

30 Donald MacLeod, "The Gender Divide," in *Guardian Education* (June 17, 1997), 3, as quoted in Kevan Bleach, "Why the Likely Lads Lag Behind," in *Raising Boys' Achievement in Schools*, Kevan Bleach, ed. (Stoke-on-Trent, UK: Trentham Books, 1998), 4; American Association of University Women (AAUW), *Gender Gaps: Where Schools Still Fail Our Children* (New York: Marlowe and Company, 1999), 6.

31 Jewelle T. Gibbs, ed., *Young, Black, and Male in America: An Endangered Species* (Westport, CT: Auburn House, 1988); Khaula Murtadha-Watts, "Theorizing Urban Black Masculinity Construction in an African-Centered School," in *Masculinities at School*, Nancy Lesko, ed. (Thousand Oaks, CA: Sage Publications 2000), 49–71; Nancy Lesko, "Introduction," in *Masculinities at School*, xi, xiv; and Odette Parry, *Male Underachievement in High School Education* (Barbados: Canoe Press, 2000); and "The Monitor's View: Responding to Littleton," *Christian Science Monitor*, Thursday, April 22, 1999, at http://www.csmonitor.com/1999/0422/p10s1.html (accessed on August 30, 2010).

32 Debbie Epstein et al. (eds), "Schoolboys Frictions: Feminism and 'Failing' Boys," in *Failing Boys? Issues in Gender and Achievement*, (Philadelphia: Open University Press, 1998), 3–10.

33 Michèle Cohen, "'A Habit of Healthy Idleness': Boys' Underachievement in Historical Perspective," in Epstein et al., 19–34.

34 Paul Willis, *Learning to Labour: How Working Class Kids Get Working Class Jobs* (Aldershot: Saxon House, 1977); J. Martino, "'Cool Boys,' 'Party Animals,' 'Squids' and 'Poofters': Interrogating the Dynamics and Politics of Adolescent Masculinities at School," in *British Journal of Sociology of Education*, vol. 20, no. 2: 240–263 (June 1999); and Becky Francis, *Boys, Girls, And Achievement: Addressing the Classroom Issues* (London: Routledge Falmer, 2000), 124–131.

35 Patricia Cayo Sexton, *The Feminized Male: Classrooms, White Collars, and the Decline of Manliness* (New York: Random House, 1969), 3–11, 24–28, 30–34, 134–135, and 163–166.

36 Francis, 124–131.

37 See Sheelagh Drudy et al., *Men and the Classroom: Gender Imbalances in Teaching* (London and New York: Routledge, 2005).

38 Gilbert Herdt, "Issues in the Cross-Cultural Study of Homosexuality," in *Textbook of Homosexuality and Mental Health*, Robert P. Cabaj and Terry S. Stein, eds (Washington, DC: American Psychiatric Press, 1996), 68; and William Byne, "Biology and Homosexuality," in *Textbook of Homosexuality and Mental Health*, 132–133.

39 Lawrence Hartmann, "Foreword," in *Textbook of Homosexuality and Mental Health*, xxv–xxxi.

40 Stuart Michaels, "The Prevalence of Homosexuality in the United States," in *Textbook of Homosexuality and Mental Health*, 61; and Hilda F. Besner and Charlotte I. Spungin, *Gay and Lesbian Students: Understanding Their Needs* (Washington, DC: Taylor and Francis, 1995), 13–25.

41 Mindy Blaise, *Playing It Straight: Uncovering Gender Discourses in the Early Childhood Classroom* (New York: Routledge: 2005) 22; William J. Letts, IV and James T. Sears, eds, *Queering Elementary Education: Advancing the Dialogue about Sexualities and Schooling* (Lanham, MD: Rowman and Littlefield Publishers, 1999), 165–204, and 207–256; and Madiha Didi Khayatt, *Lesbian Teachers: An Invisible Presence* (Albany: State University of New York Press, 1992).

42 Susan Birden, *Rethinking Sexual Identity in Education* (Lanham, MD: Rowman and Littlefield Publishers, 2005), 1.

43 David Campos, *Diverse Sexuality and Schools: A Reference Handbook* (Santa Barbara, CA: ABC-CLIO, 2003), 9.

44 Besner and Spungin, 67–96.

45 David Campos, *Understanding Gay and Lesbian Youth: Lessons for Straight School Teachers, Counselors, and Administrators* (Lanham, MD: Rowman and Littlefield Education, 2005), 20, 97–100.

46 Betty Levy and Judith Stacey, "Sexism in the Elementary School: A Backward and Forward Look," *Phi Delta Kappan* 50, no. 2: 105–109 (October 1973).

47 AAUW, *Gender Gaps*, 68–69.

48 Kay Kohlhaas et al., "Science Equity in Third Grade," *Elementary School Journal*, vol. 110, no. 3: 393–407 (March 2010); and Barbara A. Marinek and Linda B. Gambrell, "Reading Motivation: Exploring the Elementary Gender Gap," *Literacy Research and Instruction*, vol. 49, no. 2: 129–141 (2010).

49 See Sara Cunningham, "Male teachers scarce: Fewer men serve as role models; experts split on impact," *Courier Journal*, Louisville, KY (May 8, 2010), at (http://pqasb.pqarchiver.com/courier_journal/access/2030370551.html?FMT=ABS&date=May+08%2C+2010 (accessed on July 29, 2010); and Annie Pleshette-Murphy, "Number of Male Teachers Shrinking Fast," ABC, Good Morning America (October 20, 2008), at http://abcnews.go.com/GMA/Parenting/story?id=6070282&page=1 (accessed on July 20, 2010). See also "Duncan: Black male teachers needed," CNN Newsroom Blog Archive (June 21, 2010), at http://newsroom.blogs.cnn.com/2010/06/21/duncan-black-male-teachers-needed-2/ (accessed on August 10, 2010).

50 NCES, "Table 33. Historical summary of public elementary and secondary school statistics, 1869–7 through 2006–07," *Digest of Education Statistics* (2009), at http://nces.ed.gov/programs/digest/d09/tables/dt09_033.asp?referrer=list (accessed July 28, 2010).

51 James R. King, "The Problem(s) of Men in Early Education," in *Masculinities at School*, Nancy Lesko, ed. (Thousand Oaks, CA: Sage Publication, 2000), 3–25.

52 Christine Skelton et al., "Gender 'matters' in the primary classroom: pupils' and teachers' perspectives," *British Educational Research Journal*, vol. 35, no. 2: 187–204 (April 2009); Herbert W. Marsh et al., "A Multilevel Perspective on Gender in Classroom Motivation and Climate: Potential Benefits of Male Teachers for Boys?" *Journal of Educational Psychology*, 2008, vol. 100, no. 1: 78–95 (February 2008); and Chance W. Lewis, "African American Male Teachers in Public Schools: An Examination of Three Urban School Districts," *Teachers College Record*, vol. 108, no. 2: 224–245 (February 2006).

53 Karen Hunter Quartz et al., "Careers in Motion: A Longitudinal Retention Study of Role Changing among Early-Career Urban Educators," *Teachers College Record*, vol. 110, no. 1: 218–250 (January 2008).

54 Francis, 117–120.

55 Peggy Orenstein, *SchoolGirls: Young Women, Self-Esteem, and the Confidence Gap* (New York: Anchor Books, 1994), 51–66 and 91–105.

56 William S. Pollack and Todd Shuster, *Real Boys' Voices* (New York: Penguin Books, 2000), 297–312; Timothy Egan, "Body-Conscious Boys Adopt Athletes' Taste for Steroids," *The New York Times*, November 22, 2002, at http://www.nytimes.com/2002/11/22/us/body-conscious-boys-adopt-athletes-taste-for-steroids.html (accessed on October 16, 2010); and Aaron Patnode, "Many Body-Conscious Teens Use Supplements to Improve Physique," Press Room, Children's Hospital Boston (August 1, 2005), at http://www.childrenshospital.org/newsroom/Site1339/mainpageS1339P1sub-level158.html (accessed on October 16, 2010).

57 Jeremy N. Price, "Peer (Dis)Connections, School, and African American Masculinities, in *Masculinities at School*, 127–159.

58 Francis, 120–121.

59 NCES, *America's High School Graduates: Results from the 2005 NAEP High School Transcript Study*, at http://nces.ed.gov/pubsearch/pubsinfo.asp?pubid=2007467 (accessed on July 16, 2010).

60 NCES, *The Nation's Report Card: America's High School Graduates* (2007), at http://nces.ed.gov/nationsreportcard/pdf/studies/2007467_4.pdf (accessed on July 20, 2010); College Board, *Program Summary Report* (2009). http://professionals.collegeboard.com/profdownload/program-summary-report-09.pdf (accessed on July 20, 2010); and Christianne Corbett et al., *Why So Few?: Women in Science, Technology, Engineering, and Mathematics* (Washington, DC: American Association of University Women, 2010).

61 Judith A. Bazler and Doris A. Simonis, "Are High School Chemistry Textbooks Gender Fair??" *Journal of Research in Science Teaching*, vol. 28, no. 4: 353–362 (April 1991); and Jessica J. Good et al., "The Effects of Gender-Stereotypic Textbook Images on Science Performance," *Journal of Social Psychology*, vol. 150, no. 2: 132–147 (2010).

62 NCES, *Trends in Educational Equity of Girls and Women: 2004, Extracurricular Activities*, 8–9, at http://nces.ed.gov/pubs2005/equity/Section6.asp (accessed on July 20, 2010).

63 Ibid., 94–107.

64 National Center for Women & Information Technology (NCWIT). *By the numbers* (2009), at http://www.ncwit.org/pdf/BytheNumbers09.pdf (accessed on July 16, 2010).

65 U.S. Bureau of Labor Statistics, *Highlights of Women's Earnings in 2009* (June 2010), at http://www.bls.gov/cps/cpswom2009.pdf (accessed on July 20, 2010).

66 AAUW, *Gender Gaps*, 108–119.

67 AAUW and Harris/Scholastic Research, *Hostile Hallways: The AAUW Survey on Sexual Harassment in America's Schools*. (Washington, DC: American Association of University Women Educational Foundation, 1993); and Nan Stein. *Classrooms and Courtrooms: Facing Sexual Harassment in K–12 Schools* (New York: Teachers College Press, 1999), 3–5, 21.

68 AAUW, *Harassment-free Hallways: How to Stop Harassment in Schools* (Washington, DC: American Association of University Women Educational Foundation, 2004), 8.

69 Ibid., 1, 25–29, and 115; "Title IX," Education Amendments of 1972, at http://www.dol.gov/oasam/regs/statutes/titleix.htm (accessed on July 20, 2010); *Franklin v. Gwinnett County Public Schools*, 503 U.S. 60, at http://www.law.cornell.edu/supct/html/historics/USSC_CR_0503_0060_ZS.html (accessed on July 20, 2010); *Gebser v. Lago Vista Independent School District* (96–1866), 106 F.3d 1223, at http://www.law.cornell.edu/supct/html/96–1866.ZO.html (accessed on July 20, 2010); and *Davis v. Monroe County Board of Education*, at http://www.law.cornell.edu/supct/html/97–843.ZS.html (accessed on July 20, 2010).

70 AAUW, *Harrassment Free Hallways*, 66–67.

71 Michael Gurian and Kathy Stevens, "Foreword," in *Debating Single-Sex Education*, Frances R. Spielhagen, ed. (Lanham, MD: Rowman and Littlefield Education, 2008), 1.

72 AAUW, *Separated by Sex: A Critical Look at Single-Sex Education for Girls* (Washington, DC: American Association of University Women Educational Foundation, 1998), 2–3.

73 "Australia," *The World Factbook*, at https://www.cia.gov/library/publications/the-world-factbook/geos/as.html#top (accessed on July 23, 2010).

74 Australian Bureau of Statistics (ABS), "NSSC Table 42a—All Full-time and Part-time Students—by State and Territory Affiliation, Sex, Grade and Years (1995–2009), click on "NSSC T42a – Full-time + Part-time STUDENTS (All) (1995 to 2009), XLS" at http://abs.gov.au/AUSSTATS/abs@.nsf/DetailsPage/4221.02009?OpenDocument (accessed on June 17, 2010); Kathryn Edwards, "OLPC [One Laptop Per Child] boosts outback education with laptop deployment: Australia's Indigenous Communities to Benefit from New Educational Tools," *Computerworld* (May 27, 2009), at http://www.computerworld.com.au/article/304648/olpc_boosts_outback_education_laptop_deployment/ (accessed on June 21, 2010); and Stephanie Fitzpatrick, "Outback Education Shake-up Worries Parents," ABC News (Australia) (June 3, 2010), at http://www.abc.net.au/news/stories/2010/06/03/2916908.htm (accessed on June 21, 2010).

75 Department of Education, Employment, and Workplace Relations (DEERW), "Schooling: Overview," at http://www.deewr.gov.au/Schooling/Pages/overview.aspx (accessed on June 21, 2010); and Australian Education International, "Overview of Education System, Australia," at http://www.aei.gov.au/AEI/CEP/Australia/EducationSystem/Overview/default.htm (accessed on June 21, 2010).

76 Lyn Yates, "Feminism and Australian State Policy: Some Questions for the 1990s," in *Feminism and Social Justice in Education: International Perspectives*, Madeline Arnot and Kathleen Weiler, eds (Washington, DC: The Falmer Press, 1993), 170–173.

77 Yates, 174–181.

78 Terry Evans, *A Gender Agenda: A Sociological Study of Teachers, Parents and Pupils in their Primary Schools* (Sydney: Allen and Unwin, 1988), 137–140 and 141–147.

79 Rob Gilbert and Pam Gilbert, *Masculinity Goes to School* (New York: Routledge, 1998), 4–8, 30–36, 49, and 57–78; and Amanda Keddie, "National Gender Equity and Schooling Policy in Australia: Struggles for a Non-identitarian Feminist Politics," *Australian Educational Researcher* (August, 2009), at http://findarticles.com/p/articles/mi_6929/is_2_36/ai_n35632412/ (accessed on June 14, 2010).

80 ABS, "Australian Social Trends: Are Young People Earning or Learning?" (March 2010), 3, at http://www.ausstats.abs.gov.au/ausstats/subscriber.nsf/LookupAttach/4102.0Publication16.03.105/$File/41020_LearningorEarning.pdf (accessed on June 18, 2010).

81 Kevin Rudd, "Comments" concerning the release of the draft National Curriculum (March 1, 2010), at http://www.pm.gov.au/node/6531 (accessed on June 16, 2010); Press release announcing the availability of the draft, at http://www.pm.gov.au/node/6517 (accessed on June 16, 2010). At the time of this writing, the draft National Curriculum was available at http://www.australiancurriculum.edu.au/Documents/SeniorYears/History/Modern%20History.pdf (accessed on June 16, 2010).

82 ABS, "NSSC Table 42a—All Full-Time and Part-Time Students—by States and Territories, Affiliation, Sex, Grade and Years (1995 to 2009)," click on the Excel version and scroll to the 2008 figures, at http://abs.gov.au/AUSSTATS/abs@.nsf/DetailsPage/4221.02009?OpenDocument (accessed on June 16, 2010); and DEERWA, Students, Selected Higher Education Statistics, under "2008 Full Year Student Summary Tables," click on "All Higher Education Providers (XLS 109KB)," see "Table (i): Summary of 2008 Student Numbers (a)," at http://www.deewr.gov.au/HigherEducation/Publications/HEStatistics/Publications/Pages/2008FullYear.aspx (accessed on June 21, 2010); DEERWA, "Previous Issues—Selected Higher Education Statistics 2008, click on "2008 Full Year Student Summary (PDF 21KB), see "Attachment A – Summary of the 2008 Higher Education Student Statistics,) at http://www.deewr.gov.au/HigherEducation/Publications/HEStatistics/Publications/Pages/Students.aspx (accessed on June 21, 2010); and Organization for Economic Co-operation and Development (OECD), *Education at a Glance: 2009, OECD Indicators* (OECD 2009), 45, 47, and 65, at http://www.oecd.org/dataoecd/41/25/43636332.pdf (accessed on June 22, 2010).

7

Education of People with Disabilities

Chapter contents

Chapter objectives

Readers should:

- Become aware of issues connected with the education of students with disabilities.
- Appreciate the social, political, and economic complexities of inclusion.
- Understand the history and present-day issues of education of people with disabilities.
- Become informed about the legal bases of inclusion, such as relevant laws and court decisions.
- Understand major findings on the effectiveness of inclusion, particularly those concerning teacher, student, and parental responses.
- Appreciate the ethical dimensions of inclusion.
- Become aware of reform efforts in other countries and how those efforts are similar and different depending on national context.
- Develop a better understanding of the issues involved in the education of people with disabilities.

Opening questions

1. What role does the education of people with disabilities play in the daily life of a classroom teacher?

2. What are the issues that raise particular concern among educators and make the issue of inclusion so controversial?
3. How can we learn from the history of educating students with disabilities in order to understand current questions about mainstreaming and inclusion?
4. What do we need to know about the legal basis as well as current research findings on the effectiveness of inclusion in order to begin our preparation for dealing with the issue in the classroom?
5. How do inclusion and the education of people with disabilities tie into larger philosophical concerns about equal opportunities for all students?
6. How does the United States compare with other countries in regard to inclusion and the education of students with disabilities?

The issue

In early times, children with disabilities, particularly the more severe kinds, seldom survived infancy, and those that did usually faced uncertain futures. In some historical eras, people with disabilities might be considered deficient in rationality, while in others they might be viewed as "touched" by divine intervention, perhaps possessing special powers or serving as warnings to others about divine retribution. In some cultures, disabilities might be perceived as sources of evil, while in others they might be treated with pity and charity.[1] In short, history reveals a variety of ways people in the more distant past viewed and dealt with disabilities.

From about 1820 to 1860, important American reform movements were set in motion that met with varying degrees of success (the abolition of slavery, prison reform, state hospitals for mental illness, and state systems of public schools). One such movement concerned the education of people with disabilities, but at that time policy decisions were made to educate them separately from other children. In some cases this meant isolated residential institutions, in others it meant separate day schools or at least separate classes in regular schools, due not only to traditional prejudices but also to well- intentioned beliefs that the needs of people with disabilities could best be met in separate facilities. However, institutions often became places of permanent abode, particularly for those with severe disabilities. Many institutions suffered from inadequate funding, which meant ineffective care and education, a problem also experienced by separate day schools and separate classrooms in regular schools. Some locales were unable or simply refused to educate children with special needs, particularly those with severe disabilities. By the mid-twentieth century, the perception was growing that such separation was, like racial segregation, not only morally unfair and undemocratic but unconstitutional as well. Separate education isolated children from interaction with the larger society, which did little to foster greater independence. Critics pointed out that, while some needed long-term support, other children with special needs could become independent. In addition, researchers were finding that many disabilities once considered educationally hopeless could be ameliorated with better, more appropriate educational intervention.

Mainstreaming and *inclusion* are late twentieth-century terms applied to integrating students with disabilities into regular schools and classrooms. The terms represent general concepts rather than specific teaching techniques or curricular programs, and they are outgrowths of the larger movement to reduce or abolish separate education for children with special needs. Despite the fact that mainstreaming was designed primarily for students with mild disabilities and inclusion was intended to take in students with moderate to severe disabilities, the two concepts are similar. Both are grounded in civil rights, embrace the placement of students with disabilities in general education settings, and share similar aspects of implementation. The essential idea is the integration of students with disabilities into regular schools and classrooms, with any exceptions carefully considered according to individual need and context.

It is sometimes easy to assume that earlier times were backward while the present is enlightened. Progress has been made, of course, but change rarely occurs without controversy and uncertainty. Today, many school systems across the United States have become inclusive settings in which students, both those with and without disabilities, are educated together as much as possible in common environments. At the same time, problems and issues remain that educators, students, parents, and citizens must face in the process.

WEB: Suggested Reading 7.1.

For Further Reflection: How may we create a society that allows all people, including those with disabilities, to lead fulfilling, active lives?

Background

If the United States had its revolution in the late eighteenth century, it experienced another "revolution" in the early nineteenth century through energetic institution building. As Alexis de Tocqueville observed upon his visit to the United States in 1831, Americans from all walks of life constantly formed associations, "to give entertainments, to found seminaries, to build inns, to construct churches, to diffuse books, to send missionaries to the antipodes; they found in this manner hospitals, prisons, and schools."[2] To de Tocqueville, it seemed that whenever Americans encountered a problem, they founded an institution to deal with it. This tendency was readily apparent in how Americans approached education, including the education of people with disabilities. At that time, the special needs most often recognized were those readily observed according to physical conditions and outward behavior, such as sight, hearing, and mental disabilities.

Education and hearing disabilities

A pioneer in American education for people with hearing disabilities was Thomas Hopkins Gallaudet, a young minister who attempted to teach nine-year-old Alice Cogswell, a neighbor's child who was deaf. He turned this interest into his life's work. Gallaudet went to France to study under Abbé Roche-Ambroise Cucurron Sicard, head of the Institution Nationale des Sourds-Muets (National Institution for Deaf-Mutes), where he became an advocate of **sign language** as the most appropriate mode of education for people with hearing disabilities. In the meantime, Dr. Mason Fitch Cogswell (the father of Alice) secured an act of incorporation from the Connecticut legislature in 1817 to establish the Connecticut Asylum for the Education and Instruction of Deaf and Dumb Persons.[3]

Before returning to the United States, Gallaudet convinced Laurent Clerc, a student of Sicard and also a prominent teacher at France's National Institution, to come with him. Clerc had participated in developing a system of writing, hand signs, and grammatical rules that later influenced the development of American Sign Language (ASL). He lost his hearing in infancy, but when he became a student at the National Institution at age 12, he progressed rapidly. Sicard soon made him an assistant and eventually a teacher. Clerc became a major advocate of sign language and of the idea of a **deaf community**, with students taught by instructors who were also deaf.[4] In the United States, both Gallaudet and Clerc wanted the Connecticut Asylum (later renamed the American School for the Deaf) to become a model school for the education of people with hearing impairments.[5]

Gallaudet's son Edward was instrumental in securing an act of Congress in 1864 to establish a college for students with hearing disabilities in Washington, D.C. That institution, today called Gallaudet University, was the first higher education institution in the world designed specifically for students with hearing disabilities, and it enhanced the growth of the notion of a deaf community".[6]

Sign language approach

Under the Gallaudet-Clerc approach, sign language became a part of the culture and community of many deaf Americans. Where the larger society saw deafness as an affliction, many people in the deaf community came to view themselves as a linguistic minority, a viewpoint enhanced by sign language and by residential schools providing the means and the nurturing environment where students could share cultural outlooks and values as a minority group within the larger society. To this day, the idea of a deaf culture and community endures: In autumn 2006, students and faculty at Gallaudet University were able to force that institution's governing board to rescind its decision to hire a new president because, among other things, the candidate was deemed not "adequately committed to American Sign Language."[7]

Oralist approach

The **oralist approach** or speech approach also had its own tradition going back at least to sixteenth century Spain, but oralism was boosted by Édouard Séguin, a prominent French physician-educator, who emigrated in 1848. Although Séguin's area of expertise was mental retardation, he was sympathetic to oralism because it emphasized the senses of touch and sight to help students learn to speak. At least one residential school, the Virginia School for the Deaf and Blind, emphasized speech to help its students earn a living. The school opened in 1839, with Joseph D. Tyler, who was himself deaf, as its first principal.[8]

The most famous oralist in the United States, by far, however, was Alexander Graham Bell. Bell was born in Scotland and immigrated to the United States in 1871. He is known worldwide for inventing the telephone, but what is less known about him is his interest in hearing and speech that led to it. Bell's grandfather and father were well-known teachers of elocution, and his mother had a hearing disability, as did his wife, Mabel Hubbard. His mother inspired him to employ teaching techniques that used music and dancing to show the rhythms of speech. In 1872, Bell founded a school for deaf-mutes in Boston that soon became a part of Boston University, where he was the professor of vocal physiology. He attempted to build a "phono-autograph" to enable deaf students to observe the vibrations of spoken words on an electrified membrane that moved a mechanical lever. The device failed, but from it Bell would invent the telephone in 1876.[9]

Bell not only believed that some forms of deafness were hereditary, but he alienated the deaf community with his view that couples with congenital deafness should not have children. Bell's belief that sign language was inferior to speech was also criticized, but his influence boosted oralism, and by the time he died in 1922, most American schools for the deaf taught at least some speech, even though the deaf community continued to question Bell's views.[10]

An example of an oralist school began in 1864 as a small private school at Chelmsford, Massachusetts. Although founded by Harriet Rogers, the school was named the Clarke Institution for Deaf Mutes because wealthy industrialist John Clarke made a substantial donation. The school also secured state funding and allied itself closely with the public schools, took children as early as age five, and lengthened the period of instruction to ten years. The Clarke School (as it came to be called) reflected middle-class standards and projected a familial, surrogate mother image to its students rather than the more impersonal learning environment the large residential sign language schools had cultivated. Although the Clarke School promoted oralism as a competitor to sign language, oralism never achieved the long-term dominance that sign language did.[11]

For Further Reflection: Do debates such as the one between advocates of sign language and advocates of oralism advance or hinder the cause of education? Can the strengths and weaknesses of arguments be examined without debate? Consider the best ways to resolve disagreements.

Education and sight disabilities

American education for people with sight disabilities followed a pattern similar to that for hearing disabilities. When Bostonian John Fisher was a medical student in Paris in the 1820s, he became familiar with the work of Valentin Haüy. Haüy developed a system of teaching that used the sense of touch, including reading by means of raised letters. He also taught vocational skills related to touch, such as basket weaving. Impressed by Haüy's work, Fisher returned to Boston determined to establish an American institution along similar lines. Armed with data from a survey on the numbers of people with sight disabilities who needed education, Fisher and his supporters obtained an act of incorporation to establish the New England Asylum for the Blind in 1829, although the school did not actually begin operation until 1832. Other states soon followed: New York in 1832, Pennsylvania in 1833, Ohio in 1837, Tennessee in 1838, and Virginia in 1839. By 1890, there were 18 state schools for students with sight disabilities, but none had quite the impact of the Massachusetts institution founded by Fisher and brought to prominence by Samuel Gridley Howe.[12]

Samuel Gridley Howe

Howe, a physician and passionate social activist, assumed active leadership of the new institution in 1832, beginning with six indigent students in his home. Impressed by his work, the Massachusetts legislature provided annual funding. When a wealthy supporter named Thomas H. Perkins made a substantial donation, the school moved to more spacious quarters in South Boston and changed its name to the Perkins Institute and Massachusetts School for the Blind. Howe modeled his curriculum after the common schools, but he also included vocational training in music and handicrafts. Music, in particular, offered his students occupational opportunities, several becoming church organists. The school band also became popular, and students helped raise funds for the school through concerts.[13]

Reading through the sense of touch

Students learned to read with plaster-cast letters and raised-print reading materials, and Howe taught writing through two approaches: writing with pencils on grooved paper and writing with letters pricked into paper. He taught geography using maps with raised borders and physical features, and he taught arithmetic on boards with raised figures and letters. By 1836, he had students who were able to study French, higher mathematics, and natural philosophy. He also taught traditional handicrafts such as mat, basket, and mattress making. Always short of funds, the school maintained a department where student-made items were on sale to the public.[14]

Perhaps the single most important technical development fostered by Howe was his raised-letter printing method. Apparently unaware at the time of the work of Louis Braille in France, Howe developed a phonetic alphabet employing both stenographic symbols and the common alphabet. He set up a press that produced raised-letter reading materials that were cheaper and smaller in size than European braille. In the late 1830s, he published raised-letter editions of the Old and New Testaments as well as numerous raised-letter textbooks. Inadequate funds hampered Howe's publishing efforts, but his operation printed more reading material for blind people than any other school in the English-speaking world at that time.[15]

For Further Reflection: Why did American educators rely so heavily on European models for educating people with disabilities?

Suggested Activity: Explore the biographical materials on Samuel Gridley Howe, and present an oral report (individual or small group) to the class on why he was such a dominant figure in the education of people with disabilities in the United States in his day.

Education and mental disabilities

Reforms in the education of people with sight and hearing disabilities helped direct attention to the education of people with mental retardation. In 1839, a child with both sight and mental disabilities was brought to Howe for instruction at the Perkins Institute. Reflecting the prejudices of the times, Howe was convinced that "feebleminded" children could be educated, and he improvised an instructional approach he intended to become a part of the institute's program, but nothing came of it at first. In 1846, the governor of Massachusetts established a commission to investigate the condition of *idiots* (the classification term used at that time) in the state, and he appointed Howe as the chair. The commissioners shared a belief that "idiocy" might be caused by the sins of the parents, but they also believed it could be alleviated by humane care and education; consequently, the commission succeeded in getting the Massachusetts legislature to fund a school for "feebleminded" children.[16]

In 1850, the Massachusetts School for Idiotic and Feeble-Minded Children became the first state-financed public school for the education of students with such learning dificulties in the United States. It was to move from the Perkins Institute into its own quarters in 1856, and it served as a model for other states to open their own schools, including Rhode Island in 1850, New York in 1851, Pennsylvania in 1852, Ohio in 1857, and Kentucky in 1860. By 1888, at least 11 states were operating schools for children considered mentally retarded.[17]

Édouard Onesimus Séguin

The education of people with mental disabilities was influenced significantly by Édouard Onesimus Séguin.[18] Séguin studied medicine under Jean Marc Gaspard Itard, a physician at France's National Institution who gained recognition for his educational work with a "feral" or abandoned boy who exhibited characteristics of "idiocy," the so-called "Wild Boy of Aveyron."[19]

Itard and the Wild Boy of Aveyron

Jean Marc Gaspard Itard was a physician at France's Institution Nationale des Sourds-Muets (National Institution for Deaf-Mutes) who strongly believed that a cure could be found for deafness. Although he never achieved such a cure, his name is recognized today in medical circles for his invention of the eustachian catheter (sometimes called Itard's catheter) and his work in identifying Tourette's syndrome, among other accomplishments. Itard gained fame, however, for his educational work with the Wild Boy of Aveyron, an abandoned boy found in a remote rural area of France in 1799. Itard was influenced by Enlightenment thinkers who taught that people could be changed if environmental conditions were altered and proper education used. They emphasized the role of sense experience in learning and argued that learning best occurred from interactions with natural environmental surroundings. Some of them developed this into a sensationalist learning theory, or learning through the five senses from one's experiences of natural conditions and from social interactions. Some also believed that human progress would be advanced with greater attention to the natural developmental processes of childhood. Living in an intellectual environment in which these ideas had currency, Itard thought the "wild boy" was a promising example to demonstrate what could be done with proper environment and instruction. In 1800, he began working with the boy, who was about ten or 11 years old at the time; the boy appeared to be congenitally deaf and mute, and some observers believed he also had congenital mental retardation. Itard thought the boy was retarded primarily because of his previous isolation from human nurture and socialization. He named him Victor, because he hoped to show the victory of education over what was then called idiocy. A woman named Madame Guerin took care of Victor in her home while Itard worked with him in a variety of carefully planned educational activities organized around socialization, sensory stimulation, concept formation, speech development, and transfer of training. Itard worked with Victor from 1800 to 1804, and Victor learned to discriminate objects and conditions through touch, taste, smell, sight, and hearing, but he never learned to speak beyond simple sounds and gestures. Victor also learned social skills, and he developed emotional attachments to both Itard and Madame Guerin, but Itard concluded that his work with Victor was a failure and that disabilities such as Victor's could not be cured. Despite Itard's pessimism, his work proved to be an important foundation for later advances, and today he is considered to be one of the key founders of special education.

Sources: Jean Marc Gaspard Itard, *The Wild Boy of Aveyron*, George and Muriel Humphrey, trans. (New York: Appleton-Century-Croft, 1962); Harlan L. Lane, *The Wild Boy of Aveyron* (Cambridge: Harvard University Press, 1976).

At the National Institution, Séguin was an apt student of both education and medicine. He was also influenced by the belief that people had a right to education regardless of their station in life. Under Itard's guidance, Séguin specialized in the education of "idiots," and from his study and subsequent professional practice he developed what he called the **physiological method** of motor and physical sensory training, language and speech training, and socialization. Working at the Hospice des Incurables at Bicêtre, Séguin taught students to use language, to count, and to develop memory. He advocated separating the mentally retarded from the mentally ill because he believed that idiocy was not caused by disease or sin but rather by **developmentally delayed** growth of the brain, a condition he thought could be ameliorated by education. By the time he immigrated to the United States in 1848, Séguin had an international reputation and had influenced the thinking of Howe and other American educators.[20]

Howe persuaded Séguin to come to his Massachusetts school to use the physiological method of teaching. These two strong personalities clashed, however, and after only three months Séguin resigned and left Massachusetts. Despite Séguin's reputation, Howe grumpily wrote a friend that "'I have found out that in the matter of idiocy they do not know so much in England as they do in France, & in France not half so much as they & the rest of the world think they do.'"[21] Undeterred, Séguin continued teaching his approach to other educators in Pennsylvania and New York. In 1866, he published his most important book, *Idiocy and Its Treatment by the Physiological Method*. Although he carefully noted that science had yet to determine the cause of "idiocy," Séguin defined it as "a specific infirmity of the cranio-spinal axis, produced by deficiency of nutrition *in utero* and in *neo-nati*."[22] He also described ways to manage institutions, select and train teachers, and investigate mental disabilities with both a medical and educational rationale. His neurological investigations helped advance the scientific study of mental disorders, and in his later years he researched fever as a causal factor of mental disabilities. Séguin was steadfast in his commitment to education as a human right and a means of social reform, and while he never held a permanent school post, he made significant contributions through his publications, his teaching, and his advising of fellow educators. Today he is generally credited with being a leading founder of special education in the United States.[23]

> **For Further Reflection:** Why was Séguin's view that some disabilities were due to delayed development rather than mysterious forces a major contribution to educational theory?

The era of special education

Generally speaking, by the close of the nineteenth century much of the education of people with disabilities took place in separate institutions, which most people at the time thought the best approach. Indeed, it has also been suggested that the way special education institutions developed served to separate them from general education, and the preponderance of the **medical model** helped keep special education a separate field within education.

> **Suggested Activity:** Investigate what is meant by "the medical model" in special education. How has it helped or hindered the development of the education of people with disabilities?

Origins of separate special education

The Enlightenment's belief in progress and romanticism's distrust of tradition and its love of institution building all had impacts. In addition, the Industrial Revolution also generated large-scale system building in the form of factories and the beginning of industrial corporations. The resulting growth in communication and transportation technology brought forth telegraphs, highways, canals, streetcars, and railroad systems, and by the late nineteenth century, telephone and electrical power systems. A note of caution is needed about the complexity of historical events, however, for while statewide systems of public schools also developed during the time, they were accompanied by another set of institutions that was neither orderly nor particularly systematic. These were the hospitals for the mentally ill, almshouses for the destitute, orphanages, and residential educational institutions for those with disabilities, and they developed not as systems but as single institutions. Each institution stood alone with its own board of directors, and while a number of such institutions received public funding, philanthropy and voluntarism were also significant sources of income. Thus, institutions for people with special needs developed separately from public school systems, and each institution established its own traditions that, once in place, proved difficult to change. For example, when Cogswell and Gallaudet opened their school for deaf students in 1817, they followed a model of organization called corporate voluntarism, that is, a group of citizens simply formed a legal corporation to establish an entity, in this case a school for children with hearing disabilities. Over time such institutions appeared across the country, and schools for students with disabilities continued to be seen as separate institutions rather than integral parts of public school systems. They were usually built in remote rural areas, even as society was becoming more industrialized and urban, and they had names that rang of separate status: asylum, training school, and even colony.[24]

It has been argued that two trends in the last few centuries were largely responsible for the separate schools, one intellectual (the **medicalized theory of deviance**) and the other social (demographic and socioeconomic changes).

Eighteenth-century scholars, influenced by Enlightenment ideas, came to see deviance not as wilful behavior to be controlled by coercion but as unintentional behavior requiring treatment and/or therapy. This intellectual shift led to the medicalized theory of deviance, which had a profound impact on how we educate children with special needs. In the nineteenth century, this view helped promote "child-saving institutions" for pupils with blindness, deafness, and some types of mental disability. By the twentieth century, there was a greater sense of responsibility for low-achieving pupils, with **learning difficulties** also coming under the sway of the medicalization trend. The demographic and socioeconomic trend included population growth and new ways of earning a living through wage labor and manufacturing in densely populated urban areas, which increased the number and diversity of children entering the school systems and a rise in public expectations that everyone should be educated, including those with disabilities. These two trends provided fertile ground for the growth of special education, although still separated from regular education.[25]

Motivations behind separate special education ranged from the humanitarian to the economic and political. A plethora of **labels** such as backwardness, incorrigibility, and mental retardation emerged. Some educators maintained that placement in regular classrooms had a negative effect on students with disabilities, while others argued that the classification and segregation of students by disability was desirable for both humanitarian and economic reasons. Although the change from an older "deviance as wilful behavior" to "deviance as a neurological condition" produced a new consciousness of **disabilities as treatable conditions**, reformers still maintained that social control was needed, and education was the best way to provide it. Educators were not alone in promoting educational therapy for deviant behavior; they were joined by penologists and criminologists as well. Similarly, not only did physicians spread the medicalized view of deviance, but psychiatrists, psychologists, and educators did as well. It was only a matter of time before such views found their way into the schools, and the early decades of the twentieth century witnessed the appearance of guidance counselors, school psychologists, and special education professionals who brought with them such techniques as group counseling, testing, and behavior modification techniques. As the century progressed, definitions of childhood disabilities expanded to include not only mental retardation but also emotional disturbance and learning disabilities.[26]

For Further Reflection: How did the American tendency to form associations and institutions affect the development of education for people with disabilities? In hindsight, did separate institutions help or hinder people with disabilities?

Advent of psychological testing

By the early twentieth century, the new discipline of psychology was seeking to establish its scientific reputation, and it hoped to discover the inner workings of the mind and to develop better treatments for mental disabilities. However, psychology faced the entrenched position of medicine as the "healing" profession with an established track record in special education (physicians such as Itard, Séguin, and Howe). Since psychologists sought to establish their area of specialization as legitimate, they went about doing so (though never so securely as physicians) through **mental measurement** or **psychological testing**. Pioneers included Wilhelm Wundt in Germany; Sir Francis Galton in Britain; Alfred Binet in France; and James McKeen Cattell, G. Stanley Hall, Lewis Madison Terman, and Henry Herbert Goddard in the United States. Cattell was an early advocate of mental measurement, but existing techniques measured physiological responses to stimuli by way of blood pressure and breathing rate. Called brass instrument psychology because of its mechanical apparatuses, this form of measurement was cumbersome. Hall favored child study through clinical observation, but two of his students, Lewis Terman and Henry Goddard, became avid leaders in the testing movement. In France, Alfred Binet and Theodore Simon developed an **intelligence scale** to measure varying levels of "idiocy" in 1904, and by 1908 they had also developed a battery of tests for "normal" children. Cheap and easily administered, the new tests quickly replaced mechanical measurement. Binet wanted his tests used on an individual and small-scale basis, but many other psychologists wanted large quantities of data to lend scientific objectivity to their efforts.[27]

WEB: Suggested Reading 7.2.

For Further Reflection: How have testing and mental measurement affected the education of people with disabilities?

Mental measurement and special education

Before psychology and mental measurement became prominent in special education, however, they were pulled in some now-discredited directions by other developments. In the late nineteenth and early twentieth centuries, the United

States was experiencing a major population increase from immigration, and many of the newcomers had difficulty adjusting to urban crowding and industrial work. The sheer numbers threatened to overwhelm existing educational institutions. For example, New York City saw a 60 percent increase in school enrollments from 1890 to 1914, which drastically strained school facilities, personnel, instructional materials, and funding. To some critics, the newcomers were "strangers" who were culturally different and who posed threats to "the body politic."[28]

For Cross-Reference: See the section on social Darwinism in Chapter 3, Social Class, pp. 116–117, for additional background information.

Suggested Activity: Individually or in a small group, read up on social Darwinism and eugenics. How did they affect the education of people with disabilities? Do remnants of these outlooks still exist, and do they still impact the education of people with disabilities? If so, how and to what effect?

WEB: Suggested Reading 7.3.

Under the influence of social Darwinism and its doctrine of survival of the fittest, a new theory emerged called *eugenics*, a term coined by British psychologist Sir Francis Galton in the 1880s. It combined Mendelian genetics and social Darwinism into a system promoting the mentally healthy, or "the fit," and segregating or sometimes even sterilizing the "unfit." Not only did eugenicists adopt the medical metaphors of disease, germ, and infection but also some psychologists who saw themselves as scientific experts believed they could "doctor" society and prevent "social infections" from spreading through the body politic. Just as society quarantined people with infectious diseases, eugenicists urged, it must also quarantine the "misfits" from infecting society with the "germ" of deviancy. Society must be "disinfected" through institutionalization and even sterilization. For example, Walter Fernald of the Massachusetts Institute for the Feebleminded was concerned that "feebleminded" females could spread the "contagion" if they were allowed to procreate, while education psychologist

E. L. Thorndike held that children with special defects should be put in separate schools described as educational hospitals. Advocates saw the new intelligence tests as the way to discover who should be segregated because, they claimed, the test results were scientific and objective. They seemed to ignore evidence that tests were not always trustworthy, and they optimistically believed the Binet scale was akin to a fine surgical instrument, if administered and interpreted by trained professionals such as themselves.[29]

One leading American advocate of mental measurement was Henry Goddard. First a teacher and then a principal, Goddard was influenced by the writings of G. Stanley Hall. He completed his PhD in 1899 at Clark University (where Hall was president) and became a zealous disciple of scientific psychology. He took a position at the Training School for Feebleminded Girls and Boys at Vineland, New Jersey, where he translated the Binet-Simon scale into English and promoted its widespread use. After Lewis Terman of Stanford University revised the Binet-Simon scale in 1916, millions of people were tested with the new Stanford-Binet IQ test over the next several decades, and Goddard was one of its leading advocates.[30]

Goddard understood that the people with mental disabilities were a diverse group, and he wanted a better classification system. Some people were born with mental disabilities while others acquired them by illness or trauma, and traditional classifications such as idiot, imbecile, and feebleminded were too inexact. Persons with serious mental disabilities were easiest to classify, while the most difficult were persons who seemed "normal" in appearance and behavior but were unable to learn elementary material. The latter individuals tantalized Goddard because he believed they could be educated within certain limits. At first, he thought mental disabilities were largely due to environmental conditions, but under the sway of eugenics he turned to inner conditions as the probable causes. Using the Binet-Simon scale as a departure point, Goddard compared the test taker's chronological age with the scale's "mental age" and came up with the following classification system: an "idiot" tested below the mental age of three, an "imbecile" with a mental age of three to seven, and a *moron* (Goddard's own invented term for a person with arrested mental development) with a mental age of eight to 12 years.[31]

In 1907, Goddard accepted that "feeblemindedness" was educational and psychological in nature, but by the time he wrote *The Kallikak Family: A Study in the Heredity of Feeble-Mindedness* (1912) and *Feeble-Mindedness: Its Causes and Consequences* (1914), he thought eugenics offered the best explanation for inner causal factors. In *The Kallikak Family*, he traced the offspring of Martin Kallikak, who "dallied" with a "lowly barmaid" but married a "wholesome Quaker woman." According to Goddard, the Kallikak descendants of the barmaid were disabled while descendants of the Quaker wife were productive citizens. He associated mental disability with criminality, alcoholism, prostitution, pauperism, and truancy. For *The Kallikak Family*, Goddard conducted case studies of 327 families he classified as "feebleminded," and he concluded that more than 70 percent of it could be attributed to heredity. He strongly recommended that people with such hereditary disability should be prevented from reproducing, perhaps by sterilization but certainly by being "colonized" in separate institutions guided "by high eugenic ideals." He thought such measures would diminish the condition, but he also recognized that those who became "feebleminded" from accidental trauma or disease could not possibly transmit their condition through reproduction. Although he made important contributions, Goddard interjected personal views into purportedly objective findings and offered simplistic explanations for complex sociocultural conditions.[32]

Despite their inherent flaws, social Darwinism and eugenics influenced attitudes, public policies, and educational practices in ways that prolonged the separation of people with disabilities segregated from the larger society. Eventually, however, it became increasingly clear that those most often separated into special institutions or programs were disproportionately poor, from racial and cultural minorities. The drive to identify, test, label, and segregate people with disabilities, while it had humanitarian impulses to help and to educate behind it, was flawed by misrepresentations of Darwinian natural selection and the unfounded claims of eugenics, as well as motivations reflecting class, race, and anti-immigrant biases.[33]

For Further Reflection: How have so-called scientific and objective claims often negatively impacted the development of educational theory and practice? Are similar claims still being made today, and if so, what impact do they have?

Separate special education

Eventually separate special education institutions attracted a growing number of critics. If people with disabilities were placed in institutions that segregated them from the larger society, they were denied sufficient opportunities to learn from and interact with that society; likewise, the larger society was cut off from the understandings and interactions to be gained from direct contact with those who were institutionalized. Actually, Samuel Howe made this point back in 1849 when he realized that the segregation of blind children in separate institutions had some deleterious effects, but his complaint gained little public notice.[34]

Gradually, criticism of separate institutions gained a wider audience as more people came to believe that, while some forms of disability were so severe that institutionalization might be a reasonable choice, children with less severe conditions would have greater opportunities and lead happier lives as part of the larger society, if given the chance.

Learning disabilities

As Séguin understood back in the nineteenth century, some students were easily identified as needing special education, but many others with learning difficulties had no apparent abnormalities. Nevertheless, the specific classification called **learning disabilities** did not emerge until the 1930s when researchers concluded that not all learning disorders could be attributed to mental retardation, particularly disorders in the development of language, speech, reading, and other communication skills. By 1967, Samuel A. Kirk and a group of like-minded colleagues were using the term *learning disability* to designate "a retardation, disorder, or delayed development" in speech, language, reading, writing, arithmetic, or other school subjects, "a psychological handicap" related to "cerebral dysfunction and/or emotional or behavioral disturbances."[35]

Although some researchers believed all learning disabilities were due to brain injury of one kind or another, Kirk maintained that learning disabilities had various origins, some due to brain injury but others to psychological disorders affecting such things as language processing. At a meeting in Chicago in 1968, Kirk chaired the National Advisory Committee on Handicapped Children, which developed a definition of learning disability as "a disorder in one or more of the basic psychological processes" such as "listening, thinking, talking, reading, writing, spelling, or arithmetic." The disorders included "perceptual handicaps, brain injury, minimal brain dysfunction, dyslexia, developmental aphasia, etc.,"[36] a list that excluded the traditionally recognized disabilities of blindness, deafness, mental retardation, and emotional disturbance. The committee hoped its general definition would clarify understanding and lead to better school programs for students with disabilities.

What appeared to be a promising development soon encountered opposition, however. Some critics accused the learning disabilities movement of inventing a disease that had no discernible physical or biochemical characteristics, and others dismissed it as being pushed by professionally self-interested medical, psychological, educational, and pharmaceutical interests. Still others claimed that learning disabilities was a new label for middle-class children with academic difficulties, while lower-class children with the same difficulties continued to be labeled mentally retarded or emotionally disturbed. Some critics argued that greater attention was needed on effective teaching, not new labels to classify and separate them. Within the field of learning disabilities itself, there was criticism of overzealous advocates who failed to understand the history of the problem and too quickly discarded educational techniques still useful with some children.[37] Despite the critics, the learning disabilities idea gained acceptance and became an established view in education.

In the 1950s, the education of people with disabilities seemed securely divided into several options: There were still separate institutions for the blind and deaf, most of which had reasonably strong educational programs. Institutions for those with mental disabilities were facing increasing criticism, particularly those providing only custodial and protective services. A number of states also had other specialized institutions, such as those for children with disabilities such as epilepsy, and for incarcerated youngsters. The variety of institutions and disabilities, the levels of severity, the range of ages, and the diversity of institutions (ranging from schools to hospitals to custodial and even penal institutions) made standardization and systematization virtually impossible.[38]

By the 1960s, the education of people with disabilities was ready for major reform. One development, the idea of **normalization**, came in response to the issue of labeling people with disabilities as deviant. It originated in Europe and was popularized in the United States by people such as Wolf Wolfensberger, who noted how persons can be perceived as deviant if they differ significantly from those considered normal, particularly if the differences are viewed negatively. Various definitions of deviancy have emerged from different historical and cultural contexts, and societies have differed in how they treat people with disabilities, ranging from destroying "deviant" persons to segregating them to attempting to reverse or cure their perceived conditions. The idea of normalization was intended to help people with mental disabilities achieve a life as close to normal as possible. Normalization also addressed how labels and stereotypes influenced behavior, as when pupils considered mentally retarded were placed in separate special education classrooms, they usually did not perform as well as when placed in general education classrooms. In short, normalization meant the physical and social integration of persons with disabilities into the general population, with both physical integration (including accessibility to service facilities) and social integration (inclusion in regular child care and general education classrooms as much as possible).[39]

Mainstreaming and inclusion

There was growing pressure to desegregate special education students and include them in regular schools and classrooms where possible. The 1970s witnessed efforts to abolish traditional labels such as mentally retarded and emotionally disturbed on the grounds that they were simplistic, negative stereotypes. Many critics of old-style special education argued that labels and the separation into special classes or schools actually made education more difficult to achieve.[40]

For Further Reflection: How can schools ensure equal educational opportunity while simultaneously meeting individual needs? Does equality mean sameness?

Legal bases

The U.S. Constitution enunciates a legal view of equality under the **equal protection of the laws** that is as significant in education as in other aspects of life. In the past, persons with disabilities were often denied equal protection of the laws not only by being sequestered in separate institutions or classrooms but sometimes by not receiving any educational services at all. When the mainstreaming movement gained traction in the mid-1970s, it was estimated that children with disabilities comprised between 10 and 13 percent of the total school population.[41] The argument was that equal educational opportunity was needed for this significant minority, and mainstreaming came about through a combination of efforts by advocates and the application of "the equal protection of the laws" clause in the Constitution.

Court decisions

Perhaps the landmark decision on equal protection of the laws was *Brown v. Board of Education* (1954), in which the U.S. Supreme Court declared racially segregated public schools in violation of the Constitution. While race was central in that case, the court's decision articulated a broad principle that would eventually be applied to the education of children with disabilities. Under the U.S. Constitution, the power to establish public schools is an implied state power delegated under the Tenth Amendment, and the equal protection of the laws provided by the Constitution's Fourteenth Amendment is also a responsibility of the states. In the *Brown* ruling, the Supreme Court affirmed state responsibility for both education and equal protection of the laws: If a state provides public schools for its citizens, then it cannot deny them equal access to those schools in the absence of compelling reasons, and race is not a compelling reason.[42]

Over subsequent years the principle of equal access was broadened by the courts to include other circumstances, including physical, mental, emotional, and learning disabilities. For example, a Pennsylvania district court in

Pennsylvania Association for Retarded Children (PARC) v. Commonwealth of Pennsylvania (1972) ruled that Pennsylvania, having undertaken to provide a free public education to all of its children, "including its mentally retarded children," must not deny to "any mentally retarded child access to a free public program of education and training." In short, mental retardation was not a compelling reason. Shortly thereafter, in *Mills v. Board of Education* (1972), a Washington, D.C., district court held that publicly supported education could not be denied to "exceptional children." This interpretation was broadened in *Maryland Association for Retarded Children v. State of Maryland* (1974), when the circuit court declared that the public schools must include "children with handicaps, and particularly mentally retarded children."[43] These rulings illustrate the evolving legal right of equal access to public schools.

Legislation

The inclusion of students with disabilities in public schools and classrooms was not generated solely by judicial decisions, however. Parents of children with disabilities, with the help and support of special education professionals and other interested citizens, played central roles not only in moving the action to the courts but also to state legislatures and the U.S. Congress, which passed laws requiring better and more equitable educational opportunities for children with disabilities.

By far the most important legislative act to show the changing climate of public opinion was the **Education for All Handicapped Children Act (Public Law 94–142)**, passed by Congress and signed into law by President Gerald Ford on November 29, 1975. It defined handicapped children as the "mentally retarded, hard of hearing, deaf, orthopedically impaired, other health impaired, speech impaired, visually handicapped, seriously emotionally disturbed, or children with specific learning disabilities" who needed "special education and related services."[44]

When Congress passed PL 94–142, the intent was to mainstream at least the "mildly educationally handicapped" into general education classrooms. Placement was to be determined by the needs of the pupil, such as academic remediation, social skills development, auditory training, perceptual and motor exercises, speech correction, occupational therapy, physical therapy, and so forth. Each placement must also be accompanied by an **individualized education program (IEP)**, a key feature that has been maintained through all subsequent revisions of the law. The IEP is an educational plan limited to a student's unique requirements. It must also be mutually agreeable to the school administrator, the teacher, the parent or guardian, and the student (where appropriate). The IEP must include an assessment of the student's performance, a statement of annual goals, and a statement of expected duration. It may also involve related services such as transportation and corrective and supportive services like speech pathology and physical and occupational therapy.[45]

Other significant features of the law was the requirement that local school systems receiving federal funds must establish **free appropriate public education** for all applicable children between the ages of 3 and 21, or between 5 and 18 under some state laws and court orders.[46] Still another was the requirement of the **least restrictive environment (LRE)**, intended to avoid the problem of indiscriminate placement. To bolster these features, federal regulations accompanying the law required that "to the maximum extent appropriate, handicapped children in public or private institutions or other care facilities, . . . [shall be] educated with children who are not handicapped." Special classes, separate schools, or other means of separating children with disabilities from regular educational environments were allowable "only when the nature or severity of the handicap is such that education in regular classes with the use of supplementary aids and services cannot be achieved satisfactorily."[47]

Since the passage of P.L. 94–142, the law has been revised several times in both terminology and provisions. In October 1990, Congress broadened the act's provisions and changed its title to **Individuals with Disabilities Education Act (IDEA)** in P.L. 101–476. The term *handicapped* was replaced with "individuals with disabilities" as a more appropriate descriptor. The law has since been amended several times, the latest version being P.L 108–446, the Individuals with Disabilities Education Improvement Act of 2004. It is important to note that in all its different versions some key ingredients were maintained, including "free appropriate public education," "individualized education program," and "least restrictive environment."[48]

By the mid-1990s, approximately 70 percent of all students with disabilities were placed for at least a portion of each day in general education classrooms. There was a decrease in the number of pupils in separate schools, a slight increase in separate classrooms in regular schools, and an increase in the overall number of students identified as learning disabled during the same period. In general, placement of students with disabilities varied across the 50 states: Some states placed the majority of students with learning disabilities in general education classrooms, while others continued to place some in either separate classrooms or schools. Still, the majority of students considered disabled were being included in general classrooms and schools.[49]

Contemporary conditions

Where inclusion was once an issue in debates about the education of students with disabilities, by the twenty-first century the central topic seemed to be not whether inclusion was a good idea but how best to conduct it in general education environments. The 1997 revision of the Individuals with Disabilities Education Act signaled that schools must ensure that all students received a quality education, with special and general educators collaborating on such matters as student instruction, assessment, and evaluation. The scope was extended in the No Child Left Behind (NCLB) legislation in 2001, which required all school districts to set proficiency goals and test all their students on an annual basis, creating new pressures for the schools to improve student outcomes.[50]

By the 2007–2008 school year, the total number of children 3 to 21 years old in federally supported programs for disabilities was 6.6 million. There were programs for specific learning disabilities, speech or language impairments, mental retardation, emotional disturbance, hearing impairments, visual impairments, multiple disabilities, deaf-blindness, autism, traumatic brain injury, developmental delay, and other health impairments (such as heart conditions, tuberculosis, rheumatic fever, nephritis, asthma, sickle cell anemia, hemophilia, epilepsy, lead poisoning, leukemia, and diabetes). Today, the vast majority of students with disabilities are educated in general public education settings. For example, by autumn 2007 approximately 95 percent of 6- to 21-year-old students with disabilities were served in general education public schools, with only 3 percent in separate special schools, 1 percent in general education private schools, and less than 1 percent in separate residential facilities, homes or hospitals, or correctional facilities.[51]

Why inclusion? Some ethical considerations

Inclusion is an educational movement that seeks, among other things, to break down segregation based on disabilities and to promote the idea that all persons should have equal access to education and other personal and social opportunities. In this sense, the ideal of inclusion belongs within the American tradition of equal rights, a tradition that also values education as a common good. At the same time, while we affirm our moral and political equality, everyday experience tells us that people differ in intellectual capacity, creativity, and physical ability, for example, and disagreements often arise over the best ways to meet those differences.

The idea of inclusion can be supported by two historic ethical ideas: **respect for persons** and **equal educational opportunity**. Part of the reason inclusion came about may be due to their role in a slowly developing realization that class, race, ethnicity, gender, disability, and other such conditions are insufficient reasons to deny respect for persons and equal educational opportunity; instead, they support helping people participate in personal and social life.

There are many sources for respect for persons and equal educational opportunity, but for present purposes two philosophical viewpoints will serve to illustrate evolving outlooks about the human condition, one historical and the other contemporary.

Respect for persons

One of the more influential views on respect for persons may be found in the ethical writings of Immanuel Kant, a teacher and philosopher in Germany during the late Enlightenment period. Kant argued that every human is equal in his or her humanity and each is a personality of absolute worth; thus, every child needs to develop its full potential, and education is a necessary ingredient in making that happen. He believed that the highest educational objectives should involve learning to live according to universal principles of right and good, which requires discipline, culture, discretion, and moral training. Such an education should reflect the ethical principle of respect for persons, that is, we should always treat other persons as ends and never as mere means to ends.[52]

Kant lived at a time when serfdom was only a memory but slavery was still alive and even growing in such places as the United States. Kant was a teacher and scholar, not a revolutionary, but the quality of his thought and the influence of his writings helped spread his ideas. Of course, respect for persons long predated Kant and his era, but his particular formulation helped stimulate new levels of thought about the ethical treatment of others, just as it continues to impact ethical thought today.

Conflicts often arise over how people differ, and pertinent ethical concerns Kant helped elevate include "What is right and good?" and "What is fair and just?" In a society with democratic goals, questions about rightness and fairness soon lead to the question, "How do we provide equal respect and equal opportunities for all persons, regardless of their differences?" It could be argued that at every historic juncture when education became available to more people (whether involving class, race, ethnicity, gender, or disabilities), ethical concerns about rightness, fairness, and justice were significant elements.

Equal educational opportunity

An influential present-day view on equal opportunity is provided by American philosopher John Rawls, who critiqued how some people are born advantaged while others are born disadvantaged, circumstances that impact their life chances from birth (or some could become disadvantaged from catastrophic events or disease, for example). He sought to develop a better concept of **distributive justice**, and his general concept in its simplest form is that all social values (such as liberty, opportunity, wealth, the social supports of self-respect) should be distributed equally unless an unequal distribution of one or more such values is to everyone's advantage. Two refinements form what Rawls calls **the difference principle**: any privileges or benefits attached to offices and positions must be open to all under fair equality of opportunity, and any resulting inequalities must provide the greatest benefit to the least advantaged members of society.[53]

At first glance, this may appear extreme, but there is ample evidence that liberty, opportunity, wealth, and position are currently distributed unequally to the most advantaged members of society, which almost guarantees that their advantages will continue or possibly compound. Under such unequal distributions, most disadvantaged persons will probably never realize any equal rights to basic liberties.

Rawls's views encompass any disadvantaged individuals or groups, not just those with disabilities, but his recommendations reflect some existing policies and programs for people with disabilities that are widely evident, such as barrier-free access to public facilities to benefit people with physical disabilities or special services in the schools to benefit students with learning disabilities. Such measures are examples of unequal distributions that benefit disadvantaged people along the lines Rawls recommends. Critics may object that if unequal distribution is made only to benefit the least advantaged, over time it will raise them to most advantaged status, and the formerly advantaged will be reduced to least advantaged status; this would churn society and probably produce social anxieties leading to violent upheavals. Perhaps, but when, for example, the rich get richer and the poor get poorer, violent upheavals also sometimes occur, as witnessed by historic revolutions. Moreover, Rawls argues against precipitous, all-at-once redistributions and recommends carefully planned and executed programs designed to improve the long-term prospects of the least advantaged, an approach that does not require the destitution of any other group. Rawls also recommends redistributions to benefit everyone, such as the preservation of important gains made in society and civilization, the development of better means of production, and better investments in education and learning.[54]

The difference principle and education

According to Rawls, it is difficult for education to redress injustice immediately because it is far better at improving people's long-term prospects, including those of the least favored. Some critics might insist that educational resources should be distributed unequally in favor of those with high ability and intelligence. Rawls thinks this is permissible, but if and only if it serves to improve the long-term prospects of the least favored. Education is often touted for its economic benefits, but for Rawls it is far more important in helping people enjoy and participate in their society and helping them develop a secure sense of self-respect, both of which also involve moral ideals, a sense of right and justice, and respect for others. Self-respect is a primary good because without it, people are plagued by self-doubt and a lack of will to strive. Thus, a society committed to democratic equality of opportunity will cultivate social conditions that promote self-respect among all its members, and it will seek to prevent the undermining of the social supports of self-respect almost at any cost.[55]

Conflict, language, labels, and ethical consequences

History is full of examples of opposed points of view struggling against each other. Philosopher John Dewey made the resolution of such opposing ideas (he called them dualisms) an important part his philosophy. He particularly noted the harm done to education when controversial issues split people into contending camps over the differences between such things as what kinds of knowledge should be taught and what societal interests should be served. He also decried the harmful effects of the division of society into "more or less rigidly marked-off classes and groups," and the resulting "social ruptures of continuity" brought on when contentious dualisms remain unresolved.[56]

The education community experienced some ruptures over contending views about separate special education and inclusion. As inclusion became a public issue, there were criticisms about how societal divisions seemed to have undue influence on special education placements. There was also considerable debate about whether separate special education was right or whether it unfairly segregated students on the basis of disabilities. It is impossible to ascertain how the vagaries and misuse of language contributed to all of this, but a good case can be made that it did contribute to some extent.

In 1974, mainstreaming was described by one of its advocates as providing "high quality special education" to exceptional children in regular grades for as much of the school day as possible. In 2008, a U.S. Department of Education document also described a new instructional approach as "high-quality" instruction in inclusive settings.[57] Descriptors such as "high-quality" are abundant, but sometimes they explain less than meets the eye. What is high quality? Presumably, it is the best, but there can be much disagreement over what is best. Traditionally, what was called special education was for children with mental, emotional, and physical disabilities, but the addition of learning disabilities broadened the meaning considerably. The term *learning disabilities* proved helpful in many ways, but it also helped increase rancorous disagreement and debate as well. In the past, the term *exceptional* was used, and sometimes still is, to refer to persons with disabilities who need special education services, but it has also been used to refer to students of supposedly "superior" abilities too. Other potentially confusing terms are *regular*, *normal*, and *general* when they are applied to curriculum programs apparently designed for persons who are not deemed special, exceptional, or disabled. As can be seen, various descriptive terms and labels historically connected to inclusion help illustrate how words, terms, and labels can contribute to confusing linguistic mazes.

Such is an issue not only in the American context but in other countries as well. For example, a critique of terms used in inclusive schooling in England found that inclusion, inclusive education and inclusive schools had very loose meanings, while terms such as *special educational needs* suggested deficits specific to the learner unless given precise definition.[58]

A ready suggestion might be that things are far better now than back when words such as *idiot* and *feebleminded* were used by professionals as acceptable descriptors. In the ensuing years, valuable strides have been made to devise terminology that respects persons and attempts to limit the harm that thoughtless expressions can inflict. Still, it is also helpful to remember that language itself is a system of communicative symbols that have immense variability. Words can be used to communicate with some precision, but so many words have multiple meanings, with additional shadings added by vocal tone and emphasis. Such features make language both delightful and frustrating, but as French philosopher Jacques Derrida points out, we should become sensitive to the vagaries of language, because language is not only variable but unstable and inexact.[59]

Human actions have ethical consequences, and in efforts to achieve the right and the good it is also necessary to consider the possibility of unintended consequences as well. Careful thought and planning arc needed before acting, and assessments and readjustments must be made as we act, including our use of terminology and language. An important ethical concern is whether students—both those with and those without disabilities—have both respect as individuals and equality of educational opportunity and whether they actually benefit from inclusion.

The sorting or separating of children in schools has a fairly long history, and schools have been called "sorting machines,"[60] although not just because of special education classifications. At the same time, educators need to take stock of student differences and provide appropriate educational experiences that accommodate or develop those differences, which may sometimes necessitate separate individual and small group instruction. Where such separations go wrong is when they become longlasting, because—as experience seems to show—this tends to sharpen perceived differences, encourage innocuous labeling, promote self-fulfilling prophecies, and encourage the pupils caught up in it (and sometimes their teachers) to think of individuals in terms of group labels, all of which can give the "special" (and also "gifted") pupils a limited (or exaggerated) sense of their own capacities, thereby affecting their efforts to develop healthy self-respect and respect for others.[61]

Part of the problem students with disabilities face, particularly those who do not receive the services they need, can stem not only from inadequate resource allocations but also from inadequate assessment and description of individual needs, an issue that better identification, assessment, and placement seek to address.[62] This underlines the ethical duty for educators to show respect for persons, individually and collectively, by delivering competent educational services that extend equal educational opportunities to every student.

For Further Reflection: Recall experiences with labeling in your own education. Did you know someone who was labeled? Were you ever labeled? How, in your experience, do labels affect people? How may labeling be avoided?

WEB Suggested Reading 7.4.

Inclusion and special education services

As applied in education, the term *inclusion* refers to students with disabilities having access to the standard curriculum in general education classrooms; however, the manner in which inclusion is accomplished varies from one state or locale to another. In some instances, pull-in programs are used where students receive all education services in the general education classroom, such as when a speech pathologist comes to the general education classroom to work with an individual student. Another version of inclusion is co-teaching, meaning special education teachers coming to general education classrooms to work with students who have special needs. There are also pull-out programs in which students leave regular classrooms to go to resource rooms, partially self-contained classes, or self-contained special classes to receive special services.[63]

Some leading aspects of inclusive education

Inclusive education is backed by legal and policy requirements that differ from most traditional forms of education. The following provides selected terms with brief descriptions.

- **Evidence-Based Practices:** Use of teaching interventions/strategies shown to be effective by rigorous and systematic research, which may differ from those in general education and which typically focus on individuals as much or more than groups, such as seeking skill mastery rather than in-depth understanding.

- **Family Involvement:** Expectation that each child's parent/guardian will be involved in the child's education to a greater extent than for children without disabilities, including membership on the child's individualized education plan (IEP) team and also partnership in planning and decision making, with rights to challenge IEPs for their child and for services not typically offered to students without disabilities.
- **Free Appropriate Public Education (FAPE)**: Right to appropriate educational services at no cost to the student, parent, or guardian.
- **Frequent Monitoring of Progress:** Frequent, systematic assessments/evaluations of how students with disabilities respond to plans/practices used to develop student skills and comprehensions, and the linkage of instruction with such assessments.
- **Individualized Education Program (IEP)**. For individuals with disabilities ages three to 21, to ensure appropriate educational services designed by an IEP team for each individual student, composed of the student's parent/guardian, general and special education teachers, other individuals with expertise relevant to the student's situation, and where appropriate, the student with the disability.
- **Individualized Family Service Plan (IFSP).** For infants and toddlers with disabilities through age two, to ensure early identification, assessment, and provision of appropriate services according to a plan developed by a multidisciplinary team (with parental participation and informed consent for implementation) to support the child's transition to preschool or other educational services.
- **Least Restrictive Environment (LRE)**: Right to be educated with nondisabled peers to the maximum extent possible, with separation from general education classrooms only when the kind or severity of a disability requires it (including services general education classrooms cannot provide, such as skills and comprehensions best learned in community settings and on-the-job sites).
- **Related Services:** Additional services to help students with disabilities in general education schools, such as: paraprofessionals for individualized assistance; multidisciplinary teams for family therapy, occupational therapy, and physical therapy; and other professional services (school nurses, social workers).
- **Systematic Identification Procedures:** To improve identification of individuals needing special education services, determination of appropriate services, and avoidance of overidentifications due to ethnic, cultural, and linguistic factors, or underidentifications associated with gifts and talents. Designed to enhance expertise of general educators to ensure a student's general education difficulties not caused by regular interventions/strategies that fail to produce desired performance and behavioral outcomes.

Sources: Diane P. Bryant et al., *Teaching Students with Special Needs in Inclusive Classrooms* (Boston: Pearson, 2008), 23–31, 183; and U.S. Department of Education, "Building the Legacy: IDEA 2004," at http://idea.ed.gov/explore/view/p (accessed on August 24, 2010).

WEB: Suggested Reading 7.5.

Curriculum, instruction, and universal design for learning

Various curricular and instructional approaches have been developed to achieve a more inclusive education. One of them is **assistive technology**, which seeks to enable students to achieve in ways that might otherwise be difficult or impossible by increasing learning through technology that helps reduce obstacles encountered by individuals with disabilities in instructional settings. This includes traditional devices such as walkers and wheelchairs, but it also encompasses new technologies such as computer hardware, software, and related technological developments.[64]

Another is **response to instruction (RTI)**, sometimes called response to intervention, which requires high-quality research-validated instructional interventions in core subjects (such as reading) in general education classrooms. RTI starts with careful screening to identify those with learning disabilities who need special interventions. Interventions must be research backed and provided for a specific period of time, and as student progress is made the intervention must intensify to improve the student's achievement. In addition, progress monitoring must occur along the way to evaluate student advancement and response to instruction in order to determine next steps.[65]

Idea of universal design

The universal design concept probably originated in architectural and engineering efforts to design structures, fixtures, and accommodations that benefit the widest possible range of users and usages. Common examples include buildings with electronic door openers, accessible restroom facilities, and ramps and elevators. In regard to the use of universal design in higher education, federal legislation defines it as "a scientifically valid framework" to guide educational practice in ways that not only provide flexibility in how information is presented, how students acquire knowledge and skills, and how students are engaged in the process but also reduce instructional barriers, provide appropriate accommodations, and support high achievement expectations for all students, including those with disabilities and those with limited English proficiency. It also must use curricula specifically designed to meet the needs of as many users as possible.[66]

Universal design for learning

Probably the most general educational development that encompasses the efforts described in the preceding section is **universal design for learning (UDL)**. It is based on curriculum and instruction that employ multiple ways of presenting subject matter in formats that recognize sensory and cognitive differences among learners. For example, students with sight impairments may be provided with assistive technology to enhance their audio and tactile capacities through the use of computer hardware and software capable of transmitting screen text to a board that raises and lowers pins to produce text in braille. Similarly, students with certain hand impairments might use voice-activated switches and software instead of a keyboard and mouse to access computers. With the UDL approach, curriculum content can be provided in a variety of formats so that students are able to work individually or in small groups and configurations that include both students with disabilities and those without.[67]

In effect, UDL attempts to address the longstanding problem of a traditional, one-size-fits-all curriculum that is unable to accommodate many individual learning styles. UDL takes its descriptor "universal" from its intention to benefit all students and to harm no one, but the term *universal* should not be taken to mean a final and complete educational design that applies to everyone perfectly. There is no such universal curriculum or instructional strategy, and the variety of individual differences (learning styles, backgrounds, interests, or abilities) means that diversity rather than homogeneity is typical of both individuals and groups.[68] However, individual differences do not make separate species, and members of the human race share far more in common than not. Moreover, the moral/ethical and political concepts of human equality and equal educational opportunity are central values in any democratic society.

Who needs to learn? Universal design for learning and assistive technologies

The goal of UDL is to reach all learners, but some groups are especially underserved. Lack of access to technology often correlates not only with disabilities but also socioeconomic status, ethnicity, language, educational level, and age. Digital access is important today because so much information and so many services are now readily available through digital resources. Some groups particularly need attention:

- Low-Income and Minority Learners. They often have less access to computers, the internet, and to family and immediate community resources that provide technology-based learning at home. An example includes extending the hours of use of networked computers in schools, libraries, and community centers.
- English Language Learners. English predominates as the language of instruction in most schools and on most websites. The acquisition of essential knowledge and skills needed today is hampered when English is not one's first language. Properly designed translation technology helps reduce language barriers and offers help with English and unfamiliar vocabulary or syntax through translation and other assistive technologies.

- Learners with Disabilities. Many learners with physical and sensory disabilities need assistive technologies to achieve along with their peers. Examples include electronic mobility switches and alternative keyboards for students with physical disabilities; computer screen enlargers, text-to-speech devices, and screen readers for individuals with visual disabilities; electronic sign-language dictionaries and signing avatars for learners with hearing disabilities; and calculators and spellcheckers for individuals with learning disabilities. Many UDL digital resources are possible through assistive technologies.
- Pre-K Learners. Learning gaps in literacy begin in early childhood and become increasingly difficult to surmount over time. Early intervention is crucial for underserved children to keep pace with their peers, especially to augment the linguistic, visual, and symbolic worlds they experience. One example is technology-based resources that target school readiness skills.
- Adult Workforce. Many working people are underproductive and face limited job opportunities because of insufficient skill development. They may also lack the time or opportunity for the sustained learning that skill development requires. Technological avenues such as online courses expand worker opportunities for when and where they may learn. Not only do individual workers benefit from increased worker productivity but companies and agencies do as well.
- Seniors. Many older adults develop visual, hearing, motor, and cognitive disabilities as they age, just as they also have special strengths of accumulated wisdom and experience. Improving their strengths through lifelong learning opportunities requires careful design and the use of assistive technologies so that the disabilities of aging do not become obstacles to continued learning, independence, and social life.

Source: USDOE, "Who Needs to Learn?" at http://www.ed.gov/technology/netp-2010/who-needs-to-learn (accessed on September 13, 2010).

Suggested Activity: Interview an experienced classroom teacher about the inclusion of students with disabilities in the general education classroom. Seek insight on the strategies used, enablers and barriers encountered in the process, and successes and failures.

Suggested Activity: Conduct an interview with parents of students with or without disabilities. Analyze their perceptions of inclusion and its effect on their child. What do your results show?

Teacher roles and responsibilities

School personnel are key to the success of inclusion. Obviously, inclusive education has its best effects if certain essential conditions are met: Educators must be well prepared and committed to inclusion; they must be provided with adequate materials, support services, and equipment; appropriate physical accommodations must be made; and sufficient funding and active family involvement must also be present. In regard to the latter, families of students with disabilities not only need to be involved in their children's schooling, they also may need support themselves. To improve the chances of successful inclusion, then, educators need to be cooperative, empathetic, and respectful of parents while providing the leadership necessary to meet the needs of all their students.[69]

It should be noted, however, that general education teachers have not always received the training, assistance, or the information needed to implement inclusion effectively. Past research indicates that most teachers supported the idea of inclusion, but a sizable portion felt most comfortable working with students with mild rather than severe disabilities. Many teachers believed they did not have the necessary background training or essential resources; the more severe the disability, the less confident they felt. Research also indicates that as teachers gained experience with students with disabilities, they usually moved beyond their initial concerns and came to appreciate how special services aided their work, not only with students with disabilities but also with students who needed but did not qualify for special services. Similarly, parents—whether of children with or without disabilities—became more accepting of inclusion once they became familiar with how it worked and what effects it had.[70]

Comprehensive staff development programs, flexible time for school personnel to meet and plan together, and supplemental support are important. Well-prepared teachers report positive outcomes for students, an enhanced sense of professional competence, and a new pattern of collegial cooperation. Teamwork is seen as the key strategy if inclusive education is to work for all children, regardless of disability. A first step toward successful teamwork is the building of trust, because collaborative efforts among school personnel are essential for successful inclusion programs in schools.[71]

The general education teacher's role has changed in today's inclusive classrooms. Prior to inclusion, regular classroom teachers usually identified the students they thought had special needs and referred them for separate special education provisions. In inclusive classrooms, however, the general education teacher is usually expected to provide educational services for almost all students, aided by special education teachers and support specialists who may co-teach, collaborate, and/or provide consultative support. As a result of inclusion, the general education teacher has had to learn new skills, such as serving on IEP committees, interacting with parents of children with special needs, providing greater individualization of instruction, applying a greater variety of instructional techniques, and using more diverse applications of new technology.[72]

Inclusion and its impact on teacher education

Debate about inclusion is not confined to the United States, because it has shaped educational policies and practices internationally. Consequently, a growing body of research is investigating the changes occurring in different countries' teacher preparation programs, often engaging in international comparisons.[73]

Pressures for change

In the United States, the inclusion movement has clearly impacted the preparation of teachers, but much more needs to be done. Pressures for change are contained in IDEA and NCLB, but there are also those who have been pushing change for years. A persistent teacher education challenge has been the need for interdisciplinary and interdepartmental cooperation, especially between special and general education. Collaboration is an essential ingredient in schools that successfully implement inclusion. Many teacher education reformers maintain that such collaboration should be first rooted in the preparatory programs in the colleges and universities.[74]

Research on teacher education in higher education indicates that to improve teacher candidates' knowledge about students with disabilities and inclusive education, preparation programs must include coursework and related learning activities on collaboration and cooperative participation that cuts across education departments and programs, particularly such developments as team-teaching experiences that cross majors, co-teaching experiences within majors that combine contributions from both general and special education, and field experiences for all candidates that emphasize cross-major and -discipline collaborations. It would also be beneficial if teacher education faculty outside special education increased their knowledge and experience concerning special education services and collaboration. A general need is for more resources, funding, and time allocations for teacher education faculty to provide their students with better preparation for inclusive classrooms and schools.[75]

Some teacher education reformers want to go beyond programmatic changes. One view is that both inclusion and curriculum detracking help call into question all policies and practices that sort, rank, and label learners. Divisive they may be, but they continue to be entrenched in many ways. To help counteract harmful practices, teacher preparation programs need to help candidates question the assumptions behind differentiations of learners that undermine respect for persons and equal educational opportunities for all.[76]

Some possible directions

Promising approaches include the following: providing future teachers with the tools for observing learners in open-minded ways, engaging them in critical inquiry into traditional and current standards, and ensuring that they have experiences critiquing and developing curricular and pedagogical strategies that promote equality of educational opportunity by meeting diverse student needs.[77]

The first component, tools for understanding learners, is based on the idea that teachers need to assess students in ways that emphasize student potential as starting points for teaching and learning strategies directed toward growth in learning. The goal is to enable future teachers to recognize the potentials and complexities of students, not to prejudge and categorize them by such things as test scores interpreted on the basis of some "normalized" statistical curve. Instead, teacher candidates need to become professionals who approach their work by recognizing student strengths to learn and then developing teaching and learning practices that build on those strengths to help students further expand their potentials. Such an orientation is part of a "capacity-oriented" framework for effective inclusion practices.[78]

The second orientation is critical inquiry into the standards against which students are measured. Teachers today face a dilemma: Under NCLB, they must respond to diverse learning styles, but they must also help all students meet the standards. To address this quandary, teacher candidates must learn not simply to align their teaching with prescribed standards but to also carefully analyze the standards for the kinds of knowledge, learning styles, and ways of knowing that are most valued within the standards. Such inquiry helps teacher candidates reflect thoughtfully on how the standards can be used to expand their curricular, pedagogical, and assessment practices and help them create more effective learning environments for their students.[79]

Finally, teacher candidates need to understand the relationship between schooling and inequality, just as they also need to know how to develop relationships with families and communities to better comprehend the cultural, competency, and knowledge expectations of the local communities surrounding the schools in which they teach. In other words, rather than rely on common stereotypes about communities, prospective teachers need to develop cultural understandings that help them develop relevant instructional plans for their students. Advocates maintain that such approaches are necessary if teacher education is to prepare the kinds of teachers needed by schools in the present and foreseeable future.[80]

Although there have been efforts to prepare both general and special educators to meet the needs of diverse learners, some critics might argue that the inclusion movement has not impacted teacher education strongly enough. There is still insufficient attention to cross-program and -departmental collaboration, and much remains to be done concerning entrenched attitudes and cultural assumptions regarding the inclusion of diverse learners. Maybe the difficulties are simply due to stubborn biases and fear of change, but perhaps it is more likely that fundamental changes to long-established attitudes and cultural assumptions simply take patience and persistence.

Student outcomes

Effective inclusive schools are characterized by an emphasis on the learning of all students, and an essential benchmark of success is when students with disabilities in general classrooms progress as much or more than they would in separate settings. Inclusive education is not problem free, but it is possible for important academic, behavioral, and social benefits to be gained by all students (and their teachers) if effective teaching and learning strategies are used. Not only is it possible for students with disabilities to learn new skills and experience new interactions and friendships but also for general education students who may experience positive outcomes in classrooms where students with disabilities are their classmates.[81]

Positive student outcomes are not easy to achieve. For example, consider ten-year-old fourth grader Don, who was identified as "profoundly learning disabled." He lacked the fine motor skills necessary for writing and experienced difficulty reading and understanding text. In addition, he was frequently absent due to severe bouts of asthma. While Don was usually working with a learning disabilities specialist outside the general science classroom, his teachers made arrangements to include him in a special program of study. Soon, positive learning outcomes could be observed. When the class examined what objects sink or float, he was actively engaged in problem solving, constructed a diver system more quickly than some of his peers, and triumphantly shared his learning. In addition, he was able to write about, revise and elaborate on his thinking with minimal adult assistance. Still, challenges became obvious. One was that Don struggled socially, especially in a small group activity where his contributions were either ignored or rebuffed. While such occurrences might have gone undetected by the general education teacher busy with 28 students, if a specialist shadowing Don had been present, such events might have been noticed, and assistance immediately given. In addition, this specialist could have assisted the general education teacher in modeling group interactions that allow all students to equally participate, such as taking turns.[82] Don's case illustrates what has been emphasized before: The inclusion of students with disabilities in general education settings has much to offer and can be highly successful, although inclusion is not without its challenges. Certain conditions must be met to make inclusion work for all concerned, both academically and socially, and close collaboration among educators is one essential prerequisite if the goal is to achieve optimal learning outcomes for students like Don and his classmates.

Suggested Activity: Interview a student or former student (with or without disabilities) about experiences of inclusion in his or her own education.

International comparison: Denmark

The education of children with disabilities has gained recognition around the world, but despite rhetorical commitments in many countries children with special needs continue to be underserved or even excluded from schooling. The extent and implementation of educational programs for students with disabilities varies greatly among and within nations. Internationally, the number of special schools that provide segregated education for children with disabilities has decreased significantly, indicating a greater level of inclusion. For example, in Australia, Denmark, Greece, Norway, and Spain less than 1 percent of children are educated in special schools; however, in developing countries, most of which were never able to establish special schools or classrooms for persons with disabilities, traditional indigenous modes of education continue to operate.[83]

In Europe, the great diversity of national educational systems makes generalizations difficult. In Denmark, only 0.5 percent of students are educated outside a general education environment, whereas in the Netherlands, 95 percent of children with special needs attend special schools. Denmark has a high level of physical integration of special needs students, but there is an ongoing debate about how to go beyond integration to ensure that the education of special needs students is meaningful.[84]

Denmark is a relatively small country located in northern Europe between the North Sea and the Baltic Sea and bordering Germany to the south. Denmark's landmass consists of the Jutland Peninsula and 406 islands, 78 of which are inhabited. It also has two overseas island possessions that are internally self-governing but dependent on the Kingdom of Denmark for foreign affairs: the Faroe Islands, lying roughly halfway between Norway and Iceland in the Norwegian Sea; and Greenland, the world's largest island, lying off the coast of North America between the Arctic Ocean and the North Atlantic Ocean. According to a July 2010 estimate, Denmark had slightly more than 5.5 million inhabitants. Its capital is Copenhagen, and it is both a constitutional monarchy and a modern democracy, with a unicameral parliamentary form of government.[85]

Danish education

Most pupils with disabilities are included in the general education schools of Denmark. The move toward integration started in the 1940s and 1950s with discussions about ending the differentiation of students. The legislation that moved Danish education most directly toward inclusive education was probably the 1993 revision of the Folkeskole Act, which focused on changing the general education environment to ensure that all children experienced an appropriate educational development. One issue was to eliminate the phenomenon of "bubble kids," or students with disabilities being physically included in the schools but separated from general education students. A related issue was how general and special educators could integrate practice and maintain a sense of community while also recognizing student diversity. In Denmark, a special education teacher is trained as both a generalist and a specialist, and the challenge is to develop a truly integrated school rather than a "school within a school."[86]

Among the countries in the European Union (EU) there has been a trend toward greater inclusion of pupils with special educational needs in "mainstream" schools. There has also been an increase in teacher supports (in the form of supplementary staff, in-service training, and additional materials and equipment). Three general patterns may be seen. First, some countries (Spain, Italy, Portugal, Sweden, Iceland, and Norway) use a one-track approach, that is, they have policies and practices that include almost all pupils within regular or mainstream schools, supported by numerous special education services. Second, some countries (Denmark, France, Luxembourg, Austria, Finland, and the United Kingdom) use a multitrack approach, that is, they use a variety of inclusive approaches and provide a variety of services to help pupils move between mainstream and special needs education. Third, there are countries (Switzerland, Germany, the Netherlands, and Belgium) that use a two-track approach, that is, special education is well developed but is mostly delivered in special schools or special classes.

All EU countries have inclusive education, but the level of its development varies among them. For example, Sweden, Denmark, Italy, and Norway were leaders in developing inclusive legislation and policies in earlier years, while most of the other countries undertook such changes at later times.[87]

Children with special needs

In Denmark, children with special needs are taught in mainstream schools to the greatest extent possible, and all children are entitled to instruction adapted to their particular needs and capacities. Parents have the right to enroll their children in a *Folkeskole* (a term applied to the entire Danish public school system and to each individual public school) in the municipality or district where they reside or in any other municipality of their choice. Children may be enrolled in either a regular Folkeskole or in one with specific programs designed for pupils with special needs, the only limitation being that the chosen school must have the relevant support and programming needed by the individual child. Generally, most pupils with special needs attend regular schools and receive special education in one or more subjects to supplement instruction in regular classes. Some pupils may attend either mainstream classes or special classes, and some may be taught in both types of classes. Special classes are provided for pupils with, for example, intellectual disabilities, dyslexia, visual impairment, hearing impairment, and physical impairment.[88]

Denmark requires ten years of compulsory education, which may be satisfied by completing the Folkeskole. Other options include private school attendance and also home schooling as long as national standards are met. Most Danish children attend the Folkeskole, which is divided into one year of preschool, six years of primary, two years of lower secondary education, and an optional tenth year of public school for those wishing to improve their scholastic performance or clarify their vocational choice in order to attend upper secondary education. Upper secondary options include general education to qualify for higher education or vocational-technical education to qualify for the job market.[89]

Denmark is a signatory of the Salamanca Statement, a declaration made on June 10, 1994, by delgates from 92 governments and 25 international organizations at the World Conference on Special Needs Education held in Salamanca, Spain. The statement called on governments and the international community to recognize the necessity for inclusive education and to facilitate within their regular educational provisions appropriate educational opportunities for "children, youth and adults with special educational needs."[90]

For the most part, Danish students with special needs attend mainstream schools and classes, receiving special education provisions as supplements to general instruction. Generally, these provisions include differential teaching, counseling, technical aid, and personal assistance. However, some students might not benefit from every aspect of the mainstream experience and might need special education instruction in one or more subjects, which may be gained in special classes in a mainstream school or even in a special school. Special classes are sometimes organized specifically for students with intellectual disabilities, dyslexia, hearing problems, and similar conditions.[91]

National education standards

The Folkeskole Act applies to all students in regard to such matters as aims, curriculum, evaluations, tests, and leaving exams; consequently, students with special needs face the same expectations as other students. Seven compulsory final examinations are required of all students before leaving the ninth grade, but under certain special circumstances a principal may exempt students with severe disabilities or students who lack sufficient command of the Danish language.[92]

Denmark requires an annual written student plan for each student at all levels of the Folkeskole stage, which must also be shared with parents or guardians. Each plan must include information about evaluations of the student's progress in every subject, as well as decisions about remediations or advancements based on the evaluation results. The requirement is national, but the exact format of a plan and the manner of reporting the plans to parents are the responsibility of each local municipal board of education.[93]

Suggested Activity: Interview an international student on your campus about inclusion in his or her home country. Compare and contrast the responses with what you know about inclusion in the United States. Consider that education of persons with disabilities may be handled differently from country to country, in particular the significant differences between the Netherlands and Denmark. Can you think of justifications for both practices in the name of fairness and equal educational opportunity?

Summary and conclusions

The education of children with disabilities shows a long process of trial and error, proceeding from the more obvious disabilities (such as deafness or blindness), to less obvious ones (such as learning disabilities). Among the most striking historical changes was the move from viewing people with disabilities as uneducable, then to providing education in separate institutions and classrooms designed for specific disabilities, and finally to the inclusion of nonmainstream students on a large scale in ordinary educational institutions and processes among people not considered disabled. Today, the education of people with disabilities is still far from perfect, but progress has been made, and it seems unlikely that society will revert back to prior levels of neglect.

Despite such progress, how we educate people with disabilities is still hampered by some seemingly intractable problems. One of them is a continuing tendency to categorize and classify people, which can define individuals according to disability rather than their other human qualities. At the same time, there are practical needs to be descriptive in order to provide services where needed. For good care and service, it is necessary to research, assess, and devise appropriate educational plans for specific needs and differences.

A person's right to an education, regardless of disability, has been guaranteed and protected by legislation and judicial decision. Parents of children with disabilities, interested citizens, educators and other human service professionals, community leaders and lawmakers, and a host of other people all played significant roles in making this possible at both the state and national levels. The law requires that students with disabilities must have equal access to the schools, with due regard for individual needs and appropriate educational provisions. Equal educational opportunity is a historic ideal, but the inclusion of people with disabilities is a relatively recent addition to the debate, due in part to the realization that persons with disabilities could be educated far beyond most people's previous expectations but also to greater awareness of the ethical demands of fairness and democratic equity.

By the twenty-first century, inclusive education was widely recognized in the United States, with separate education reduced but not completely gone. Public schools were expected to take in all students and were held accountable to meet the demands of federal and state education laws in regard to inclusive education. While inclusive education seemed to be settled policy, there were still issues concerning funding and the better preparation of teachers as well as the degree and exact form inclusive education should take.

Inclusion has international ramifications, but there is great variation among countries. The number of separate special schools has decreased, but many poor countries have never been able to provide much more than family care and local community charity for individuals with special needs. Inclusion has taken firm root in Europe, but implementation varies from country to country. In Denmark, for instance, most students with disabilities attend general education schools and classrooms.

Vocabulary

assistive technology
deaf community
developmentally delayed
difference principle
disabilities as treatable conditions
distributive justice
Education for All Handicapped Children Act (Public Law 94–142)
equal educational opportunity
equal protection of the laws
eugenics
free appropriate public education
inclusion
individualized education program (IEP)
Individuals with Disabilities Education Act (IDEA)
intelligence scale
labels
learning difficulties
learning disabilities
least restrictive environment (LRE)
mainstreaming
medical model
medicalized theory of deviance
mental measurement
normalization
oralist approach
physiological method
psychological testing
respect for persons
response to instruction (RTI)
sign language
universal design for learning (UDL)

Notes

1 Herbert C. Covey, *Social Perceptions of People with Disabilities in History* (Springfield, IL: Charles C. Thomas, 1998), 6–8.

2 Alexis de Tocqueville, *Democracy in America*, Richard D. Heffner, ed. (New York: Mentor Books, New American Library, 1956), 198.

3 Cathryn Carroll, "A Father, a Son, and a University: Thomas Hopkins Gallaudet," at http://clerccenter.gallaudet.edu/InfoToGo/751.html (accessed on August 18, 2010).

4 Philip L. Safford and Elizabeth J. Safford, *A History of Childhood and Disability* (New York: Teachers College Press, 1996), 3, 41–42.

5 Covey, 219–223; Safford and Safford, 40–41.

6 Margaret A. Winzer, *The History of Special Education: From Isolation to Integration* (Washington, DC: Gallaudet Press, 1993), 21–22, and 99; and Safford and Safford, 92–96.

7 Lubna Takruri, "Gallaudet Exposes Debate over Deafness," The Associated Press, October 30, 2006, at http://www.washingtonpost.com/wp-dyn/content/article/2006/10/30/AR2006103000087.html; Susan Kinzie, "New Gallaudet President Met with Protest," *The Washington Post*, May 2, 2006, A01, at http://www.washingtonpost.com/wp-dyn/content/article/2006/05/01/AR2006050100770.html; Susan Kinzie et al., "Gallaudet Board Ousts Fernandes," *The Washington Post*, October 30, 2006, A-1, at http://www.washingtonpost.com/wp-dyn/content/article/2006/10/29/AR2006102900533.html?nav=emailpage; and Sue Ann Pressly and Susan Kinzie, "Trustees Seek Student and Faculty Input Before Leadership Search," *The Washington Post*, November 12, 2006, C-06, at http://www.washingtonpost.com/wp-dyn/content/article/2006/11/11/AR2006111100781.html?nav=emailpage (all accessed on August 18, 2010).

8 Safford and Safford, 96–99.

9 Michael E. Gorman, "Alexander Graham Bell's Path to the Telephone," at http://www3.iath.virginia.edu/albell/homepage.html (accessed on August 18, 2010).

10 Safford and Safford, 100–101; Winzer, 53–55, 154–155, and 195–196.

11 Winzer, 126–129. See also, "About CLARKE: History," at http://www.clarkeschools.org/about/welcome (accessed on August 18, 2010).

12 Winzer, 104, 109.

13 Harold Schwartz, *Samuel Gridley Howe: Social Reformer* (Cambridge: Harvard University Press, 1956), 49–58. See also "History," Perkins School for the Blind, at http://www.perkins.org/about-us/history (accessed on August 18, 2010).

14 Schwartz, 49–58.

15 Ibid., 59–61.

16 Samuel G. Howe et al., *On the Causes of Idiocy; Being the Supplement to a Report by Dr. S. G. Howe and the Other Commissioners Appointed by the Governor of Massachusetts to Inquire into the Condition of the Idiots of the Commonwealth, February 26, 1848* (reprint; New York: Arno Press, 1972), xv–xvi ff.; Schwartz, 140–142.

17 Schwartz, 142–144; Winzer, 115.

18 The authors acknowledge indebtedness to Joy L. Johnson, "Edouard Seguin's Contributions in Education for Children with Mental Retardation," unpublished paper, Virginia Commonwealth University, 1998. For contemporaneous views of Séguin, see "In Memory of Edouard Seguin, M.D." (1880), at http://www.disabilitymuseum.org/lib/docs/1924.htm (accessed on August 18, 2010).

19 Jean-Marc Gaspard Itard, *The Wild Boy of Aveyron*, George and Muriel Humphrey, trans. (New York: Appleton-Century-Croft, 1962).

20 Mabel E. Talbot, *Édouard Seguin: A Study of an Educational Approach to the Treatment of Mentally Defective Children* (New York: Teachers College Press, 1964), 1–12.

21 As quoted in Schwartz, 146.

22 As quoted in Talbot, 69. Seguin developed a tripartite classification system of "idiot" (arrested development), "retarded" (delayed development), and "imbecile" (defects in social development).

23 Talbot, 74–76, 78–80.

24 Winzer, 93–96.

25 Barry M. Franklin, *From Backwardness to "At-Risk": Childhood Learning Difficulties and the Contradictions of School Reform* (Albany: State University of New York Press, 1994), xii–xiii.

26 Franklin, 6, 11–12.

27 JoAnne Brown, *The Definition of a Profession: The Authority of Metaphor in the History of Intelligence Testing, 1890–1930* (Princeton: Princeton University Press, 1992), 35–40.

28 Brown, 46–48.

29 Ibid., 80–83, 92–94. The authors also wish to acknowledge background material on eugenics from Stephen R. Hall, *Oscar McCulloch and Indiana Eugenics*, Thesis (PhD), Virginia Commonwealth University, 1993. See also Richard Hofstadter, *Social Darwinism in American Thought* (1944 reprint, Boston: Beacon Press, 1992); and Herbert Spencer, "Progress: Its Law and Cause," at *Modern History Sourcebook*: "Herbert Spencer: Social Darwinism (1857)," at http://www.fordham.edu/halsall/mod/spencer-darwin.html (accessed on August 18, 2010).

30 Leila Zenderland, *Measuring Minds: Henry Herbert Goddard and the Origins of American Intelligence Testing* (New York: Cambridge University Press, 1998), 17–18, 20–23, 25–43. See also "Henry Herbert Goddard," (2003), at http://www.indiana.edu/~intell/goddard.shtml; and "Goddard and Eugenics," at http://www.vineland.org/history/trainingschool/history/eugenics.htm (both accessed on August 18, 2010).

31 Zenderland, 71–104.

32 Henry Herbert Goddard, *Feeble-Mindedness: Its Causes and Consequences* (reprint, New York: Arno Press, 1973 [1926]), 566; *The Kallikak Family: A Study in the Heredity of Feeble-Mindedness* (New York: Arno Press, 1912), 105–107; and Zenderland, 353.

33 Steven Selden, *Inheriting Shame: The Story of Eugenics and Racism in America* (New York: Teachers College Press, 1999), 1–21; and Beth A. Ferri and David J. Connor, *Reading Resistance: Discourses of Exclusion in Desegregation & Inclusion Debates* (New York: Peter Wang, 2006), 26–39.

34 Schwartz, 271–274.

35 Scott B. Sigmon, *Radical Analysis of Special Education: Focus on Historical Development and Learning Disabilities* (New York: Falmer Press, 1987), 12.

36 As quoted in Franklin, 68. See also J. Lee Wiederholt, "Historical Perspectives on the Education of the Learning Disabled," in *The Second Review of Special Education*, Lester Mann and David A. Sabatino, eds (Philadelphia: JSE Press, 1974), 142–143.

37 See, for example, Peter Schrag and Diane Divoky, *The Myth of the Hyperactive Child: And Other Means of Child Control* (NY: Pantheon, 1975), 30–31; Christine E. Sleeter, "Learning Disabilities: The Social Construction of a Special Education Group," *Critical Voices on Special Education: Problems and Progress Concerning the Mildly Handicapped*, Scott B. Sigmon, ed. (Albany: State University of New York Press, 1990), 33; and William M. Cruickshank, *Disputable Decisions in Special Education* (Ann Arbor: The University of Michigan Press, 1986), 6.

38 Robert L. Osgood, The History of Inclusion in the United States (Washington: Gallaudet University Press, 2005), 34–61.

39 Wolf Wolfensberger, *Normalization: The Principle of Normalization in Human Services* (Toronto: National Institute of Mental Retardation, 1972), 13, 25, 27, and 31. See also Osgood, 94–95.

40 Sigmon, 28, 30.

41 Alan Abeson, "Legal Forces and Pressures," in *Mainstreaming and the Minority Child*, Reginald L. Jones ed. (Minneapolis: Leadership Training Institute/ Special Education, 1976), 15.

42 Brown v. Board of Education of Topeka (1954), 347U.S. 383, at http://supct.law.cornell.edu/supct/search/display.html?terms=Brown%20v.%20Board%20of%20Education&url=/supct/html/historics/USSC_CR_0347_0483_ZO.html (accessed on August 18, 2010).

43 Abeson, 18. For the full decisions, see also *Brown v. Board of Education*, 1954, 347 U.S. 483; *Pennsylvania Association for Retarded Children v. Commonwealth of Pennsylvania*, 343 F. Supp. 279; *Mills v. Board of Education of the District of Columbia*, 348, F. Supp. 866 (Dist. D. C. 1972); *Maryland Association for Retarded Children v. State of Maryland*, Equity No. 100-182-77676 (Circuit Court, Baltimore, Maryland, 1974).

44 U.S. Congress, Public Law 94–142, "Education for All Handicapped Children," 29 November 1975 (sec. 4).

45 Ibid., 42, Section 4(a), 16–17.

46 Ibid., Section 3(c).

47 "Education of All Handicapped Children, Part II," *Federal Register*, 42, no. 163 (Tuesday, August 23, 1977):42497–. Italics added.

48 "Education of the Handicapped Act Amendments of 1990," in *United States Statutes at Large, 1990*, vol. 104, part 2 (Washington, DC: U.S. Government Printing Office, 1991), 1103–1151. For the "Individuals with Disabilities Education Act Amendments of 1991," see *United States Statutes at Large, 1991*, vol. 105 (Washington, DC: U.S. Government Printing Office, 1992), 587–608. For the latest version of the law as of this writing, see P.L 108–446, Individuals with Disabilities Education Improvement Act of 2004, at http://frwebgate.access.gpo.gov/cgi-bin/getdoc.cgi?dbname=108_cong_public_laws&docid=f:publ446.108 (accessed on July 7, 2010).

49 Tom E. C. Smith et al., *Teaching Students with Special Needs in Inclusive Settings*, 2nd edn (Boston: Allyn & Bacon, 1998), 31.

50 Robert A. Gable and Jo M. Hendrickson, "Teaching all the students: A mandate for educators," in *Successful Inclusive Teaching: Proven Ways to Detect and Correct Special Needs*, 4th edn, Joyce S. Choate, ed. (Boston: Pearson, 2004), 2–4.

51 National Center for Education Statistics (NCES), *Digest of Education Statistics, 2009*, at http://nces.ed.gov/fastfacts/display.asp?id=64 (accessed on August 8, 2010).

52 Immanuel Kant, *Education*, Annette Churton, trans. (Ann Arbor: University of Michigan Press, 1960).

53 John Rawls, *A Theory of Justice*, rev. edn (Cambridge: Belknap Press of Harvard University Press, 1999), 53–54; and *Political Liberalism* (New York: Columbia University Press, 1993), 291.

54 *Political Liberalism*, 65–70, 252 specifically and chapters 4, 5, and 6 generally.

55 Ibid., 87, 92, 386–391, 452.

56 John Dewey, *Democracy and Education: An Introduction to the Philosophy of Education* (New York: The Macmillan Company, 1916), 340, 377.

57 For the 1974 mainstreaming reference, see J.W. Birch, *Mainstreaming: Educable Mentally Retarded Children in Regular Classes* (Reston, Virginia: The Council for Exceptional Children, 1974), 2; for the 2008 reference to RTI, see United States Department of Education (USDOE), Office of Special Education and Rehabilitation Services, "Coordinated Early Intervening Services (CEIS) Guidance," 6, at http://www2.ed.gov/policy/speced/guid/idea/ceis-guidance.pdf (accessed on September 23, 2010).

58 Alan Dyson and Alan Millward, *Schools and Special Needs: Issues of Innovation and Inclusion* (London: Paul Chapman Publishing, Ltd., 2000), viii.

59 Howard Ozmon and Samuel M. Craver, *Philosophical Foundations of Education*, 7th edn (Columbus, OH: Merrill Prentice Hall, 2003), 342–345.

60 David L. Kirp, "The Great Sorting Machine," *Phi Delta Kappan*, 8, No. 5: 522–524 (April, 1974). See also Joel Spring, *The Sorting Machine Revisited: National Educational Policy Since 1945*, updated edn (New York: Longman, 1989).

61 Robert L. Osgood, *The History of Inclusion in the United States* (Washington, DC: Gallaudet University Press, 2005), 2–12.

62 Cathleen G. Spinelli, *Classroom Assessment for Students with Special Needs in Inclusive Settings* (Upper Saddle River, NJ: Pearson/Merrill/Prentice Hall, 2006).

63 Diane P. Bryant et al., *Teaching Students with Special Needs in Inclusive Classrooms* (Boston: Pearson, 2008), 32–34.

64 "What is Assistive Technology?" The National Center on Accessible Information Technology in Education, at http://www.washington.edu/accessit/articles?109 (accessed on September 14, 2010).

65 USDOE, "CEIS and Response to Intervention (RTI), at http://www2.ed.gov/policy/speced/ guid/ idea/ceis_pg4.html (accessed on September 13, 2010); and Nicole Strangeman et al., "Response-to-Instruction and Universal Design for Learning: How Might They Intersect in the General Education Classroom?" LD OnLine, at http://www.ldonline.org/article/13002?theme= print (accessed on September 13, 2010).

66 "Universal Design for Learning," Title I, § 103, ¶ 24, of the Higher Education Opportunity Act (P.L. 110–315—August 14, 2008), 122 Stat. 3088, at http://frwebgate.access.gpo.gov/cgi-bin/ getdoc.cgi?dbname=110_cong_public_laws&docid=f:publ315.110.pdf (accessed on September 13, 2010).

67 "What is Universal Design for Learning?" Center for Applied Special Technology, at http://www.cast. org/research/udl/index.html (accessed on August 18, 2010); "What is a Refreshable Braille Display?" Center for Universal Design in Education (CUDE), at http://www.washington.edu/doit/CUDE/ articles?140 (accessed on September 14, 2010); and Diane P. Bryant et al., *Teaching Students with Special Needs in Inclusive Classrooms* (Boston, MA: Pearson, 2008), 22, 204, 205.

68 "Universal Design . . . What It Is and What It Isn't," Trace Center, at http://trace.wisc.edu/docs/ whats_ud/whats_ud.htm (accessed on September 14, 2010).

69 Joyce S. Choate and Dorothy C. Schween, "Special Needs of Diverse Learners," in *Successful Inclusive Teaching: Proven Ways to Detect and Correct Special Needs*, 4th edn, Joyce S. Choate, ed. (Boston: Pearson, Allyn and Bacon, 2004), chapter 2; Katie Blenk and Doris L. Fine, *Making School Inclusion Work* (Cambridge, MA: Brookline Books, 1995), 213; and Larry D. Bartlett et al., *Successful Inclusion for Educational Leaders* (Upper Saddle River, NJ: 2002), 27.

70 Peggy Dettmer et al., *Consultation, Collaboration, and Teamwork for Students with Special Needs* (Boston: Pearson Education, 2005), 41, 220; Thomas E. Scruggs and Margo Mastropieri, "Teacher Perceptions of Mainstreaming/Inclusion, 1958–1995: A Research Synthesis," *Exceptional Children*, vol. 63, no. 1: 59–74 (Fall 1996); and NCERI, 14, 20.

71 National Center on Educational Restructuring and Inclusion (NCERI), *National Study of Inclusive Education*, 2nd edn (New York: CUNY, 1995), 2; June E. Downing and Joanne Eichinger, "Educating Students with Diverse Strengths and Needs Together," in *Including Students with Severe and Multiple Disabilities in Typical Classrooms: Practical Strategies for Teachers*, June E. Downing, ed. (Baltimore: P.H. Brookes Publishing Co., 2002), 11; and Pam Hunt and Lori Goetz, "Research on Inclusive Educational Programs, Practices, and Outcomes with Students with Severe Disabilities," *Journal of Special Education*, vol. 31, no. 1: 26 (Spring 1997).

72 Smith et al., 29.

73 Chris Forlin et al., "Demographic Differences in Changing Pre-service Teachers' Attitudes, Sentiments and Concerns about Inclusive Education," *International Journal of Inclusive Education*, vol. 13, no. 2: 195–209 (March 2009).

74 Michael W. Harvey et al., "Pre-service Teacher Preparation for Inclusion: An Exploration of Higher Education Teacher-Training Institutions," *Remedial and Special Education*, vol. 31, no. 1: 24–33 (January/February 2010); Mary T. Brownell et al., "Critical Features of Special Education Teacher Preparation: A Comparison with General Teacher Education," *The Journal of Special Education*, vol. 38, no. 4: 242–252 (February 2005); Nancy Burstein et al., "Moving toward inclusive practices," *Remedial and Special Education*, vol. 25, no. 2: 104–116 (March/April 2004).

75 Harvey et al., 28–31.

76   Woo-Sik Jung. "Pre-service Teacher Training for Successful Inclusion." *Education*, vol. 128, no. 1: 106–113 (Fall 2007).

77   Thea Renda Abu El-Haj and Beth C. Rubin, "Realizing the Equity-Minded Aspirations of Detracking and Inclusion: Toward a Capacity-Oriented Framework for Teacher Education," *Curriculum Inquiry*, vol. 39, no. 3: 435–463 (June 2009).

78   Ibid., 453–454.

79   Ibid., 454–456.

80   Ibid., 456–458.

81   Dettmer et al., 41; Hunt and Goetz, 25–26; Jeanette Klingner and Sharon Vaughn, "Students' Perceptions of Instruction in Inclusion Classrooms: Implications for Students with Learning Disabilities," *Exceptional Children*, vol. 66, no. 1: 23 (Fall, 1999); Dorothy K. Lipsky and Alan Gartner, *Inclusion and School Reform* (Baltimore: Paul H. Brookes Publishing, 1997), 197; and Margaret Tomasik, "Effective Inclusion Activities for High School Students with Multiple Disabilities," *Journal of Visual Impairment & Blindness*, vol. 101, no. 10: 657–659 (October. 2007).

82   Annemarie S. Palinscar et al., "Investigating the engagement and learning of students with learning disabilities in guided inquiry science teaching," *Language, Speech, and Hearing Services in Schools*, vol. 31, no. 3: 240–251 (July 2000).

83   United Nations Educational, Scientific, and Cultural Organization (UNESCO), "Including the Excluded: One School for All," EFA 2000, no. 32 (July-September, 1998), 3–7.

84   Seamus Hegarty, "Challenges to Inclusive Education: A European Perspective," in *Inclusive Schooling—National and International Perspectives*, Stanley J. Vitello and Dennis E. Mithaug, eds (Mahwah, NJ: Lawrence Erlbaum Associates, 1998), 151–165; and Patrick Daunt, "Introduction: Integration Practice and Policy for Children with Special Needs in Europe," in *Inclusive Education in Europe*, Christine O'Hanlon, ed. (London: David Fulton Publishers, 1995), 1–8.

85   "Denmark," *The World Factbook*, at https://www.cia.gov/library/publications/the-world-factbook/geos/da.html (accessed on July 9, 2010); "Faroe Islands," *World Factbook*, at https://www.cia.gov/library/publications/the-world-factbook/geos/fo.html (accessed on July 9, 2010); and "Greenland," *World Factbook*, at https://www.cia.gov/library/publications/the-world-factbook/geos/gl.html (accessed on July 9, 2010).

86   European Agency for Development in Special Needs Education, "Development of Inclusion- Denmark," at http://european-agency.org/nat_ovs/denmark/6.html (accessed on August 18, 2010); Anette Ipsen and Jørgen Thorslund, "Curriculum Reform and Life Skills in Denmark," in *Curriculum Change and Social Inclusion: Perspectives from the Baltic and Scandinavian Countries*, International Bureau of Education, UNESCO (2001), 64, at http://www.ibe.unesco.org/fileadmin/user_upload/archive/curriculum/Balticpdf/vilnius.pdf (accessed on August 25, 2010); and Susan Tetler, "The Danish Efforts in Integration," in *Inclusive Education in Europe*, 9–23.

87   Cor J.W. Meijer, "Special Needs Education in Europe: Inclusive Policies and Practices," European Agency for Development in Special Needs Education (2010), at http://www.inklusion-online.net/index.php/inklusion/article/viewArticle/56/60 (accessed on July 14, 2010).

88   European Agency for Development in Special Needs Education, "Special needs education within the education system – Denmark" (updated March 26, 2010), at http://www.european-agency.org/country-information/denmark/national-overview/special-needs-education-within-the-education-system (accessed on July 12, 2010).

89   Ministry of Education, "Welcome to the Danish Folkeskole," 2010, at http://www.eng.uvm.dk/~/media/Publikationer/2010/Folkeskolen/Velkommen%20til%20den%20danske%20folkeskole/pdf/Folkeskolen_ENG_web.ashx (accessed on July 16, 2010); and Ministry of Education, "Upper Secondary Education," at http://www.eng.uvm.dk/~/media/Publikationer/2010/Folkeskolen/Velkommen%20til%20den%20danske%20folkeskole/pdf/Folkeskolen_ENG_web.ashx (accessed on July 16, 2010).

90 United Nations Educational, Scientific, and Cultural Organization (UNESCO), *The Salamanca Statement and Framework for Action on Special Needs Education* (Salamanca, Spain, June 7–10, 1994), vii–xii, at http://www.unesco.de/fileadmin/medien/Dokumente/Bildung/Salamanca_Declaration.pdf (accessed on July 16, 2010).

91 Ministry of Education, "The Folkeskole: Additional Information," at http://www.eng.uvm.dk/Uddannelse/Primary%20and%20Lower%20Secondary%20Education/The%20Folkeskole/Additional%20Information.aspx (accessed on July 16, 2010).

92 European Agency for Development in Special Needs Education, "Special needs education within the education system—Denmark," (March 26, 2010), at http://www.european-agency.org/country-information/denmark/national-overview/special-needs-education-within-the-education-system (accessed on July 16, 2010).

93 Ministry of Education, "The Folkeskole: Evaluation, Tests, and Student Plans," at http://www.eng.uvm.dk/Uddannelse/Primary%20and%20Lower%20Secondary%20Education/The%20Folkeskole/Evaluation%20Tests%20Student%20Plans.aspx (accessed on July 14, 2010).

Religion and Education

Chapter objectives

Readers should be able to:

- gain an understanding of the history of religion and education.
- appreciate the precursors of the controversies surrounding the issue today.
- understand the role of religion in schools and varying viewpoints on it.
- analyze policies related to religion in schools.
- understand some of the legal aspects associated with religion and public education, particularly the separation of church and state.
- gain insight into political controversies concerning religion in public education.
- develop perspective through international comparison.

Opening questions

1. How has the relationship of religion and education changed over time?
2. What aspects of the relationship changed the most, the least, and why?

3. What are the leading religion-education controversies today, and why are they controversial?
4. How have some major court decisions on religion and public education impacted public policy?
5. How have religion-education controversies and legal rulings most impacted curriculum and instruction in the daily operation of the schools?
6. How is the religion-education relationship in the United States similar to or different from that in other countries, and why?

The issue

The preceding chapters examine important facets of how sociocultural conditions serve to define people (such as class and race) and how education is impacted as a result. Another facet is religion, and it not only encompasses ideas about people but also beliefs about origins and destinies. People may accept, reject, or be indifferent about religion, but it continues to impact human behavior with far-reaching educational consequences.

Education conceived as the conscious effort to inform people about their origins and what their possible destinies are began long ago. Exactly when this effort first appeared remains uncertain, but it seems that deliberate education emerged from the need not only to pass on knowledge about survival in the natural environment but also about accumulated understandings of how life should be lived, as well as curiosities about what came before and what might lie beyond life.

Similarly, the exact origins of schools remain unclear, but the evidence suggests that schools emerged soon after writing systems developed. Certainly writing and schooling were significant advances for humankind. As religions developed complicated views, writing proved a convenient way to store and retrieve various rules and doctrines. The word *scripture* is usually taken to mean "sacred writings." Thus, religion, writing, and schools found mutual connections.

What role religion should have in schools, however, has long been a topic of debate. Throughout American history, not only have scholars and policy makers joined in those debates but members of the general public as well, often with considerable passion. Thus, the relationship between religion and education has been long and contentious.

Background

As human societies developed, their accumulated wisdom could no longer be committed to memory alone. Better ways of storing and retrieving information were needed, and systems of symbols representing ideas and information emerged. Writing probably started with scratches, notches, and symbolic markings that conveyed meanings, including numbers and representations of objects. Such efforts evolved into abstract writing systems, which made them more useful but also more difficult to master. Schools probably emerged following the appearance of writing because group instruction proved an efficient way to teach it. Writing and schools did not develop all at once but in halting steps in different locales around the globe, usually in fertile areas where urbanization also occurred.[1]

Mesopotamia and Egypt

One of the earliest forms of writing was **cuneiform**, which probably originated around 3100 B.C.E. in the Mesopotamian city of Sumer. Cuneiform writing was imprinted with wedge-shaped reeds on damp handheld clay tablets, and its mastery involved lengthy preparation and a high degree of skill. By 2500 B.C.E., cuneiform contained more than 400 symbols, a complexity that likely gave rise to Sumerian schools called *edubbas,* literally "houses of clay." A central purpose of edubbas was to train **scribes**, a small, literate group of persons who could record, store, and retrieve all sorts of data and ideas. Archaeologists have uncovered thousands of surviving clay tablets that include grammar texts, dictionaries, and even corrected student exercises. The tablets reveal that students not only learned cuneiform script but also drawing, laws, mathematical tables, and botanical, zoological, geographical, and mineralogical information. They learned about deities, scriptures, legends, and rules that supported these deities; thus, Sumerian education had both secular and religious objectives.[2] Mesopotamia also influenced the Babylonian, Assyrian, Chaldean, and Persian civilizations, all with roots in Sumerian culture and education.

> **Suggested Activity:** For examples of early cuneiform materials and student writings, see "Scribal Activity, School and Learning," 13.1–13.2, The Schoyen Collection, at http://www.schoyencollection.com/scribes.htm (accessed on August16, 2010).

Education and religion were firmly joined in ancient Egypt, as well. Around the time cuneiform appeared in Mesopotamia, Egypt produced a writing system called **hieroglyphics**. Originating from pictographs, hieroglyphs were used for scriptures (such as the *Book of the Dead*) and for inscriptions on temples, tombs, and public monuments. For practical uses, a derivative script called hieratic was written in ink on papyrus sheets. Egyptian scribes were also priests; consequently, they not only controlled access to writing but also to the scriptures regarding deities and the afterlife. As Egyptian culture expanded so did the need for scribes to record secular matters, such as governmental and economic records, and the demand for scribes necessitated government-sponsored schools by about 1500 B.C.E. However, Egypt's religious system discouraged change, and Egypt was eventually overrun by the Persians in the early sixth century, the Greeks in the fourth century, and the Romans in the first century B.C.E.[3]

Suggested Activity: For photo images of important Egyptian artifacts related to scribal life housed in the British Museum, see http://www.ancientegypt.co.uk/writing/home.html (accessed on August 16, 2010). For a brief account of how modern scholars finally learned to decipher Egyptian hieroglyphics, see http://www.mnsu.edu/emuseum/prehistory/egypt/hieroglyphics/rosettastone.html (accessed on August 16, 2010).

Greece and Rome

Ancient Greek religion centered on the Olympians, gods and goddesses who exhibited humanlike traits and foibles. At first, stories about them were orally transmitted by long epic poems, particularly the *Iliad* and the *Odyssey*, which were put in written form around 800 B.C.E. Such Olympian **mythology** was central to Greek education, for it provided moral and cultural lessons about what it meant to be Greek. For this reason, Greek religion has been called a "religion of culture."[4]

The Greek writing system appeared in the ninth century B.C.E., and while it was influenced by Mesopotamia and Egypt, the Greeks borrowed heavily from the Phoenician alphabet. The resulting Greek alphabet was an improvement that, with occasional changes, has been used ever since and has strongly influenced our own. During the classical period when Athens was at its height (the fifth century B.C.E.), the education of free citizens was a major emphasis. The curriculum involved not only literacy but also **rhetoric** (an in-depth study of language, with a philosophical emphasis). Pericles, the leader of Athens during its golden age, argued that citizens should be educated to participate in developing public policies. Philosophers such as Socrates, Plato, and Aristotle inquired into the nature of the good society and developed philosophies on what education would help bring a more just society into existence.[5]

> WEB: Additional Information 8.1.:
> GRECO-ROMAN MYTHOLOGY AND ITS CONTINUING IMPACT

The Romans adopted freely from the Greeks, including their ideas about religion and education. Many Romans were bilingual in Greek and Latin, particularly the upper classes; however, where Athens wanted free-minded citizens, Rome wanted citizens loyal to the state; where Greeks excelled at philosophical education, Romans favored **oratorical education** and practical rhetoric. One of Rome's greatest intellectuals, Cicero, thought education should produce responsible servants of the Roman republic, men who were persuasive and knowledgeable leaders. Roman education included some religion but overall had a secular orientation.[6]

Christianity

For centuries, Rome dominated Europe, Asia Minor, and North Africa. Roman power provided law and order, and it spread Greco-Roman educational ideas. As Rome declined, Christianity became dominant, particularly after Emperor Constantine gave it official recognition in 313 C.E. Constantine also divided the empire into two parts, east and west, and he moved the government seat to Byzantium in the east, renaming it Constantinople. Constantinople became the capitol of the Byzantine Empire, with the Eastern Orthodox faith as its official religion.

The Roman Catholic Church retained its base in the city of Rome. The church wanted to extend its influence over education, but it needed doctrinal consistency. Church leaders such as Jerome and Augustine discouraged familiarity with pagan Greco-Roman writings and insisted on devotion to Christian scriptures. Roman citizens by birth and educated in classical schools, both men became Christians as adults and also prominent church leaders, but Jerome feared the classics would lure people away from the Bible, and Augustine wanted classical readings restricted to physics, logic, and mathematics, which he thought would not threaten Christian teachings.[7] Unfortunately, their fears of pagan influence helped discourage Christian inquiry into and preservation of Greco-Roman writings.

Suggested Activity: Interested students may electronically access a number of ancient authors and their works at "The Internet Classics Archive," at http://classics. mit.edu/ (accessed on 28 August 2010).

The Middle Ages

Before the fall of the western Empire in the late fifth century C.E., there were large migrations of people from the north and east (Goths, Vandals, Huns, and Saxons, to name a few). This created social upheaval across Europe, but even as the western Empire slowly collapsed there were efforts to maintain cultural and educational continuity. Martianus Capella (early to mid-fifth century), a pagan from Carthage, wrote an influential book, *The Marriage of Philology and Mercury*, in which he described classical knowledge as comprised of seven **liberal arts**: the *quadrivium* (arithmetic, geometry, astronomy, and music or harmony) and the *trivium* (grammar, rhetoric, and logic or dialectic). In the sixth century a Christianized version was defended by churchmen such as Flavius Magnus Cassiodorus, who founded a monastery in Italy dedicated to preserving both classical and Christian manuscripts.[8] During the Dark Ages (the sixth to eighth centuries), some monasteries preserved enough classical learning to help re-energize liberal arts education in the Middle Ages.

Emerging European views

As the Roman Catholic Church and the socioeconomic system called feudalism became dominant, loyalty to Rome was replaced by loyalty to the church. Medieval education settled into the transmission and right interpretation of church-approved knowledge, with the church the defining force behind education.[9]

Although the church first used education to instruct converts in its beliefs, it soon expanded into academic education, particularly after the classical schools disappeared. For example, under the influence of the Rule of Benedict (developed by Benedict of Nursia), **monastic schools** stressed reading, book copying, and other scholarly activities, although not every monastery had a school. Some monastic schools became recognized centers of learning. Almost every cathedral (the administrative center of a church diocese, headed by a bishop) had a preparatory school for priests, and some of these **cathedral**

schools evolved into **universities** by the twelfth century. Some parishes had **parish schools** to teach such things as reading, writing, and sacred music. Ambitious towns developed **municipal schools**, and prominent craft guilds also developed **guild schools**, which offered elementary and secondary education serving the secular purposes of businesses and the skilled trades.[10] By the end of the Middle Ages, there were a variety of educational institutions ranging from parish, municipal, and guild schools to monastic schools, cathedral schools, and universities, most of which were either controlled or at least influenced by the church, even lay schools with secular purposes; however, the majority of people remained illiterate and unschooled.

Educational changes

Some key developments occurred in the eighth and ninth centuries. For example, Charlemagne, a successful military and political leader, was crowned by the pope in 800 as emperor of the Frankish kingdoms (a large swath of western Europe), the so-called Holy Roman Empire. Convinced of the need for education, Charlemagne persuaded the monk Alcuin, a renowned cathedral schoolteacher from York, England, to become his educational advisor. Reforms were initiated to upgrade monastic and cathedral schools and to improve local parish schools, but after Charlemagne's death political instability returned.[11]

> ### Suggested Reading 8.1.

Other reformers included Rabanus Maurus, the archbishop of Mainz, who pushed educational development in Germany, and Alfred the Great, an English king who reformed education in both Latin and English. Educational development was also encouraged by various popes, particularly parish and cathedral schools.[12]

> ### WEB: Additional Information 8.2.:
> ### ISLAMIC SCHOLARSHIP AND EUROPEAN EDUCATION

Universities

From the eleventh through the thirteenth centuries, Europe experienced significant social, economic, and educational growth. In the upper levels of education, the recovery of important Greek writings helped revive elements of **classical education**. Of particular importance was the rise of the universities, which usually evolved from cathedral schools with a strong academic program called the *studium generale* (general studies in the liberal arts). Cathedral schools were headed by chancellors, and a pope might grant a chancellor the right to issue the *licentia docendi* ("license to teach"). When this system became abused by church officials practicing simony (selling licenses rather than awarding them on merit), some of the cathedral schools sought to protect their scholarly reputations by forming guilds. Some schools with exceptional reputations received papal charters to award teaching licenses on their own, and from among their number some became separate institutions called universities. They were freed from cathedral control but still under the aegis of the church, and they offered undergraduate (or bachelor's) degrees in the liberal arts and graduate (or master's) degrees in law, medicine, theology, and the liberal arts. Universities became important for several reasons, including fulfilling the church's need for educated priests for important church offices, governments' need for educated administrators, and the needs of learned professions and other important enterprises for educated professionals. Sometimes conflict arose between school and society, but the universities served vital societal interests and received church and civil protection in return.[13]

An example of university service to society was the controversy over **faith and reason**, which threatened to split the church apart. The dispute was between realism (the traditional church-approved Platonic view that human reasoning must be based on timeless universal truths of divine origin) and nominalism (an Aristotelian view that truth is found in the rational study of specifics from which universal truths may be drawn). Peter Abelard, a prominent philosophy and theology teacher at a cathedral school in Paris (from which the University of Paris later emerged), helped found **scholasticism**, an educational method based on lectures and logical disputations that became prominent in medieval universities. Abelard's predilections were nominalist, but he tried to steer a middle ground by arguing that both realism and nominalism had elements of truth that demanded thoughtful analysis before coming to defensible conclusions. His efforts helped, but probably the best effort at reconciliation came from Thomas Aquinas, a philosophy and theology professor at the University of Paris, who argued that philosophy and science dealt with natural truth, while theology dealt with faith and revealed truth, or the supernatural realm. If God is the source of both, then reason and faith can be applied to all questions—if it is recognized that some elements of faith are beyond rational demonstration.[14] The syntheses attempted by Abelard and Aquinas helped soothe the uproar over faith and reason, and it also helped make universities integral parts of medieval society.

Renaissance and Reformation

Educational development and the recovery of important classical works contributed to a rebirth of humanistic thought during the **Renaissance**. While not rejecting religion, Renaissance education embraced worldly concerns. A new social order was surfacing in the growth of cities and populations, the beginnings of modern nation-states, and the emerging economies in which money was the chief medium of exchange. Educational development was also fueled by the invention of the movable-type printing press, which made reading materials cheap and widely available; and the "discovery" of the New World revolutionized European concepts of geography, distance, and time.

Educational development

The Renaissance educational ideal centered on well-rounded knowledge of the liberal arts in both classical and vernacular languages. Growth occurred in secondary education, notably in England, Germany, and France. Most Renaissance thinkers rejected scholasticism in favor of a reborn classical humanist view of "man as the measure of all things"; however, many Renaissance humanists continued to view humans as God's creations.

Two notable educators were Desiderius Erasmus and Juan Luis Vives. Erasmus was educated in both cathedral and monastic schools and was ordained a priest in 1492. Although critical of the church, he remained a priest and refused to join the Protestant movement. A professor at the University of Paris, Erasmus translated Greek and Latin classics and wrote philosophical and religious treatises. He also authored important works on education, but his educational focus was on the ruling class. Juan Luis Vives was educated at the University of Valencia (Spain) and the University of Paris. As a professor, Vives valued classical learning but thought it should be combined with vernacular studies. He argued for the education of females as well as males, and he championed education that served the good of humanity.[15]

For Further Reflection: In a corporation-driven world set on accountability, to what extent do educational institutions still make it their explicit goal to "serve the good of humanity"? Does the corporation-minded outlook serve the good of humanity, or does it primarily serve the corporate profit motive? Is any balance possible? Why or why not?

Impact of the Reformation and Counter-Reformation

In the sixteenth and seventeenth centuries, Catholicism was confronted by the **Protestant Reformation**, which shook it to its core and changed the map of Europe. Economically, there were major industrial expansions fed by colonial empires with vast natural resources. Socially, there was the emergence of the upper middle class and a growing restiveness among the lower classes as socio-economic changes began wiping out the last vestiges of feudalism. Intellectually, there was increased secularization of human thought spurred by technological innovation and scientific development.

The printing press made reading materials much cheaper, and both Protestantism and Catholicism took advantage of this new technology. Through Protestantism's emphasis on widespread literacy to encourage Bible reading, elementary education was expanded; through Catholicism's **Counter-Reformation** their secondary and higher education were rejuvenated as well. Both the Reformation and the Counter-Reformation affected educational opportunity.

Martin Luther stands as a prime example of Protestant thinking. He vigorously opposed the Catholic Church, but he also warned Protestantism not to let schools formerly supported by the church die out. He favored the study of classical languages but was better known for advocating the use of vernaculars. One of the first things he did after breaking with Catholicism was to translate the Bible from Latin into German. Based on his view of the **priesthood of all believers**, Luther argued that everyone should have basic education, with the most promising students receiving advanced education. He pushed for new schools and libraries, and he believed the burden of education should not be borne by parents alone but by governments as well.[16]

The Catholic Church responded to Protestantism through several approaches, one of which was the Order of Jesuits founded in 1539 by Ignatius of Loyola. The Jesuits developed a detailed plan of study for secondary and higher education, with special attention to the role of teachers. Published in 1599, the *Ratio Studiorum* has endured with only minor revisions since. **Jesuit schools** spread in Catholic areas of Europe and as far westward as the Americas and as far eastward as India. Their network of schools taught both Jesuit recruits and lay students.[17]

Education and religion: the American experience

Europeans brought educational traditions that linked religion and education back to the dawn of history, traditions deeply embedded in habitual and institutional patterns passed down over generations and accepted as the way education should be pursued. All was not habitual, however, because many consciously chosen goals gave direction to educational efforts.

Forging a new nation of diverse people, the Americans inevitably faced the question "Who are we?" Their response may be seen in two broad themes: On the one hand were "moral dreams" about civic ideals (inspired, as Abraham Lincoln put it, "by the better angels of our nature") that lay behind such developments as the revolution of 1776, the abolition of slavery in the 1860s, or the civil rights movement of the 1950s and 1960s. On the other hand were "moral fevers" stoked by threatening changes such as economic upheavals or large immigration waves. Change seems to provide for every generation an "un-American them" that must be controlled and an "American us" that must be strengthened. What holds these dueling tensions in an uneasy relationship, and why does religion continue to impact American education? A clue is that many Americans retain religious beliefs, and while some nations have a few religions tightly woven into their societies, American religions tend to "restlessly shift, split, and spread in a kind of ecclesiastical uproar."[18] Perhaps these shifting tendencies to "control them" and "strengthen us" help explain why entanglements of American politics and religion periodically become uproars that complicate public education.

Suggested Activity: Brainstorm current examples of American politics and religion being entangled in ways that impact public education. What do you make of such entanglements?

Colonial beginnings

As the first colonies became established, attention soon focused on long-term needs in which education played a major role. The first attempt to found a college in the English colonies occurred in Virginia in the early 1620s at a place called Henrico Town (or Henricus) located near present-day Richmond. There were plans to move the center of government from Jamestown up the James River to Henrico Town, because Jamestown lacked an adequate freshwater supply and was susceptible to raids by Spanish warships. Henrico Town was situated far upstream, across the river from a fortified village where Pocahontas was kept (after the English took her from Chief Powhatan), and where she learned Christianity, was baptized, and later married John Rolfe in 1614. A goal of the envisioned college at Henrico Town was to Christianize the natives, teach them "useful trades," and prepare them to become missionaries among their own people. As one observer put it, however, native parents proved "'very loathe . . . to part with their children,'" and threatened by the increase of land-hungry whites, Powhatan's people rose up in 1622, killed more than 300 settlers, and burned many settlements, including Henrico Town and its partially constructed college (from which neither ever recovered).[19]

Cross-Reference: See Chapter 5, Ethnicity and Education, pp. 212–218, and 231–232, for an extended discussion of Native Americans and their views on education.

When Virginia's colonial legislature addressed the need for education in its 1631–32 session, it required ministers to "examine, catechise, and instruct the youth and ignorant persons" in "the ten commandments, the articles of belief, . . . the Lord's prayer . . . and . . . the catechism, set forth in the book of common prayer." In the 1642–43 session, legislation required guardians and overseers to teach destitute orphans the "Christian religion and . . . the rudiments of learning."[20]

For Discussion: To what extent does society today see religious instruction as an effective educational tool? Should religion be taught in schools, and if so, should it be taught as one academic subject among others, or should it be taught to induce beliefs? Why or why not?

In New England, however, educational efforts were more substantial. The Puritans of the Massachusetts Bay Colony successfully founded not only elementary and secondary schools but a college as well. One suggestion why New Englanders undertook such commitments was their strong sense of religious mission. Governor John Winthrop urged them to see their colony as "a Citty upon a Hill" with the eyes of the world on them. A central goal in the founding of Harvard College was to "advance Learning and perpetuate it to Posterity; dreading to leave an illiterate Ministry to the Churches, when our present Ministers shall lie in the Dust."[21]

Fearful that Satan would "keep men from the knowledge of the Scriptures," the Massachusetts Bay lawmakers passed the **Old Deluder Act** (1647) to ensure that children were taught to read the Bible and be wary of "false glosses of saint-seeming deceivers," presumably those of non-Puritan leanings. Similar to the Harvard founders, the lawmakers also feared that, unless children were properly educated, learning would be "buried in the grave of our fathers in the church and commonwealth."[22]

Meanwhile, mindful of the 1622 failure in Virginia, a determined Scottish preacher named James Blair, sent to Virginia by the bishop of London in 1685 to revive the colony's struggling churches, soon realized that success depended on better-trained ministers, and in 1691 he returned to England to seek a charter and funds for a new college. Favorably disposed, Queen Mary directed the Crown's attorney general and treasury commissioner, Sir Edward Seymour, to draw up a charter and provide Blair with funds. When Seymour sharply questioned Blair as to why Virginia of all places needed a college, Blair replied that, as in England, Virginia also had souls to be saved. "Souls!" Seymour reportedly exclaimed, "Damn your souls. Make tobacco."[23] Seymour notwithstanding, Blair returned to Virginia in 1693 with both a charter and funds in hand. The new school was built at Middle Plantation (later Williamsburg), and was named the College of William and Mary.[24]

The Enlightenment

Primarily a European intellectual movement, the **Enlightenment** pushed the view that through reason, scientific investigation, and social reform it was possible to achieve human progress. Enlightenment thinkers tended to ignore traditional religious views of humanity as forever tainted by original sin and human progress as a vain hope; instead, they argued that knowledge and education, if properly used, could actually bring about both progress and happiness, that is, the natural and social worlds could be shaped and molded for the better through scientific investigation and widespread education. The Enlightenment exerted a major influence on the United States, especially in the events leading up to the revolution and the founding of the new nation in the late eighteenth century and the scientific, industrial, and educational advancements of the early nineteenth century.

Sir Francis Bacon was an Enlightenment thinker who maintained that knowledge is power and progress is possible in human affairs. Bacon championed the use of inductive thought and the systematic, scientific study of nature. This nature theme was prominent among many Enlightenment thinkers, including John Locke, who saw the child as fundamentally shaped through experience of the natural and social world. Such **naturalism** did not mean either Bacon or Locke rejected all aspects of religion, but they did not think education and religion should be as tightly intertwined as tradition had it, because both wanted more tolerance and freedom of thought than religious tradition allowed.[25] For

Enlightened thinkers, knowledge was not innate in the soul or mind but something acquired from the external world through the natural senses of sight, hearing, taste, smell, and touch and aided by active inquiry and sound reasoning. Education about nature and for the good of society was central to Enlightenment thought.

Perhaps the Enlightenment merely reflected Greek and Roman traditions about the civic importance of education, but it was something more. For example, Benjamin Franklin supported a view of education designed specifically for American social, political, and economic development. He did not believe education should be controlled by religion, and he favored educational goals directed toward secular rather than sectarian religious ends. People such as Franklin helped produce greater variety in American outlooks about the relationship of religion and education.[26]

The Great Awakening

Enlightenment secularism did not drive all before it, however. From the beginning of the eighteenth century, change created anxieties that affected religion as much as other aspects of life. A religious revival called the **Great Awakening** got under way in the English colonies, reaching its peak in the 1740s and exerting strong educational influence. It came out of European evangelical pietism, the view that true Christian living emerged from believers' inner personal experiences of God. English evangelical revivalists such as George Whitefield came to the colonies, attracted large crowds, and won over many converts. There were also homegrown revivalists, such as Jonathan Edwards, a student of Enlightenment thought who attempted to synthesize Protestant theology with Isaac Newton's physics and John Locke's psychology. Some revivalists feared the Enlightenment would overwhelm religious faith, but as Edwards saw it, the "advancement of learning" went hand in hand with "true religion."[27]

Traditional Puritan-style religion encouraged rationalistic views, but many of the new evangelical reformers emphasized a personal-emotional religion. Staunch traditionalists saw this as anti-intellectual religious passion, and "old side" educators at schools such as Harvard and Yale shied away from Great Awakening reformers who advocated "new side" schools called log colleges, small schools for preparing ministers dedicated to evangelical revivalism. One long-term benefit of the log college movement was the founding of the College of New Jersey (later Princeton University), the College of Rhode Island (later Brown University), and Queen's College (later Rutgers University).[28]

Despite differences, the Enlightenment and the Great Awakening shared some similarities: Each wanted to remake society, although in different ways; each also wanted education in modern languages and useful knowledge to bring about social change. The net result: American education was never quite the same afterward, for where it previously sought to preserve traditional knowledge and culture, it came to be valued as an agent of social change, too, and this was nowhere better seen than in education's promise to help produce a new social order.[29]

For Further Reflection: Does the advancement of religion go hand in hand with true learning? What is the relationship between science and belief?

Separation of church and state

The American Revolution created a new nation and social order, and one of the first political controversies was the issue of an "established church," an officially recognized, tax-subsidized church that was a holdover from British colonial law. For example, in Virginia the Episcopal Church was the established church: Some people wanted to maintain the tradition, but others wanted to abolish all tax support for religion and make a new law putting all religions on equal standing. Americans influenced by the Enlightenment, particularly Thomas Jefferson and James Madison, successfully moved a Bill for Religious Freedom through the Virginia legislature in 1786, an act that had far-reaching consequences as the separation of church and state found acceptance in other states as well.[30]

One result was the addition of **religious freedom** to the U.S. Constitution when the First Amendment was added in 1791. It included the following words: "Congress shall make no law respecting an establishment of religion, or prohibiting the free exercise thereof. . . ." Both Jefferson and Madison understood this language to require the **separation of church and state**, that is, the wording of the First Amendment strictly prohibits the U.S. government from making any laws involving or interfering with religious institutions, beliefs, or exercises. On the face of it, the doctrine of separation seems clear enough: It has survived for more than 200 years and has also been adopted by many other countries; nevertheless, the doctrine has become a contested issue, particularly concerning public education.[31]

Religion and the public common schools

By the early nineteenth century, the separation of church and state seemed tolerable to most Americans, but the established church tradition remained strong in New England. In 1818, however, Baptists, Methodists, and other like-minded denominations joined with the Jeffersonians to disestablish the

Congregationalist Church in Connecticut, with Massachusetts and New Hampshire following suit a decade later.[32]

As the public common school movement got under way, Massachusetts became a key site of contention in 1837. Although it had disestablished the Congregational Church, the belief remained strong that children's education should have a religious component. As secretary to the Massachusetts state board of education, Horace Mann found religious contentiousness to be a particularly challenging problem. Mann was reared a Congregationalist and became a Unitarian as an adult. He understood that the Constitution set a new direction among nations with its First Amendment religious freedom, but as a state official he was bound by an 1827 Massachusetts law requiring religion to be taught without sectarian bias in the schools. Mann believed schools should avoid religious controversy, but this proved impossible when critics insisted that their views on religion must be taught in the schools. The compromise Mann embraced was to teach religion through Bible readings on broad Christian principles, but (as the law required) to be delivered without sectarian comment or bias. He thought this would leave children free to decide what, if any, sectarian views they might embrace as adults. If sectarian instruction was desired, then it should be provided privately by children's families and the churches of their choice, and Mann believed his plan was lawful, fair, and reasonable.[33]

Even Thomas Jefferson believed religion had a place in education, but since young children could easily be confused by abstract religious concepts, religion studies should be reserved for higher education. At the University of Virginia, Jefferson opposed any imposition of religious belief, but he recognized a place for the academic study of religion in history and classical language courses.[34]

Perhaps Mann was partially following Jefferson when he advocated an abbreviated approach for younger students of simple Bible readings without commentary, but Mann's critics charged him with reflecting Unitarian biases. Perhaps he was, but in his defense it should be noted that Massachusetts was becoming more religiously diverse at the time: Congregationalism split into two camps (conservative Trinitarians and liberal Unitarians), while Episcopalians, Methodists, Baptists, Roman Catholics, and the followers of other beliefs were rapidly increasing. In addition, many public school supporters were Whigs who favored centralized state control of education; many critics were Democrats who wanted local control over education, including religion's place in the curriculum. In an anticentralization push in 1840, the Democrats tried to abolish the state board of education (and Secretary Mann's position, too); however, they lost, and Mann continued as secretary until 1848 when, after 12 years in office, he resigned to run for Congress.[35]

Mann's Bible-reading "compromise" never solved the problem because the issue continued to resurface. For one thing, the King James Version was the approved Bible for school readings, and while it was widely favored by Protestants, Roman Catholics preferred the Douay Version. In addition, there were Protestant and Catholic critics alike who argued that reading the Bible without sectarian comment took religious substance out of the exercise, and mere readings reduced the Bible to its historical, cultural, and literary value, not its religious significance.[36]

Suggested Activity: Discuss Horace Mann's compromise. Consider whether it is possible today to achieve a compromise on religion in the public schools. Justify your positions by taking contrary points of view into account.

The Catholic dilemma

The first European country to establish a lasting colonial foothold in North America was Roman Catholic Spain, in Florida at a place named St. Augustine. Spain also sprinkled mission settlements across South America, Central America, and the southwestern portions of what is today the United States. In contrast, the English stronghold was its settlements along the eastern coast of North America, all predominantly Protestant. Catholics were a distinct minority in the English colonies, at first predominantly located in Maryland where they established some Catholic schools in the mid-seventeenth century. By the nineteenth century, however, Catholics were widely dispersed and their number grew as the public common school movement got under way, particularly with the influx of Catholic immigrants fleeing the potato blight famine in Ireland. Roughly 1.5 million Irish immigrants arrived between 1846 and 1855.[37]

One of Horace Mann's chief foes on nonsectarian religious education was Orestes Brownson, a Protestant convert to Catholicism. Although Brownson was a devoted advocate of **universal education**, he was skeptical of the way the public schools were run. He appreciated the delicate task the schools faced in a society of diverse religious views, but he argued that moral education was not possible without strong religious foundations. Because Brownson was a journalist who published his own periodical (*Brownson's Quarterly Review*), his ideas received wide public circulation as he sought to implant the kind of religious education he believed necessary for the public schools.[38]

Brownson floated several options, but the one he finally settled on was sectarian public schools, that is, control of individual public schools by either

Protestants or Catholics, each controlling a sufficient number of schools to accommodate their children. As Brownson saw it, this would preserve public schools but under local sectarian control with both secular and religious instruction provided as each group saw fit. Brownson hoped this idea would alleviate the injustices Catholics encountered in Protestant-dominated schools, but he also hoped it would satisfy Protestants and preserve the idea of universal public education. It satisfied neither: Catholic leaders saw the plan as a threat to private Catholic parochial schools. What they wanted from Brownson was condemnation of public schools and enthusiastic endorsement of public tax monies for parochial schools. Protestant reaction was little better: Most Protestants believed the existing public schools already met their needs, so why change?[39]

Catholics were as interested in education as Protestants, but many disliked public schools organized and controlled by the Protestant majority. Not only did Catholics dislike King James Bible readings, their efforts to be excused from them often met with indifference, denial, and sometimes outright hostility. Catholic leaders insisted on separate Catholic schools; poor Catholic parents could ill afford to pay parochial school tuition fees, but they found it difficult to disobey their church leaders. Catholic efforts to get a portion of school taxes redirected to parochial schools were strongly resisted by the Protestant majority. Pleas for compromise were drowned out by extreme elements on both sides. There were episodes of violence, including riots and even bloodshed. The Civil War blunted religious tempers, but tensions continued to simmer below the surface.[40]

Religion, politics, and education

There is a tendency to depict the history of Protestant-Catholic tensions over the schools as one of unremitting rancor. True, there were tensions exploited by extremists: Some praised the supposed religious neutrality of the public schools and heaped criticism on private and parochial school advocates, while others claimed the Catholics were forcefully driven from the public schools and that all Catholics were in absolute agreement on the need for tax-supported parochial schools. In truth, such arguments were inaccurate. For example, in the nineteenth century the public schools of New York were rarely battlegrounds of religious strife because primary control of the schools resided with localities, not the state. While some strife was present and not always handled perfectly at the local levels, it was still handled peacefully enough.[41]

Today, there are also those on both the right and left wings of the political spectrum who seem to view the nineteenth century as a time when religious education was prominent in all American public schools. For example, the right wing looks back to a golden era when Bible reading and prayer were daily parts

374 Foundations of Education

of all public schooling; the left sees widespread Bible reading, too, but for religious indoctrination at the expense of freedom and diversity. On the contrary, Bible reading was neither as universal nor as uniformly applied as is claimed; from the 1840s to 1900, practices were varied, inconsistent, and subject to change. Fears of sectarian rivalries and other social tensions led many schools systems to restrict Bible readings to brief "without comment" exercises, some chose to restrict it to classes such as literature and history, and a few, such as Cincinnati, banned it altogether, an action upheld by Ohio's supreme court in 1869. U.S. commissioner of education reports in the late 1890s note that Bible reading was less common in larger cities than smaller ones, and it was more common in the northern and southern states than in the central or western states. Moreover, of 49 western cities responding to a school survey, only 14 reported Bible reading and only 11 reported prayer.[42]

For further reflection: Historical realities tend to get distorted for political gain, as in the case of Bible reading. Think of other examples where politics and education mix in an unfortunate way.

The Constitution, church and state, and education

The Constitution was put before the American public and adopted in 1789, but many people felt it did not go far enough to protect fundamental rights and liberties. Ten amendments were soon approved by Congress and submitted to the states for ratification, which was successfully completed in 1791. The First Amendment was of special interest because it protected some of the basic freedoms central in the revolutionary generation's cause: "Congress shall make no law respecting an establishment of religion, or prohibiting the free exercise thereof; or abridging the freedom of speech, or of the press; or the right of the people peaceably to assemble, and to petition the government for a redress of grievances."

The First Amendment was almost a bill of rights in itself, containing five of the basic freedoms: freedom of religion, speech, press, peaceable assembly, and petition.

The framers of the Constitution and its First Amendment were aware of the history of intertwined governments and religions; they understood the mixture could suppress political and religious freedoms and corrupt both government and religion in the process. Most of the First Amendment's framers viewed religion as a matter of individual conscience and embraced the idea of religious freedom. They also believed that all First Amendment rights must be outside the reach of government, so they carefully limited the national government's powers over those rights.[43]

Most framers were also influenced to one degree or another by Enlightenment views that individual liberty should be elevated while government authority should be restricted; therefore, the First Amendment opens with "*Congress* shall make *no* law . . ." (italics added for emphasis). That part seems clear enough, but "respecting an establishment of religion" and "prohibiting the free exercise thereof" are the clauses subject to controversy and litigation.

Indeed, the **establishment clause** and the **free exercise clause** have been central to most religion-connected education cases to come before the U.S. Supreme Court. Another part of the Constitution involved in religion and education is Section 1 of the Fourteenth Amendment, which brought state governments under the Constitution: "No *state* shall make or enforce any law which shall abridge the privileges or immunities of citizens of the United States; nor shall any *state* deprive any person of life, liberty, or property, without due process of law; nor deny to any person within its jurisdiction the equal protection of the laws." (Italics added for emphasis). In effect, the Fourteenth Amendment requires that *state* governments also shall make no law respecting an establishment of religion or prohibiting its free exercise. Since public schools are creations of state governments, then under the Fourteenth Amendment they, too, must conform. Of course, much depends on how constitutional requirements are defined and interpreted by the courts, especially the U.S. Supreme Court. In most disputes to come before the Supreme Court concerning a religion-connected education issue, both the First and the Fourteenth amendments might be central points of law.

Public schools, religion, and the courts

After the initial controversies over the role of religion in the public common schools in the nineteenth century, the schools experienced an uneasy peace the remainder of that century, but as the twentieth century unfolded the tensions resurfaced and—fortunately—most of them hit the courtrooms rather than the streets.

Although there were numerous lower court decisions, some of the most significant cases made their way to the U.S. Supreme Court. That body's decisions sometimes stir strong feelings among portions of the population, stimulating actions intended to change the court's directions. The most compelling method is by constitutional amendment, but that is complicated and time consuming. A proposed amendment must first achieve a two-thirds majority in Congress and then be ratified by three-fourths of the 50 state legislatures before it becomes part of the Constitution. The framers designed the amendment process to be slow to avoid constitutional changes forced by turbulent passions of the moment. Perhaps the quickest way to change court directions is through presidential appointment of new Supreme Court justices when opportunities arise, although appointees sometimes do not maintain the ideological expectations of their appointers. All new appointments affect the court in various ways, and some of them have helped establish important new directions in American jurisprudence.

Early cases

Despite the general trends of the more recent religion-based education cases, those in the early twentieth century only tangentially touched religion and were decided on Fourteenth Amendment rights to liberty and property, not First Amendment religious freedoms; nonetheless, they set numerous precedents affecting many subsequent religion and education cases. Three of the most significant rulings are *Meyer v. Nebraska* (1923), *Pierce v. Society of Sisters* (1925), and *Cochran v. Louisiana* (1930).

First, *Meyer v. Nebraska* (1923) concerned a 1919 Nebraska law prohibiting the teaching of languages other than English to children up through the eighth grade. Meyer, a teacher in a private Lutheran school, was convicted of teaching German to a fifth grader during free time. (Recall that the United States entered World War I against Germany, 1917–18, which created lingering anti-German feelings). The Supreme Court ruled that the Nebraska law violated the Fourteenth Amendment right to liberty, including Meyer's right to teach and parents' rights to hire instruction for their children.[44]

The second case, *Pierce v. Society of Sisters* (1925), involved a 1922 Oregon law requiring all children ages eight to 16 to attend public schools. The Supreme Court held that a state can compel school attendance, but not exclusively in public schools; cannot ignore the liberty of parents and guardians to oversee their children's education, including sending them to private schools; and cannot destroy private schools as businesses or properties by imposing unconstitutional attendance restrictions.[45]

The third case of significance was *Cochran v. Louisiana* (1930), arising from a 1928 Louisiana law requiring the state to purchase textbooks for loan to all Louisiana children to use in schools. Cochran claimed that Louisiana used tax monies to purchase textbooks that could be loaned to children attending private parochial schools, which resulted in public aid being funnelled to private institutions. However, the Supreme Court held that Louisiana loaned the books to all children for school-related uses, without specifying private, parochial, or public schools; therefore, the court concluded, the books served a public purpose of benefiting the child, not the institutions.[46]

In sum, *Meyer* and *Pierce* both clarified and limited state authority over teacher occupational rights, parental oversight rights, and private school property rights. *Cochran* introduced a new element of interpretation to education law, sometimes called the **child benefit theory**, which proved to be a factor in several subsequent cases.

For Further Reflection: Consider both sides in *Cochran v. Louisiana*. Put the lawsuit in its historical context, remembering that it occurred in 1930, during the Great Depression, and considering how the pertinent issues would have been framed then. How might they be different today, and what difference, if any, should it make in considering "child benefit" then and now?

The free exercise clause

Fewer education cases have come before the Supreme Court on free exercise than on establishment grounds; nevertheless, the free exercise cases involved important rulings. In 1940, the Gobitis family brought suit against the school board in Minersville, Pennsylvania, for requiring the flag salute (or Pledge of Allegiance) to instill patriotism. The board argued that the pledge was a civil, not a religious, requirement. The Gobitis family, who were Jehovah's Witnesses, claimed the requirement forced them to worship a graven image in violation of their free exercise of religion beliefs. In *Minersville School District v. Gobitis* (1940), the Supreme Court held that if the Minersville school board decided the exercise was important for learning patriotism, it could require it. However, just three years later the court reversed itself in *West Virginia State Board of Education v. Barnette* (1943). The West Virginia state board of education required the flag salute and took action against children and parents who refused. The court ruled that the First Amendment guaranteed religious freedom, and the state could not deprive individual citizens of this right. While the state could protect what it deemed to be the general welfare, it must do so within the bounds of permissible constitutional limits.[47] There were some reasons for *Barnette's* reversal of *Gobitis*, including the fact that some court members felt the *Gobitis* decision went too far. Also, membership on the court had changed slightly, thereby enabling a different outcome. Parenthetically, it is also worth noting that the *Barnette* decision was made in 1943, in the middle of World War II, at a time when patriotic feelings were running high, yet little controversy resulted from the decision.

It was 30 years before the court decided another education-related, free exercise case, this time in *Wisconsin v. Yoder* (1972). The state of Wisconsin had a compulsory education law requiring attendance beyond the eighth grade, which conflicted with the Yoder family's Amish views that public high schools promoted values undermining Amish religious and communal life. Upon appeal, the Supreme Court ruled in Yoder's favor, holding that the state had the right to compel school attendance to uphold the well- being of the whole community, but the right to compel attendance could not take precedence over the First Amendment right of free exercise.[48] Thus, in both *Barnette* and *Yoder*, the First Amendment right of free exercise of religion was deemed more binding than a state's power to conduct public education.

In some cases, the First Amendment's establishment and free exercise clauses are intermingled. For example, *Lee v. Weisman* (1992) was a suit brought by Daniel Weisman on behalf of his daughter, Deborah, over a prayer offered by a rabbi at official graduation ceremonies at her public middle school in Providence, Rhode Island. Weisman claimed this was government involvement in a religious establishment. In its majority decision, the court recognized that there are times when religious values, practices, or persons might interact with public schools and students, but when First Amendment freedoms are involved, government may neither persuade nor compel anyone to participate: "No holding by this Court suggests that a school can persuade or compel a student to participate in a religious exercise. That is being done here, and it is forbidden by the Establishment Clause."[49] In this instance, the majority recognized a free exercise element, but found the school's official involvement in planning the ceremony and its religious elements to more directly violate the establishment clause.

The establishment clause

Although the establishment clause did not come to the forefront until the mid-twentieth century, one can see possibilities for it in earlier cases, particularly *Cochran* and its child benefit ruling. The establishment clause proved central in virtually every religion-based "benefit" case involving education thereafter.

The first major education-related establishment clause case was *Everson v. Board of Education of Ewing* (1947). New Jersey authorized local school districts to provide transportation for schoolchildren by reimbursing parents for the cost, including parents of children attending private and parochial schools. Everson filed suit on both First and Fourteenth Amendment grounds that New Jersey was using tax monies to support transportation to Catholic parochial schools, a form of government aid to an establishment of religion. The Supreme Court ruled that the transportation aid in *Everson* benefited the child, not the school. Thus, child benefit was upheld in *Everson*, but dissent was strong, with the court split 5 to 4.[50]

Two additional cases soon followed: *McCollum v. Board of Education* (1948) and *Zorach v. Clauson* (1952). *McCollum* involved a Champaign, Illinois, practice of allowing religion classes in public school for grades four through nine, conducted by instructors provided by local churches or religious institutions. Admission was by written parental permission, participating children attended classes on their respective faiths, and those opting not to attend were assigned to study halls. This approach was called **released time**. McCollum claimed it violated the First and Fourteenth amendments because it used tax-supported public school facilities to support establishments of religion. The Supreme Court agreed and held that in this case church and state were not being kept separate, and the practice aided the establishment of religion.[51]

In *Zorach v. Clauson* (1952), however, the court approved released time under a different set of circumstances. This case involved a New York program in which children were released from school to attend religious classes off campus. Attendance was voluntary, parental permission was required, and local religious groups provided the instruction at nearby off-campus locations. Participating students had to register, local providers had to report attendance figures, and those not attending had to remain at school engaged in their studies. The Supreme Court found this type of released time permissible because it used no public school facilities and violated neither the establishment nor the free exercise clauses.[52] This type of released time remains legal and continues to be used in some local school systems today.

Suggested Activity: Released time programs that follow the requirements in *Zorach* are legal in the United States. Numerous organizations exist to support and enhance released time programs. Do an internet search to see how programs are described, explained, and conducted. Some suggested sites are:

- "Released Time Bible Education," School Ministries, Inc., at http://www.released-time.org/sitert/besthtml/best_about.htm (accessed on August 16, 2010).
- "Religion in the Public Schools: Released Time Programs," AntiDefamation League, at http://www.adl.org/religion_ps_2004/timeprograms.asp (accessed on August 16, 2010).
- "Released Time Education," Fellowship of Christian Released Time Ministries, at http://www.rtce.org/ (accessed on August 16, 2010).
- James D. McWilliams, "Overview: Released Time," The First Amendment Center, at http://www.firstamendmentcenter.org/rel_liberty/publicschools/topic.aspx?topic=released_time (accessed on August 16, 2010).

School prayer, bible reading, and the neutrality doctrine

One of the most controversial Supreme Court decisions was rendered in the so-called prayer ban case of *Engel v. Vitale* 370 US 421 (1962). The New York Board of Regents composed a "nondenominational" prayer to be used in the schools. The wording was as follows: "Almighty God, we acknowledge our dependence upon thee, and we beg thy blessings upon us, our parents, our teachers, and our country." Some parents challenged the prayer as contrary to their beliefs and an unconstitutional involvement of state government in an establishment of religion. The Supreme Court found New York in violation of the First and Fourteenth amendments because the Regents—a state government body—prescribed the prayer for New York's public schools, and this breached the separation of church and state. Although the prayer was voluntary, the "constitutional prohibition against laws respecting an establishment of religion" meant that "it is no part of the business of government to compose official prayers for any group of the American people to recite as a part of a religious program carried on by government."[53] The court's judgment was a 6 to 1 decision (two justices did not participate).

The *Engle* decision raised a storm of public protest, including agitations to get a school prayer amendment added to the Constitution. Condemnations poured in on those who brought the suit and the court's justices who joined in the majority decision. There were calls for the impeachment of certain justices and a free-flowing use of epithets hurled at the court and those bringing suit, accusing them of being agnostics, atheists, and communists (and these were among the tamer expressions). Despite the furor, no groundswell of public support arose to push an amendment to successful conclusion. Perhaps most people wanted neither a prayer amendment in the Constitution nor state-required religious exercises in the public schools, and this included many religious believers. Still, advocates for a prayer amendment continued to persist.[54]

Fears of lurking forces bent on eradicating religion in the schools were stoked by another Supreme Court decision the following year, *School District of Abington Township v. Schempp* 374 US 203 (1963). The facts of this case included a 1959 Pennsylvania law that required daily readings of at least ten Bible verses without comment, reciting the Lord's Prayer, and saluting the flag in every public school during opening exercises. At Abington Senior High School, the exercise was broadcast into every homeroom over the intercom system, and students could be excused from the exercise with written parental permission. Suit was brought by the Schempps, who as Unitarians objected on grounds of religious freedom. In an 8-1 decision, the Supreme Court ruled that the exercise, even if voluntary, was government support of a religious establishment. In an attempt to clarify First and Fourteenth Amendment religious freedom requirements for both federal and state governments, the court declared that government must be neutral—it must neither advance nor prohibit religion. However, in enunciating this **neutrality principle**, the court also clearly recognized a place in school curriculum for the study of comparative religion and the history of religion and also the study of the Bible for its literary and historical merits.[55]

Despite the fury against the two decisions, *Engle* and *Schempp* did not ban all prayer and Bible reading from the public schools; instead, they banned *government*-composed prayers and *government*-required Bible readings. The practical effects of both *Engle* and *Schempp* might have dampened legitimate school instruction about religion, but in *Schempp* the court clearly approved the study of religion's historical significance and the literary merits of scriptures. Nevertheless, opponents of the *Engle* and *Schempp* decisions stepped up their efforts pushing constitutional amendments, particularly concerning prayer.[56]

Excessive entanglement

Where the line should be drawn between child benefit and establishment of religion (or between church and state in its broader application) continued to be a problem. The child benefit theory initiated by *Cochran,* allowing the state to loan textbooks to all children, was broadened in *Everson* to include transportation costs. Broadening continued in *Board of Education v. Allen* (1968), which concerned a New York State law requiring school districts to lend textbooks free of charge to all students grades seven through 12, regardless of the school attended. The Supreme Court upheld the practice under the child benefit doctrine, if the books were used for secular purposes.[57]

In *Lemon v. Kurtzman* (1971), however, the court tightened parameters around what was permissible. This case involved the purchase by both Rhode Island and Pennsylvania of the "secular services" of parochial instructors to teach secular subjects in the public schools as long as they used materials approved by the public schools. The court set up a three-part test drawn from previous case history: Any law respecting an establishment of religion must have a secular purpose, neither advance nor inhibit religion, and avoid excessive government entanglement with religion. The court did not question the value of religious schools to society; rather, it questioned how state aid to such schools squared with the Constitution's establishment and free exercise requirements. The court concluded that the practices in Pennsylvanian and Rhode Island involved too much government supervision (bookkeeping and other kinds of oversight); hence, it was **excessive entanglement** of government and religion.[58] Almost any government aid affecting the education of children could potentially be justified as a benefit, but *Lemon's* "excessive entanglement" ruling restricted how far such arguments could be pushed.

Several cases followed involving the excessive entanglement doctrine. For example, in 1973 there was another New York case concerning state financial aid to nonpublic schools for maintenance and repairs of schools with a high percentage of low-income students, including tuition reimbursement for low-income parents with children in those schools. In 1975, a Pennsylvania case involved a state-approved program in which public schools shared with parochial schools such things as counseling services and audio-visual equipment and materials. Similarly, a 1977 Ohio case concerned state funds for nonpublic students for materials, equipment, and transportation. In all three cases, the Supreme Court found excessive entanglement.[59] It would appear that the excessive entanglement doctrine was well established; however, from the late 1970s through the turn of the century, conservative political outlooks gained ground in both the presidency and Congress.

Politics, religion, education, and the Supreme Court

The election of Ronald Reagan as president in 1980 signaled a rightward swing in American politics, and the support sought by Reagan from conservative religious organizations was one of the factors. Their political muscle now apparent, these organizations went by such descriptors as the Moral Majority, fundamentalists, and evangelical conservatives that, for present purposes, shall simply be called the **religious right**. One of their particular targets was what they called **secular humanism**, which they claimed had taken over the public schools and was indoctrinating students into liberalism, evolution, socialism, and sexual permissiveness. In their view, atheistic, anti-Christian secular humanism had even spread its influence to the U.S. Supreme Court, as witnessed by its bans on prayer, Bible reading, and other aspects of religion in the public schools. They called for amending the Constitution to allow religious observance in the schools (particularly prayer), and they demanded tax support of private and parochial schools through school vouchers. Some advocates even charged that secular humanism itself was a religion, one that not only defied Christian values and parental authority but also the U.S. Constitution in ways that bordered on treason.[60]

For further reflection: Compare and contrast statements on such sites as "Contender Ministries" at http://www.contenderministries.org/discrepancies/discrepancies. php (accessed on August 16, 2010), with those on "The American Humanist Association," at http://www.americanhumanist.org/about/briefintro.php (accessed on August 16, 2010).

In your opinion, do these views represent majority or minority views in the United States, and why or why not?

Suggested Activity: Perform an internet search to sample the opinion swirling around religion and education. Some suggested sites showing the opposing positions are given below:[a]

Humanist Sites:

Council for Secular Humanism http://www.secularhumanism.org/
American Humanist Association http://www.americanhumanist.org/index.html

Religious Right Sites:

Moral Majority Coalition http://www.moralmajority.us/
Christian Coalition of America http://www.cc.org/

[a]All sites accessible as of August 16, 2010.

While the rhetoric and objectives of the religious right generated both support and opposition, most political observers recognized the right's increased political sophistication. As president, Ronald Reagan supported three different congressional resolutions that attempted to amend the Constitution to allow school prayer (two in 1981 and another in 1984). All three resolutions fell short of the Constitution's required two-thirds majority for Congress to forward a proposed amendment to state legislatures for ratification or rejection. However, Presidents Reagan, George H. W. Bush (his immediate successor), and George W. Bush actually influenced Supreme Court decisions through another constitutional provision: Article II gives the president the power "by and with the Advice and Consent of the Senate" to appoint "Judges of the Supreme Court."[61]

During their 12 years in office, Presidents Reagan and George H. W. Bush, both Republicans, replaced three of the nine justices on the Supreme Court.

Table 8.1 Membership of the U.S. Supreme Court by Year of Oath, September 1, 2010

Name of justice	Appointed by (Party)	Birth date	Seated
Antonin Scalia	Reagan (R)	03/11/36	1986
Anthony M. Kennedy	Reagan (R)	07/23/36	1988
Clarence Thomas	Bush[a] (R)	06/23/48	1991
Ruth Bader Ginsberg	Clinton (D)	03/15/33	1993
Steven G. Breyer	Clinton (D)	08/15/38	1994
John G. Roberts, Jr.[c]	Bush[b] (R)	01/27/55	2005
Samuel A. Alito, Jr.	Bush[b] (R)	04/01/50	2006
Sonia M. Sotomayor	Obama (D)	06/25/54	2009
Elena Kagan	Obama (D)	04/28/60	2010

Notes:
[a]President George H.W. Bush.
[b]President George W. Bush.
[c]Chief Justice.

Source: "Members of the Supreme Court of the United States," at http://www.supremecourt.gov/about/members.aspx (accessed on August 16, 2010).

President William J. Clinton, a Democrat, appointed two; President George W. Bush, a Republican, appointed two (one of them the current chief justice); and President Barack Obama, a Democrat, appointed two. As shown in Table 8.1, by 2010 Republican presidents had appointed five and Democratic presidents four of the nine current sitting justices.[62]

Sometimes the power of appointment can be significant in the long-term interpretational directions of Supreme Court decisions. The *Barnette* decision is one example where membership change probably affected the court's reversal of its own recent decision concerning a state's right to compel flag salutes, but such reversals are rare in comparison to the influence exerted on the court by precedents established in prior cases. Exactly what the changes in court membership would mean in the twenty-first century was by no means clear at the time.

As the second decade of the twenty-first century began, religion retained important societal influence. While it no longer exercised the direct power and control it once held in medieval Europe or colonial America, it continued to have an impact, particularly on public education.

Contemporary conditions and reform

Because the United States is a diverse nation, many different religions are represented among its people. Such diversity is reflected in the nation's institutions, among them the schools. In order to protect the interests of all, including religious minorities and those who do not subscribe to any religion, schools are enjoined from sponsoring or officially endorsing a religion. Some groups are of the opinion that these attempts to protect minorities are discriminatory against people with different beliefs. Banning prayer, according to them, is but one example of secularism going too far and denying many believers their right of religious expression. The counterargument is that school- sponsored prayer and other religious expressions in schools violate the Constitution's provisions for religious freedom. It has been argued that such officially approved practices as prayer unduly entangle government and religion, and rather than helping religion, these entanglements could just as well wind up with government control of religion. Thus, the separation of church and state protects religion as much as (if not more than) it protects government.

The main issues in contention around the role of religion in schools involve school prayer, released time for religious activities, school access by religious groups, flag salutes, religion in the public school curriculum, and tax support of denominational schools.[63] One can add others as well, such as the display of religious symbols, the treatment of religious holidays, the distribution of religious literature, and the wearing of religious attire in schools. It could be argued that religion has been the subject of many of the most rancorous disputes embroiling public education.

Prayer in school

Legally speaking, school-sponsored prayer violates the Constitution (*Engel v. Vitale*), but individual students can exercise their right to pray or discuss religious beliefs at appropriate times and places and under conditions that do not affect ordinary school activities and operations. At times, it is not easy to discern whether an activity is religious in nature. For example, controversy surrounds the issue of a **moment of silence**, which is permissible in some states. Questions also surround whether and under what conditions student-led prayers or other related activities can be unofficial parts of graduation exercises, athletic events, and other school-sponsored activities.[64]

In *Santa Fe Independent School District v. Doe* (2000), the U.S. Supreme Court found that certain kinds of school-approved student-led invocations before football games violated the establishment clause. Suit was filed by some Mormon and Catholic students and their mothers (the Does in the case name), who claimed that the Santa Fe Independent School District was involved in "promoting attendance at a Baptist revival meeting, encouraging membership in religious clubs, chastising children who held minority religious beliefs, and distributing Gideon Bibles on school premises," as well as promoting "overtly Christian prayers over the public address system at home football games." The latter complaint, on which the case eventually hinged, involved a school district policy that encouraged prayers offered by an elected "student council chaplain" over the public address system before every scheduled varsity football game at Santa Fe High School. The district claimed the exercise was private student speech, not public speech. Even as the case was being tried in the lower courts, however, the district changed its pregame policy by altering the student election process and dropping the word *prayer* and substituting the words *messages, statements,* and *invocations* in its policy. When the case reached the Supreme Court, it held that the district's policy alterations did not change the fact that "These invocations are authorized by a government policy and take place on government property at government-sponsored school-related events." Moreover, the school district's actions of changing official student elections and changing the wording in its policy only served to reveal the level of "excessive entanglement." The court concluded that the district's policy violated the First Amendment's establishment clause, because the policy "establishes an improper majoritarian election on religion, and unquestionably has the purpose and creates the perception of encouraging the delivery of prayer at a series of important school events."[65]

Religion in the curriculum

Because the curriculum is at the heart of what goes on in school, it can be highly contested terrain on any number of issues. What is included in the curriculum and what is not, whether and how a certain subject or topic is taught, what values are openly espoused or endorsed through obvious or subtle means, what textbooks and other materials are used—all significantly define the academic part of schooling. It is not surprising, then, that controversies about the role of religion in the curriculum continue to be passionately waged.

Those on the religious right tend to be vigorous in voicing their views. They oppose curriculum content about such things as drug education, global education, socialism, the theory of evolution, environmentalism, and disarmament. While the religious right has raised important issues and generated considerable political support, their rhetoric is often opposed for being unnecessarily reactionary and divisive. At the same time, the religious right's distrust of science and modern knowledge finds sympathy among other elements of society that, while not devoutly religious, are concerned about the moral structure of society and skeptical of many scientific claims.[66]

> WEB: Additional Information 8.3.:
> CITIZENS FOR EXCELLENCE IN EDUCATION and
> PEOPLE FOR THE AMERICAN WAY

While some argue for the need for religion in the curriculum, others question religion itself. For example, Sam Harris argues that religious faith is "the one species of human ignorance" that will not recognize even "the *possibility* of correction" because it is generally sheltered from criticism. At best, faith makes rational thought impossible and, at worst, it serves as a never-ending source of violence. Under religion's influence, people have sacrificed happiness, compassion, and justice in this world for a fantasy world in the beyond. Even education does not guarantee rationality, because many educated people choose to "cling to the blood-soaked heirloom of a previous age." The solution to this problem not only involves society coming to grips with extremist minorities but also finding approaches to ethics and spirituality that do not depend on religious faith, which needs to be replaced by the power of reason.[67]

Such a view might qualify for what has been called an "antireligious diatribe." Robert Nash maintains that, given the great power of religion in people's lives, students need opportunities to analyze the role of faith (or its absence) in their own lives as well as in society. There are those who refuse to acknowledge anything positive about religion and argue that the existence of God is impossible to prove scientifically, but millions of people choose to live as though God exists and view their lives and the lives of others around them as improved by such faith. Furthermore, complex human societies cannot be adequately understood without also considering religion's role, including both the good and the bad it might produce.[68]

Religion as a school study

The study of world religions is more prevalent today than in the past, but schools rarely promote in-depth analysis by students concerning religion's influence on the cultural, political, and moral fabric of societies. For example, many textbooks try not to offend readers, so the content often remains shallow as a result. Most texts provide insufficient depth concerning how religions sometime promote peace, sometimes war. Textbooks present past religions through contemporary analytical lenses, which may be unavoidable, but they also need to help readers understand the various contexts in which religion influenced people's experiences. In short, religion continues to impact people's lives and moral compasses, and it needs to be understood and not litigated completely out of the curriculum.[69]

Other observers maintain that the current heated discussion over the role of religion in education is "not about the books." Instead, it is a about basic beliefs and values that go beyond textbook debates to include questions of the good and the bad in society and its institutions. Considering how religion is central in many people's moral convictions and worldviews, it is not surprising that debates over religion in the schools tend to become oppositional, with one side called fundamentalists and the other secular humanists. Fruitful exchange and compromise become difficult. Consider, for example, the following scenario: Parents are concerned about a story in a textbook where a person steals an item and goes unpunished; furthermore, the students are asked to think about how stealing might be defensible in certain situations. Some parents might reach the conclusion that the story and class analysis are nothing but an effort to promote stealing. Judgment is rushed, and the potential value of a lesson is quickly dismissed by either-or thinking. The end result could well silence thoughtful dialogue. Furthermore, such polarization could undermine the need for the rational kinds of discussion the public ought to have about curriculum content and parental roles in its determination.[70]

Suggested Activity: In a group discussion, compare your schooling experience with those of others. Did religious content play a role? If so, in what ways? Given the reflections above, would you like to see those practices changed?

A philosophical viewpoint

Education philosopher Nel Noddings has long been concerned about the lack of discussion about spiritual and moral/ethical concerns in the schools. Students suffer when public schools are obsessively careful to avoid offending school patrons and citizens (and to avoid expensive lawsuits) over religious and moral issues, focusing instead on safe and noncontroversial parts of the curriculum. According to Noddings, it is not religious instruction per se that is needed, but stimulating and relevant conversations in classrooms about many issues. What is important is the tone of the conversation, with adults striving to be respectful of one another and of child participants. (In some ways, a respectful conversation is more important than the topic, argument, or conclusion). Not only do respectful interchanges help teach important skills needed for rational public discussions conducted with trust and confidence, they are almost always the best vehicles to achieve wise public policies.

> **For Further Reflection:** Think about examples of moral issues that can be used as both a basis for discussion of moral education as well as a launching pad into a unit in math, English, social studies, science, or any other discipline.

There may be reluctance for teachers to engage students in class conversation about moral issues for fear that it might lead to indoctrination of students or waste precious instructional time. Noddings finds the distrust of teachers to be unwarranted and maintains that such distrust is only one indication of the moral malaise our society experiences today. This condition interferes with the development of character in young people by limiting their opportunities to grow in moral understanding. Teachers, however, are in a unique position to spark moral discussion and thoughtful reflection while linking these activities to academic studies. If societal fears and teacher restrictions prevent moral and academic instruction to take place effectively, then teachers need to engage students in important moral conversations, many of which arise out of the academic curriculum itself (such as issues of peace, war, and justice encountered in history or the moral quandaries of characters portrayed in good literature). If teachers take such steps, new academic goals will likely emerge.[71]

> **Suggested Activity:** Ask a teacher to what extent engagement in conversations about moral issues is both possible and desirable in public schools. What is the reality teachers face in this respect? Are approaches such as character education truly effective? In your opinion, what reform ideas (such as Noddings's) might improve the situation?

Not only are moral conversations needed to facilitate student growth, but teachers should model the kinds of ethical behaviors that help create learning environments that allow people to "be good." Here the emphasis is on establishing conditions that support moral life. For example, novelist George Orwell captured some of his educational experiences in his description of school conditions where it was "not *possible* for me to be good" and in which he was "more wicked than

I had imagined."[72] The point is simple but powerful: People are fundamentally shaped by their conditions in life, and simply having moral convictions does not always translate into virtuous social behavior in an unjust environment. One merely has to think about oppressive institutions and conditions (such as abusive families, concentration camps, warfare, and famine) to understand how conditions can bring out the worst in people (of course they sometimes also produce acts of moral courage). Social institutions in themselves are not evil, and most of them are intended to meet human needs and improve life. The specifics of a given culture, its social, economic, and political environments and the people who live in them, all have a hand in shaping its institutions, be they potential sources of good (such as schools and hospitals) or moral monstrosities (such as concentration camps). The point is it takes conscious, deliberate efforts to make schools good places for learning, not only academically but morally too. There may be obstacles in the institutional structure of a school (such as overt authoritarianism) that permeate its environment and make it difficult for students to "be good." It is the task of society, including education professionals, to change poor conditions to ensure that schools are good environments to promote the growth of students, academically and morally.

Suggested Activity:

1. Recall your K–12 school days. Make two lists of institutional characteristics you believe both helped and hindered your moral development. What was it about school that helped you to be honest and empathetic? What might have tempted you to cut corners, cheat, bully others or engage in other bad behaviors? Make sure you list only institutional characteristics (such as the culture, policies, and structural arrangements), not singular occurrences or personal idiosyncrasies (such as "the one bad teacher.") An example: Does school emphasis on grades and testing encourage cheating?

2. Compare, contrast, and discuss the lists with your classmates. Analyze what changes in the institutional character of schools would have been necessary in order to minimize the barriers to and maximize the enablers of morally good behavior.

3. Consider what impact reforms have had since you graduated from high school. Have they gone in the right direction? Have they helped bring out the best in students, or is the reverse true? Justify your position.

Religious expression and public schools

Courts have consistently found that officially sponsored religious displays in schools violate the establishment clause of the Constitution and are therefore not permissible. For example, neither the display of the Ten Commandments nor depictions of religious figures are lawful in public schools. Likewise, public schools are prohibited from sponsoring religious exercises. While teachers may teach about religious holidays, holiday programs in public schools are supposed to serve educational aims, not religious ones. They must also not make students feel excluded due to their religious affiliations or lack thereof. Holiday programs in December, for example, may contain religious themes as long as they do not dominate and as long as they promote cultural understandings rather than sectarian religious beliefs. While holiday displays are permitted to make use of religious symbols, they have to be temporary, diverse, and not used to force student participation in religious activities. Students have the right to be excused from discussions and activities related to holidays with religious origins (such as Halloween) if those observances violate their religious convictions.[73]

For Further Reflection: One of the central missions of public schools is to provide a broad education and to expose students to knowledge and insights they may not encounter in their families and communities. To what extent is this mission undermined when students are excused even from academic discussions about religious traditions? Do parental rights to religious self-determination and the need for a broad education ever come into conflict?

Individual expressions of religious beliefs in school may create situations that bring the establishment, free exercise, and free speech clauses of the Constitution into conflict. Students, for example, have the right to free speech, but student speech may be curtailed if it is seen as harmful (hate speech) or if it unnecessarily disrupts teaching and learning.

Greater restrictions apply to freedom of speech for teachers than for students because, as paid professionals employed by the local board of education, teachers are considered a part of government; therefore, what teachers say and do as teachers must always be lawful, age appropriate, directly connected to the approved curriculum, and within the educator's area of expertise. In regard to specifically religious matters, public schools must ensure that they do not sponsor religious beliefs, even when it curtails the free speech of teachers. For example, in *Peloza v. Capistrano Unified School District* (1994), John E. Peloza was a high school biology teacher who brought action against the Capistrano Unified School District, challenging its requirement that he teach evolution and its order barring him from discussing his religious beliefs with students. The district court dismissed the claims as frivolous and awarded attorney fees to the school district. On appeal, the ninth circuit court of appeals rejected Peloza's claim that the district requirement for him to teach evolution violated the establishment clause. The circuit court observed that evolution was not a religion but simply a scientific theory that higher life forms evolved from lower ones. Likewise, the district was simply upholding the establishment clause when it directed Peloza not to discuss his religious beliefs with students during the school day; however, the circuit court found that Peloza's appeal was not entirely frivolous since free speech is such an important right, and it overturned the lower court's award of attorney fees to the school district.[74]

Acting as private citizens, teachers are as free to engage in religious activities and express their personal views as any other citizen, but when acting as professional educators employed by public schools, certain ethical obligations are imposed on teachers to obey the laws and to teach the curriculum as their contract requires. In other words, the permissible boundaries of freedom may differ for teachers when acting in their professional capacities than in their private personal capacities.

Released time for religious activities

Since *Zorach v. Clauson* (1952), released time programs that allow public school students to leave school grounds in order to attend properly designated religious education locations are permissible. Typically, such activities take place at nearby churches or other off-campus sites and are upheld by the courts as long as they take place under appropriate conditions that protect the safety and well-being of the students. Released time programs remain controversial, however. Proponents argue that they are reasonable accommodation of their needs, while opponents argue that they discriminate against non -participating students, who may spend the time in study halls.[75]

For Further Reflection: Discuss the concept of released time in public schools for religious purposes. Do you see arguments for and against this practice?

Student voices

While much has been written about how both scholars and the courts see the role of religion in schools, far less is known about student opinion on the issue. Annette Hemmings studied the "coming of age" of students at three high schools that differed in racial makeup, class background, and achievement. Although public schools are legally bound by First Amendment restriction, she found religion played an important role in the lives of many students: They were sorting out their religious identities, holding on to or breaking away from various views and generally wrestling with questions of morality and spirituality. Some were self-proclaimed **true believers** and practitioners of their beliefs, and others saw religion as an anchor for their social lives or connection to family heritage. One student turned away from religion altogether after the death of a loved one, while another who described himself as agnostic was highly critical of what he perceived to be church hypocrisy and money-mindedness. Hemings concluded that student ways of thinking about religion were diverse and variable, but they still exhibited levels of preoccupation over spiritual concerns that should not be ignored.[76]

Some students joined religious groups while others were victimized by religious dogmas, such as a homosexual student rejected by his parents because his sexual orientation violated their religious beliefs. Similarly, some students viewed their Catholic faith as overly controlling, while others welcomed church doctrines as sources of direction. Some students engaged in new age religious movements, some adopted Eastern beliefs such as Hinduism or Buddhism; still others found meaning in medieval astrology or American Indian pantheism. One student was fascinated by "paranormal experiences" in her family and sought to communicate with the dead. Some Christian students disliked new age beliefs, while at least one student perceived the Christian God as the "horned devil" when compared with Taoism and Confucianism. Other groups included skinheads who wore Christian crucifixes and Nazi swastikas and "goth" students who wore black clothing, lipstick, and eye shadow in combination with images of the Virgin Mary.[77]

In their struggles with **religious identity formation**, adolescents grappled with the religious customs (or lack thereof) in their own homes. They sometimes resisted family religious rituals as well as the moral codes and expectations of their parents and church. Some students did not object to religious restrictions, such as an immigrant student who readily obeyed the rules of her Islamic family and was willing for her parents to arrange a marriage for her. She also believed that Americans misunderstood the Muslim tradition of wearing veils, thinking it a mistreatment of women; instead, she believed veils protected Muslim women from being seen as sex objects, although she herself did not wear one, possibly because she was reassessing her beliefs or did not want appear as rejecting American customs. These examples indicate how complicated religious beliefs can be for adolescents.[78]

Despite these adolescent experiences with religious beliefs and symbols, there seemed to be a "spiritual void" in school. Not only was religion an instructional taboo, but teachers shied away from meaningful discussions involving morality, even if the school itself adhered to a formal philosophy subscribing to values of community and care. School authorities seemed less concerned with forming morally sound citizens than controlling student behavior, rule violations, and avoiding lawsuits, while students were left with few adult-directed alternatives. Under such circumstances, students might conclude that school and society have no worthy moral values to transmit, leaving them to deal with issues of meaning and identity on their own.[79]

> **For Further Reflection:** Schools reflect the religious diversity that exists in society at large. What are some implications for teachers and the ways schools operate?

Some observers see a need to reconsider the place of religion in the academic curriculum of schools. One way or another, religion continues to affect individuals, institutions, and societies, and it seems reasonable to suggest that school curricula include religion topics in appropriate academic studies, with this caveat: The purpose must not be indoctrination and conversion but a better understanding of people, cultures, and the world we all inhabit.

Public funds and religious schools

Most private schools in the United States are affiliated with religion (Catholic, Protestant, Judaic, and Islamic). Often perceiving themselves to be strapped for funds, some religious bodies seek public funding for their operation, activities that invite debates and lawsuits over the separation of church and state. Despite a fairly long legal tradition of separation of church and state, initiatives to divert public resources to private schools have recently been put on the political front burner once again, just as the schools are grappling with a new population growth of diverse origins and are hampered by a lack of adequate funding to meet pressing educational needs. Space permits only brief treatment here, but two recent decisions stand out, *Mitchell v. Helms* 530 U.S. 793 (2000) and *Zelman v. Simmons-Harris* 536 U.S. 639 (2002).

Mitchell v. Helms

It might be said that the majority decision reached in *Mitchell v. Helms* (2000) was an attempt to make a decisive change on public funding of private religious schools, although the decision was split six to three. This case involved federal legislation that allowed educational materials and equipment to be loaned to both public and private schools, provided the items were neutral and nonideological.

Jefferson Parish in Louisiana used approximately 30 percent of its allocation on items for church-affiliated private schools. A group of taxpayers sued on grounds of an advancement of religion in violation of the establishment clause. The court ruled that the law was not an establishment violation and that Jefferson Parish need not exclude religious schools from the program. Moreover, if certain previous court decisions conflicted with their conclusion, the majority opinion stated, "we overrule them." The minority opinion argued that the majority reached "an erroneous result" but had not staged the "doctrinal coup" they intended.[80] Perhaps not, but the majority decision challenged a substantial history of legal precedents, and court membership would undergo some dramatic changes after the *Mitchell* decision of 2000 (see Table 8.1).

Zelman v. Simmons-Harris

Doctrinal direction was joined again in the case of *Zelman v. Simmons-Harris* (2002), this time in a five-to-four split decision. In 1995, a federal district court in Ohio declared the Cleveland public schools in crisis and placed them under state control. Ohio enacted the Pilot Project Scholarship Program that provided tuition vouchers to poor families with children in any Ohio school district placed under state control by federal court order. (Interestingly, Cleveland was the only district in that category.) The act approved state-funded vouchers for qualifying low-income families seeking better educational opportunities for their children than provided by Cleveland public schools. Parents could choose from the following: qualifying private schools, religious or nonreligious; non-traditional public magnet schools and state-financed public charter schools in Cleveland; and participating public schools located in adjacent school districts. Families with incomes below 200 percent of the poverty line were given priority, and eligible families could receive up to 90 percent of a private school's tuition (not to exceed $2,250 per child, with any private school fees not to exceed $250 per child). By the 1999–2000 school year, 56 private schools participated, of which 46 (or 82 percent) were religious schools. Of the 3,700 students who participated, 96 percent were enrolled in religious schools.[81]

Some Cleveland citizens brought suit against the Pilot Project Scholarship Program for violating the establishment clause, claiming it provided unrestricted state funds to religious schools, with choices structured so that most parents chose religious schools. The district court ruled in favor of the claimants, the circuit court of appeals affirmed that judgment, but the U.S. Supreme Court reversed these decisions, finding Ohio's program did not violate the establishment clause.[82] *Zelman* was unusual in at least two respects: It attempted a bold departure from a half century of important religion-education decisions, but there was a greater variation of opinions on the court than usual.

Writing for the majority, Chief Justice William Rehnquist held that the Ohio program did not violate the establishment clause, because it had secular purposes of assisting low-income families with children in a failing public school system; it provided assistance directly to citizens exercising private choices about the schools where the vouchers were spent, with any advancement of religion coming from those choices, not government actions; and it met prior court rulings requiring neutrality by providing aid directly to a group of individuals without coercion and without regard for their religious beliefs. The majority opinion declared the program provided a neutral, "true private choice" that neither favored nor discriminated against any religion. That most participating private schools had religious affiliations merely reflected the makeup of most private schools in most American cities.[83]

Justice David Souter dissented, focusing on three flaws: The majority departed from longstanding court precedents by allowing substantial public aid to religious schools, as if this had no constitutional consequences; it employed mere formalistic meanings to "neutrality" and "choice" by affirming that the simple passage of public vouchers through private hands to religious schools met all establishment clause requirements; and it ignored government entanglements accompanying public funds given to the private religious schools, such as forbidding the consideration of religious preferences in the admission of students and the employment of professional personnel. When 96 percent of the participating students attended religious schools, Souter stated, something was at work besides choice alone. In addition, the maximum of $2,500 per voucher per student was inadequate, since it did not pay the actual operating costs per child at either the private or the public schools. In sum, the dissent concluded, the majority's claim of program neutrality and "true private choice" simply lacked merit.[84]

Suggested Activity: Research whether religion-affiliated schools in your area get public tax support in any way. What is your opinion on this?

The long-term impact of *Zelman v. Simmons-Harris* is difficult to predict, but some tentative observations have been made. *Zelman* received enthusiastic approval from school choice advocates, some claiming it "lifted the cloud of constitutional doubt" and presented "a clear set of rules for crafting constitutional school choice programs." However, since the majority in *Zelman* concluded that government can fund the religious education of students through vouchers, the ruling may have opened a legal precedent for government *having* to fund religious schools to one degree or another.[85]

Opposition to Zelman included the view that, while the school choice movement might involve important values concerning freedom of choice and parental rights, there is an equally strong need for common educational experiences, and a balance should be struck between individual freedoms and public needs for equity and social cohesion. *Zelman* gave much attention to school choice but virtually none to social cohesion.[86]

Some observers raised questions about *Zelman's* impact on school choice. For example, when the decision was made, approximately 50,000 students were educated nationwide under tax-funded vouchers, or one thousandth of one percent (.001 percent) of all American schoolchildren. Thus, vouchers were not as serious a part of the school choice movement as home schooling, which included roughly a million students. In addition, the court's majority declared that vouchers met establishment clause requirements, but they might not meet various state constitutional requirements where the main responsibility for public education rests.[87]

New directions?

How all of this Supreme Court drama will affect religion in public education issues is unclear, but an additional case indicates some possibilities. Although not directly involving public schools, the decision in *Hein v. Freedom from Religion Foundation, Inc.* (2007) concerned federal taxpayer standing to sue executive branch officials over alleged establishment clause violations. The district court dismissed the original suit, holding that taxpayer standing is limited to establishment clause suits over congressional appropriation powers, not executive branch actions. The seventh circuit court of appeals reversed, ruling that taxpayers may bring establishment clause suits against any program financed by Congress, including executive branch expenses, when taxpayer costs are greater than zero. The Supreme Court reversed the circuit court in a plurality decision, that is, five justices agreed to reverse, but they lacked sufficient agreement to form a majority decision.[88] A plurality decision may not make good law, but the decision in *Hein* restricts taxpayer rights to bring establishment clause suits.

Hein has been criticized for its apparent disregard of precedent, particularly when the court never previously distinguished between the legislative and executive branches in establishment clause cases. The decision apparently gives the executive branch freer rein to test the limits on such matters, and it has already stopped some suits and could prevent significant future establishment clause suits from ever starting.[89]

At the same time, *Hein* may have opened the door for new suits contesting taxpayer standing against school vouchers. At this writing, at least one was being considered in the court's October 2010 session, *Arizona Christian School Tuition Organization v. Winn*.[90] Whatever the results, however, it seems likely that religion-education controversies will continue.

International comparison: Turkey

The Republic of Turkey lies in southeastern Europe and southwestern Asia. It is composed of Thrace (in Europe) and Anatolia (in Asia), with Thrace comprising 8 percent and Anatolia the other 92 percent of Turkey's landmass. The two parts are divided by the Bosporus Strait, a narrow channel of water that connects the Black Sea to the Sea of Marmara, which connects to the Mediterranean Sea. The city of Istanbul straddles the Bosporus Strait, and it is heavily populated along both shores. The republic was founded on October 29, 1923, following the fall of the Ottoman Empire in World War I. Its capital city is Ankara, and its population totals approximately 76.8 million (July 2010 estimate). Turkey is a country with many links to ancient history: Its largest city, Istanbul, is the former Constantinople, which was the headquarters of the Roman emperor Constantine and later the seat of the Byzantine Empire, a Christian (Eastern Orthodox) empire that lasted until 1453, when the Ottoman Empire conquered Turkey and made Islam its official religion.[91]

After gaining independence in 1923, Turkey established a secular form of government under its first president, Mustafa Kemal, who wanted Turkey to become a **secular state** with an elected parliamentary form of government. Kemal was honored with the surname Atatürk by an act of the Turkish National Parliament in 1934. He remained in office until his death in 1938, and Turkey continues to follow a political ideology variously called Kemalism or Atatürk nationalism.[92]

Turkish education

Atatürk believed that Turkey's success depended on a secular education that would bring about scientific, cultural, and economic development. He thought it would also help abolish superstition and promote nationalism. According to Turkey's Ministry of National Education, educational institutions today are open to all citizens regardless of gender, religion, language, or race, while educational service is provided according to the desires and abilities of citizens and the needs of Turkish society. In the mid-twentieth century, "religious culture and moral teachings" were added to the curriculum on a limited basis, and the ministry maintains control of all religion-related instruction in the nation under its General Directorate of Religious Education. Turkish government policy is to promote moral values that yield a strong and stable society, while political and ideological agitations against Kemalism (or Atatürk nationalism) are not allowed.[93]

Religion as an issue in Turkish education

There are critics who maintain that any religion content in Turkish schools is a violation of Turkey's separation of religion and state. Religion advocates counter that the limited amount of moral teaching in the schools is the only religious instruction available for most children, particularly because private religious schools (**medreses or madrasas**) were closed by the Law of Unification of National Education in 1924.[94]

By 1927, all religious content in the curriculum was abolished and did not reappear until 1949, when an optional religion course was established for the fourth and fifth grades. In 1956, optional religion study was reintroduced in the secondary schools, and following the military coup in 1980, a "religious culture and moral teachings" curriculum became required in grades four through eight (two hours of instruction weekly), and in secondary schools (one hour weekly). Roughly half of the content was devoted to Islam and other religions (including Judaism, Christianity, Hinduism, and Buddhism), while the other half explored topics ranging from ethical values and etiquette to secularism and humanism. Religion advocates argued that both the content and the allotted time were simply not enough. With a new political party in power by 2000, a plan was launched to make the religion courses center on Islam and to strengthen teacher preparation, materials, and facilities.[95]

Suggested Activity: Visit the Religious Freedom Page at http://religiousfreedom.lib. virginia.edu/ (accessed on April 11, 2007), click on "Nations Profiles," scroll down the page, and click on some countries of interest. What are some of the issues in other countries, and do these issues relate to education? How are other countries dealing with religious differences, and how does education play a role? Discuss your findings in class or with individual classmates.

Politics, religion, and education

Kemalism claimed secularism as one of its basic values, but today more than 99 percent of the Turkish population are Islamic, of which 75 percent are Sunni Muslims and almost 25 percent are Alevi (a small branch of Islam found mostly in Turkey). Less than 1 percent of the population are Christians, Jews, or other. Thus, it is fair to say that secularism and Islam coexist in an uneasy relationship in Turkey, an uneasiness that seems to be affecting education and politics today. Some of this may help account for political instability in Turkey in the last half of the twentieth century, including three military coups, the first occurring in 1960, the next in 1971, and the most recent in 1980.[96]

Efforts have been made to modernize Turkey and increase the nation's world standing, a push that continues at present. Education was a chief tool used by Atatürk for modernization, of course, and Turkey has continued to build its system ever since. For example, in 1973 it extended primary education from five to eight grades, in 1981 it integrated all higher education institutions into a single system, and in 1997 it required "uninterrupted basic education" in an effort to prevent students from dropping out before completion of that phase.[97]

Turkey has sought membership in the European Union (EU), a development that could have economic and political benefits. This calls for significant expenditures, and educational development is one of the important EU criteria for admission. In a nationwide referendum, Turkey recently passed 26 new constitutional amendments, and while the EU found this development promising, it still called for additional reforms in such areas as freedom of expression and religion.[98] As with many nations today, Turkey is challenged by globalization, international competition, technological innovation, immigration (particularly from Iraq and Afghanistan), and the need for educational development, just as it also faces long-held domestic tensions over religion-related passions that impact society and its educational institutions.

Summary and conclusions

Throughout history, religion has impacted human ideas and institutions. The first schools probably developed with the appearance of writing and the need to produce scribes who could record many aspects of life, including religious matters. In ancient times, education and religion were interrelated in virtually every society. In Egyptian education, religion was a dominant force, while in Greek education civic purposes became dominant, with religion enhancing the understanding of Greek culture. Rome, heavily influenced by Greece, spread Greco-Roman culture and education across its empire. As imperial Rome declined, Christian influence grew, and the Roman Catholic Church became the primary sponsor of educational development, including universities. Christian influence was supreme, but elements of classical education were retained in the liberal arts and became distinguishing features of European education.

The Renaissance rejuvenated interest in humanistic education. It retained a religious orientation, but it also helped change the relation of education and secular society. Increasing dissatisfaction with church authority helped bring about the Protestant Reformation, which championed literacy education and the ideal of universal education for all. The Counter-Reformation also had education as a major emphasis, taking new initiatives to spread education.

Such were the educational traditions European colonists brought to America. The education-religion connection was retained, but secular society's needs were never out of sight. As education developed in the English colonies, the European tradition of education as a responsibility of home and church had to yield to new conditions and needs. Government involvement in spreading educational benefits increased, although both religious and secular purposes continued to be served.

Under the Enlightenment influence, focus was placed on social progress through human reason, scientific study, and educational development to achieve a better life for everyone. These emphases found fertile soil as American social, political, and economic growth occurred. Some Great Awakening revivalists were attuned to Enlightenment ideas, and under both secular and religious influences American education grew apace.

Following the American Revolution, appreciation for religious freedom led to its inclusion in the Constitution, with calls for a **wall of separation** between church and state. As the public school movement got under way in the nineteenth century, the country experienced increased immigration and diversity, and the social purposes of education gained importance. Religion retained a controversial place in the curriculum, particularly around Bible reading, prayer, and Darwinian evolution, creating tensions that extended into the twentieth and even the twenty-first centuries.

Despite the possibility of violent disagreements over religion, most educational disputes have been handled more or less peacefully, despite strong passions. From the 1920s to the recent past, most religion-education controversies were adjudicated in courts of law, with most of them coming in the second half of the twentieth century, mostly involving the First Amendment's free exercise and establishment clauses. The main themes of religion-education court decisions concern what the Constitution permits or forbids when it comes to such things as state aid to religious institutions, state-required observances or practices of religious establishment, and state authority to require or compel acts or behaviors that interfere with religious freedom. For most of that history, the courts have restricted or prohibited government acts that affect an establishment of religion or the free exercise of religion. A doctrine that government must be neutral and neither advance nor restrict religion seemed to be ascendant, but in recent decisions, the U.S. Supreme Court has loosened some previous restrictions and prohibitions.

In the contemporary United States, tensions surrounding the role of religion in public schools have involved school prayer, released time for religious activities, flag salutes, religious content in the curriculum, and government aid to religious schools. Court cases continue to arise over what is permissible in terms of school requirements and activities that lead to religious observances. Other issues surface over what is permitted or forbidden in the curriculum.

Sometimes religion itself becomes the issue, as with observers who want to eliminate all religious material and ideas. Then there are those who think religion ought to be studied not so much to develop "true belief" as to understand how religion has impacted individuals and societies, with the study of world religions a case in point. Others advocate the exploration of religion's role in moral and ethical ideas, with schools becoming places where people's conceptions of right and wrong are examined in greater depth.

Intellectual freedom is essential for good education because it is necessary for genuine discussions and understandings concerning regular curriculum content as well as for explorations of current events. Because freedom of belief is a crucial American right, it needs to be placed in the context of the law and professional ethical obligations. Schools and their personnel need to avoid promoting or inhibiting religion in illegal or unethical ways. Students have a right to religious freedom, including freedom from religion.

How other countries handle their religion-education concerns is instructive. The Republic of Turkey is a country in which the majority of the population identifies with Islam. Turkey established a secular government shortly after gaining independence in 1923; today, its educational system remains secular, but this position is experiencing direct challenges, socially and politically. There is a certain amount of religion in the curriculum, and secularists see it as too much while religionists see it as too little. The study of that curriculum content is mostly devoted to Islam, but a portion also deals with world religions.

Vocabulary

cathedral schools
child benefit theory
classical education
Counter-Reformation
cuneiform
Enlightenment
establishment clause
excessive entanglement
faith and reason
free exercise clause
Great Awakening
guild schools
hieroglyphics
Jesuit schools
liberal arts
medreses or madrasas
moment of silence
monastic schools
municipal schools
mythology
naturalism
neutrality principle
Old Deluder Act
oratorical education
parish schools
priesthood of all believers
Protestant Reformation
released time
religious freedom
religious identity formation
religious right
Renaissance
rhetoric

scholasticism
scribes
secular humanism
secular state
separation of church and state
true believers
universal education
universities
wall of separation

Notes

1 R. Freeman Butts, *The Education of the West: A Formative Chapter in the History of Civilization* (New York: McGraw-Hill, 1973), 3–74; and Peter Damerow, "The Origins of Writing as a Problem of Historical Epistemology" (March 1999), at http://www.mpiwg-berlin.mpg.de/Preprints/P114.PDF (accessed on August 16, 2010).

2 Wayne M. Senner, ed., *The Origins of Writing* (Lincoln: University of Nebraska Press, 1991); and Florian Coulmas, *Writing Systems of the World* (New York: Blackwell Publishing, 1989), 57–60. For Sumer specifically, see Samuel Noah Kramer, *The Sumerians: Their History, Culture, and Character* (Chicago: University of Chicago Press, 1963), 237–240, 245–246.

3 James Mulhern, *A History of Education: A Social Interpretation* (New York: The Ronald Press, 1959), 63–78; Butts, 55, 57–58, 63–65; and David Crystal, *The Cambridge Encyclopedia of Language* (New York: Cambridge University Press, 1987), 199.

4 Henri I. Marrou, *A History of Education in Antiquity,* George Lamb, trans. (Madison: University of Wisconsin Press, 1956), 100–101. See also Lewis Jewsbury, "Homeric Epics," at http://history-world.org/Homerepics.htm (accessed on August 16, 2010); and "Greek Mythology," at http://isthmia.osu.edu/arched/mythology.html (accessed on August 16, 2010).

5 "Athens: Education in the Archaic Age," in *Education in the History of Western Civilization: Selected Readings,* Frederick M. Binder, ed. (New York: Macmillan, 1970), 16–18. This source of selected readings will hereafter be referred to as 'Binder.' See also, "Pericles' Funeral Oration," at http://www.fordham.edu/halsall/ancient/pericles-funeralspeech.html (accessed on August 16, 2010). For Plato, see *The Republic,* "Book II: The Individual, the State, and Education," at http://www.ilt.columbia.edu/publications/Projects/digitexts/plato/the_republic/book02.html (accessed on August 16, 2010).

6 Marrou, 234–237, 258–262; and "Cicero, Model for the Ages," in Binder, 50–52.

7 See "St. Jerome," *Catholic Encyclopedia,* at http://www.newadvent.org/cathen/08341a.htm (accessed on August 16, 2010); "Life of "Saint Augustine of Hippo," *Catholic Encyclopedia,* at http://www.newadvent.org/cathen/02084a.htm (accessed on August 16, 2010); "Church Fathers Proclaim the Superiority of the Scriptures" (see "St. Jerome . . ."), in Binder, 69–70; and "St. Augustine and the Bounds of Christian Scholarship," in Binder, 71–72.

8 William Harris Stahl et al., *Martianus Capella and the Seven Liberal Arts* (New York: Columbia University Press, 1971); Ralph W. Mathieson, "Bishops, Barbarians, and the Dark Ages: The Fate of Late Roman Educational Institutions in Late Antique Gaul," in Medieval Education, Ronald B. Begley and Joseph W. Koterski, S.J., eds (New York: Fordham University Press, 2005), 3–19; "Cassiodorus, Father of Literary Monasticism," in Binder, 81–82; and James J. O'Donnell, *Cassiodorus*

(Berkeley: University of California Press, 1979), electronically available at http://www9. georgetown. edu/faculty/jod/texts/cassbook/toc.html (accessed on August 16, 2010).

9   Robert Ulich, "The Medieval Church," in *Three Thousand Years of Educational Wisdom: Selections from Great Documents,* 2nd edn, edited and commented upon by Robert Ulich (Cambridge: Harvard University Press, 1954), 172. This source of primary readings will hereafter be referred to as "Ulich."

10 See "Catechumenal Training" and "St. Benedict's Rule," in Binder, 76–77, 79–80; and Nicholas Orme, *Medieval Schools: Roman Britain to Renaissance England* (New Haven: Yale University Press, 2006).

11 "Charlemagne . . ." in Binder, 84–85; Einhard, *The Life of Charlemagne,* Samuel Epes Turner, trans. (New York: Harper & Brothers, 1880), at http://www.fordham.edu/halsall/basis/einhard. html#Public%20Works (accessed on August 16, 2010); "Carolingian Schools," Catholic Encyclopedia on CD-ROM, at http://www.newadvent.org/cathen/03349c.htm (accessed on August 16, 2010); and "Cathedral Schools and Chantry Colleges at Salisbury," at http://salisbury.art.virginia.edu/cathedral. text.uva10298613658895 (accessed on August 16, 2010).

12 "Rabanus Maurus," in Ulich, 174–179; "King Alfred greets Bishop Werfrith . . ." in Binder, 88–89; "Alfred the Great"" at http://www.royal.gov.uk/output/Page25.asp http://www.royal.gov.uk/History-oftheMonarchy/KingsandQueensofEngland/TheAnglo-Saxonkings/AlfredtheGreat.aspx (accessed on October 18, 2010); and Gaines Post, "Alexander III, the Licentia Docendi and the Rise of Universities," in *Anniversary Essays in Medieval History* (1929), 255, at http://books.google.com/ books?id=cNANgxkr5kYC&pg=PA255&lpg=PA255&dq=licentia+docendi&source=web& ots=HraZJHEsGK&sig=esDc4Ec-X8xZ7OKMnkfRGORpNxE#PPA255,M1 (accessed on August 16, 2010).

13 Christopher Lucas, *Our Western Educational Heritage* (New York: Macmillan, 1972), 235ff; and Binder, 105–112.

14 See "The Scholastic Movement," in Binder, 99, 100; "Peter Abelard," *Stanford Encylopedia of Philosophy,* at http://plato.stanford.edu/entries/abelard/ (accessed on October 18, 2010); and "St. Thomas Aquinas," *Stanford Encyclopedia of Philosophy,* at http://plato.stanford.edu/entries/ aquinas/ (accessed on October 18, 2010).

15 Desiderius Erasmus, De Ratione Studii (Upon the Right Method of Instruction) (1511), in *Desiderius Erasmus Concerning the Aim and Method of Education,* William Harrison Woodward, ed., Classics in Education, No. 19 (New York: Teachers College Press, 1964), 162–165; and Juan Luis Vives, *Vive's Introduction to Wisdom: A Renaissance Textbook,* Marian Leona Tobriner, ed., Classics in Education, No. 35 (New York: Teachers College Press, 1968), 85–86.

16 Martin Luther, "Letter to the Mayors and Aldermen of all the Cities of Germany in behalf of Christian Schools" (1524), from *Great Pedagogical Essays, Plato to Spencer,* F. V. N. Painter, ed. (1905), as reprinted in Binder, 160–165.

17 "Biography of St. Ignatius of Loyola," at http://www.ccel.org/i/ignatius (accessed on August 16, 2010); and "The Jesuit Ratio Studiorum of 1599," Boston College Libraries, at http://www.bc.edu/bc_org/ avp/ulib/digi/ratio/ratiohome.html (accessed on August 16, 2010).

18 James A. Morone, *Hellfire Nation: The Politics of Sin in American History* (New Haven: Yale University Press, 2003), 3, 497. The quote from Abraham Lincoln comes from his "First Inaugural Address," Monday, March 4, 1861, at http://www.bartleby.com/124/pres31.html (accessed on August 16, 2010).

19 Louis H. Manarin and Clifford Dowdey, *The History of Henrico County* (Charlottesville: University Press of Virginia, 1984), 25–28; and Mary Miley Theobald, "Henricus: A New and Improved Jamestown," *Colonial Williamsburg Journal* (Winter 2004–2005), at http://www.history.org/foundation/ journal/Winter04-05/henricus.cfm (accessed on August 16, 2010). See also Louis H. Manarin and Clifford Dowdey, *The History of Henrico County* (Charlottesville: University of Virginia Press, 1984),

24–28; and Helen C. Rountree, *The Powhatan Indians of Virginia: Their Traditional Culture* (Norman: University of Oklahoma Press, 1989).

20 "Piety for Virginia Households [Laws of Virginia, Feb. 1631–2]," in *The Educating of Americans: A Documentary History,* Daniel Calhoun, ed. (Boston: Houghton Mifflin Company, 1969), 17, hereafter referred to as Calhoun; "Protection for Public Wards [Laws of Virginia, March 1642–43]," in *Educational Ideas in America: A Documentary History,* S. Alexander Rippa, ed. (New York: David McKay Co., Inc., 1969), 17, hereafter referred to as Rippa; "Enforcement of Pious Teaching [Laws of Virginia, March 1645–6]," in Calhoun, 18.

21 John Winthrop, "A Modell of Christian Charity [1630]," in Rippa, 45; and "New England's First Fruits [1643]," in *American Higher Education: A Documentary History,* vol. 1, Richard Hofstadter and Wilson Smith, eds (Chicago: University of Chicago Press, 1961), 5–6.

22 "The Massachusetts School Law of 1647," in Rippa, 162.

23 See, for example, Benjamin Franklin, The Life of Benjamin Franklin, Written by Himself, vol. 3, 272, at   http://books.google.com/books?id=ufb8UFwNSqkC&pg=RA2-PA272&lpg=RA2-PA272&dq= souls+and+tobacco&source=web&ots=lFcPN_bFJt&sig=9HX1z71CwohKOIwD-KKS9SdnuAM (accessed on August 16, 2010); Virginius Dabney, *Virginia, The New Dominion: A History from 1607 to the Present* (Garden City, NY: Doubleday and Co., 1971), 74; and Edward L. Bond, *Damned Souls in a Tobacco Colony: Religion in Seventeenth-Century Virginia* (Macon, GA: Mercer University Press, 2000), 194.

24 "William & Mary 1618–1699," at http://www.wm.edu/about/history/chronology/1618to1699/index. php (accessed on August 16, 2010).

25 Francis Bacon, "Novum Organum," in Ulich, 306–310; and John Locke, "Some Thoughts Concerning Education," in *John Locke on Education,* Peter Gay, ed., Classics in Education, no. 20 (New York: Teachers College Bureau of Publications, 1964), 19–20, 25–26, 33, 34, 35, 42, 65, 88–89. See also, "Francis Bacon," at http://www.iep.utm.edu/b/bacon.htm; and "John Locke," at http://www.iep.utm. edu/l/locke.htm#Educational%20Writings (both accessed on August 16, 2010).

26 Benjamin Franklin, "Proposals Relating to the Education of Youth in Pensilvania [1749]," in Rippa, 108.

27 "Jonathan Edwards: Biography," the Jonathan Edwards Center at Yale University, at http://edwards. yale.edu/research/about-edwards/biography (accessed on October 18, 2010); and Jonathan Edwards, "On the Great Awakening," at http://www.nhinet.org/ccs/docs/awaken.htm (accessed on October 18, 2010).

28 Douglas Sloan, "The Great Awakening and American Education," in *The Great Awakening and American Education: A Documentary History,* Douglas Sloan, ed., Classics in Education, no. 46, Lawrence A Cremin, gen. ed. (New York: Teachers College Press, 1973), 1–28, 33–35, 41–43.

29 Ibid., 47–48.

30 James W. Fraser, *Between Church and State: Religion and Public Education in a Multicultural Society* (New York: St. Martin's Press, 1999), 18–20; Thomas Jefferson, "A Bill for Establishing Religious Freedom," at http://www.teachingamericanhistory.org/library/index.asp?document=23 (accessed on October 18, 2010); and James Madison, "Memorial and Remonstrance against Religious Assessments," at http://religiousfreedom.lib.virginia.edu/sacred/madison_m&r_1785.html (accessed on October 18, 2010).

31 Fraser, 20.

32 Ibid., 24.

33 Ibid., 25–27.

34 Jennings L. Wagoner, *Jefferson and Education* (Charlottesville: Thomas Jefferson Foundation, 2004), 33–36, 139–141; Robert M. Healey, *Jefferson on Religion in Public Education* (New Haven: Yale University Press and Archon Books, [1962] 1970), 205–226.

35 Fraser, 28–31; and Raymond B. Culver, *Horace Mann and Religion in the Massachusetts Public Schools* (New York: Arno Press and the New York Times, 1969), 21–28.

36 R. Laurence Moore, "Bible Reading and Nonsectarian Schooling: The Failure of Religious Instruction in Nineteenth-Century Public Education," *The Journal of American History,* vol. 86, no. 4: 1587–1588 (March 2000).

37 Kevin Kenny, "Irish Immigration in the United States," (February 13, 2008), at http://www.america.gov/st/peopleplace-english/2008/February/20080307131416ebyessedo0.6800043.html (accessed on August 28, 2010).

38 Power, 104–116.

39 Ibid., 118–122.

40 Neil G. McCluskey, "America and the Catholic School," in *Catholic Education in America: A Documentary History,* Neil G. McCluskey, S. J., ed. (New York: Bureau of Publications, Teachers College, 1964), 12–15.

41 Benjamin Justice, *The War That Wasn't: Religious Conflict and Compromise in the Common Schools of New York State, 1865–1900* (Albany: State University of New York Press, 2005), 5.

42 Moore, 1583–1586.

43 Mark Douglas McGarvie, *One Nation Under Law: America's Early National Struggles to Separate Church and State* (Dekalb: Northern Illinois Universiy Press, 2004), 49–58.

44 Meyer v. Nebraska 262 US 390 (1923), at http://www.law.cornell.edu/supct/html/historics/USSC_CR_0262_0390_ZO.html (accessed on October 18, 2010).

45 Pierce v. Society of Sisters 268 U.S. 510 (1925), at http://www.law.cornell.edu/supct/html/historics/USSC_CR_0268_0510_ZS.html (accessed on October 18, 2010).

46 Cochran v. Louisiana 281 US 370 (1930), http://caselaw.lp.findlaw.com/cgi-bin/getcase.pl?court=US&vol=281&invol=370 (accessed on October 18, 2010).

47 Minersville School District v. Gobitis 310 US 586 (1940), http://supreme.justia.com/us/310/586/index.html (accessed on October 18, 2010); and West Virginia State Board of Education v. Barnette 319 US 624 (1943), http://www.law.cornell.edu/supct/html/historics/USSC_CR_0319_0624_ZO.html (accessed on October 18, 2010).

48 Wisconsin v. Yoder 406 US 205 (1972), at http://www.law.cornell.edu/supct/html/historics/USSC_CR_0406_0205_ZS.html (accessed on October 18, 2010).

49 Lee v. Weisman, 505 U.S. 577, 599 (1992), at http://supreme.justia.com/us/505/577/case.html (accessed on August 17, 2010).

50 Everson v. Board of Education, 330 US 1 (1947), at http://www.law.cornell.edu/supct/html/historics/USSC_CR_0330_0001_ZO.html (accessed on October 18, 2010).

51 McCollum v. Board of Education, 333 US 203 (1948), http://caselaw.lp.findlaw.com/cgi-bin/getcase.pl?court=US&vol=333&invol=203 (accessed on October 18, 2010).

52 Zorach v. Clauson 343 US 306 (1952), http://www.law.cornell.edu/supct/html/historics/USSC_CR_0343_0306_ZO.html (accessed on October 18, 2010).

53 Engel v. Vitale 370 US 421 (1962), http://www.law.cornell.edu/supct/html/historics/USSC_CR_0370_0421_ZO.html (accessed on October 18, 2010).

54 Morone, 403–404; Fraser, 219–221; and Provenzo, 75–79.

55 Sch. Distr. of Abington Township v. Schempp 374 US 203 (1963), particularly 222–225, at http://www.law.cornell.edu/supct/html/historics/USSC_CR_0374_0203_ZO.html (accessed on October 18, 2010).

56 Fraser, 217–221; and Schempp, 225, at http://www.law.cornell.edu/supct/html/historics/USSC_CR_0374_0203_ZO.html (accessed on October 18, 2010).

57 Board of Education v. Allen 392 US 296 (1968), at http://www.law.cornell.edu/supct/html/historics/USSC_CR_0392_0236_ZO.html (accessed on October 18, 2010).

58 Lemon v. Kurtzman, 403 US 602 (1971), at http://www.law.cornell.edu/supct/html/historics/USSC_CR_0403_0602_ZS.html (accessed on October 18, 2010).

59 Committee for Public Education and Religious Liberty v. Nyquist 413 US 756 (1973), at http://caselaw.lp.findlaw.com/scripts/getcase.pl?court=US&vol=413&invol=756 (accessed on October 18, 2010); Meek v. Pettinger, 421 U.S. 349 (1975), at http://caselaw.lp.findlaw.com/scripts/getcase.pl?court=US&vol=421&invol=349 (accessed on October 18, 2010); and Wolman v. Walter 433 US 229 (1977), at http://supreme.justia.com/us/433/229/case.html (accessed on October 18, 2010).

60 Eugene F. Provenzo, Jr., *Religious Fundamentalism and American Education*, SUNY Series in Philosophy of Education, Philip L. Smith, ed. (Albany: State University of New York Press, 1990), xii–xviii.

61 See the analysis by D. A. Ackerman and K. D. Jones, *The Law of Church and State in the Supreme Court Revisited* (New York: Nova Science Publishers, Inc., 2006), 2–3.

62 "Members of the Supreme Court of the United States," at http://www.supremecourt.gov/about/members.aspx (accessed on October 18, 2010).

63 James John Jurinski, *Religion in the Schools* (Santa Barbara, CA: Contemporary World Issues, 1998), 2–6.

64 Julie Underwood and L. Dean Webb, *School Law for Teachers: Concepts and Applications* (Upper Saddle River, NJ: Pearson Education, Inc., 2006), 212–214.

65 Santa Fe Independent School District v. Doe 530 U.S. 290 (2000), 290, 293, 295, 298, and 317, at http://supreme.justia.com/us/530/290/case.html (accessed on October 18, 2010).

66 Gilbert T. Sewall, "Religion and the Textbooks," in *Curriculum, Religion, and Public Education: Conversations for and enlarging the Public Square,* James T. Sears with James C. Carper, eds (New York: Teachers College Press), 78, 79.

67 Sam Harris, *The End of Faith: Religion, Terror, and the End of Reason* (New York: W. W. Norton: 2005), 20–21, 223–224.

68 Robert J. Nash, *Faith, Hype & Clarity: Teaching about Religion in American Schools and Colleges* (New York: Teachers College Press, 1999), 3–4.

69 Sewall, 81, 83.

70 F. Dan Marshall and Jo Kincheloe, "It's Not about the Books: Textbooks Conversations and the Need for Uncertain Conversations," in *Curriculum, Religion, and Public Education,* 85–91.

71 Nel Noddings, "Moral Education as a Form of Life," in *Curriculum, Religion, and Public Education,* 116–124.

72 Nel Noddings. *Educating Moral People: A Caring Alternative to Character Education* (New York: Teachers College Press, 2002), 9. The quote is from George Orwell, *A Collection of Essays* (San Diego, CA: Harcourt Brace [1946] 1981), 5.

73 Underwood and Webb, 215–216.

74 John E. Peloza v. Capistrano Unified School District, Nos. 92–55228, 92–55644 (Ninth Circuit Court of Appeals, 1994) at http://www.talkorigins.org/faqs/peloza.html (accessed on April 12, 2007).

75 Jurinski, 13–16.

76 Annette Hemmings, *Coming of Age in U.S. High Schools: Economic, Kinship, Religious, and Political Crosscurrents.* (Mahwah, NJ: Lawrence Erlbaum Associates: 2004), 111–115.

77 Ibid., 117–122,124–125, 137–138.

78 Ibid., 132–134.

79 Ibid., 135–141.

80 Mitchell v. Helms 530 U.S. 793 (2000), 835, 837–838, and 911, at http://supreme.justia.com/us/530/793/case.html (accessed on October 18, 2010).

81 Zelman v. Simmons-Harris 536 U.S. 639 (2002), at http://supreme.justia.com/us/536/639/case.html (accessed on October 18, 2010), 641–42, and 644–48; and John E. Ferguson Jr., "Public Funds

and Religious Schools: The Next Prayer Debate?" in *Democracy and Religion: Free Exercise and Diverse Visions*, David Odell-Scott, ed. (Kent and London: The Kent State University Press, 2004), 48–70, 77.

82 Zelman v. Simmons-Harris, 639–642.

83 Ibid., 643–669.

84 Ibid., 698–711, and n. 15, 705.

85 Marie Gryphon, "True Private Choice; A Practical Guide to School Choice after Zelman v. Simmons-Harris," *Policy Analysis*, no. 466 (February 4, 2003), 1, 11, at http://www.cato.org/pubs/pas/pa-466es. html (accessed on October 18, 2010); and Joshua Edelstein, "Zelman, Davey, and the Case for Mandatory Government Funding for Religious Education," *Arizona Law Review*, vol. 45, no. 1: 899, 921, and 924 (2004).

86 Henry M. Levin, "A Comprehensive Framework for Evaluating Educational Vouchers," *Educational Evaluation and Policy Analysis*, vol. 24, no. 3: 161–162, 169 (Fall 2002).

87 Chad D'Entremont and Luis A. Huerta, "Irreconcilable Differences? Education Vouchers and the Suburban Response," *Educational Policy*, vol. 21, no. 1: 41, 50–52 (January 2007).

88 "Syllabus," Hein v. Foundation for Freedom from Religion, Inc. (2007), at http://www.law.cornell. edu/supct/html/06-157.ZS.html (accessed on November 11, 2010); and "Plurality Opinion Law & Legal Definition," USLegal, Inc., at http://definitions.uslegal.com/p/plurality-opinion/ (accessed on November 11, 2010).

89 See, for example, "Taxpayers' Right to Sue over Church-State Violations," The Roundtable on Religion and Social Welfare Policy, at http://www.religionandsocialpolicy.org/resources/HeinvFFRF. cfm (accessed on November 11, 2010), and Ira C. Lupu and Robert W. Tuttle, The State of the Law 2008: A Cumulative Report on Legal Developments Affecting Government Partnerships with Faith-Based Organizations, The Roundtable on Religion and Social Welfare Policy, ii, 51–57, at http://www. religionandsocialpolicy.org/docs/legal/state_ofthe_law_2008.pdf (accessed on November 11, 2010).

90 Arizona Christian School Tuition Organization v. Winn, Docket # 09-987; Argument Date: November 3, 2010; Opinion Date: To Be Decided; SCOTUSblog, at http://www.scotusblog. com/case-files/cases/arizona-christian-school-tuition-organization-v-winn-garriott-v-winn/ (accessed on October 18, 2010).

91 "Turkey," *The World Factbook*, at https://www.cia.gov/library/publications/the-world-factbook/geos/ tu.html (accessed on October 6, 2010).

92 "Ataturk's Life," at http://www.turkishnews.com/Ataturk/life.htm (accessed on October 6, 2010).

93 "Atatürk's Views on Education," at http://www.meb.gov.tr/Stats/apk2001ing/Section_0/Ataturks-Viewon.htm; and "General Principles Regulating the Turkish National Education System," at http:// www.meb.gov.tr/Stats/apk2001ing/Section_1/1Generalprincipals.htm (both accessed on October 6, 2010).

94 Hadi Adanali, "The Many Dimensions of Religious Instruction in Turkey," in *Religious Education in Schools: Ideas and Experiences from Around the World* (Oxford: International Association for Religious Freedom, 2002), 15–19, at http://www.iarf.net/REBooklet/Turkey.htm (accessed on October 6, 2010).

95 Ibid.; and "Innovations in the Education System: 6. New Approaches in Religious Education," Ministry of National Education, at http://www.meb.gov.tr/Stats/apk2002ing/apage107–117.htm#6 (accessed on October 6, 2010).

96 Ertan Aydin and Yilmaz Çolak, "Dilemmas of Turkish Democracy: The Encounter between Kemalist Laicism and Islamism in 1990s Turkey," in *Democracy and Religion: Free Exercise and Diverse Visions*, David O'Dell-Scott, ed. (Kent, OH: Kent State University Press, 2004), 206–208; "Turkey: Religions," at http://lexicorient.com/e.o/turkey_4.htm; David Zeidan, "The Alevi of Anatolia," at http://

www.angelfire.com/az/rescon/ALEVI.html; and "Military Interventions in Turkey," at http://www.allaboutturkey.com/darbe.htm (all accessed on October 6, 2010).

97 Özcan Demirel, "Education in Turkey: Modern and Contemporary," in *Globalization, Modernization, and Education in Muslim Countries,* Rukzana Zia, ed. (New York: Nova Science Publishers, 2006), 275–278.

98 CNN Wire Staff, "Turkey needs more reform, European Union says after vote," September 13, 2010, at http://www.cnn.com/2010/WORLD/europe/09/13/turkey.referendum/indcx.html?iref=allsearch (accessed on October 6, 2010).

Index

Parents Involved in Community Schools v. Seattle School District No. 1 et al (2007) 190–1
parish schools 222, 362
parochial schools 220, 248, 373, 376, 378, 382
passive resistance 179
Peabody Education Fund 173
peer culture 289
Peloza v. Capistrano Unified School District (1994) 391
Pennsylvania 58, 62, 112, 216, 326–7, 377, 380, 381
Pennsylvania Association for Retarded Children (PARC) v. Commonwealth of Pennsylvania (1972) 327
Pericles (495–429 B.C.E.) 359, 404n. 5
Perkins Institute 314–15
Pestalozzi, Johann Heinrich (1746–1827) 11, 65, 100n. 20
Phelps-Stokes Fund 173
physiological method 316–17
Piaget, Jean (1896–1980) 275
Pierce v. Society of Sisters (1925) 376
Plato (428–348 B.C.E.) 106, 274, 359, 363, 149n. 1, 404n. 5
Pledge of Allegiance 377
Plessy v. Ferguson (1896) 164, 175, 200
pluralists 219
Poland 220, 234
Potter, Alonzo (1800–1865) 11
power of the purse 75, 86
Powhatan, Chief 366
Powhatan tribal confederacy 108
Pratt, Richard Henry (1840–1924) 216, 251n. 15
Pratt, Robert 186, 204n. 44, n. 47, n. 54, 206n. 75
prayer 30, 367, 373–4, 378, 380–3, 385–6, 401
priesthood of all believers 365
Prince Edward County, Virginia 177–8
principal 17, 27, 78, 82, 90, 97, 166, 178, 185, 228, 312, 322, 346
printing press, educational impact of 5, 364–5
progressive education reforms 64
   administrative progressives 68
   pedagogical progressives 65, 66–7
proposition 227 (California) 241

Protestant-Catholic tensions 373
Protestant Reformation 365
pull-in and pull out programs 334

quid pro quo harassment 293

race 17–18, 67, 77, 89, 115, 117, 156–207, 227, 243, 259, 284, 323, 326, 329–30, 337, 357, 398
   concept of 157–60, 178
   racial prejudice 158, 191, 249
   racialization 182, 199
   racism 157, 180–2, 188, 191, 195, 199, 279
Randolph, Virginia E. (1870–1958) 173
Ravitch, Diane 88, 153n. 62, 255n. 74
Rawls, John (1921–2002) 331, 351n. 53
Reagan, Ronald (1911–2004) 21, 74, 382–4
reciprocity of effort 33
reconstruction 124, 160–1, 199
reflective professional communities 40
Refugee Act (1980) 225
Rehnquist, William 396
released time 379, 385, 392, 385, 402
religious identity formation 393
religious right 382–3, 386
Renaissance 4–5, 364, 401
resegregation 180, 186–7, 189, 191
respect for persons 329–30, 334, 341
response to instruction (rti) 336
rhetoric, study of 4, 359–61
Rhode Island 57, 264, 315, 369, 378, 381
Rockefeller, John D. (1839–1907) 116, 172
Roman Catholic Church 4, 220, 360–1, 371, 401
Roosevelt, Eleanor (1884–1962) 270
Roosevelt, Franklin (1882–1945) 122
Rosenwald Fund 173–4
Rousseau, Jean-Jacques (1712–1778) 11, 65, 100n. 19
rudiments 108, 110, 262, 367
Ruffner, William Henry (1824–1908) 162
Rush, Benjamin (1746–1813) 9, 262

St. Louis, Missouri 17, 61, 114, 134
Santa Fe Independent School District v. Doe (2000) 385